Landscape planning and environmental impact design

2nd edition

The Natural and Built Environment series

Editors: Professor Michael J. Bruton, The Residuary Body for Wales
Professor John Glasson, Oxford Brookes University

1. *Introduction to environmental impact assessment*
    John Glasson, Riki Therivel, Andrew Chadwick

2. *Methods of environmental impact assessment*
    Peter Morris & Riki Therivel (editors)

3. *Public transport*
    Peter White

4. *Planning, the market and private housebuilding*
    Glen Bramley, Will Bartlett, Christine Lambert

5. *Housing policy in Britain and Europe*
    Gavin McCrone & Mark Stephens

6. *Partnership agencies in British urban policy*
    Nick Bailey (with Alison Barker and Kelvin MacDonald)

7. *British planning policy in transition*
    Mark Tewdwr-Jones (editor)

8. *Urban planning and real estate development*
    John Ratcliffe & Michael Stubbs

9. *Controlling development*
    Philip Booth

10. *Development control*
    Keith Thomas

11. *Landscape planning and environmental impact design, 2nd edition*
    Tom Turner

Landscape planning and environmental impact design

2nd edition

Tom Turner

Routledge
Taylor & Francis Group

LONDON AND NEW YORK

First published in 1998 by Routledge

Reprinted 2003 by Routledge
2 Park Square, Milton Park,
Abingdon, Oxon, OX14 4 RN

Transferred to Digital Printing 2009

*Routledge is an imprint of the
Taylor & Francis Group*

British Library Cataloguing in Publication Data
A catalogue record for this book is available from the British Library.

Library of Congress Cataloguing-in-Publication Data are available.

ISBNs:
1-85728-321-X HB
1-85728-322-8 PB

Publisher's Note
The publisher has gone to great lengths to ensure the quality of this reprint
but points out that some imperfections in the original may be apparent.

Contents

Preface   vii

PART 1   1
Landscape Planning

1 Will planning die?   3
2 Landscape plans   28
3 Context theories   73

PART 2   109
Environmental Impact Design

4 Public open space   113
5 Reservoirs   155
6 Mineral working   185
7 Agriculture   217
8 Forests   246
9 Rivers and floods   280
10 Transport   318
11 Urbanization   353

Appendix: Environmental impact questions   394

References   402

Index   417

Preface

In town and in country there must be landscapes where we can walk in safety, pick fruit, cycle, work, sleep, swim, listen to the birds, bask in the sun, run through the trees and laze beside cool waters. Some should be busy; others solitary. Rivers should be prised out of their concrete coffins and foul ditches. Quarries should be planned as new landscapes. Forests should provide us with recreation, timber and wildlife habitats. Wastes should be used to build green hills. Routeways should be designed for all types of user, not just for motor vehicles. Old towns should be revitalized and new villages made. When growing food, farmers should conserve and remake the countryside. Buildings should stop behaving like spoilt brats: each should contribute to an urban or rural landscape. But what is a landscape? In this book, the word is used to mean "a good outdoor place": useful, beautiful, sustainable, productive and spiritually rewarding.

To achieve these goals, there is but one necessity: when preparing and approving plans for new places, or spending money on old places, we must look beyond the confines of each and every project. Gazing at these wider horizons, we shall see that development projects are initiated by specialists who have been imprisoned within "closely drawn technical limits" and "narrowly drawn territorial boundaries" (Weddle 1967: vii). It is not the specialists' fault. But if their approach results in single-objective projects, the collective landscape suffers.

> Ill fares the land, to hast'ning ills a prey,
> Where wealth accumulates, and men decay. (Goldsmith 1770)

Professionals should be trained to take both narrow and broad views. This book is addressed to members of the public, to let them know what they should request, and to the many professions involved in landscape-making: planners, designers, architects, engineers, farmers, foresters and others. The task has aesthetic, functional, economic, political and philosophical dimensions.

Economists distinguish between private and public goods. Private goods, such as cars, houses and farms, are the province of private individuals, private organizations and single-minded professionals. Public goods, such as fresh air and beautiful views, belong to us all and are the responsibility of us all. Multi-objective design and planning can ensure that society obtains both private and public goods from our collective landscape.

Financial appraisal concentrates on private goods. Environmental assessment encompasses public goods and has become a growth industry. But what happens, too often, is that the environmental assessment process squanders time and money. After a lengthy assessment procedure, projects are either permitted or refused. Much money is spent and few benefits are won. More attention should be given to environmental impact *design*, for which the abbreviation EID is used in this book. Instead of wearily mitigating the endless negative impacts of land use, projects should be planned with generosity and imagination, to yield positive impacts on the stock of public goods and contribute to community objectives. The land uses discussed in this book are at different points on the long journey from single-objective planning to multi-objective planning (Fig. 0.1).

Since it is scarcely possible for planning to be politically neutral, I should like to state an enthusiasm which underlies this book: for the mixed economy. Wherever *possible*, land users should be free to do their own thing in their own way. Wherever *necessary*, they should be regulated in the public interest. A doctrinaire attachment to either principle is insupportable. Even the great opponent of state planning, Friedrich von Hayek, in *The road to serfdom*, acknowledged:

> Where, for example, it is impracticable to make the enjoyment of certain services dependent on the payment of a price, competition will not produce the services . . . Nor can certain harmful effects of deforestation, or of some methods of farming, or of the smoke and

	10%	20%	30%	40%	50%	60%	70%	80%	90%	100%
Public open space										
Reservoirs										
Mineral workings										
Agriculture										
Forestry										
River works										
Transport										
Housing										
Commerce										
Manufacturing										
Nature conservation										

Figure 0.1 Estimates of relative progress towards fully multi-use planning by those responsible for land management in the UK, 1945–95.

noise of factories, be confined to the owner of the property in question. In such instances we must find some substitute for regulation by the price mechanism. (Hayek 1979: 28)

Yes, yes and yes again. This book reviews some of the substitutes for "regulation by the price mechanism". Societies must find and implement different solutions, ranging from "all public" to "all private", depending on context and circumstances. Environmental impact design is an example of the mixed economy in action. Private developers may be asked to modify their designs in the interests of the public welfare; public developers may be asked to modifiy their designs in the interests of firms and individuals. To the degree that town planners serve public interests and architects serve private interests, this approach treats landscape planning as "planning writ small" and "architecture writ large".

Thomas Hobbes, a leading theorist of liberal democracy, is remembered for having described the "state of nature" as follows:

No arts; no letters; no society; and which is worst of all, continual fear and danger of violent death; and the life of man, solitary, poor, nasty, brutish and short. (Hobbes 1651: Ch. 13)

Hobbes believed this wretched condition, so prevalent in his lifetime, could be ended only by the rule of law and the establishment of a civil society which fosters private ownership of property. In those countries where these measures have been taken, Hobbes has been proved correct. Fukuyama even detects an "end of history", not for any gloomy reason, but because he believes the advance of liberal democracy has brought an end to the era of war between the great powers (Fukuyama 1992). Today, we face a challenge which requires the dilution of private property rights. As our numbers have grown, the impact of humanity upon the environment has become so heavy that we are in danger of being returned to that very "state of nature" from which Hobbes helped us escape.

Perhaps we can learn from non-human communities. Some of this book's background and organization is explained by the start of my interest in the subject. I think it began with a book on seashore ecology given to me at the age of 12, by an artist. The book explained seashore zonation and I attempted a zoning diagram of the beach near our home. The zones ran from a hardy periwinkle zone, which was splashed only by the largest waves at the highest tides, to a laminaria zone, known to us as the underwater forest, which was hardly exposed by the lowest tides. The wonder of the beach was the rock pools. After watching the breakers roar in from the North Sea, one could walk the shore at low tide and view the most perfect assemblies of plants and animals. Each pool was a symbiotic community. No pool was colonized exclusively by periwinkles, coral, breadcrumb sponge or bladder wrack. Different species lived together and gained from each other's presence, as should land-users.

Terrestrial habitats have more species diversity than rock pools, with interlocking food chains of producers and decomposers. When human societies attempt to bring order out of nature's chaos, they have a depressing tendency towards monoculture (cultivation of only one crop). Vast areas are allocated to spruce *or* larch *or* wheat *or* potatoes *or* housing *or* industry *or* recreation. Compared with the rock pool, there is little diversity, little symbiosis, little sustainability and little beauty. Part 1 of this book, which is plan-oriented, gazes at the whole pool; Part 2, which is project-oriented, examines the niche relationships between land-uses. "Planning" is used in the title of Part 1 and "Design" in the title of Part 2. The distinction between the two activities is not firm, though planning projects tend to be larger in scale, longer in duration, inclusive of several land-uses, more concerned with public than with private goods and more to do with function than with aesthetics.

Part 1 is new to this edition. In Part 2, there are new chapters on transport and agriculture. The remaining six chapters are updated from the first edition, the previous chapters on New Towns and Urban Renewal having coalesced into a chapter on Urbanization – which advocates the foundation of new villages. The appendix contains a list of environmental impact design questions which summarize the book's content. The questions can be used by community groups and planners to help carry out an environmental audit of the relationship between a new project and the existing environment. Environment is used to mean surroundings. For clarity, the questions are terse.

It is a characteristic of landscape planning that the aims, because of their long-term nature, can be attained only in part: the land existed before *Homo sapiens* evolved and will continue to exist when our species is extinct. Each landscape plan is for a small intervention in an endless process. We make footprints in the sands of time. No end-state can be known or planned. The background to this approach is summarized in the first chapter of this book and discussed at greater length in a set of essays *City as landscape* (Turner 1996).

The term environmental impact design, as used in Part 2, embraces development control, design control and impact mitigation. "Environmental Impact Design" was chosen for the title for several reasons: it is broad; it covers modifications to both urban and rural projects; it does not have the unfavourable connotations of the other labels – "development control" suggests an anti-development bias; "design control", like "aesthetic control" suggests an over-emphasis on visual matters and a regulatory approach to creativity; "impact mitigation" suggests we can but fiddle while Rome burns.

It is difficult for statutory plans to deal with the long-term and high-level concepts which should lead and inspire the planning process: beauty, harmony, composition, sustainability, health, spirituality. Landscape planning can and must deal with these concepts. Environmental impact design is too detailed for public authorities to carry out on their own. It requires joint working between the public, landowners and professionals. Only those who use and study individual parcels of land can gain a full appreciation of the potential. Environmental assessment procedures must, therefore, be integrated with land-use planning procedures.

So does the planning of good landscapes require new laws, new bureaucracies and new taxes? No. Most of the developed countries have sufficient legislation on their statute books. They should continue with environmental protection, which is the husbandry of a diminishing resource, but they should aquire more skill in the art of environmental improvement, which can create valuable public goods.

Part 1

Landscape Planning

Introduction

To conserve and create a good environment, societies need:

- Information
- Ideals
- Theories of context
- Laws

Chapter 1 discusses the strategic role of information in the planning process. Chapter 2 reviews the ideals and the plans which may guide us in the conservation and development of fine landscape, as a lighthouse guides ships. Chapter 3 considers the laws and theories of context which can help fit projects to their environmental niches.

CHAPTER 1
Will planning die?

Specialisation . . . is the mortal sin

Karl Popper (1945)

Will planning die away, then?

Environmental planning has been too scientific, too man-centred, too past-fixated and two-dimensional. In *Cities of tomorrow* Peter Hall asks "Will planning die away, then?" (Hall 1988: 360). His answer is markedly cautious: "Not entirely". The thirst for liberalism and economic growth, which pushed back planning in the 1980s and smashed the Berlin Wall, now threatens all types of government planning. But, argues Hall, a core is likely to survive. This is because:

> Good environment, as the economists would say, is an income-elastic good: as people, and societies generally, get richer, they demand proportionally ever more of it. And, apart from building private estates with walls around them, the only way they are going to get it is through public action. The fact that people are willing and even anxious to spend more and more of their precious time in defending their own environment, through membership of all kinds of voluntary organisations and through attendance at public inquiries, is testimony to that fact. (Hall 1988: 360)

This chapter looks at the factors that have caused our doubts about planning, and at how they might be resolved. The argument, in summary, is that geography created the opportunity for physical planning, that geography revolutionized planning at the start of the twentieth century, and that geography can revolutionize planning once again. A development of profound importance, the computer-based Geographical Information System (GIS), is set fair to be the revolution's handmaiden. Modern geography and modernist planning are giving way to a future in which there will be a myriad of thematic maps, pluralist plans and non-statutory action by user groups 'willing and even anxious to spend more and more of their precious time' on the environment.

A good environment, like good health, is easy to recognize but hard to define. And "health is not valued till sickness comes". To conserve and improve our health, doctors must understand the workings of the body. To conserve and improve our environment, planners must understand the geographical equivalents of anatomy, physiology and biochemistry. Doctors found it easier to investigate surface anatomy than the interior. Planners found it easier to investigate the physical environment than its workings. But one cannot treat the inside of the body by treating the skin, and one cannot improve the environment by dealing only with the visible. Knowledge, ideas, beliefs and skills are required.

Gender and planning

Planning has been "too masculine": it has concentrated on the way of the hunter and neglected the way of the nester.

Abstract thought characterizes the way of the hunter and, hitherto, the way of the planner. Hunters identify a goal, formulate a plan and decide upon a course of action. In most human societies, this has been a masculine role (Betsky 1995). It requires dominance and it has led societies to privilege the way of the hunter over the way of the nester. In this sense, planning has been too masculine and too preoccupied with a never-present future. In times of scarcity, hunting may take precedence over other activities. In times of plenty, the nester can give thought to the long-term wellbeing of the species, while the hunter continues to sacrifice everything for a single objective. Modern planning has over-emphasized both man-the-hunter and man-the-species.

In the 1780s Lord Kames, an important figure in the history of aesthetic philosophy, wished to "improve" Kincardine Moss for agriculture. He therefore diverted a river and washed so much peat into the Firth of Forth that the estuarine shore was made brown and sticky for a decade. Standards have changed. Such a policy would now be judged unethical and illegal. There was an international outcry when the wreck of the *Exxon Valdez* washed an oil slick onto the pristine shore of Prince William's Sound in the 1980s. Aldo Leopold compares the advent of a land ethic to the changed relationship between the sexes:

> When the God-like Odysseus returned from the wars in Troy, he hanged all on one rope a dozen slave-girls of his household whom he suspected of misbehaviour during his absence. (Leopold 1970)

They were his property – to be disposed of as he wished. Ethical standards now embrace relations between man and environment. To the regret of some, land can no longer be treated as a woman or a slave, to be raped and destroyed at will. The creation of a good environment requires the way of the hunter to be fused with the way of the nester. Planning needs to be less dictatorial and more inspirational.

Science and planning

Planning has been "too scientific" in the sense of trying to project trends and deduce policies from empirical studies of what exists.

It is right that diagnosis should come before treatment, but prescriptive plans cannot be derived from scientific studies of what exists. David Hume, the empiricist philosopher, declared that *ought* cannot be derived from *is*. His subject was morality. His point has continuing importance for planning:

> In every system of morality which I have hitherto met with I have always remarked that the author proceeds for some time in the ordinary way of reasoning, and establishes the being of a God, or makes observations concerning human affairs; when of a sudden I am surprised to find that, instead of the usual copulations of propositions, *is* and *is not*, I meet with no proposition that is not connected with an *ought*, or an *ought not*. The change is imperceptible; but is, however, of the last consequence. (Hume 1974 edn, III(i): 1)

Take the case of highway planning. Surveys will show the trend in vehicle movements to be rising. Analysis of origins and destinations will show where vehicles come from and whither they are bound. Alternative alignments for new roads can be mapped. Public consultation takes place. The best route is chosen. The road should be built on this alignment. Money will be allocated next year. By imperceptible degrees, highway planners develop the case for new roads. If this mode of reasoning is accepted, similar studies will go on leading to similar conclusions, until all the cities in all the world are blacktop deserts with isolated buildings surrounded by cars – standing as bleak monuments to the folly of pseudo-scientific planning.

Science is characterized by the application of reason and observation. They are matchless tools, but of limited efficacy. Plato's analogy of The

Cave dealt with the limits to human knowledge and understanding. Men, he suggested, are like prisoners in a cave, able to look only at shadows on the wall, never at the objects that cast the shadows (Fig. 1.1) Nor is modern science able to reach beyond the walls of the cave, although our cave is larger. In the absence of certain knowledge as to why the human race exists and how its members ought to behave, it is necessary to rely on judgement and belief. Can science, for example, advise on whether it is right to let a species of animal, say the tsetse fly, become extinct?

Our descendants may come to see the twentieth century as the Age of Science. It opened with widespread confidence in the Enlightenment belief that scientific reasoning would usher in a golden age. With ignorance, poverty and disease banished, the Four Horsemen of the Apocalypse should have been confined to their barracks for evermore. But our confidence was unseated, by two world wars, by some 300 lesser wars between 1945 and 1990, and by a century of environmental despoliation, in which science and technology saddled the Horsemen. Many people now feel that we live in what George Steiner described as Bluebeard's Castle (Steiner 1971). We keep opening doors to gain knowledge, and in so doing we draw nearer and nearer to that fatal final door which, once opened, will lead to our own destruction. The remedy is not to destroy the Castle of Knowledge. It is to restrain Bluebeard. We must assert the pre-eminence of human values over spurious facts. In planning, rationality must be guided by morality and imagination.

Lack of imagination has been a significant failing of scientific planning. The UK government's Chief Planning Inspector wrote that:

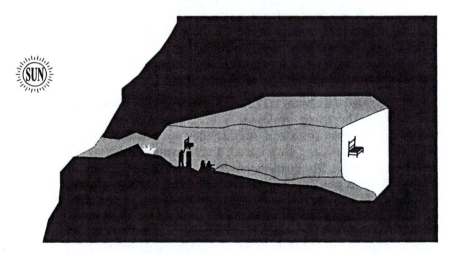

Figure 1.1 Plato's Cave Analogy suggests that we live as prisoners, chained in an underground cave, only seeing shadows cast on the cave wall.

In particular, at the regional and strategic level, [planning] has been very tentative. Few regional plans or structure plans examine imaginative options for the future, or try to consider in any meaningful way what life in the twenty-first century will be like. (Shepley 1995)

The plans lack imaginative content.

Geography and planning

Three-dimensional design, and the natural tendency for places to evolve and change, have been comparatively neglected by planners.

Map-making and planning have ebbed and flowed together. They declined with the Roman Empire and resumed their advance with the Renaissance. Surveying and cartography have a profound influence on geography and planning. Our verb "to plan" derives from the noun "plan", meaning a two-dimensional projection on a plane surface (Fig. 1.2). The word "geography" comes from *geo*, meaning "the earth" and *graphein*, meaning "to write". Geography is the science that describes the Earth's surface and explains how it acquired its present character. Before the age of Darwin, Christendom believed the Earth to have been created in six days. Darwin's theory of evolution changed this belief. When geologists examined the evidence, it was found that the Earth had evolved by infinite degrees on a geological timescale. Ruskin, when he sat to contemplate God and Nature, kept hearing "those terrible hammers" chipping away at the bedrock of his faith.

Figure 1.2 In origin, "to plan" means to make a two-dimensional projection on a plane surface.

Geikie, a geologist, adopted and adapted the word "landscape" to impart an evolutionary worldview (Fig. 1.3). The *Oxford English Dictionary* cites one of his books, published in 1886, as the first place in which "landscape" was used in its predominant modern sense: "a tract of land with its distinguishing characteristics and features, esp. considered as a product of shaping processes and agents (usually natural)" (Burchfield 1976). The descriptive use of the word became predominant. Before Geikie, landscape was used in a sense which derived from the Neoplatonic theory of art, to mean "an ideal place". It was an evaluative word, eminently suited to characterizing a goal of the planning and design process. Landscape painters sought to represent an ideal world on canvas (Fig. 1.4). Landscape designers sought to make landscapes of country estates (Fig. 1.5). However, the evaluative connotations of "landscape" were never entirely discarded: if we speak of a wretched landscape, the phrase has a deliberate internal tension.

Once the concept of landscape evolution had been grasped, it was natural for planners to look beyond city boundaries. They considered a wide range of geographical phenomena and extended their professional interests beyond the types of plan produced by cartographers, surveyors, architects and engineers. Patrick Geddes, inspired by French geography, was the most

Figure 1.3 The geographers' use of "landscape" – Siccar Point in Berwickshire. Towards the end of the nineteenth century biologists and geographers began to use landscape to mean "a tract of land, considered as a product of shaping processes and agents". The geological non-conformity at Siccar Point was used, by James Hutton, to prove that the world was made over an immense period of time.

Figure 1.4 The artists' use of "landscape" – Claude's *Jacob with Laban and his daughters*. Artists used the word landscape to mean "a picture representing natural inland scenery". Such paintings usually contained buildings and showed men living in harmony with nature. (Courtesy of the Governors of Dulwich Picture Gallery.)

influential agent of this change. He had trained as a biologist with Darwin's collaborator Thomas Huxley. Geddes was also the first British citizen to use "landscape architect" as a professional title. He became a founder member of Britain's Town Planning Institute and his Survey-Analysis-Plan

Figure 1.5 The designers' use of "landscape" – Blenheim Park is one of the great eighteenth-century English landscapes. It was designed, by Lancelot Brown, to be an ideal place where the owner could live in harmony with nature.

9

methodology formalized the link between modern geography and modern planning. The American Institute of Planners was an offshoot of the American Society of Landscape Architects.

Modern planning

Modern planning tended towards the creation of similar places all over the world.

The belief that science, education and planning would inevitably make the world a better place derives from the Enlightenment of the eighteenth century. During the nineteenth century, planning became rooted in health, roads and other public projects. This type of planning was especially well developed in Germany. During the twentieth century, planning became more ambitious, aiming to integrate transport, housing, industry, forestry, agriculture and other land-uses. The wide environmental horizon was good, but the technocrats' scientific approach had drawbacks. Planners were lured into trend planning, into single-use zoning and into the habit of deriving "ought"' from "is". The three stages of modern planning can be named, like architectural styles.

Early-modern planning

In the first half of the twentieth century, before the influence of Geddes and Mumford made itself felt, planning had an engineering and architectural bias. This is described as the "*beaux-arts*" or "city beautiful" era. Design and drawing effort were lavished on the environmental equivalents of anatomical drawings, chiefly concerned with the outside appearance of cities. Planning was conceived as "architecture writ large", extending beyond the confines of individual buildings to focus on the design of streets and façades (Fig. 1.6).

High-modern planning

In the 1920s and 1930s, with a better understanding of evolutionary geography, planners produced master plans, zoning plans and land-use plans, showing the "parts of the body" as separate compartments. Despite Geddes, they paid less attention to the biology of the environment than to its physics. The main elements in high-modern planning were written documents and two-dimensional plans, known as zoning plans, land-use plans or

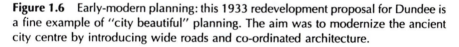

DUNDEE—REDEVELOPMENT PROPOSALS, 1933

Figure 1.6   Early-modern planning: this 1933 redevelopment proposal for Dundee is a fine example of "city beautiful" planning. The aim was to modernize the ancient city centre by introducing wide roads and co-ordinated architecture.

just town plans. High-modern planning went beyond architecture and aimed to produce land-use plans which would, for example, prevent houses being built beside factories or on valuable agricultural land. This led to a conception of planning focused on land-use plans, density regulations and lines of communication. Cities were seen as nodes, with definable land-use zones, axial communication lines and density gradients from centre to the periphery (Fig. 1.7).

With the advent of high-modern planning, the planning profession was engulfed by practitioners from a social science background who knew about geography, politics, economics and statistics. The goals of the profession then became so wide, and went so far beyond architecture, that planning became "government writ small" instead of "architecture writ large". Physical planning and design became neglected arts.

Late-modern planning

In the 1960s and 1970s, planners developed an approach which embraced biological and ecological ideas, but still focused on land-uses and road

11

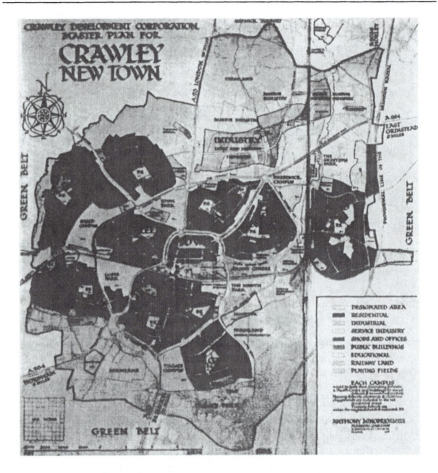

Figure 1.7 High-modern planning: the 1948 plan for Crawley New Town demarcated the land into zones for town centre, residential, industrial, parkland and other land-use zones.

transport. It was variously known as policy planning, comprehensive planning, systems planning, corporate planning or administrative planning. Planners saw themselves as impartial experts who would co-ordinate the work of other experts, in order to solve problems, resolve conflicts, "conduct the orchestra" of the built environment professions and thus produce the best of all possible worlds. McLoughlin (1970) and Chadwick (1978) were powerful advocates of this approach (Fig. 1.8). The problems planners set out to solve were at a high level: of economic efficiency, justice, land-use and transport.

12

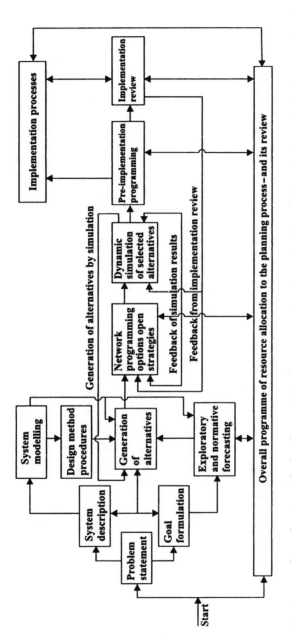

Figure 1.8 Late-modern planning: Chadwick used this diagram to show the principle of "A rational method of systematic planning, derived from scientific method" (Chadwick 1978: 378). (Courtesy of the author.)

Each phase of modernist planning embraced the assumption that planning could have a unitary vision for the future condition of a town or region: one way, one truth, one method. Following science, planning became universal. This approach led to common plans, regardless of whether they were for towns in Europe, Asia, Africa or the Americas. Such minor variations as there were between the visions of the future encapsulated in plans for different places depended more on the dates of their conception than upon the character of the localities or the wishes of local inhabitants.

One year the fashion would be green belts and ring roads. Then town expansion schemes based on avenues. Then city centre redevelopment projects based on ring roads. Then conservation areas. Then park-and-ride schemes. Then business parks and shopping malls. Then traffic calming. Most of the plans came from a narrow social group. We can see them as having been middle-class, car-owning and aged between 30 and 60, with social-democratic tendencies and certificates from professional bodies to affirm their grasp of the conventional wisdom. They were too ambitious in what they sought to control, too limited in the range of community interests they sought to embrace and possessed of too little power to achieve their objectives, even in Stalinist regimes. Happily, the age of narrowly scientific government and rigidly scientific planning is passing away.

Single-purpose planning

Great harm was done to the environment by single-use planning.

When working on the first edition of this book, I made a discovery which surprised me at the time but seems obvious in retrospect: there is a common pattern to the recent history of each land-use – and it is a product of scientific modernism:

1 At some point, around 1900, management of the land-use came within the province of a specialized skill.
2 A learned society took control of the land-use.
3 Educational courses were set up and text books written.
4 The land-use came as near to being a single-purpose activity as possible.
5 Side-effects, whether harmful or beneficial, were excluded from consideration.
6 There was a public outcry in the 1970s.
7 Experts spent the 1980s attending conferences and developing new techniques which used the vocabulary of multi-objective planning.

8 Few changes were made, but higher fees were charged, glossier brochures were produced and managers began to boast of their 1990s-style environmental awareness.

This is the story of planning for forests, roads, rivers, industry, commerce, agriculture, minerals and urban renewal, as will be discussed in Part 2. Other land-uses, such as parks and nature reserves, have been run in a single-purpose manner but have been less criticized, so far. Writing about T. E. Lawrence, Liddell Hart made a related point:

> The increasing specialisation of warfare is largely responsible for the sterilisation of generalship. It is likely to become worse as warfare becomes more scientific. It can only be overcome by wide thought and hard work. (Hart, 1936: 478)

Single-purposism results in roads planned only for motor vehicles, forests for timber production, farms for food, rivers for flood water, bus stops for standing in queues, parks for recreation, stations for getting off trains and buildings for sleeping *or* working. Single-purposism is obviously bad for the environment. If students are isolated on a campus, they lack shops, entertainment, part-time jobs and a variety of accommodation. If places to work in are isolated from places to live in, everyone must commute. If houses are isolated from reservoirs, parks and natural areas, people cannot choose to live in contact with nature. If rivers are planned as industrial corridors, they cannot fulfil their potential as wildlife habitats or public open spaces.

Multi-purpose planning

Modern use-categories should be deconstructed

The arrangement of land-uses can be subject to philosophical analysis, aided by Venn diagrams and structuralist and deconstructionist concepts.

Venn diagrams were devised by an English logician, John Venn, as a means of representing classes and logical statements pictorially. Circles or ellipses are used to depict categories and relationships between categories. Thus an isolated circle can depict a single land-use, the overlap between two circles an area that has two land-uses, the overlap between three circles an area that has three land-uses. The relationships between Venn diagrams, overlay maps and database tables are shown by Figs 2.9a and 2.9b.

Before the age of planning, land-uses were mixed indiscriminately (Fig. 1.9a). If someone built a tannery or a blacksmith's shop next to your home, this was unfortunate: the former gave off a sickening odour, the latter a devil's rattle. In the early days of planning, problems of "negative side

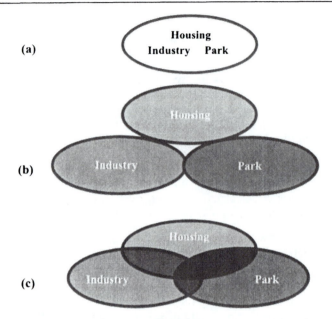

Figure 1.9 Three alternative ways of arranging land-uses, shown by Venn diagrams: (a) mixed, (b) singular zoning, (c) plural zoning.

effects", or pollution, were solved by single-use zoning (Fig. 1.9b). Today, the aim is to allow "good neighbour" land-uses to enjoy a beneficial relationship (Fig. 1.9c) and to place "bad neighbour" land-uses in industrial zones. The task of fitting land-uses together and forming harmonious relationships requires skill and ingenuity, as does match-making between people. The first step is to review each project to discover its potential for:

- adaptation to the production of public goods (see Chapter 2);
- adaption to neighbouring land-uses and the local context (see Chapter 3).

As discussed in the preceding section, the use of scientific procedures led to an emphasis on single-use planning. This was a cause of urban sprawl. It also tended to produce a hierarchical relationship between land-uses: roads have a privileged relationship to planning, planning to architecture, architecture to landscape architecture, flood control to nature conservation, forestry to amenity. The way these land-uses are planned and designed is a sign that reveals underlying social structures. They are structures that can be interpreted with the aid of two philosophical approaches, structuralism and deconstruction.

Structuralism is a broad twentieth-century intellectual movement, which seeks to discover structures in everyday life and in language. It developed from semiotics, which is the study of signs. A sign comprises a signifier and a signified. The signifier is an indicator; the signified is the meaning. An arrow (the signifier) tells you which way to go (the signified). An oversized door signifies "main entrance". Social customs can also be signifiers. For example, the custom of cooking food signifies that "Man is different from nature." The sign is a human construct to signify how we understand the world and expect people to behave. Binary pairs such as *cooked:uncooked, mown:unmown,* and *married:unmarried* are surface structures which tell of deep structures in human society.

Deconstruction is a development of structuralism. Followers of Jacques Derrida have argued that in each binary opposition one term is hierarchically privileged. Culture is better than nature, cooked is better than uncooked, mown is better than unmown, male is better than female, speech is better than writing, a novelist is better than a critic, a moral poem is better than a naïve poem, reason is better than emotion. Deconstruction began as a way of reading philosophical texts to uncover hidden structures and contradictions. Use of the technique was extended from philosophy to literature and then to the visual arts. It is a sceptical procedure, which questions hierarchical relationships. The words master and chairman, for example, are said to contain the meaning that men have a hierarchical dominance over women. Noting that architectural function is privileged over architectural form, Jacques Derrida recommended deconstructing the relationship. At Parc de la Villette, Bernard Tschumi designed the form of the park buildings *before* planning their functions. He also deconstructed the very idea of a park and proclaimed that la Villette would be "the largest discontinuous building in the world". His clients wittily re-deconstructed his proclamation, and the place is known as Parc de la Villette (Turner 1996: 208).

A deconstructive procedure can also be used to challenge relationships between development projects and their contexts. The man-made environment has been profoundly affected by hierarchical relationships, not unlike those discussed in structuralist and deconstructionist texts. It has many examples of relationships that have been brought to the surface, as a crude artificial language and landscape. Relph describes the effects of zoning policies on the North American townscape:

> The result on the ground is segregated landscapes – here a zone of high-rise apartments, there a zone of detached houses, beyond a zone of retailing revealed as a plaza. And the boundaries between zones on the maps appear no less clearly as boundaries in urban landscapes – a six-foot-high fence marks the line between a residential zone and a retail zone, an arterial road separates industrial and residential uses . . . in those parts of cities where everything old has been carefully eradicated, zoning has directly contributed to the creation of a tight visual order in which landscapes correspond almost exactly to the land use zones set out in plans. (Relph 1987: 69)

Instead of the ecotones and easy transitions that characterize the natural environment, we have demarcated strips and parcels of land for road, river, housing, open space, industry, shopping, recreation, forestry, ecological area (Fig. 1.10). In the following pairs, the first member normally has a privileged position:

road : housing
river : housing
housing : open space
recreation : ecological area
forestry : recreation

Everywhere one looks, there are similar examples. Land-uses have been parcelled. Boundaries have become binary divides. Everything must be A or not-A, B or not-B. The fantastic workings of a living organism are severed by the butcher's knife, as in Tunnard's montage (Fig. 1.11). Smooth transitions are forced into culturally imposed formal structures. Happy is the river that is not a property line, not a local government boundary, not an engineer's "watercourse". The butchery was done by people with an inadequate appreciation of environmental structure. Many of the privileges, concealed in language and custom, date from early times and have no relevance to the conditions of modern life. In the following examples an advantage can be gained by reversing the hierarchy, but the reversal should not be institutionalized:

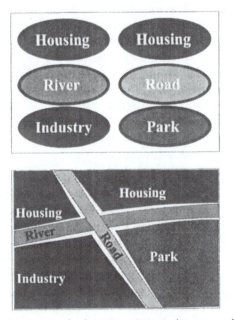

Figure 1.10 Singular zoning for housing, river, industry, road and park.

Figure 1.11 The fantastic workings of a living organism ought not to be severed with a butcher's knife (from Christopher Tunnard *Gardens in the modern landscape*).

Roads : Planning When planning a ring road, give land-use decisions precedence over highway decisions.

Planning : Architecture Let the design of an important building change the town plan.

Landscape : Architecture Let the planning of the outdoor landscape take precedence over the building design.

River engineering : Nature conservation When designing flood control works, let the interests of the river's fauna, and of recreational users, be the prime considerations.

Forestry : Recreation When designing a forest, let timber production be regarded a useful byproduct, not the main objective.

Some land-uses, notably highways, are notorious for their hierarchically dominant behaviour. As public resentment has grown, a few concessions have been made. Like the "reforms" granted by Nicholas III in pre-revolutionary Russia, they have been grudging and inadequate, too little and too late. Some roads have been delayed and others diverted. But when the roads come to be built, it is still done in accordance with a standard set of so-called "design criteria", which cover a host of details: horizontal and vertical curves, kerbs and drainage, the location of junctions, storm detention basins, sight lines at junctions, fencing and bank profiles. Although the UK Highways Agency permits a few minor "relaxations" and "departures", the consequence of the "design criteria" is that roads do not respond to local conditions or the wishes of local people. Nor can they be integrated with urban design or the local environment. At one time, a Cornish road was very different from a Northumbrian road. Now they are the same. It is like the Stalinist practice of constructing identical blocks of flats in the Crimea, Siberia and Germany.

The aspirations and skills of local people and community groups deserve a central place in the planning process. Ornithological clubs can plan for birds, conservation societies for conservation, angling clubs for fishing, bus companies for buses, schools for children's travel, ethnic minorities for their own communities, chambers of commerce for business, cycling clubs for cycling. Each group can contribute a layer to the planning process and each must respect the other layers in the cake. The community groups must obtain geographical information and then produce plans.

GIS-based planning

Computer-based geographic information systems (GISs) have the potential to revitalize planning, when they are used as conceptual models, rather than maps or decision-making tools.

Geography made planning possible, and geography is set to revolutionize planning, especially landscape planning. The GIS will allow a host of new messages to be heard and spoken. It assists multi-purpose planning by allowing the relationships between land-uses to be recorded and analyzed (Fig. 1.12). McLuhan's dictum that "the medium is the message", related to the successive impacts of printing, radio, film and television on society. They led to new ways of seeing, understanding, influencing and controlling the world. So will geographical information systems.

A GIS is a computer-based system for storing, retrieving and analyzing geographical information. Like its famous predecessor, the map, it is a store of data (Fig. 1.13). Spatial information can be held as points, lines and areas, defined by co-ordinate geometry. Unlike a map, a GIS permits the rapid modification and reproduction of plans, at any scale, with extraordinary precision. Non-spatial information, known as attribute data, can be held as words and figures. Subject to the constraints of data collection, data storage and data processing, a GIS allows the physical world to be mapped in any number of ways for any number of purposes. Readers who have used a spreadsheet but not a GIS may find an analogy helpful. If a TV screen or a newspaper photograph is enlarged, it will be found to comprise a large number of dots, known as pixels. These dots can be thought of as the cells of a spreadsheet or database programme. On a TV screen, the dots receive information about colours. In a GIS, they can also contain other types of information: heights, temperatures, pressures, population statistics, soil types, plant species, animal species, anything. Like the information

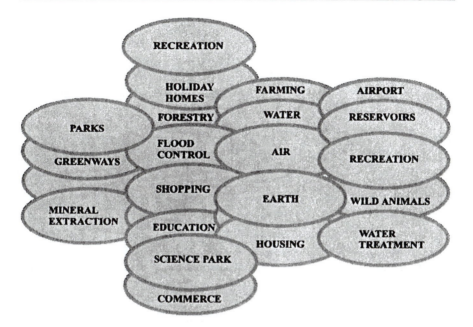

Figure 1.12 A GIS enables relationships between land-uses to be mapped and analyzed as a set of Venn diagrams.

displayed on a TV screen, GIS data can be stored digitally on magnetic media. It can then be recalled whenever it is wanted and displayed in fresh combinations.

When a new technology becomes available, it is often used in the first instance to do the same job as an older technology. Early printing presses were used to print bibles; the first automobiles were treated like horse-drawn carriages; the first tanks were used as mobile guns. But it is also possible to use new technologies in new ways. This is the challenge. The GIS will do for landscape planning what the pocket calculator did for arithmetic: it will make previously complicated operations easy to perform. But a GIS will not convert planning from an art of judgement into a deductive science. As with any computer system, there is a direct relationship between inputs and outputs. Facts in, facts out. Values in, values out. Wisdom in, wisdom out. Garbage in, garbage out!

GIS will provide new conceptual models to help us think about planning. Like physical models (Fig. 1.14), they can represent the past or the future. Physical models display shapes and colours. GIS models can show all sorts of other qualities: traffic, water flows, air flows, materials, vegetation, population, property values, any topic on which data are available. For each layer, the GIS can show both the existing situation, a predicted situation

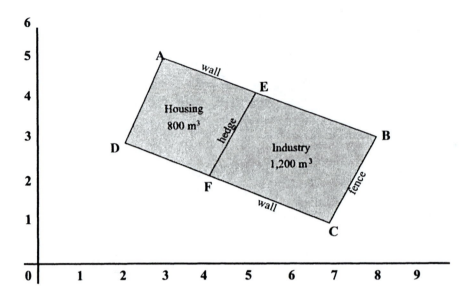

Polygons	Area	Land-use		
ABCD	2,000 square metres	Urban		
AEFD	800 square metres	Housing		
BCFE	1,200 square metres	Industry		
Points			Co-ordinates	
		x	y	
A		3	5	
B		8	3	
C		7	1	
D		2	3	
E		5	4	
F		4	2	
			Co-ordinates	
Lines	Boundary type	x	y	x	y
AB	Wall	3	5	8	3
BC	Fence	8	3	7	1
CD	Wall	7	1	2	3
DA	Wall	2	3	3	5
EF	Hedge	5	4	4	2

Figure 1.13 A GIS is a spatial database. Areas on a map are produced from database tables, and vice versa.

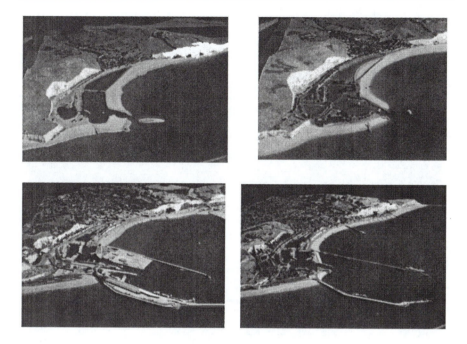

Figure 1.14 Physical models, like GIS models, can show what the land was like in the past and what it could be like in the future. These models are of Dover. (Courtesy of Dover Museum.)

and a proposed future condition. GIS can also store the information that land managers use (Fig. 1.15).

Diagrams in textbooks often represent a GIS as a glass box with a series of layers. If the GIS is to contain only information about the existing landscape, this is a reasonable analogy. The date the information was collected is the date on the box. But if the GIS also deals with future plans, then a tank of water is a better analogy, with new material arriving all the time. Better still, imagine a column reaching up through the earth's bedrock, on through the sea, up towards the outer atmosphere (Fig. 1.16). Layer upon layer of material arrives, sinking gradually through the swirling airs and waters to form the existing landscape. High above are the forces of nature, human intentions and dreams. Some will settle, others will be swept away. Pre-GIS planning used only two layers: one for the existing landscape, one for the proposed landscape.

Post-GIS planning will be multi-dimensional and multi-layered. Plans will be able to reach high levels of indefinability. Metaphorically, they will lie below the seabed and above the waves. Health can be partially defined by

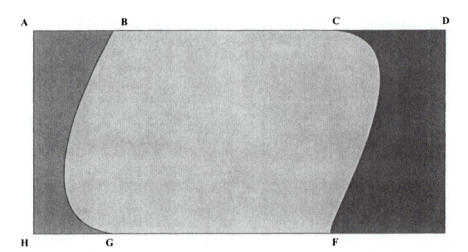

Polygon	Area	Operation	Cost	Total
ADEH	4000 m^2	Collect litter	£1.00/m^2	£4,000
BCFG	2600 m^2	Mow grass	£	£
ABGH	600 m^2	Weed flower bed	£	£
CDEF	800 m^2	Weed shrub bed	£	£

Figure 1.15 A GIS can store the information that administrators and businesses require.

quantifiable measures: temperature, pulse rate, cholesterol levels, physical strength and so forth. But these are seabed measures and they are not the only ones. Spiritual, social and mental states also contribute to good health and to a good environment.

In many countries the environmental impact assessment system is separate from the planning system. GIS has the technical capability to integrate the two systems. It should become easy to ask zoning, location and impact questions. A further strength of GIS is that information from photography and remote sensing can be utilized. But the real significance of GISs is conceptual. They model the environment and help us to *think* about development and the environment.

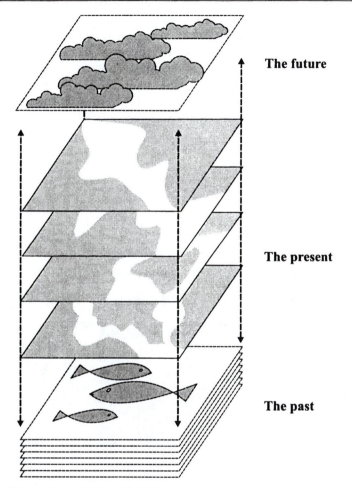

Figure 1.16 A GIS can be used to model the past, the present and the future.

Although computer memories can be vast, GIS models will always be small in relation to the complexity of the real world. The only accurate model of the world is the world itself. Individual atoms, protons and neutrons, which would have to be referenced in a complete GIS model, are placed into colossal categories: hill, town, house, meadow, farm, bog, forest. The categories, known as entities or objects in a GIS, are chosen because of the ways in which humans live. Other animals and other human societies would have different ways of categorizing the world. If hedgehogs could set up a GIS, one surmises their categories would be based on olfactory perceptions of food, safety and sex.

Classifications are always made for a purpose. At present there are strict limits, imposed by laws and the limitations of maps and mapping conventions, on what can be shown on approved town plans. Only the "most important" land-uses appear: housing, industry, roads, commercial areas and parks. When computer-based geographical information systems replace maps, there will be fewer restraints on what is mapped, planned and designed. Planning-on-paper will be replaced by planning-by-database (Fig. 1.17).

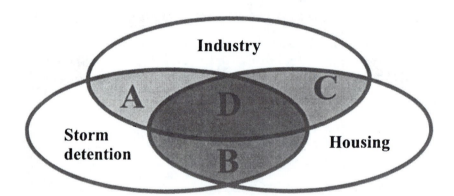

Area	Primary land-use	Other land-use(s)	Planning objective(s)
A	Industry	Storm detention	An industrial area with lush vegetation and buildings with the cabability to resist flooding
B	Housing	Storm detention	Scenic housing with views over public open space
C	Housing	Industry	Live-in workshops for residential use combined with good-neighbour industry
D	Recreation	Housing Industry Storm detention	Public open space designed to accommodate storm water, occasional commercial/industrial use and occasional residential use (e.g. for tourists in summer)

Figure 1.17 Planning-on-paper will be replaced with planning-by-database, using areas, relationships and attributes.

So will planning die?

GIS to the rescue.

On the contrary, I believe it will grow. But the way of the hunter must be married to the way of the nester. The age of the pre-eminent development plan, master plan or unitary land-use zoning plan is passing away. The fall of the Berlin Wall in 1989 was a symbolic end to a period in which scientifically trained technocratic elites aspired to the formulation of Five-Year Plans. In the foreseeable future, all kinds of plans will be produced by all kinds of groups. This book is concerned with plans for the conservation and improvement of the landscape as perceived by the individual, the walker, the cyclist, the swimmer, the ornithologist, the parent, the traveller, the photographer, the home-maker, the employer, the employee. It is not concerned with the planning of statistical aggregates.

Planning will become more plural. Forward-looking plans and backward looking plans will be wanted by many groups within society. Some will be able to prepare their own plans. Others will need help. The planners' job will become that of making plans, of assisting others to make plans, of fitting plans together, of supplying information, of resolving conflicts, of helping with implementation. Where conflict resolution proves impossible, or where public funding proves necessary, decisions must be taken by democratic or judicial bodies. Land-use plans and master plans will be joined by mistress plans, servant plans, hedgehog plans, water plans and vision plans, among others.

The forum for all this activity will be the geographical information system, accessed through the Internet. The lower layers of the GIS model will represent the existing environment. The upper layers will represent plans, ideals and aspirations. Conventional plans look downwards to the existing world and project current trends in a depressing manner. Future plans will also look upwards to the world of hopes and dreams. Development projects should consider the welfare of the existing environment and be creative with regard to future environments. GIS technology will enable both to be modelled and displayed.

CHAPTER 2
Landscape plans

Our whole life is governed by ideals, good and bad, whether we know it or not. North, south, east and west are only ideals of direction: you will never absolutely get there; yet you can never get anywhere, save indeed straight down into a hole, without them.

Patrick Geddes

Through his own work and through Lewis Mumford, the influence of Patrick Geddes on twentieth century town and country planning has been profound. He is remembered as an advocate of survey-analysis-plan scientific planning, but, as the above quotation reveals, Geddes also had a full appreciation of the importance of ideals and imagination in guiding the planning process.

Lighthouse plans

Plans are required for public goods.

Landscape quality is a public good. The distinction between private and public goods is that the former can be purchased, owned and consumed. Houses, apples and seats at the opera are examples of private goods. The characteristics of public goods are non-depletability and non-chargeability. A lighthouse is the traditional shining example (Fig. 2.1)! However many people benefit, the source of light and safety is not depleted. A lighthouse has to be paid for, but it is impracticable to levy a charge on the individual sailors who are warned away from dangerous rocks in tempestuous seas. In cities, the following points about public goods should be kept in mind:

- We cannot charge for fresh air, beautiful views, clean rain, fine townscape, access to public space, listening to the birds or the presence of hedgehogs.

Figure 2.1 A lighthouse distributes a public good which costs money, which is not depleted by over-use and for which no charge is made.

- We want public goods but cannot, as individuals, decide to purchase more of them.
- The fact that I benefit from a public good (e.g. clean rain) does not reduce your opportunity to benefit from the same good.
- A large stock of public goods makes some cities more desirable than others as places to live in, work in and visit.
- If public goods are not protected, they tend to decay.
- If new public goods are to be created, plans must be agreed and implemented.

The distinction between public and private goods is useful in clarifying the objectives of planning, but it is not hard and fast. Roadspace is usually made available as a public good, but it can be subject to tolls. Available roadspace can also be depleted, by abrasion or congestion.

29

To protect and enhance public goods, communities need plans. This chapter will review some of types of landscape plan required. They can be thought of as lighthouse plans, because they show directions for movement. Some public goods will only benefit some sections of the public and may harm the interests of other sections. Therefore planning must be subject to plural control by democratic bodies, community groups and individuals.

Ecology, economics and planning

Negative side effects are the environment's wicked stepmother; positive side effects are her fairy godmother.

The twin disciplines of economics and ecology provide a theoretical framework within which to discuss the landscape implications of public goods. Both take their name from the Greek root *oikos*, meaning home. Economists restrict their concern to the "home of man". Ecologists study all relationships between living things and the environment. "Ecology is really an extension of economics to the whole world of life" (Wells et al. 1931). In a developed ecosystem each species has a place in the community structure and depends on resources provided by other plants and animals. Energy is collected by green plants and distributed through food chains and food webs to herbivores, carnivores and decomposers. Each plant and each animal adapts to a special place in the habitat, known as a niche (Fig. 2.2). The habitat itself belongs to all its inhabitants. Elton wrote that

> . . . the "niche" of an animal means its place in the biotic environ-
> ment, its relations to food and enemies . . . when an ecologist says
> "there goes a badger" he should include in his thoughts some definite
> idea of the animal's place in the community to which it belongs, just as
> if he had said "there goes the vicar". (Elton 1966a: 64)

Some land-uses, such as lighthouses and churches (Fig. 2.3), have distinct niches in the land-use pattern, from which they radiate public goods. Only a few modern buildings have an equally beneficial relationship with their surroundings (Fig. 2.4). Private ownership boundaries are all too obvious and one rarely senses that enthusiasm which Elton so plainly felt for the forest community: "No sensitive person can enter a forest without feeling that here is the supreme development of nature on land" (Elton 1966b: 190). Though dominant in the ecosystem, trees are massive providers of public goods. Birds and other animals live among their branches; insects and mammals use them as a vertical transport route and benefit from their shelter. Trees prevent erosion and draw moisture from the water table. When blown over, trees provide a habitat for insects and fungi. But it is

Sumer is icumen in,
Lhude sing cuccu!
Groweth sed, and bloweth med,
And springth the wude nu—
Sing cuccu!

Figure 2.2 Each species has a niche in the habitat and depends on resources provided by other species.

not the primary aim of trees to provide shelter, of insects to transport pollen, or of fungi to make topsoil. Such benefits are *positive side effects* of their primary activities.

Good landscape planning should achieve comparable patterns of benefit by arranging niches for human land-uses. This is not an argument against the private ownership of land; it is an argument for being considerate and generous to one's neighbours and for seeking to plan the outdoor environment as a home, for plants, animals and humans. The endeavour can be described as *oikos*-planning, eco-planning, home-planning or eco-city-planning.

Studies of economic relationships also take account of side-effects. Alfred Marshall was the first to recognize their importance. He was particularly interested in the favourable impact of external *economies* on economic growth. When firms of a similar character are concentrated in a locality they develop interdependencies. Each firm gains from the widening pool of skilled staff, specialist knowledge, new techniques and shared facilities.

31

Figure 2.3 Old churches often have a niche in a settlement, from which they radiate public goods.

As in natural communities, the benefits become available to others as side-effects of the firms' primary activities (Marshall 1961: 217). Since Marshall's time economists have become more interested in the external *diseconomies* of industry: the unwanted side-effects, which impose a cost on surrounding land-users (Samuelson 1973: 476, 810). Smoky chimneys are the favourite example. Manufacturers produce smoke as a waste product and impose a cost on their neighbours, who must pay for higher laundry bills, more health care, extra window cleaning and repairs to buildings that have been damaged by air-borne acids. Other famous examples of external diseconomies are soil erosion after forest clearance, effluent discharge and the obstruction of beautiful views.

When external effects influence the environment, they are known as *environmental impacts* (Fig. 2.5). A report on the environmental consequences of a development project is known as an environmental impact statement (EIS). The idea was introduced to America by the National Environmental Policy Act of 1969 and to Europe by the EC Directive 85/337 (Commission of the European Communities, 1985). A distinction can be made between two sub-categories of environmental impact. *Landscape impacts* "are changes to the fabric, character and quality of the landscape as a result of development". *Visual impacts*, a subset of landscape impacts, "relate solely to changes in available views of the landscape" (Landscape Institute & Institute of Environmental Assessment, 1995).

Figure 2.4 Some modern buildings, like the Sydney Opera House, radiate public goods. It is loved by millions of people who do not love opera. (Courtesy of Australian Tourist Commission.)

Collectively, external diseconomies can be thought of as the environment's wicked stepmother (Fig. 2.6). Luckily she also has a fairy godmother, the external *economies* that first attracted Marshall's notice. Street trees, parks and some building projects, such as the Sydney Opera House, produce positive side-effects and confer public goods on the wider landscape. Inattention to positive side-effects wastes resources and destroys landscape quality. Two types of measure can encourage fairy godmothers:

1 Area-wide landscape plans for the environmental public goods, as discussed in this chapter, require an injection of ideals into the planning process.

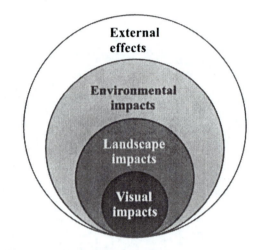

Figure 2.5 The external effects of a land-use can be sub-categorized as environmental impacts, landscape impacts and visual impacts.

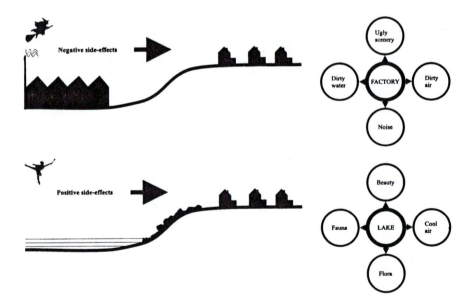

Figure 2.6 The environment has both a wicked stepmother (above) and a fairy godmother (below).

2 Single-objective projects can be modified to improve their contextual relationships. In environmental assessment circles this is known as impact mitigation.

Development projects should be modified in order to produce multi-objective project designs. Design modifications can prevent negative environmental impacts and foster positive environmental impacts.

Landscape plans

Landscape plans should deal with environmental public goods.

As a lighthouse guides ships, plans for public goods should guide the process of environmental planning and design. Ships need to be safe; land dwellers have many objectives. The environmental public goods can be placed in three groups, akin to the Vitruvian objectives for the private goods to be obtained from architecture (commodity, firmness and delight). The simplest classification of the environmental public goods is *natural*, *social*, and *visual*, but they can be classified in other ways (Fig. 2.7). In *Methods of environmental impact assessment*, Morris and Therivel use an extensive classification of environmental impacts: socio-economic, noise, traffic, landscape, archaeological and cultural, air and climate, soils and geology, water, terrestrial ecology, freshwater ecology and coastal ecology (Morris & Therivel 1995). They pay less attention to the impacts of a development project on surrounding land-uses.

Environmental objectives are of vital concern to the community at large; they reach beyond the partisan interests of private landowners and private land-users; they tend to decay when not planned; they need not be depleted as consumption rises; they tend to improve when well planned; one cannot levy a charge for them; they are classic examples of public goods.

The German Federal Nature Conservation Act of 1976 was a pioneering example of legislation to protect and enhance the environmental public goods (Schmid 1989). The act requires the preparation of landscape plans

Firmness	Ecological	Natural	Environmental
Commodity	Functional	Social	Human
Delight	Aesthetic	Visual	Artistic
Price	Financial	Economic	Sustainable

Figure 2.7 The environmental public goods can be categorized.

to deal with three categories of public goods: nature conservation, scenic quality and public recreation.

The following types of landscape plan can help to create and conserve environmental public goods:

- Natural process plans
  - landform plans   to protect and enhance a distinctive and convenient landform;
  - waterspace plans   to provide space for water storage, water transport and water recreation;
  - habitat plans   to protect and enhance the pattern of natural and semi-natural habitats;
  - air plans   to provide fresh air, clean air and shelter.

- Social process plans
  - Alexander plans   to show the archetypal patterns that should exist in a neighbourhood;
  - Greenspace plans   to provide public access to environmentally good space in urban and rural areas;
  - Special area plans   to protect and create areas of special character;
  - Recreation plans   to increase opportunities for outdoor recreation: footpaths, bridleways, cycleways, campsites, food-gathering places;
  - Sustainability plans   to make human life more sustainable, both in town and country.

- Visual plans
  - Scenic plans   to protect and create good scenery and good views, both in town and country;
  - Spatial plans   to protect and create good spatial patterns;
  - Skyline plans   to protect and create good skylines;
  - Urban roofscape contours   to give city roofscapes a distinctive shape.

The above types of landscape plan are discussed at greater length in the remainder of this chapter, and there are further examples of the plan-types in Part 2.

Natural process plans

Landform plans

Landform plans should indicate areas for protection, excavation and deposition.

Historic cities often grew on sites where the topography was significant for trade or defence: beside a natural harbour, on a hill, at the mouth of a valley, round a castle, at the lowest bridging point of a river. The scenic qualities of these sites came to be appreciated. Church and castle builders often accentuated the character of the landform by building the tallest structures on the highest land. New settlements can also be related to the existing landform, but often this is not done.

Modern man has tended to conceal or destroy the landform of cities. We have found it easy to adjust land-shape for various purposes and, in making a city, enormous volumes of earth are moved from site to site. It is usually done without any comprehensive plan and requires the use of vast energy resources. Holes are dug to obtain useful minerals or to make space for sub-structures. Huge quantities of sand and gravel are dug to make concrete. Waste material, both organic and inorganic, is placed in tips. Embankments are formed for roads and other structures. All this work is done on a project-by-project basis, without co-ordination. Water channels are dug. New hills and new depressions are formed. Old hills are quarried. Old depressions are filled with rubbish. Towns lose their distinctive landform.

Yet the old landform often remains as a feature to be exploited in urban renewal. Landscape planners should seek out landform, just as Michelangelo looked at a block of marble and saw a statue concealed within. Birmingham, in the middle of England, has a significant landform, which is substantially concealed by buildings. In many American cities "the indifference to geographic contours" was "nothing short of sublime: the engineers' streets swept through swamps, embraced dump-heaps, accepted piles of slag and waste, climbed cliffs" (Mumford 1938: 185). In such places the old landform awaits rediscovery, like buried treasure.

Mineral extraction can also have a great influence on the landform of cities. At Duisberg, in Germany, the water in the port was deepened by carefully planned underground coal mining (Spirn 1984: 118). The same principle could be used to create new water bodies where underground coal is available. Subsidence is normally regarded as a constraint on mining operations. It is also an opportunity for imaginative landscape planners. At Kansas City, subsurface mining of limestone took place. This created large caverns, which have become very popular for commercial and industrial use. Rents are low, heating and cooling are inexpensive, security is high. This has changed the economic equation. Previously, the caverns were a side-effect of mineral extraction. Today, the sale of limestone is a side-effect of excavating commercial space (ibid.: 118).

With landform planning, it is not simply a case of protecting what exists or recovering what used to exist. There are heroic opportunities to create new topographic patterns, of landform, water, vegetation and buildings. Reading, in the Thames valley 65 kilometres west of London, is a case in point. It grew as a nineteenth-century railway town and is rather a dull place. But it is surrounded by sand and gravel deposits, which the mineral companies wish to extract and are extracting. The local planning authority has done its best to oppose their wishes, in the interests of "conservation". At one time the aim was to conserve agricultural land. Later, the aim was to preserve scenic quality. When permission for mineral extraction has been obtained, the companies have dug the mineral and then fenced off the water bodies for private fishing and sailing interests. Instead, they should be planning a great Water City (Fig. 2.8). There could be tongues of water running into the town and spits of housing interweaving the lakes. All the necessary powers exist. So why hasn't it been done? Lack of vision.

Cities suffer from geological hazards. Earthquake risks are now appreciated and, in the developed world, seismic building codes are in force. Shrinkable clays are less obvious but probably cause more damage. Foundations are cracked in periods of drought. Hazardous soils must be mapped, so that suitable foundations can be put in place before new structures are built. In existing urban areas the problem is exacerbated by conducting surface water off the land in drains. This accentuates the fluctuation in ground water levels and aggravates the shrinkage and swelling problem.

Every city needs a landform plan to guide future development, to gain positive side-effects, to avoid hazards. The plan should be visionary, to serve as a lighthouse for the local development process.

Waterspace plans

Water management plans should show areas for enhanced detention, infiltration and evaporation.

The rain falleth on the just and on the unjust, on the road and on the field. From the field, it seeps into the ground. From the road, it runs into drains.

Figure 2.8 Reading could become a dramatic "water city" with a mixture of land and lakes.

Man has had a great influence on surface water runoff. Since all the water that comes out of the sky has to go somewhere, and since life on earth would be impossible without water, it surely follows that plans for the management of rainwater must be prepared and implemented. It is not merely a question of drainage, stormwater management or catchment management, which is the impression given by conventional textbooks.

The old method of dealing with rainwater was engineering: if a puddle forms, dig a drain; lead the drain into a river; if the river floods, build an embankment; if it still floods, deepen the channel; if the channel is breached, clear the floodplain of buildings and vegetation; if the waters still rise, dig bypass channels and storm detention ponds. Successive schemes of this type, implemented with goodwill, have greatly accelerated the volume and speed of rainwater discharge, as will be discussed in Chapter 9. This has dried out upstream land and caused downstream floods. Wetlands have become dry-lands. Rivers no longer run. Trees have died. Ever increasing sums are required for upstream irrigation and downstream flood control.

Engineers have appreciated the problem and responded with engineering solutions. Storm detention has become popular. Rainwater is now collected in engineered ponds and underground tanks, so that it can be discharged slowly, with computer-controlled sluices, into sewer and river systems. This is an expensive and dubious policy: delaying the discharge of water prior to a flood peak may raise the eventual flood peak. The real solution depends more on planning than on engineering. We need to think globally and act locally, as advised by the Friends of the Earth. Urban water-planning must be fully integrated with urban space-planning. Planning and environmental impact controls should be used to achieve what were once thought to be engineering objectives. .

Waterspace plans are required to show the spatial dimension of surface water management. They can utilize different management policies for different areas of land, depending on subsurface and land-use conditions. The policies can be shown on diagrams (Fig. 2.9), to indicate the types of measure that may be adopted

(a) *Low density development on permeable soils* All surface water should be infiltrated within individual property boundaries. Developers should make conservation ponds within the gardens of residential properties. Runoff from roads should pass through oil traps before it is infiltrated.
(b) *High density development on permeable soils* Surface water must be detained and infiltrated. Landowners may join together to operate joint facilities. Where conditions permit, they should include a sur-face-water area for recreational use.
(c) *Low density development on impermeable soils* As much water as pos-sible should be stored on site. This may be done in boggy conditions, so

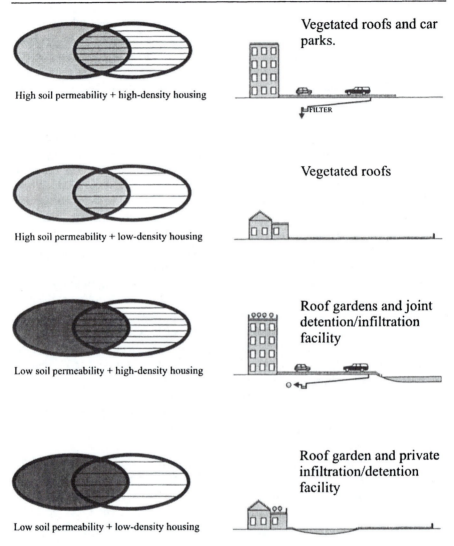

Figure 2.9 Surface-water management policies should relate the pattern of development to underground drainage conditions. These policies can be shown on Venn diagrams, cross sections, maps and tables.

that water can be evaporated and transpired. Excess water should be allowed to run off, but at no faster rate than in natural conditions.

(d) *High density development on impermeable soils* Foster evapo-transpiration. Grass roofs should be used to detain, evaporate and transpire surface water before it reaches the ground. Water should also be stored in tanks to irrigate vegetated roofs in dry weather. If the rate of surface-

SOILS

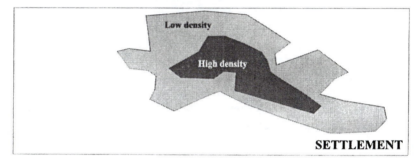

SETTLEMENT

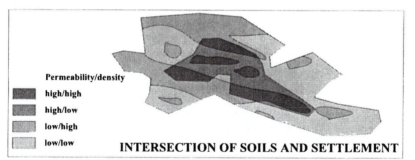

INTERSECTION OF SOILS AND SETTLEMENT

Permeability	Density	Policy
High	High	Vegetated roofs and car parks
High	Low	Vegetated roofs
Low	High	Roof gardens and joint detention/infiltration facilities
Low	Low	Roof gardens and private infiltration/detention facilities

Figure 2.9 (continued)

water discharge is accelerated, it should be conducted to surface-water infiltration sites (e.g. in parks), just as foul sewage is conducted to sewage farms.

The planning principle is that rainwater should be detained and infiltrated as near as possible to the point where it falls. This will mean that areas of less-permeable soils will have more surface water – and more potential for the creation of wetland habitats.

Recreation is another aspect of waterspace management. Every question-naire, every travel brochure, every study of trends in outdoor recreation has identified access to water as the prime goal of leisure trips. People want homes which overlook ponds, reservoirs, lakes, rivers and oceans. They want to see the rich wildlife found in wetland habitats. They want to catch fish, whether or not others approve of fishing. They want to swim in fresh unchlorinated water. They want places in which to use canoes, sailboats, modelboats, motorboats, water-skis, houseboats, leisureboats. Making adequate provision for these activities is a very important aspect of open space planning, despite the fact that waterspace has not been regarded as "open" space in any of London's open space plans (Turner 1992).

Habitat plans

Biotope management plans should indicate the desirable mix of habitats, based on historical analysis, hydrology and pedology.

Biodiversity is desirable. I do not know whether species extinction does any harm to mankind, but I do know that I would like to have a greater range of species near my home and that I would like a wide range of species to exist in other countries. Terrestrial habitats, however, are in constant flux. On a geological timescale, regions become humid and arid, marine and submar-ine, hot and cold. Our historical records go back about 5,000 years. It is surprising that only 10,000 years have passed since Britain was glaciated, the sea level was lower and one could walk from France to England. But in the last ten centuries, man has been the strongest influence on habitat change. Natural habitats, habitats free from man's influence, occupy only a tiny fraction of the land in developed countries, like England. The quantity and quality of habitat types is a proper subject for planning. Guidance on habitat mapping is provided by English Nature (Nature Conservancy Council 1990).

Since the 1960s, public consternation at the loss of "nature" to "devel-opment" has grown. Now we can redress the balance. Every region can prepare plans which show natural habitats, semi-natural habitats, proposals to re-create habitats and proposals for biological corridors to interlink habitats.

Biologists studied the characteristics of individual plants and animals before they came to study whole communities. Ecology is largely a twentieth-century development. It began by studying relationships between individuals and their environments, progressed to the study of habitats and is now examining groups of related habitats. The later study, known as landscape ecology, can encompass habitats in which man is the predominant species. According to the theory of island biogeography, "island" habitats, not linked to other habitats by biological corridors, have less biodiversity (MacArthur & Wilson 1967). Biological corridors can run through land with or without public access, beside rivers, roads, railways, canals and other public utilities (Smith & Hellmund 1993).

Habitat potential plans will indicate patches, which have the potential to be developed as new habitats, and corridors, which can provide links (Fig. 2.10). Every part of a town has habitat potential, which can be realized

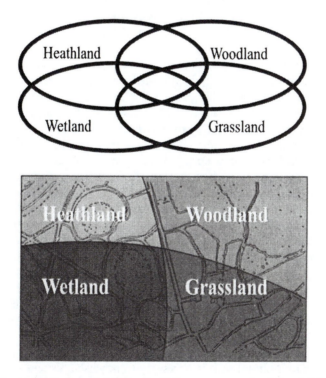

Figure 2.10 Habitat plans should indicate the presence of existing habitats and the potential to create new ones.

when particular types of development take place. If, for example, a high-volume multi-lane road is built through an existing urban area, it is likely to have vegetated embankments. If a low-volume road is built, it can be a "green lane". If a new building is erected, it can have a vegetated roof. If a shopping centre is built, it can have strips of native plants, instead of ornamental shrubs, round its car parks. Habitat potential maps will guide developers to the sorts of habitat that should be created on particular types of land. They can also guide the creation of new habitats on parkland, utility corridors, school grounds and other areas which are vegetated but which are not best suited to ornamental horticulture.

Air plans

Air management can make places healthier and more comfortable.

Air is the most public of all public goods. It passes from property to property and continent to continent with the greatest ease. Clean air is a precondition for good health. Polluted air is a serious cause of ill health. These points are agreed by all. But what can landscape planning do to improve air quality? A great deal. For cities, action can be taken at the macro-, meso- and micro-scales.

Stuttgart's air plan is the most famous example of a citywide climate plan (Fig. 2.11). Because of its valley location, the city suffers from temperature inversions, which place a "ceiling" over the valley and trap polluted air. It becomes hotter in summer and colder in winter. Climatological studies revealed that the vegetated hills around the city were reservoirs of cooler, fresher air. Building control regulations were used to protect the hills from urbanization. A radial open space system was planned to function as a network of flow channels, ducting cool fresh air downhill to break the thermal ceiling over the city centre.

At the meso-climate scale, individual streets and parks should be planned with regard to air quality. Air pollution and dust are severe problems. After developing asthma in my forties, I became very aware of air quality. On hot dusty days, walking into an exposed open space was like entering a battle-field. My lungs were under attack. Entering a cool shady space brought a great sense of relief. In unfavourable air conditions, I could hardly walk uphill. Drugs now ameliorate the symptoms, but people who have not yet developed respiratory problems are, I think, comparatively unaware of air quality issues.

The air quality requirements of open space vary according to climate and season. In hot arid climates, it is necessary to have shelter and shade: direct sun produces heat and glare; winds bring dust; pedestrians need narrow canopied streets; open space users need good tree-cover and, if possible, a

Figure 2.11 In Stuttgart, air is encouraged to flow from cool hill-top areas, shown dark, down into the town. Stuttgart suffers from temperature inversions and becomes very hot in summer.

dust-free breeze. In hot humid climates, the need for shade is equally great. In a damp climate dust is a lesser problem and humidity a greater problem, so outdoor space must be planned with regard to good ventilation. In temperate regions, air quality requirements are varied: sunny sheltered places for the winter, cool shady places for the summer. One of the more remarkable blunders of "form follows function" twentieth-century city planning was the lack of attention given to air quality and climate. Corbusian cities with isolated blocks and wide streets were built all over the world, regardless of local conditions. Better air is one of the reasons upper- and middle-income groups seek out leafy suburbs for their homes.

At the microclimate scale, significant air quality and climatic measures can be adopted. Simply put, cities should be swathed in vegetation (Fig. 2.12). In future, the environmental impact question for developers will not be "can you get some planting into this space?", but "what special case can you make for *not* vegetating this wall or this roof?" The change of policy will produce the most significant difference between twentieth- and twenty-first-century cities. Twentieth-century cities were commonly described as concrete jungles, despite being much more vegetated than their predecessors. Twenty-first century cities will be richly vegetated. Roofs will be clad in turf or other vegetation. Walls will have climbing plants. Car parking bays will

Figure 2.12 Cities should be much more richly vegetated, to improve the urban microclimate and store water. These examples from Kassel show how a road, a wall and a lighting column can be vegetated.

Figure 2.12 (continued)

have reinforced grass. Minor roads will be lightly vegetated so that they are porous to dust and water. Bare walls and roofs will become a sought-after rarity.

Social process plans

Alexander plans

Christopher Alexander argued (1977) that each building project must relate to neighbouring patterns:

> In short, no pattern is an isolated entity. Each pattern can exist in the world, only to the extent that it is supported by other patterns: the larger patterns in which it is embedded, the patterns of the same size that surround it, and the smaller patterns which are embedded in it.
>
> This is a fundamental view of the world. It says that when you build a thing you cannot merely build that thing in isolation, but must also repair the world around it, and within it, so that the larger world at that one place becomes more coherent, and more whole; and the thing

which you make takes its place in the web of nature, as you make it.
(Alexander et al. 1977: xiii)

Figure 2.13 shows how several Alexander patterns might interrelate. A
building project, bounded by the dotted line, should contribute to a set of
neighbouring patterns. The diagram's numbering follows those in *A pattern
language*. The larger patterns are *Green street* (no. 51), *Bike path and racks*
(no. 56) and *House cluster* (no. 37). The smaller patterns are *Sitting wall* (no.
234), *Seat spot* (no. 241) and *Paving with cracks between the stones* (no. 247).
A development which ignores the pattern nexus will be unneighbourly. The
subject is discussed at greater length in the next chapter (see page 99).

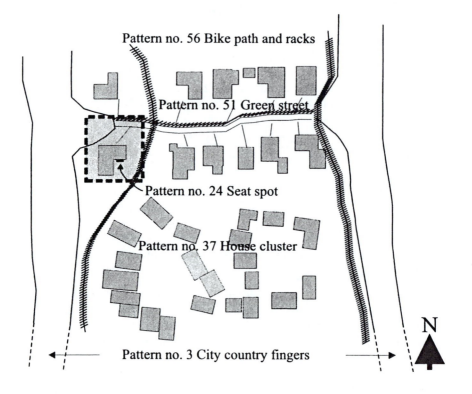

Figure 2.13 Building projects should respond to surrounding archetypes and make
provision for subsidiary archetypes.

Greenspace plans

Greenspace plans should show areas of environmentally pleasant land with public access.

It is possible to make villages, towns and cities where one can travel through greenspace to shops, schools, libraries, cinemas and railway stations – provided the green in greenspace is used to mean environmentally pleasant, rather than vegetated. This is the sense of green in green politics. Greenspace includes elegant residential streets, footpaths, park paths, riverside walks and shopping streets.

A greenspace plan should define a web of environmental space (Fig. 4.23). It will include pedestrian paths if they are of good character: clean, safe, visually attractive and not beside heavily trafficked roads. Urban squares and public parks will almost always be included, unless their planning and design are unusually bad. Riverside walks are likely to be included, as are pedestrianized shopping streets. Parts of the greenspace web will coincide with biological corridors. The greenspace web will *not* include footpaths beside high-volume roads, windswept pedestrian bridges or smelly pedestrian tunnels. Roadspace forms the current public realm in a modern city. The greenspace web should form a second public realm. It is necessary, because vehicles dominate the first public realm.

In a large city, one can purchase a street plan, showing intersections with railways, and a railway plan, showing intersections with streets. Motorists often use plans that categorize roads according to their quality and accessibility. Pedestrians need plans showing greenspace routes and intersections with other transport modes. The raised sidewalk was invented to protect pedestrians from vehicles, mud and dung, by separating them from vehicles. When traffic became faster, noisier and more dangerous, after about 1950, planners developed the idea of replacing sidewalks with a totally segregated pedestrian zone in which paths did not run beside roads and did not cross them at street level. When such zones are busy and convenient, they are popular. Inconvenient diversions to overpasses or underpasses, and the lonely journeys they necessitate, with the danger of mugging and no visual policing from passing traffic, can make them exceedingly unpopular.

From an environmental point of view, sidewalks are satisfactory when the number of vehicle movements per day is modest. Where they are high, sharing is intolerable. Roads with daily vehicle movements below 5,000 can be used as a "placenta zone". A mammalian placenta allows the interchange of food between mother and foetus. A pedestrian placenta allows interchange between passengers and vehicles.

If the ratio of vegetated to built space is low, the population will feel deprived of one of the essential amenities of modern life – the opportunity for outdoor recreation in green surroundings. If the ratio of vegetated to built space is high, the inhabitants are likely to feel that they do not live in an urban area. These considerations invite two questions. How much vegetated space should a city have? How should it be distributed? It would be madness to give standard answers to these questions, such as the old "six acres of open space per 1,000 people" rule. Alternative resolutions are appropriate in some historical, geographical and cultural contexts. But if plans are not formulated, vegetated space is likely to be badly located, badly designed, poorly managed and constantly threatened by roads and buildings.

Recreation plans

Outdoor recreation plans should look far into the future.

Every city must have outdoor space in which its people can re-create themselves after days and weeks indoors. They need fresh air, beautiful views and access to water. Some outdoor recreational activities will be run as private businesses, such as golf courses, or as public facilities, such as parks. Other activities will be non-commercial byproducts of farming, forestry, water storage and other major land-uses. These may include walking in the countryside, swimming in rivers, looking at wildlife and admiring scenery. Good planning can increase recreational resources; no planning will reduce them. Public goods may be funded by regular payments, obtained by taxation, or they may be owned. Rights of ownership may be inherited, or purchased, or acquired through legislation.

In many European countries, but not in England, there is a blanket right of access to forests and uncultivated uplands. Since the policy yields valuable public goods at very little cost to landowners, it will probably come to exist in England at some point in the future. Public access to footpaths through cultivated land is more problematic. England has a historic network of rights of way, most of which do run through agricultural land. It once served the needs of farming people, who walked to work, to school, to market and to church. Many of the routes remain in use, although they are most likely to be used for recreation. The problem is that old routes rarely suit the needs of today's population. They do not go from today's origins to today's destinations.

Footpaths across privately owned rural land are an example of a right which can be publicly owned. Recreation maps should be prepared showing an ideal network of footpaths (Fig. 7.12). New recreational rights may be acquired for the public by voluntary sale or compulsory acquisition. They may also be given or bequeathed to the public by a generous landowner. There are many examples of private landowners bequeathing land to the public. Other landowners may choose to give away rights without giving away their land. Or recreational rights could be obtained by the public as compensation for the negative side-effects of mineral working or other developments. Public rights to camp for a night, to ride a horse or to collect wild food should also be indicated on the recreation plan. The important point is that valuable rights are most likely to be acquired when they have been planned long in advance of their acquisition.

Special area plans

> *Special area plans can be used for colour, historic character, construction materials, ethnic character, land-use character and other matters.*

Municipalities can adopt plans to protect and enhance areas of special character, such as colour, building heights, construction materials and roof design (Fig. 2.14). They work best in historic settlements, such as fishing villages, which already have a high degree of unity, and in natural areas, such as forests. But since people value unity, there is every reason to encourage coherence in new settlements. The Prince of Wales admires the use of

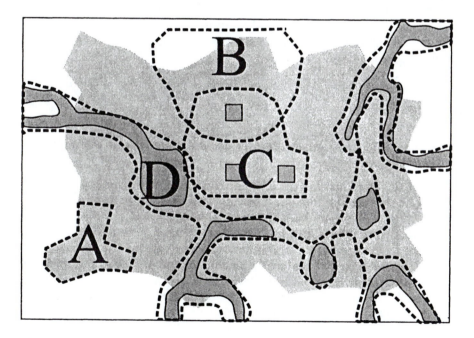

Figure 2.14 Special areas should be defined for policy purposes: A pantile and whitewash zone; B zone of restricted building height 15-m; C sandstone building zone; D greenway development zone.

rules, which he describes as "an urban code", to give coherence to the town of Seaside in Florida (Charles, HRH Prince of Wales 1989). There is also a set of rules for his development at Poundberry outside Dorchester in Dorset. Rural authorities can also adopt plans to protect and enhance special types of landscape quality, including wilderness and tranquillity (Rendel 1997).

Where special area policies have not been approved, planning authorities should require designers to submit details of the planned relationship between new structures and their surroundings. The discipline of considering side-effects leads naturally to more sensitive design proposals. Three alternative relationships between development and surroundings are discussed in Chapter 3: similarity, identity or difference (page 101). In the small proportion of our towns that merit strict conservation measures, imitation will often be the best policy. If, for example, a gap appears in a fine Georgian terrace it is normally best to infill with a new Georgian building. Limp attempts to imitate window or cornice lines are no substitute. In other places similarity or contrast will be appropriate – but designers must know what they are doing and be able to define the intended relationship between a new building and its setting.

Too many buildings are presented on design drawings which do not show the characteristics of the site or its surroundings. Towns need landmarks, but confusion reigns if all buildings are designed to contrast with their neighbours. In some cases a total contrast can be very refreshing, as in the Pompidou Centre in Paris. Partly it succeeds because it is different from its surroundings.

Sustainability plans

Sustainability plans should show "action areas" to improve the sustainability of cities.

Most of the objectives in Fig. 2.7 are well known, but a curious feature of the lists is that the "bottom line", dealing with economy in resource use, has not been part of the traditional rubric, although it has obviously been of importance throughout history. Now that we have more information and can take a global view, the importance of using resources in a sustainable manner is recognized. It is a goal different from nature conservation. Some people argue that man will not survive as a species if biodiversity is not conserved. This is both possible and doubtable. One can imagine an artificial, but nevertheless sustainable, community. One may or may not wish to live there.

The acceptance of sustainability as a planning objective marks a partial return to the values of the Middle Ages. Then as now, the motivation was both economic and religious. Peasants had to avoid waste. Monastic communities naturally took a very long view, because they expected to be immortal institutions. They had every reason to plant trees for shelter and fuel, to protect stream banks, to raise soil fertility, to develop fish stocks and to erect long-life buildings. My grandfather liked to sustain the values of his peasant forebears and was believed never to have purchased a piece of string. The Brundtland Commission's definition of sustainability as "development that meets the needs of the present without compromising the ability of future generations to meet their own needs" (Brundtland 1987) is not so clear as one might wish. It does not define the "needs of the present" and it does not help us to guess at the needs of "future generations". But several aspects of sustainability deserve consideration by planners.

Resource-use

Monastic and peasant societies had few inputs and few outputs. Almost everything came from the local ecosystem and was returned whence it came. Modern Western lifestyles, in town and country alike, are characterized by high inputs, high outputs and long transport distances. We live as feudal masters. Energy, food and materials flow to us from all quarters. After being used, they become wastes and pollutants, besmirching the land, befouling the air, defiling the waters and despoiling the environment. The basic aim of sustainability planning is to reduce inputs to and wastes from the human ecosystem (Fig. 2.15). Wastes should be recycled, water

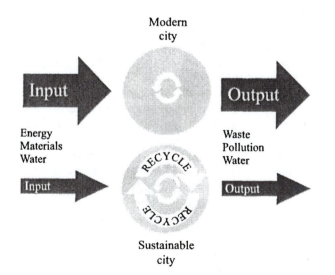

Figure 2.15   Sustainable cities have low inputs and low outputs.

53

returned to the ground, vegetation used for food and fuel, energy conserved, transport costs reduced. Nature should be revered – and conserved.

Enjoyability

Sustainability may conflict with other planning goals. Non-sustainable cities may be pleasanter than sustainable cities, especially for the rich and power-ful. Barons generally did live better than peasants. Low-density residential areas with single-family villas, double garages, large gardens and heated private swimming pools do not score well on a sustainability index. Far better to have narrow streets, walk-up apartment blocks, no private cars, thick walls and small rooms, like medieval cities. One may not actually live longer, but it will certainly feel longer. The challenge for planners and designers is to create sustainable cities which are also delightful. I believe it can be done.

Transport

An improved transport policy is the grand avenue to sustainable cities. Commuting by public transport is more sustainable than commuting by car. It requires less resource-input and produces fewer wastes. Green com-muting by human power is better still. Journeys and part-journeys to work by foot, bicycle, canoe or ice-skates are environment-friendly. They do not waste scarce energy resources, propagate air pollution or generate noise. Nor do they cause acid rain or damage the ozone layer. Green commuting can lead to tremendous savings on the public healthcare budget, by reducing stress, diminishing obesity, reducing cancer risks, curtailing road accidents, easing asthma and other respiratory diseases. It used to be said that what was good for General Motors was good for America. It wasn't true then and it's less true now. A cost–benefit analysis would show enormous positive values for policies to facilitate green commuting and discourage red com-muting. What's good for green commuters is good for America. That's it.

Journeys to work are much more likely to be made on foot or bicycle in cities that have good pedestrian and cycleway systems. Who can doubt it? Travelling beside a busy road, choked with fumes, deafened by noise and splashed by passing vehicles is a punishing experience (Fig. 2.16). One arrives feeling like an exhausted warrior needing a flask of wine. Walking or cycling down a leafy path or lane, looking at the flowers, chatting to one's friends and listening to the birds, or a personal stereo, is a great pleasure. Those who live more than half an hour from their place of work may think the journey too far to walk or cycle, but the first and last sections of their journeys can still be made by green transport modes, if cities are properly planned and designed. Every important destination, including schools, stations and shopping centres, should be the hub of foot- and cycle-paths (Fig. 2.17). Adults driving their children to school or their spouses to the station cause additional traffic congestion. This should be discouraged. If

Figure 2.16 Self-powered travel in urban areas can be dangerous and unpleasant.

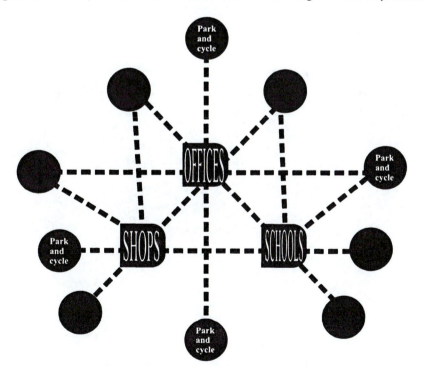

Figure 2.17 Destinations should become hubs for footpath and cyclepath networks.

developers are asked to contribute to infrastructure costs (e.g. roads and sewers) they should also be asked to contribute to the cost of green commuter routes and safe cycle storage at transport interchanges (Fig. 2.18).

Vegetation
Additional vegetation, one might think, would make cities more sustainable, because life on earth would be impossible without vegetation. But urban vegetation is often counter-sustainable. Non-renewable energy is used to cut grass, to remove leaves, to supply irrigation water, to quarry peat from natural habitats, to manufacture and dispense fertilizers, herbicides and insecticides. All these activities are carried out on useless patches of so-called "landscaping", which lower urban densities and increase commuter journeys. Well-intentioned but misguided planners have tried to improve city plans by decorating them with liberal quantities of green sauce representing strips of parkland.

Mapping
Some sustainability policies have general application. Others relate to specific geographical areas. Thermal insulation of buildings, for example, has general application and need not be mapped. But some buildings can be planned to improve climatic conditions for pedestrians, by forming arcades

Figure 2.18 Safe cycle storage is required at stations, bus stops and other transport interchanges.

and windbreaks. Places where this policy applies should be mapped. Area-specific sustainability plans should deal, among other things, with micro-climate, land, water, vegetation and transport. The aim is to map those areas where specific action can be taken. Depending on local circumstances, this could include a zone for increased infiltration, a public transport priority zone, a cycle transport network, places that can contribute to climate control, an area for urban food production.

Visual plans

Different types of plan can be prepared for the aesthetic public goods. They include scenic plans, spatial plans, image maps and skyline plans.

Scenic plans

Scenic resources need planning. Plans should define areas of high scenic value, to be conserved, and areas of low scenic value, to be improved.

We speak naturally of "our town", "our country" and "our world", believing that each individual has rights and duties which traverse ownership boundaries. We state a wish to leave the world as beautiful as we found it. This way of thinking leads to the belief that scenery is a public resource, largely the gift of nature, partly the work of our ancestors, certainly a thing of value, like water or genetic resources. If a stream runs through a chemical works, this does not confer a right to divert off the water or load it with pollutants. Nor do landowners have rights to destroy the environment's visual character. Beautiful scenery is a public good and, as Goodey observes, "most people know what they like when it comes to viewing the landscape, and frequently compose views" (Goodey 1995).

Photographs of towns, coasts, meadows and mountains attract us to foreign travel. Tourism is said to be the world's largest industry. But the scenic resource on which it depends is poorly managed, almost everywhere. Like natural forests, scenery is treated as an exploitable part of nature's bounty. Even when it is managed, the emphasis is on protection rather than creation. Scenic management requires:

- maps of scenic quality, both urban and rural;
- policies for the conservation of high scenic quality;
- policies for improvement of low scenic quality.

One may think that mapping scenic resources is more difficult than mapping other natural resources. As children of the romantic movement, many of us believe that "beauty is in the eye of the beholder". This appears to make scenic mapping impossible. But a surprising fact about scenic quality makes the task feasible. Almost every researcher has discovered a high degree of consensus about scenic quality in the natural and built environments. If you ask random groups of Burmese farmers, Japanese businessmen, Chinese fishermen, Dutch tourists and African nomads about their tastes in art, food, music and books, you will discover few correlations. But if you ask them about scenic quality, you will find a quite astonishing degree of consensus. People love views of mountains, lakes, rivers, houses set among trees, dramatic urban skylines and towns with good public spaces. This makes scenic quality assessment (SQA) feasible. As individuals, we are constantly engaged in assessing the quality of what we see, as when buying food and clothes, arranging a home, or planning a holiday. Public bodies, disliking criticism and fearing ridicule, have taken to SQA with some reluctance, but in the developed countries they have done so for the following reasons:

- to define areas of high scenic quality (e.g. national parks or urban conservation areas), for protection or for tourist development;
- to define areas of low scenic quality which merit reclamation programmes (e.g. areas that have been despoiled by industry);
- to analyze the scenic context for a major development project (e.g. a power station), so that the project design can be contextualized;
- to define scenic areas in which special management policies will apply (e.g. grants for repairing stone walls).

Assessment of scenic quality is sometimes described as landscape evaluation or visual evaluation. These terms are misleading. Most people think of landscape as a geographical term, so that an evaluation would have to include functional and biological, in addition to aesthetic, characteristics. The term "visual evaluation" has two drawbacks. First, it implies a smaller scale of concern than "scenic". Second, it refers more to perception than to appraisal. In the UK there are guidelines for "landscape assessment" (Countryside Commission 1987), meaning scenic assessment, and for "landscape and visual impact assessment", which includes other types of landscape impact (Landscape Institute & Institute of Environmental Asssessment 1995).

The two stages in effecting an SQA can be clarified by thinking of the landscape as an estate. The owner has died and land agents have been appointed to assess the value of the property. Their tasks are *inventory* and *valuation*. Scenic assessors have the same tasks, which are likely to be followed by *policy formulation*. The tasks should be done partly at one's desk, using maps and aerial photographs, partly in local art galleries, partly in the library and partly in the field, using a notebook, a sketchbook, a camera, sandwiches, a bicycle and walking gear. An overhead flight is of great assistance in taking a comprehensive view.

The *inventory* will map and catalogue the components of the landscape. On a private estate, the items in the sale catalogue are likely to be functional: farmland, woodland, fishing grounds, gardens, a house, outbuildings etc. When cataloguing the wider landscape, the units will be more topographical: hills, valleys, streams, farmsteads, sea cliffs and so forth. When urban areas are included, the list may extend to housing, industry, parks, retailing and transport. Landscape units are useful for defining policy areas, although different aspects of the landscape will result in alternative sets of units (Fig. 2.19). Maps showing non-overlapping units, for landscape quality or landscape character, are founded on an intellectual error (Fig. 2.20). Units may be defined as:

- *policy areas* Coastal management, for example, will require a map showing "zone of coastal influence", which will overlap with units defined for other purposes.
- *viewshed areas* These may be defined by ridge lines, woodlands, buildings etc. The area within a viewshed can be computed with a GIS programme and mapped as a "zone of visual influence" (ZVI).
- *natural areas* These will result from natural processes (geology, soils, hydrology, elevation, aspect etc.)
- *man-influenced areas* These will be both modern (e.g. arable land, grazing land, forestry, housing, industry) and historic (e.g. ancient settlements, farms, commons, roads, battlefields, areas associated with writers and artists).

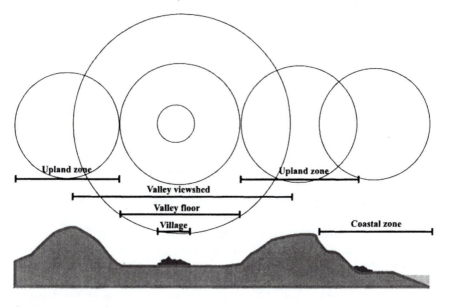

Figure 2.19 Landscape units are bound to overlap.

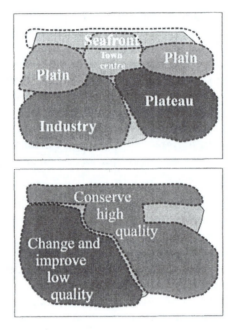

Figure 2.20 Scenic management requires inventories, evaluations and policies.

Scenic *evaluation* should be carried out when units have been defined. As with the task of definition, there should be desk studies and field studies. After spending many years planning weekend visits to areas of town and country, I have learned that a surprisingly accurate estimate of scenic quality can be made from maps. If there is a steep mountain beside a lake with a fringe of trees along a sandy shore, the natural scenic quality is likely to be high. If there is dense urban development around a castle, the historic scenic quality is likely to be high. If there is a large area of suburban housing with a repetitive geometrical pattern, the place is likely to be dull. If there is a uniform road pattern through an industrial area, it is likely to be ugly. These observations lead to the conclusion that although beauty may be subjective ("in the eye of the beholder") it is possible to base good predictions of scenic quality on objective criteria: slope, elevation, vegetation, water, geology, age of buildings and other artefacts. These elements can be included in a landscape inventory.

If objective landscape elements are regarded as predictors of scenic quality, rather than determinants, the ancient philosophical debate about whether aesthetic value is subjective or objective can be left on the sidelines. Like the rules of a game, this debate sets parameters without determining the outcome. From the time of Plato and Aristotle (*c.*400 BC) until the start of the eighteenth century, most Western philosophers believed aesthetic quality to be objective. It was judged with reference to principles, such as the Golden Section and the Rules of Taste. Further evidence for the objectivity of beauty came from the fact that certain works of art had been appreciated since ancient times. After *c*.1700, the rise of empiricism and the Romantic Movement led to the predominant modern view that aesthetic quality is a subjective matter. Taste in scenery has changed with tastes in art. We now love deep forests, mountains and rocky coasts, which used to be viewed with horror. It seems very probable that our descendants will share our taste for wildness, but we cannot know.

Scenic evaluations can be made by trained experts or by the general public, with or without special methods. The cheapest method is to employ experts. This is how, in the 1940s, Britain's national parks were selected and their boundaries defined. Since that time, many attempts have been made to involve more representative groups, by transporting people in buses or showing them colour slides in projection rooms. Public opinion surveys, of the type used to assess the popularity of TV programmes or predict election results, can also be used. One can only praise these efforts to make SQA more democratic. But so long as there is a high degree of consensus about scenic quality they are not of critical importance. The first task is to produce and publish maps. Members of the public, and other experts, will soon draw attention to contentious areas.

The information inputs to a scenic quality assessment are:

- desk studies by experts and non-experts, using maps, aerial photographs, eye-level photographs (still or video), remote sensing data;
- field studies by experts: geographers, earth scientists, social scientists, physical planners, physical designers, aestheticians.
- field studies by non-experts, chosen by statistical sampling techniques, chosen because they inhabit the area, chosen because they make tourist visits to the area;
- cultural studies by experts and non-experts: archaeologists, historians, literary critics, art critics.

The scope of the judgements made will depend on the observers' experience. This makes inter-regional and inter-national comparisons difficult. But since the purpose of the SQA will usually be to guide local planning decisions, the comparability of the assessments of regions is not the matter of first importance.

Spatial plans

Spatial plans should show the existing and proposed spatial patterns.

Spatial containment is a definable aspect of scenery. It is pleasing to walk in an urban square with contained views, in an urban space with one distant view, in a valley with seaviews, in a "lost valley" secreted within a town, in a broad avenue focused on a distant hill or monument, in a narrow space, in a broad space or on a route that sequentially narrows and widens. These experiences, which are all consequences of spatial geometry, can happen by chance, or they can be planned. Spatial planning requires concepts and policies.

There is a fundamental difference between perceiving the space, which is an empty void, and perceiving the elements which contain the space (Fig. 2.21). Architects use walls and roofs to contain indoor space. Landscape architects use mounds, trees, buildings, walls, fences and other enclosing elements to contain outdoor space. An indoor space tends to have one legal owner. Outdoor space tends to have many legal owners, which can make spatial planning difficult.

Types of spatial plan

Plans for outdoor space can be made at different levels:

Cross-sections [Fig. 2.22a] show the elements which contain space.

Ground plans [Fig. 2.22b] show what is happening at ground level, including the exact location of trees, buildings and property bound-

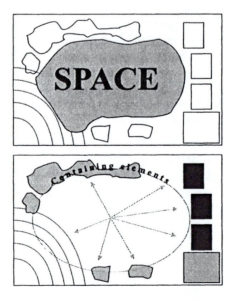

Figure 2.21 There is a fundamental difference between perceiving the space and perceiving the elements which contain the space.

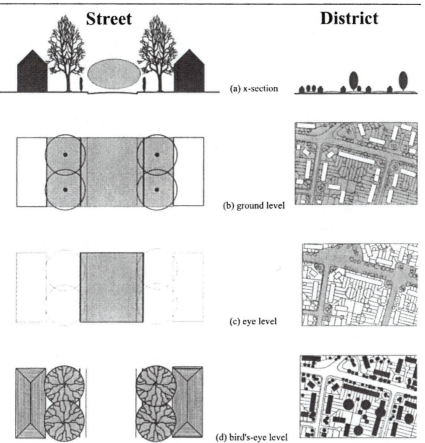

Figure 2.22 Space can be designed in cross-section (a), at ground level (b), at eye level (c), or from bird's-eye level (d).

aries. They are, in effect, cross sections taken through buildings and vegetation at ground level.

Eye-level plans [Fig. 2.22c] are drawn at a level which is intermediate between ground plans and aerial plans. They show, in principle, the boundary of the space which can be seen by an individual observer standing in a defined location and rotating their eyes through 360 degrees. Or they can show the boundary of the space which is seen by an observer moving through a space from point to point.

Aerial plans [Fig. 2.22d] can be thought of as hand-drawn aerial photographs. They are a usefully pictorial way of representing places, but they show a view of the world which is normally available only to helicopter pilots. As we who love aerial photographs know, aerial views can differ greatly from eye-level views: even familiar places can be unrecognisable.

Eye-level plans are the most appropriate tool for spatial planners. Like Giambattista Nolli's famous 1748 Plan of Rome, they show visible space in white and non-visible space in black (Trancik 1986: 99).

Urban space
Historic examples of deliberate spatial planning, as recounted in histories of urban design, come from places where power has made spatial planning possible. Power can come from a landowner, from an autocrat, from custom and tradition, from municipal codes or from democratic decisions, but it must exist. In colonies, urban power came from colonial authorities. The grid plans which the Greeks exported to Asia Minor, the Romans exported to their Empire and the Spaniards exported to South America were examples of spatial planning. Sixtus V's plan for Rome, the Grand Avenue in Paris (Fig. 2.23) and the Woods' plan for Bath are sophisticated spatial plans. The pioneer of modern urban design, Camillo Sitte, observed that

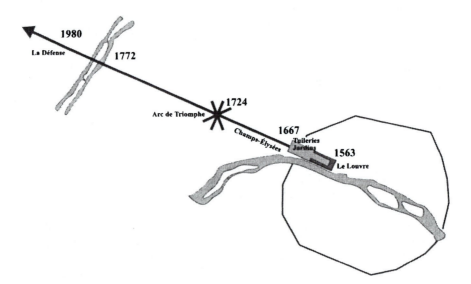

Figure 2.23 The grand avenue in Paris is one of the world's leading examples of an urban space plan. It has guided urbanization for three centuries.

In former times the open spaces – streets and plazas – were designed to have an enclosed character for a definite effect. Today we normally begin by parcelling out building sites, and whatever is left over is turned into streets and plazas. (Sitte 1979: 55)

Edmund Bacon in *Design of cities* reviews the influence of spatial concepts on a number of the world's great cities. He contends that the "human will can be exercised on our cities now, so that the form they take will be a true expression of the highest aspirations of our civilisation" (Bacon 1967: 13). His examples include the influence of the Panathenaic Way on Athens, of market places on medieval towns, of Sixtus V's obelisks on the design structure of Rome, of Le Nôtre's plan for the outward thrust of space from Paris, of the sacred axis on Peking, of the Woods' street plans on Bath, of Nash's design on the "processional route" from St James's Park to Regent's Park and of Bacon's own work on the regeneration of Philadelphia. In each case he argues that a spatial concept, based on a movement system, has had a profound influence on the urban environment. Once the space has been conceived, it serves to inspire other designers as "a dominant organising force in architectural design", with its strength lying, "not in authority but in the ability to influence growth" (ibid.: 34). The majority of Bacon's examples are of cities where linear features, such as avenues, axes and shafts of space, are used to establish the design structure. This may be because the great complexity of the task has led designers to simple solutions. In future it would be wise to remember Patrick Geddes' observation that:

City improvers, like the gardeners from whom they develop, fall into two broadly contrasted schools, which are really, just as in gardening itself, the formal and the naturalistic. Each has its own place and use. (Geddes 1904: 97)

Nash and Sitte represent the "naturalistic" school, Haussmann and Le Corbusier the "formal" school. But there are more than two styles of garden design (Turner 1986), and each can be a source of inspiration. Just as the private house is a testing ground for new architectural concepts, so the private garden is a laboratory in which to develop new spatial concepts which can be applied to the larger task of city improvement.

When offering to make such spaces in new or old towns, city improvers have an unfortunate tendency to resort to jargon. Christopher Tunnard calls for "creative urbanism" (Tunnard 1953: 386), Gordon Cullen for an "art of townscape" (Cullen 1961: 133), Lionel Brett for "macro-aesthetics"(Brett 1970: 58), Kevin Lynch for cities with "imageability" and "sensuous form" (Lynch 1960: 119), Rob Krier for a renewed effort to create "urban space" (Krier 1979: 15), and Yoshinobu Ashihara for an "aesthetic townscape" (Ashihara 1983: Ch. 2). In different ways all these authors make the point that conceiving the space itself is a different enterprise from conceiving the elements which contain the space. Ashihara quotes Lao Tzu's statement that "Though clay may be moulded into a vase, the essence of the vase is the emptiness within it" (ibid.). A potter has full control over his clay but we urban designers must set forth spatial concepts and trust that future decisions by many individuals will create good urban space.

Rural space

Spatial design for rural areas has received less attention than spatial design for urban areas. Before the eighteenth century, cities were seen as the great centres of art and civilization (Olson 1986). Appreciation of rural space developed slowly. Renaissance designers included views of the surrounding area in their garden planning. Baroque designers pushed avenues out into the countryside. English landscape designers in the eighteenth century saw that "all nature is a garden". After a century of innovation, English landscape designers formulated the first complete theory of spatial design for rural areas, which will be discussed in Chapter 3. An important residue of this theory is the modern idea that the spatial pattern for rural areas is a matter of public policy.

The scale of rural areas tends to be large, but the components are not dissimilar to those in urban areas: woods, mountains, buildings, walls, fences and hedgerows. The way in which these elements come together to make space can be appreciated in valleys. If a valley is blanketed with trees or buildings, the shape is concealed. Even if it is only the roads and paths that are lined with spatial barriers, the valley is lost to the public. It ceases to be a public good.

Image maps

Kevin Lynch believed that the visual quality of cities can be studied from the mental images held by its citizens. He was particularly interested in the quality of "legibility" and sought to represent it on image maps (Fig. 2.24):

> The contents of the city images . . . can conveniently be classified into five types of elements: paths, edges, districts, nodes and landmarks. (Lynch 1960: 46)

After using interview techniques to carry out image analysis, Lynch urged the preparation of a visual plan to:

> . . . prescribe the location or preservation of landmarks, the development of a visual hierarchy of paths, the establishment of thematic units for districts, or the creation or clarification of nodal points. (ibid.: 116)

Image maps are a good way of representing the features which compose our mental images of particular cities. They can lead to plans for improving

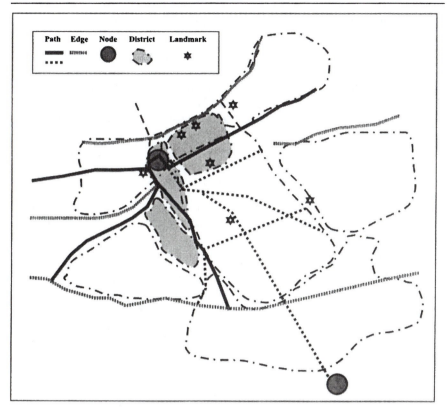

Figure 2.24 Image maps show the paths, edges, nodes, districts and landmarks.

a city's image, although Lynch acknowledged that such plans should fit in with all the other aspects of planning.

Skyline plans

Skylines are among the most memorable features of cities.

The foregoing sections, on scenic plans, spatial plans and image maps, deal with the representation of scenery on two-dimensional plans. Skylines are also important. Wayne Attoe wrote a most interesting book on the subject (Attoe 1981). He discusses skylines, in successive chapters, as collective symbols, as social indexes, as orientation aids, as features in urban rituals and as icons venerated by city inhabitants and visitors. Each of the points is persuasive, and the author concludes by discussing what should be done.

Some people welcome dramatic new buildings as a sign of progress; others hate them.

Skylines are a defining issue in urban planning. On the one hand, they are cherished public goods. On the other, it seems whimsical to halt the commercial or artistic development of a metropolis, or a locality, because it would "mar the skyline". New York and Hong Kong could not have developed if conservative skyline controls had been in existence. Florence, Paris and the dreaming spires of Oxford would be wrecked if skyline controls were relaxed. Regulation can be achieved by financial incentives, by design review boards, by urban design plans or by zoning controls. Attoe insists there is no one right answer:

> The issue is not whether to have controls, but which controls to have and where to have them apply. The principal criticism of existing skyline controls is that they are routine rather than imaginative. They accomplish too little. (Attoe 1981: 117)

From 1960 to 1980 the skyline of East London was spoiled by an unplanned spatter of high buildings. Between 1980 and 1990 a more pleasing aesthetic effect was produced by grouping high buildings together and placing an especially tall building with a pointed roof in their midst (Fig. 2.25). This happy result was not produced by a skyline policy; it came about because the Isle of Dogs was made into an Enterprise Zone in which normal planning controls were relaxed. Some people continue to dislike the Isle of Dogs skyline, and the tall buildings certainly produce a windy and chaotic effect at street level (Fig. 2.26). Yet they may come to like it in time. Abercrombie was right that different cultures and historical periods produce characteristic skylines (Fig. 2.27). We may wish to conserve historic examples and to allow the development of new skylines elsewhere. Policies can be set out in cross-section and on roof contour plans (Fig. 2.28).

Implementation

Statutory plans should be guided by non-statutory plans.

A remarkable feature of the landscape plans discussed in this chapter is that the likelihood of their being implemented may be improved if the plans do not have the force of law. This is because, in guiding human behaviour, carrots are more effective than sticks. An analysis of open space planning in London from 1925 to 1992 certainly supports this theory (Turner 1992). The statutory open space plans were painfully unimaginative and received the neglect they richly deserved. In this group, we must place the preposterous idea that each London Borough should have a prescribed area of open space

Figure 2.25 The urban island in London's Docklands was built between 1985 (top) and 1995 (below). Tall buildings look better when they are grouped together.

69

Figure 2.26 At street level, the Docklands skyline is chaotic. But compare this with Fig 3.16.

for each thousand inhabitants. This would have required mass demolition in the central business district and building on parkland in leafy suburbs. The 1976 GLC park hierarchy was also a statutory plan. It became ridiculous and ineffectual not only because it was bad planning, but also because it had to go through a Kafka-esque system of bureaucratic modification and approval.

London's non-statutory open space plan of 1943–4, the work of an inspired individual, attracted the willing support of innumerable people and is being implemented. It proposed a web of interconnected open space extending throughout the London region, to a radius of 70 kilometres. Public, private, local and national bodies have worked together on its implementation. If it had been statutory, it would have been a less visionary document and may well have attracted less support and less action. Building a lighthouse is more useful than passing a law against shipwrecks.

Conclusion

Planning requires knowledge, understanding and visions.

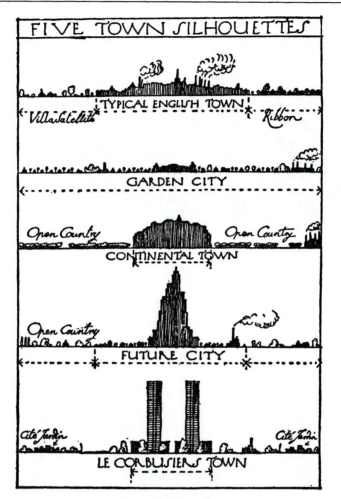

Figure 2.27 Abercrombie was interested in urban cross-sections.

The theme of this chapter has been that landscape planners should be guided by three considerations:

1 knowledge of the past;
2 understanding of the present;
3 visions of the future.

Development planners and designers should consider the environmental impact of development projects on the past, present and future. This may identify ideals and planning objectives which are in conflict. Consider a field on the periphery of a major city. The landowner wishes to construct a factory on the land. The Habitat Plan calls for the field to be restored to

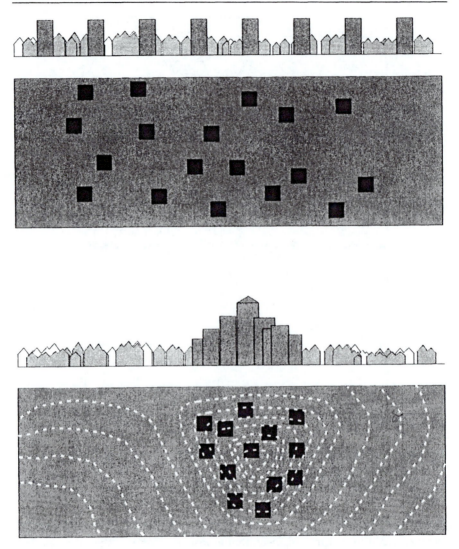

Figure 2.28 Skylines can be planned and mapped, using cross-sections and roof-scape contours.

its former condition, as a wet oakwood. The Recreation Plan calls for public access. The Rural Scenery Plan calls for its agricultural character to be conserved. The Urban Scenery Plan calls for the land to be built upon, as an extension of a city-wide development axis. Economics and politics will guide the debate. Although imaginative design can help, theories of context are also required. They are the subject of the next chapter.

CHAPTER 3
Context theories

The problem

How should a development project relate to its context?

Let us start with a dilemma. A rich Australian businessman has purchased a farm on a hill near a European capital city. He wants to endow a church and residential centre for a new religious sect, to have the buildings designed by a famous architect and to surround them with a eucalyptus forest, to remind him of New South Wales. He believes there is a local need for the development and that it will be a visual triumph, because of the glorious site and the anticipated harmony between the blue-grey foliage of the eucalyptus and the polished steel of the architecture. Local residents furiously oppose the scheme. They want the farmland to be retained and prefer local materials to stainless steel. Conservation groups like the idea of a new forest but oppose the choice of species and the buildings' architectural style. Architects believe the church design will be an important landmark in the history of their art, deserving a magnificent location. Tourism planners believe the church will attract visitors from afar. Other issues raise similar problems.

- Should new reservoirs be designed to look like natural lakes (Fig. 3.1)?
- Should new buildings in urban areas be designed to resemble their neighbours (Figs 3.2, 3.3)?
- Should the traditional character of rural buildings be used to inspire new buildings (Fig. 3.4)?
- Should road embankments be designed as farmland or as wildlife habitats (Fig. 3.5)?
- Are some sites specially suited to dramatic and monumental structures (Fig. 2.4)?
- Should new forests be planted with indigenous species, to resemble native forests (Fig. 8.8)?
- Should bridges be designed according to purely functional criteria, or should some be traditional and others modern (Figs 9.19, 9.20)?

Figure 3.1 The dam, Lake Vyrnwy: should this reservoir have been surrounded with native species and made to resemble a natural lake?

Figure 3.2 Should the building on the left have been designed to resemble its neighbours?

Figure 3.3 Should the new hotel with a turret, in the centre of the picture, have been designed in a contemporary style? (The High Street, Edinburgh).

- Should residential areas near public open spaces have a higher population density than areas distant from public open space?
- Should mineral workings be concealed? Or should they be designed to create spectacular cliff scenery (Fig. 6.6)?
- What aesthetic and ecological criteria should influence the design of new roads (Fig. 10.8)?

These questions have many dimensions: administrative, aesthetic, ecological, historical, cultural, recreational, financial, climatic, hygienic, legal and so forth. But a great question of public policy looms above them. *When should society intervene?* It might be assumed that

Figure 3.4 Should the building above, which is a water treatment works, have been designed to resemble a farm building? Is the building below, which is a nuclear power station, suited to a seaside location?

- publicly financed projects are bound to be in the public interest, so they require no regulation;
- privately financed projects are bound to be for private gain, so they require maximum regulation.

The twentieth century has proved the falsity of these assumptions. Anyone who contemplates the outrageously expensive environmental damage which

Figure 3.5 Should this road embankment have been contoured and managed to resemble the adjoining fields?

public river and drainage authorities have done to every city in the industrialized world must tremble to recollect that the assumption was ever possible. Public and private projects can be environmentally good or bad. So let us ask:

When should the public intervene?
How should the intervention take place?
What should be achieved by intervention?

These questions will be addressed in turn.

WHEN TO INTERVENE

As much as necessary but as little as possible.

Before the twentieth century, few governments would have regulated such matters as our Australian's desire for a polished steel church in a eucalyptus forest. His dream would have been regarded a private matter, like the decoration of his bedroom. Wordsworth was content "to utter a regret" about undesirable development in the English Lake District. Beside Windermere, he disliked the embankment of Belle Isle for an Italian villa, the larch plantation, which he saw as a "vegetable manufactory", and "whole acres of artificial shrubbery and exotic trees among rocks and dashing torrents, with their own wild wood in sight – where we have the whole contents of the nurseryman's catalogue jumbled together – colour at war with colour and form with form" (Wordsworth 1835: 72). Today, many people feel that merely to utter a regret is pusillanimous.

Now, it is often claimed that the world must be controlled because it is a single complex "system". Sceptics may be reminded of the arguments used in former times by ingenious theologians anxious to prove the existence of God. William Paley, for example, argued that since a watch could not be made without a watchmaker, the world could not have been made without the prior existence of a God (Paley 1970). Subsequent generations, optimistic of the good that humans might achieve through the application of reason to public policy, came to believe that governments, and planners, should assume a watchmaker's role in human society, by organizing education, spreading enlightenment and making society function more like a pocketwatch. Planners came to believe that the interconnectedness of the environment proved the need for a planning profession to control the environment.

Is there a happy medium between no intervention and maximum intervention? My view is that when a development project has a significant impact on a public good, it is a matter of public policy. Otherwise, like the Australian's bedroom, it is a matter of private taste. The aim should be to intervene as little as possible but as much as necessary.

HOW TO INTERVENE

There are three main approaches to the environmental regulation of development in a liberal democracy:

1 by means of *zoning* and *land-use plans* – this approach works from the general to the particular;
2 by means of *environmental assessment* and *control* – this approach works from the particular to the general;
3 by a combination of *zoning* and *environmental assessment* – this is the best approach.

In many countries, zoning and EA have different legislative origins and remain separate. Zoning and land-use planning derive from a positive wish to show where and how future development should take place. EA comes from a negative fear that development is likely to destroy environmental quality. Zoning looks to the future; EA looks to the past. Ahern describes them as "offensive" and "defensive" strategies (Ahern 1995). Both are necessary.

Control by zoning

Zoning plans reserve areas for defined land-uses, but fail when they are exclusive.

Zoning laws were introduced in Germany in the late nineteenth century, to separate residential from industrial development. They produce what are now known as land-use plans in Europe and zoning plans in America. The existence of such a plan confers legal certainty and fairness on contextual decisions (Department of Environment 1989: 411). A development will be approved if it accords with the plan and rejected if it does not.

The watchmaker argument for the existence of planners, as explained above, leads to the demarcation of exclusive zones for housing, industry, commerce, public open space and other land-uses. In theory, authority to develop land is given only to projects that comply with a land-use zoning plan. Under this system, our Australian friend would certainly have been allowed to carry out his project, providing the zoning plan showed a church surrounded by a eucalyptus forest. Not many zoning plans do. At Marne La Valée, before Eurodisney, the local plan made no provision for the construction of a major theme park. Nor did the 1985 development plan for Sunderland in north-east England show a site for a Nissan car plant. Both projects were granted permission, on green sites, in contravention of the approved local plans. In practice, since rich landowners often have ideas for non-conforming developments, zoning plans often change, which defeats their purpose.

Most of the large cities in Britain have been ringed by green-belt zones since the 1950s. They have slowed the pace of development, driven up urban land prices, enriched some farmers and impoverished others. But they have *not* halted the process of land development (Elson 1986). Zoning plans fall into disrepute when they are subject to constant modification, and when powerful developers clutching fistfuls of gold can negotiate lucrative amendments. This is especially so when local people wanting to build apartments for their ageing parents cannot do likewise.

Another regrettable consequence of zoning plans is that they restrict land-use diversity. In a natural habitat there is a web of interaction between individual plants and animals. The community gains mutual protection and recycles its byproducts. Interactions of this type cannot occur if there is only one species in the habitat. Monoculture is inefficient, both in natural and in human communities. If a residential area has a single use and a fixed density it will be occupied by people in a single socio-economic group. At 30 persons per hectare, the families will probably have high incomes, two children and two cars. This is less efficient than a mixed-use area with shops, businesses, schools and smaller homes for young people and old people.

Flexible zoning, as an alternative to singular zoning, is much closer to the patterns formed by natural habitats. Each habitat tends to have a dominant species (e.g. oak in an oakwood) and a wide range of associated species (birds, insects, fungi etc.). One then finds a zone of transition where one habitat merges into another. Examples of the landscape zones that should guide contextual decisions were given in the previous chapter; they include zones for waterspace development, landform enhancement, habitat creation, greenspace, climate and scenery.

For our Australian, a flexible zoning policy might accommodate his project, providing it had a favourable impact on the local environment.

Control by environmental assessment

Control by EA fails when it is too pragmatic.

When it became apparent that the zoning system was not creating or protecting zones of environmental quality, it was supplemented by a second approach. The new idea was to assess each project as it arrived on the development agenda and to discover what impact it would have on its surroundings. This became known as environmental assessment (EA) or environmental impact assessment (EIA). The idea originated in the USA, partly because of its extra-rigid system of zoning. Planning control in some American states was much less comprehensive than in Europe and there was great public concern about the harmful effect individual development projects were having on the environment. The National Environmental Policy Act (NEPA) of 1969 became a model for similar legislation throughout the world.

The principal NEPA provision was that an environmental impact statement (EIS) must be prepared for "all major Federal actions significantly affecting the quality of the human environment". The word actions included building a house, planting a forest, felling a forest, laying a pipeline and carrying out a military exercise. The great value of the EA approach was that it included *every* influence of *every* project on *every* aspect of its context (Fig. 3.6). Interaction matrices were produced (Fig. 3.7). Land-users were prompted to consider the effects of each aspect of a development on each

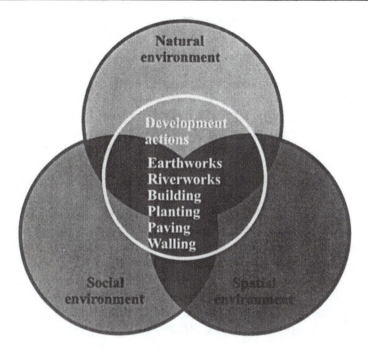

Figure 3.6 Environmental assessment should, in theory, extend to every influence of every project on every aspect of its context.

component of the natural, social and spatial environment. For example, "Soldiers defecating" was included for an EA of a military exercise in a wilderness area. For a road-building project, the component actions would include constructing a site office, removing vegetation, hiring local labour, stripping topsoil, deflowering local virgins, excavating subsoil, laying a base course, adjusting drainage patterns, and so on for ever. It was and remains a bonanza for environmental lawyers and scientists. A distinction can be

	The Environment	Natural environment		Social environment		Spatial environment		
		Physical	Biological	Circulation	Recreation	Views	Space	Skylines
The project								
Earthworks		+	+	+	+	+	+	+
Waterworks		+	+	+	+	+	o	o
Vegetation		+	+	+	+	+	+	+
Paving		+	+	+	+	+	o	o
Walling		+	+	+	+	+	+	+
Building		+	+	+	o	+	+	+

Figure 3.7 An interaction matrix prompts the land-user to consider the impact of each aspect of a project on each aspect of the environment.

drawn between strategic environmental assessment, which is concerned with the assessment of general policies, plans and programmes, and environmental impact assessment, which is carried out by organizations proposing specific development projects.

The Florida Power and Light Company, when preparing EIAs for new power stations, had to submit a 5mm-thick report in 1970, a 75mm-report in 1971, a 150mm-report in 1973 and a 600mm-report in 1977. To deal with this escalation, restrictions were placed on the total length of American environmental impact statements and on the categories of project for which they were required. The scope of the European Community directive on EIA was restricted to medium-scale projects. Small-scale buildings and large-scale forestry and agriculture were excluded. The Australian's proposal could fall within Schedule 2, Section 10 of the European Community directive, as a significant urban development project. Scientists could then identify negative impacts on fauna and flora. The hillside church would have an extensive zone of visual influence. The cultural landscape would be adversely affected. It is likely that the project would not be approved. Control by EIA has an anti-development bias. The inbuilt assumption is that the status quo ought not to change. Control by EIA has become a highly structured procedure. The authors of a textbook on it identify 15 steps in the process (Glasson et al. 1994: 3):

1 Project screening
2 Scoping
3 Consideration of alternatives
4 Description of the project/development action
5 Description of the environmental baseline
6 Identification of key impacts
7 Prediction of impacts
8 Evaluation and assessment of significance
9 Mitigation
10 Public consultation and participation
11 Environmental Impact Statement presentation
12 Review of the Environmental Impact Statement
13 Decision-making
14 Post-decision monitoring
15 Auditing.

The EIA process effectively permits some projects and halts others. It is not as effective as it ought to be in securing improvements to a project design. This is identified as stage 9 in the above list but, as the authors note, mitigation "is in fact inherent in all aspects of the process" (Glasson et al. 1994: 137).

Design control

Design control works best with the aid of forward-looking plans.

Britain's town and country planning system, as enacted in 1947, contained a novel approach to the control of development. It rested on a marriage of flexible zoning with EA-type development control. Zoning takes the form of statutory development plans, which each planning authority is required to prepare. The EA-type controls takes the form of a requirement that each landowner must obtain "planning permission" before undertaking a development project. Each project is considered by planning officials and by elected members representing the local community. They have wide discretion.

John Punter carried out a detailed study of how the system has functioned in one English city (Punter 1990). Bristol was a great seaport. From an estuary in the west of England, the city's merchant adventurers sallied forth, prospered with the "empire of the seas" and declined when that empire declined. Severe bombing during the Second World War left great scope for redevelopment and environmental improvement. The 1947 Town and Country Planning Act gave the city's authorities very considerable powers to regulate this development.

The final section of Punter's book contains a drawing (Fig. 3.8) and a photographic inventory of the 250 major office building projects from 1940 to 1990. It is deeply depressing. Each of the 250 buildings was subject to full design control. Yet most of the buildings stand out from the city like stained teeth in the gaping mouth of a poor old tired horse. Their relationship to each other and to their context lacks beauty and harmony. The drawing is a fearful indictment of the development control system. There is but one happy moment in Punter's tale: the 1977 "Townscape and Environment Topic Study". Punter writes, "This extraordinary document must be one of the most comprehensive and intelligible townscape studies ever undertaken in British planning." The objective of the study was "to revitalise the obsolete urban structure by the injection of new functions and activities and the forging of new linkages between the City and the Floating Harbour" (City of Bristol 1977). It operated in conjunction with the city's conservation policy. By defining the character of the old town centre and the historic docks, it enabled their character to be protected and enhanced. In effect, this provided:

- a pedestrian plan, for a riverside walk;
- a spatial plan, for the dock basins to have a coherent building frontage;
- an architectural plan, for new buildings to have a "dockside character";

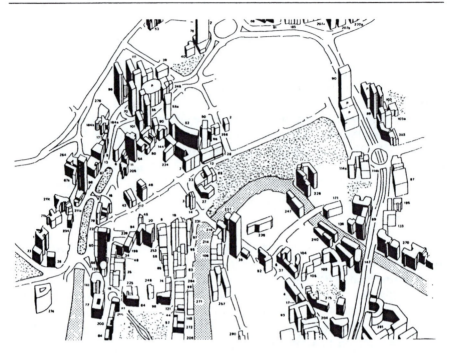

Figure 3.8 Most of the buildings erected in Bristol between 1940 and 1990 stand out like stained teeth in the mouth of an old horse. (Courtesy of John Punter).

- a colour plan, for dockside buildings to be faced in traditional red brick;
- a vegetation plan, to encourage more planting in waterside areas.

Yet the "Townscape and Environment" study is surprisingly thin on positive urban design advice. It relies on a detailed appreciation of the historic environment, and a set of diagrams (Fig. 3.9), to set forth the above principles. Compliance with some other principles would also have been desirable:

- a surface water plan, for the detention and infiltration of rainwater;
- a habitat plan, for creating new habitats for plants and animals;
- a cycling plan, for creating cycle-paths and parking facilities throughout the city;
- a seating plan, for creating a network of good sitting places.

From an EA point of view, the key feature of the above project modifications is that they relate as much to desirable future states of affairs as to the existing environment: they are not mere mitigation. The impact of the project on the re-establishment of a dockland character was just as important as

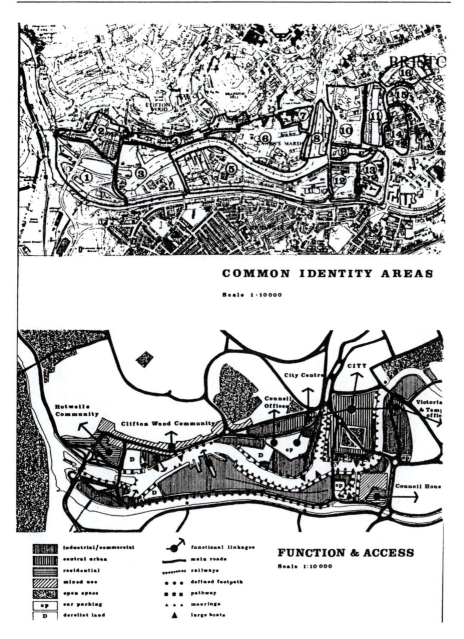

COMMON IDENTITY AREAS

Scale 1:10000

FUNCTION & ACCESS

Scale 1:10 000

industrial/commercial	functional linkages
central urban	main roads
residential	railways
mixed use	defined footpath
open space	pathway
car parking	moorings
derelict land	large boats

Figure 3.9 The Bristol townscape and environment study was founded on a survey and analysis of the existing situation. (Courtesy of Bristol City Council).

85

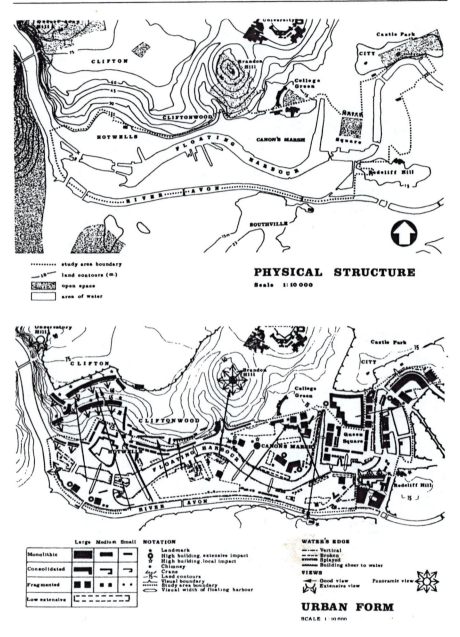

Figure 3.9 (continued)

the impact on the existing environment. As Punter comments, design control at its best is "an exercise in applied urban design". Environmental assessors must consider the impact of a project both on what does exist and on what could exist.

The Bristol "Townscape and Environment" study served as what was called a lighthouse plan in the previous chapter. It enabled the planners and the planned to chart a course through choppy waters, although sometimes they hit the rocks. At Portwall House "negotiations continued over the colour of the mortar to be used with the City preferring black but the architects preferring brown or purple" (Punter 1990: 178). One imagines a drab municipal office with tireless bureaucrats confronting devitalized architects, day after day, week after week, month after month. Since black mortar, in my opinion, looks vile with red brick, I find it impossible to see its use as a matter of public policy. The Portwall House negotiations read like a scandalous waste of professional time and public money. They help to explain why architects detest the idea of design control. Moro summarized the case against aesthetic control in 1958 (Moro 1958):

1 It stifles architectural expression.
2 It encourages uniformity and discourages contrast.
3 It causes hardship to those affected: client and architect.
4 It usually discriminates against those who are exercising their traditional right of wanting to live in a house of their time.
5 It gives undue power of judgement to officials without aesthetic training.
6 It smacks of Totalitarianism and is, in fact, a characteristic adjunct of such a form of government.
7 It is humiliating to the architect and makes nonsense of his professional status.
8 It puts those architects into an invidious position who lend themselves to the distasteful task of sitting in judgement over their colleagues.
9 It rarely stops bad conventional building.
10 It often stops good unconventional building.

With regard to Moro's fifth point it should be said that the influence of the elected chairman of a planning and development control committee can be more powerful than that of officials. Indeed, our Australian would have a very good chance of obtaining permission if he owned the golf club at which the chairman played. Punter, a planner, responded to Moro's list by giving the case *for* design control "in equally abbreviated and dogmatic form" (Punter 1990):

1 It prevents "outrages" and stops much bad building.
2 It raises the standard of much development by ensuring more thought goes into its design.

3 It encourages the architect to stand up to his client who may often want only the cheapest building to sell on to another user/owner.
4 It is a democratic process (of sorts) because it incorporates the views of the public.
5 It is accountable because decisions are made by elected representatives.
6 It provides a necessary bridge between lay and professional tastes.
7 Architecture is the most public of arts, and it is not merely the client who is forced to look at a building for many generations.

An impassioned debate along these lines has raged between Britain's architecture and planning professions for half a century. Both sides have good points. If design control leads to coherent cities with riverside walks, please can we have more of it. But if design control leads to wasteful bickering and bureaucratic interference with good architecture, let's be rid of it. In Bristol, design control succeeded in the context of an urban design strategy for the future character of the docks. So let's have more urban design strategies.

A significant aspect of the Bristol situation is that the urban strategy was historicist. It sought to recreate the spatial and architectural forms of a once-great seaport. In many places, such as Bristol, this is an excellent policy. Elsewhere, it is right to encourage new spatial structures and new architectural styles. Progress would be impossible if this were not the case. The Sydney Opera House and the Louvre Pyramid were great innovations, once doubted, now loved. On different occasions, as will be discussed in Part 2, a powerful case can be made for developments which are "similar to", "identical with" or "different from" their surroundings (Fig. 3.10). Policy

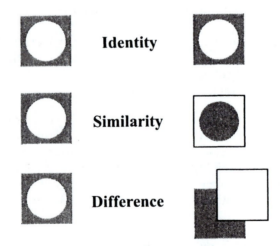

Figure 3.10 The relationship between a development and its context can be one of identity, similarity or difference.

decisions need to be made within a policy framework. Principles are required.

The Bristol study indicates that design controls, and "mitigation" under environmental assessment procedures, can be effective only when they operate within a framework of existing-site information and forward-looking "lighthouse plans". Favourable impacts need to be designed. Environmental assessment should operate in tandem with land-use planning. Without a policy framework, EA overemphasizes the status quo. Some projects may be stopped and some harmful side-effects may be mitigated, but the many ways in which the environment can be improved are not sufficiently taken into account. If we accept that governments have a right to intervene in land-use decisions, we must have theories of context to establish criteria for particular cases. Without contextual policies, our Australian will never get a fair deal.

WHAT TO ACHIEVE BY INTERVENTION

Theories of context

Contextual decisions need a theoretical context.

A theory of context should explain what factors will create a favourable relationship between development and environment. One often reads that developments should fit in with their contexts. I agree, but how? The questions posed at the start of this chapter outline the problem. If proposed development must always be similar to the existing environment, innovation will always be stifled. Conversely, if every new development is made to be different, the visual world will become utterly discordant. Theories of context should deal with this issue and also with the impact of development projects on the natural and social environment. Nine theories with the capability to guide contextual decisions will be reviewed, although few of them were launched as theories of context.

The most comprehensive theory of context dates from the late eighteenth century: the picturesque. It developed from the idea of a genius loci, who could guide development decisions. Two of the theories are mainly to do with aesthetics: critical regionalism and linguistic aestheticism. One theory is primarily ecological: design with nature. Two theories emphasize social processes: modernism and the pattern language. The identity index is proposed as an index to measure contextual similarity or difference.

Genius loci

An early eighteenth-century theory, that buildings and planting should respond to the "genius of the place", created a still-influential theory of context.

Roman civilization was superstitious and pre-Christian Rome was polytheist. When the legions established a far-flung imperial outpost they chose to placate any local gods they encountered. If none could be found, tribute was paid to the genius loci or genius of the place. Alexander Pope took up this idea in the early eighteenth century and transformed it into the most influential theory of context ever penned:

> To build, to plant, whatever you intend,
> To rear the Column, or the Arch to bend,
> To swell the Terras, or to sink the Grot;
> In all, let *Nature* never be forgot.
> Consult the *Genius* of the *Place* in all
> That tells the waters or to rise, or fall . . .
> Joins willing woods, and varies shades from shades
> Now Breaks, or now directs, th'intending Lines;
> *Paints* as you plant, and as you work, *Designs*.

This theory is encapsulated in the eternal advice to "consult the genius of the place". The modern interpretation of the theory is that projects should fit in with their context by using local styles and materials. Hough, inspired by Geddes, has written of a "regional imperative" (Hough 1990). Many people who like to see Japanese architecture in Japan and Portuguese architecture in Portugal are sad when they see local traditions being overwhelmed by rootless international styles. This leads conservationists and others to call for the genius of the place to be consulted. I am pleased to support this call. She must be consulted, always. She need not be obeyed, always. I suspect she does not favour eucalyptus forests with stainless steel churches in the more beautiful environs of European capitals.

The picturesque

Late-eighteenth-century contextual theorists held that landscapes should be designed with a picturesque transition from the works of man to the works of nature.

The aim of the picturesque, as shown in Fig. 3.11, was to create a transition from art to nature. Normally, the transition progressed from a geometrical area near a house, through a serpentine park in the manner of Capability Brown, to an irregular natural area which formed a backdrop. The theory is known as picturesque because it was inspired by the idea of organizing a landscape, like a picture, with a transition from foreground to middle-ground to background. I used the term "transition style" for layouts based on this idea in a book on English garden design (Turner 1986). It is based on landscape painting and draws from the whole eighteenth-century landscape movement.

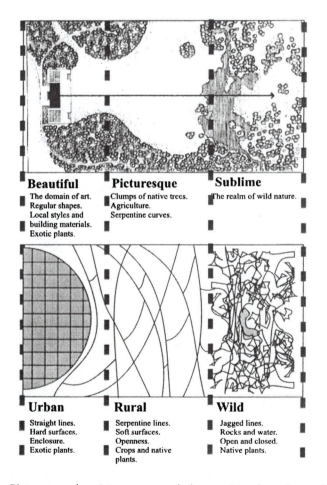

Beautiful
The domain of art.
Regular shapes.
Local styles and
building materials.
Exotic plants.

Picturesque
Clumps of native trees.
Agriculture.
Serpentine curves.

Sublime
The realm of wild nature.

Urban
Straight lines.
Hard surfaces.
Enclosure.
Exotic plants.

Rural
Serpentine lines.
Soft surfaces.
Openness.
Crops and native
plants.

Wild
Jagged lines.
Rocks and water.
Open and closed.
Native plants.

Figure 3.11 Picturesque theorists recommended a transition from the works of man to the works of nature (above). Applied to regional planning, picturesque theory suggests a transition from urban to rural to wild (below).

The Australian example can serve to explain what guidance might be obtained from picturesque theory for a proposal for a new church and forest. The design guidance would depend on the stage in the transition which the site was taken to occupy. Had it been in the first stage, the proposal would probably have been accepted. Humphry Repton, an enthusiastic advocate of Chinese and American sections in English gardens, could hardly have objected to an Australian garden, replete with eucalypts. But he would have wanted it to be near the house so that it would form part of the "domain of art". Richard Payne Knight was explicit about the desirability of planting exotics in the man-made part of an estate:

> The bright acacia, and the vivid plane,
> The rich laburnum, with its golden chain. . .

> But better are these gaudy scenes display'd
> From the high terrace or rich balustrade;

In the middle stage of a transition, Repton and Knight would probably have permitted the new church but advised native trees instead of eucalyptus. Knight expressed his planting philosophy as follows:

> Let then of oak your general masses rise,
> Wher'er the soil its nutriment supplies:
> But if dry chalk and flints, or thirsty sand,
> Compose the substance of your barren land,
> Let the light beech its gay luxuriance shew,
> And o'er the hills its brilliant verdure strew.
> (Turner 1986: 108–10)

In the third stage of the transition, wild nature herself, neither church nor eucalyptus would have been permitted. If authority were needed for this position, they need only have pointed to Salvator Rosa's paintings.

The idea of forming a graded transition from art to nature remained at the heart of English garden design from 1793 until 1947. When the 1947 Town and Country Planning Act imposed a squeeze on garden size, the transition idea leapt the garden wall and occupied the country. Planners became enthused with the notion that towns should be tightly urban in character and surrounded by a Brownian agricultural hinterland, itself giving way to wildly irregular national parks and areas of outstanding natural beauty. Strict planning controls were imposed on developments in the green belt, so that towns would become denser and the spaces between buildings could develop a townscape character, with urban squares and circuses like those of Renaissance towns.

Modernism

Modernist architectural theory held that the appearance of structures should be a consequence of social function and abstract artistic principles, not of contexts.

Modernist buildings contrasted with their Victorian predecessors. Their planning was determined by internal social function. Their exteriors were a consequence of internal function but were also influenced by the principles of abstract art. They were compositions of mass and void, line and colour, without deliberate meaning. Modernism rested on universal principles and severed the link between buildings and contexts.

Le Corbusier was the urbanist who gave most thought to form in the modern city. Coming from Switzerland, he admired mountain scenery. Working in Paris, he saw the need for high-density development. The Corbusian dream was to set great towers, as mountain peaks, against a backdrop of verdure, like valley floors (Fig. 3.12). The architectural style he advocated was unrelated to the local context. External forms were strongly influenced by internal structure and function. Corbusier and other modernist designers worked "from the inside out". This stands in total contrast to the picturesque approach, which worked "from the outside in", to give buildings a site-related style and character. Let us consider examples.

The starting point for outside-in design, say for a country house, would be a full appreciation of the local context. This would include access, views, microclimate, vegetation, materials and local character. The dwelling would be placed to take advantage of "prospect and aspect': good views would be valued, but not to the extent of placing the villa in an exposed position. If appropriate, the building would be constructed in a local stone. If the setting

Figure 3.12 Le Corbusier dreamed of urban Alps, totally unrelated to their context.

were rugged, the style would be rugged. If the site were beautiful, the style would be beautiful, or else a deliberate contrast would be made. Plants would be chosen to harmonize with the local vegetation.

An inside-out design procedure for the same house would work in the opposite direction. It would begin with the lifestyle of the inhabitants. If they were a strong family unit, one large living space would be designed round a hearth. If the parents wanted a degree of separation from the children, the bedrooms would be placed at opposite ends of the house. When the functional patterns were set, they would be wrapped in an external skin. Glass and concrete were favoured because of their flexibility as "wrapping" materials. Internal structures were expressed. The shape and appearance of the building envelope was, in theory, a product of the activities it was designed to contain. The resultant style was known as functionalist, because the form derived from the function.

Functionalism did not stop at the front door. Paths were designed to follow "desire lines". Roads were designed according to geometrical criteria for maximizing traffic flow, rivers for maximizing water flow. Universities were designed for education, farms as food factories. Functionalist doctrine, allied to the scientific method, was a powerful contributor to the single-purposism which was criticized in Chapter 1. Functional matters were privileged over both nature and society. Unfortunately, neither science nor the designers' craft could supply a sufficiently wide knowledge-base. Quantifiable functions, like traffic flow, were privileged over both natural and social processes. This was a major contribution to the poverty of modernist cityscape and landscape.

Our Australian would have had few problems with those planners who based their judgement on modernist theory. Stainless steel would have been valued for its modernity and durability, eucalyptuses for their speed of growth and whitish colour.

Design with nature

When development projects work *against* nature, it is sometimes because of ignorance, sometimes because of parsimony, and usually because it does not appear that a single project will have a significant impact on the environment. The action of one household in making 25 per cent of its land impermeable by building a roof and a road has no significant effect on the water table or on flood levels. But when a town of a million people does the same thing, underground pipes accelerate the discharge speed, the water table falls, trees die back, small streams dry up and flood peaks in larger rivers may increase tenfold. Similarly, when one householder reclaims an area of marshy land to build a house, it hardly matters. But when a whole marsh is reclaimed, populations of birds and fish are routinely destroyed. These are examples of designing against nature.

Since modernist designers tended to ignore contexts, a counter-blast to their activities came from the conservation movement. Ian McHarg, for example, showed how natural processes should influence the design process. Although his book *Design with nature* (McHarg 1971) was more concerned with planning than with design, subsequent writers, including Spirn and Hough, carried the argument further. All three writers assert that man is part of nature, and that natural processes must be central to planning and design. McHarg, Spirn and Hough give examples of how to design with nature and produce environment-friendly development projects.

If dwellings are built on gravel deposits instead of on marshland, much less habitat damage will be done, driveways can be porous, rainwater from roofs can be infiltrated directly into the ground. For mineral extraction, if full restoration and after-use plans are drawn up before operations commence, it is possible for the post-mining landscape to be as good as or better than the pre-mining landscape from both the human and ecological points of view. If forests are designed on an enlightened multi-objective basis, they can be good for wildlife, good for recreation, good for sporting interests and good for timber production. If buildings are designed with vegetated roofs, rainwater is retained and evaporated, new wildlife habitats are created, internal insulation is improved, and energy consumption reduced. If cycleways are made safe and convenient, they will prevent damage to the ozone layer, make cities quieter, reduce the incidence of asthma, reduce the amount of land needed for roads. These are examples of design *with* nature, and the case for this type of contextual design is overwhelming.

The Australian's proposal for a eucalyptus forest would receive short shrift from design with nature theorists. They would point out that eucalyptuses are not indigenous to Europe, that they are not entirely frost-hardy, and that they do not have any associated fauna or flora. The stainless steel church might receive more favourable consideration, because of its durability.

Critical regionalism

A critical response to regional context can enable local and non-local factors to play their part in planning and design.

Kenneth Frampton has proposed "critical regionalism" as a means of creating an architecture which is neither a vacantly international exercise in modern technology nor a sentimental imitation of vernacular buildings (Frampton 1987). Theoretically, the proposition is appealing. In practice it is hard to deploy. Frampton's only example of the approach is Jørn Utzon's 1976 Bagsvaerd Church in Copenhagen. This is seen as a synthesis of universal and idiosyncratic elements. The universal element is the church's regular grid and concrete frame. The idiosyncratic element is the use of a roof vault for which the only precedent is the Chinese pagoda roof. This is discussed as a subtle way of producing a religious building that does not degenerate into "the vagaries of kitsch". The example does little to make a case for an architecture that belongs to the region in which it is built.

It seems likely that the Australian's church could be designed to pass the test of critical regionalism – but the eucalyptus forest would probably be dismissed as sentimental.

Linguistic aestheticism

Linguistic philosophy provides an approach to exploring the semantic relationship between structures and contexts.

Languages comprise words and grammar. They are abstract systems of signs connected by grammatical rules to carry meaning. The built environment can be regarded as a language that uses buildings, instead of words, to convey meaning. It therefore needs grammatical rules. When looking at the landscape, it is possible to identify signs which convey meaning. Rocks, soils, vegetation and other surface features inform us about underlying geological structures, such as bedding planes and fault lines. This fact was used by the linguistic anthropologist Claude Lévi-Strauss, as an analogy to make a point about language. He argued that language is a surface code which informs us about the deep structures of human society (Fig. 3.13).

The ways twentieth-century architects have used linguistic ideas have been chronicled with admirable wit and skill by Charles Jencks. In *The language of post-modern architecture* he sees double-coding as the defining characteristic of post-modern architecture. The first code deals with function, as when building features tell us "way in", "way up", "head office". The second code is legible only to those with expert knowledge, as when a building refers to a classical predecessor, a famous architect, another building or an aspect of the locality. Linguistic analogies have helped architects to reforge the links between architecture, meanings and contexts. Others have treated the subject as a reverse cargo cult, hoping that the adornment of buildings with linguistic jargon would attract shiploads of new commissions from the South Seas.

It is hard to translate the meaning of a building into words without oversimplification. A tall building with a pointed roof in a central location expresses lofty intentions, as churches did in medieval, Renaissance and

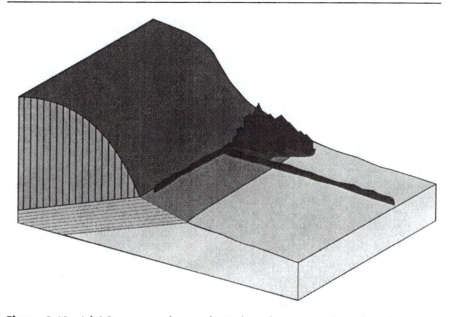

Figure 3.13 Lévi-Strauss used a geological analogy to explain the relationship between surface structure and deep structure.

Victorian cities. Financial centres have taken on this role in modern cities: London's NatWest Tower, just visible on the cover of this book, has replaced St Paul's Cathedral as the tallest building in the old City of London. Prince Charles, with obvious nostalgia for an era when churches and monarchs had greater status, has lobbied for planners to protect the position of St Paul's in London's skyline.

The use of reflective glass on a building speaks of a desire to see without being seen. A garden wall says "The land beyond this point is private property." A neat path says to the pedestrian "Use this route to enter the building; do not walk on the grass." An imposing gateway can be used to say "Important people come here." (Fig. 3.14.) Making a building stand out from its neighbours and making a building resemble its neighbours carry different meanings. Such messages, coded in the language of architecture, are welcome. The linguistic analogy, despite some eccentricities, can provide a partial basis for a theory of context.

But it is the language of the environment which should concern us, not merely the language of architecture. Roads, reservoirs and forests, like buildings, can refer to a great range of contextual factors: local climate, local materials, the structure of a town, the structure of a habitat. Each development can enter into a dialogue with its context. As in any dialogue,

Figure 3.14 An imposing gateway says "Main entrance to an important place" – note the side entrance for peasants (King's Hintock Park).

there will be a mixture of old truths restated, confusions, sharp contradictions, platitudes, enlightened commentary and inspired thinking. It is plain bad manners for a development to disregard its context, as was the norm for modernist developments. Being in a modern city is like being in a room surrounded by people shouting meaningless words at one another. Journalists call it a concrete jungle. One can easily get lost, and one never knows when a screeching noise presages a blow from an attacker, a gust of wind or the passing of a dangerous vehicle. A grey building might turn out to be a national library, a shelter for the homeless or an academy for the secret police. Surely it would be better if one could read buildings' functions from their exteriors.

A linguistic approach to architectural design would probably lend support to the Australian's proposal for a stainless steel church, partly on grounds of cultural pluralism and partly because the durability of steel proclaims the eternity of faith. The eucalyptus forest might be approved, on pluralistic grounds, as having a multi-faith message that demands tolerance.

Deconstruction

Applied to architecture, deconstruction can be used as an argument for the irrelevance of context.

Deconstruction, as discussed in Chapter 1, began as a way of reading philosophical texts to uncover hidden structures and contradictions. It can be used to explore relationships between development projects and contexts. Noting that form is privileged over function in architecture, Jacques Derrida has favoured a deconstruction of the relationship. Taking up this idea at Parc de la Villette, Bernard Tschumi designed the buildings and the spaces *before* planning their function. Some architects have welcomed this notion as an argument for liberating architecture from the several tyrannies of functionalism, historicism, environmentalism, traditionalism and contextualism.

If deconstruction is interpreted in this way, it may wreak a new terror on the built environment. *"Il n'a pas de hors texte"*, they proclaim. "There is nothing outside the text", and there is nothing outside the building. Deconstructivist buildings are designed to overcome the tyranny of context. Grids are fragmented. Horizontals are upset. Colours clash with their surroundings. The shapes and forms of revolutionary Russian constructivism are let loose on Western cities. This approach would welcome the Australian with open arms.

The pattern language

Alexander's pattern language provides a way to create functional relationships between development projects and their contexts.

The preceding theories of context have dealt with the ecological and aesthetic aspects of the relationship between projects and contexts. The pattern language, as proposed by Christopher Alexander and his colleagues, provides an approach to the social dimension, to contextual relationships between people and places. It can help planning projects to have a favourable impact on the social environment (see page 47FF).

Alexander, having studied mathematics before architecture, was initially attracted by the scientific-deductive approach to design and planning. This method was pushed to its limit in *Notes on the synthesis of form*, at which point it failed. Alexander then turned back and published a famous essay with the title "A city is not a tree". He argued that it is a fundamental error to think of cities as hierarchical tree-structures, as he had done. Human settlements, Alexander proclaimed, are semi-lattices rather than trees. Lattice theory is an abstruse branch of mathematics, which deals with the relations between different parts of the same whole. This led to the development of what became known as the pattern language (Alexander et al. 1977). The full language comprises 253 patterns, with an open invitation to readers to contribute additions. The patterns range from large to small. Pattern 1 deals with the independence of city regions. Pattern 253 deals with the display of personal bric-à-brac in your house. Each is an archetype. Some, which need not concern us here, are for the interior planning and construction of buildings. Others are for the planning and design of good outdoor space, urban and rural.

When embarking on a design or planning project, users are invited to choose from the list of 253 patterns the one that most clearly describes the project. Alexander gives the example of a project to make a front porch. Pattern 140 is chosen as the closest. It is for a "Private terrace on the street". The pattern is related to its context by using patterns from higher on the list, such as Pattern 120, "Paths and goals". The porch also creates a context for patterns lower on the list, such as Pattern 167, "Six-foot balcony", and Pattern 242, "Front door bench". When completed, "the character of the porch is given by the ten patterns in this short language" (ibid.: xxxvii). Instead of the porch being a prefabricated object, slotted into position like a shower-cubicle, it becomes a unique structure enjoying an intimate contextual relationship with its surroundings.

Alexander speaks of a pattern *language* to remind us that the patterns fit together as words in a sentence. The social environment is seen to have a structure that stands comparison with a written language, or with a machine. If a car is disassembled and all the parts laid out on the ground, it no longer has a structure. If the parts are bolted together in the wrong combinations, it may have a structure but it will not be a good structure. It will resemble a badly planned city. To make a good car, the parts must be grouped in the correct clusters, to make a body, an engine, a transmission and a passenger compartment. There is a hierarchy of assemblies and the assembly rules can be described as a language, with paragraphs, sentences and words. Language is, again, a useful analogy for the environment because there are so many different things to be said and so many types of place to be made.

The strengths and weaknesses of the pattern language approach may be summarized as follows:

Strengths:

1 The language is incrementalist. It is "piecemeal planning", not "master planning" or "blueprint planning".
2 The language makes use of archetypes.

3 The language offers a way of interrelating development projects, by responding to what has gone before and giving thought to what may come after.

Weaknesses:

1 It is claimed, unnecessarily, that each of the patterns is an objective truth. This gives a totalitarian flavour to the language.
2 Some of the patterns are eccentric and at the far left of the political spectrum. In view of the preceding point, this gives the language a menacing character to those of different political persuasions.
3 It is claimed, wrongly in my opinion, that the patterns are independent of culture and climate.
4 The language appears to use a hierarchical structure, of the type which Alexander criticized.
5 The language takes no account of natural or aesthetic patterns and does not provide a basis for commenting upon the Australian problem, as discussed above.

The weaknesses of the theory are important if the language is to be used to guide contextual design. From the viewpoint of context theory, the most significant weakness of the language is the way in which the man-made environment is privileged over the natural environment. Some of the patterns do refer to natural site characteristics (e.g. Pattern 161, "Sunny place"). But surely natural characteristics are as important or more important than man-made characteristics. McHarg's overlay approach showed how natural factors could and should be incorporated into the planning process. A pattern-based planning model has the potential to interrelate the patterns of the existing landscape with Alexander's patterns of human use and aspiration. When preparing a design for a particular location, designers should know which Alexander patterns are present on the site and what provision could be made for the establishment of other patterns.

The identity index

An index can be used to define the extent to which development projects will be similar to, different from or identical with their context.

The foregoing theories of context treat the environment in different ways: aesthetic, ecological, social. The list is incomplete, but from each standpoint the relationship between a development and its context can be one of similarity, identity or difference. Logically, these are the only possibilities. Yet a project can be identical in one respect and different in other respects, as when a skyscraper is faced in a local stone.

An identity index, using a percentage scale, is a good way to describe the degree of similarity, identity or difference between a development and an aspect of the environment. For example:

	Materials	Size	Style	Vegetation
Tower block	90%	20%	10%	30%

This example shows identity values for a stone-clad tower block in a historic stone-built town. They range from 90 per cent identity for building materials to 10 per cent identity for architectural style. Vegetation is given a score of 30 per cent, reflecting the proportion of native shrubs to exotic shrubs.

Total identity between a development and its environment is unusual, although one could get close by using identical materials in identical shapes and patterns, as when an area of disturbed ground is resown with seed gathered from the surrounding area. In time, this could produce 100 per cent identity. When a gap appeared in a row of Georgian houses it was once fashionable to carry out what was known as "sympathetic infill", using similar materials and similar shapes but in a modern idiom. Such projects might have an average identity index of 90 per cent. A low identity index would result from using unrelated materials, shapes and patterns, as in Fig. 3.15D. Project teams can be asked to state an identity index for development proposals and for the separate aspects of their proposals. Indeed, if I were drafting a planning or environmental assessment law, I would insert a

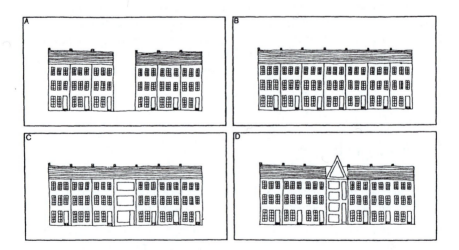

Figure 3.15 Three alternatives to filling a gap in a row of Georgian houses: similarity, identity, difference.

requirement that every application for approval must be accompanied by a statement giving an identity index for components and for the whole project. There should also be a reasoned account of how the decisions were taken.

In a conservation area, the average identity index of development projects should be weighted towards "very close resemblance". In a major redevelopment area, we could expect most of the projects to be different from the existing environment but related to each other. At La Défense, in Paris, this was achieved by encouraging tall buildings and by projecting the grand avenue from the Louvre and the Arc de Triomphe into the development area. In London's Isle of Dogs (Fig. 3.16), there is hardly any visual similarity between the buildings, but conservation of the water bodies has created a spatial pattern similar to the pre-development landscape. A new reservoir in a beautiful place should be similar to other water bodies in the region. It was right to make the Sydney Opera House different from all surrounding buildings – and to give it a kinship with the sailing ships that pass by. These examples illustrate different identity policies. Each has its place, but design teams should be *required* to explain the stances they have taken on the various aspects of identity between development and environment. Each contextual relationship requires the support of a coherent argument. Projects must be designed "from the outside in' *and* "from the inside out".

Figure 3.16 The retention of the water bodies in London Docklands has given some coherence to the architecture.

The use of an identity index need not be a factor in deciding for or against the Australian's application for a church and eucalyptus forest. It would merely define the background against which his justification of the proposed contextual relationship would have to be developed.

GIS and context

A GIS can help check the impact of development projects on natural, social and aesthetic aspects of the context. It provides the data for co-ordinating the environmental assessment and land-use planning systems.

In order to produce good contextual designs, it is necessary to have good information on:

- environmental history (e.g. former habitats, former watercourses, archaeology, ancient farming patterns);
- present environmental conditions (e.g. soils, vegetation, hydrology, land-use, visual character, Alexander patterns, street patterns);
- plans for the future environment (e.g. plans for habitat creation, scenic improvement, greenspace, river reclamation, recreational development, urbanization).

This information should be available in an environmental planning database (EPD) or planning information system (PIS). A GIS displays structures of different kinds. The "lower" layers of the model represent historic conditions. The "middle" layers show the existing situation. The "upper" layers represent possible future states of affairs. An EPD is good at answering contextual questions. What? Where? What if? For example:

Impact questions	What happens if it goes there?
	What is the impact on each aspect of the landscape?
Zoning questions	What is this area notable for?
	What is this area suitable for?
	What special considerations apply to this area of land?
	Which areas of land are homogeneous?
Location questions	Where are the location criteria satisfied?
	Which is the most scenic route?
	Which area has the lowest scenic quality?

Such questions relate to the past, present and future of the environment. By asking what?, where? and what if? questions, a GIS can bind the land-use planning system to the environmental assessment system (Fig. 3.17). The GIS offers flexibility, vast data storage and analytical capabilities. It can

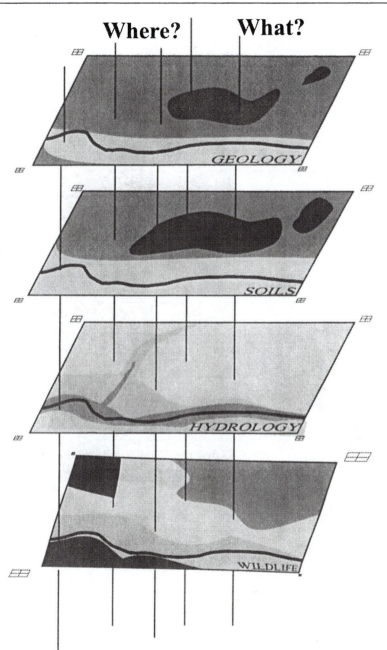

Figure 3.17 Geographical information systems use layered models. They can represent the natural environment (left) and the social environment (right), and are good at providing answers to What?, Where?, and What if? questions.

105

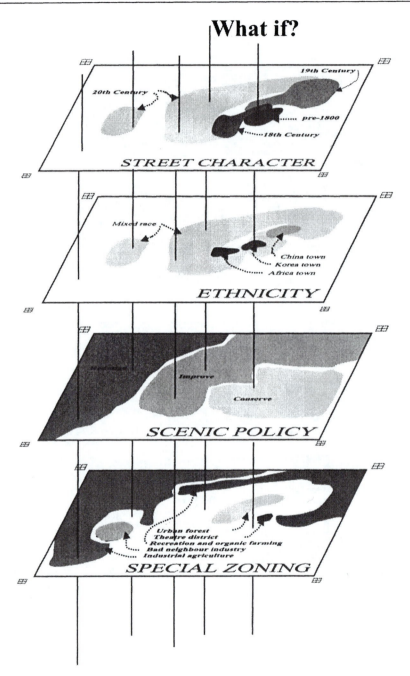

What if?

STREET CHARACTER

ETHNICITY

SCENIC POLICY

SPECIAL ZONING

Figure 3.17 (continued)

also facilitate community involvement in the planning process, as can be explained with a recondite example.

Let us assume there is a local Hedgehog Society. Members of the society can draw information from the GIS database, conduct surveys, formulate a plan and lodge it in the GIS. When a new road is being planned, the highway planners will ask the GIS about the impact of their proposal on the existing environment and on the community's aspirations. This will reveal that an area they took to be waste land is actually an important hedgehog habitat, with rotting brushwood, warm places to nest and good supplies of black crunchy beetles. Road engineers can reduce opposition to their plans by promising to manage new embankments as hedgehog habitats. We could have a low roadside fence to stop hedgehogs straying onto the highway.

Other layers of the GIS can deal with other aspects of the wood. On a two-dimensional map, existing trees would be represented by patches of green and the proposed management zone by a red line. A well-balanced EPD can go much further, by providing information and predicting the impact of alternative development scenarios. It can show the distribution of plant and animal species in the wood, proposals for water conservation and management, the location of scenic areas, the role of the wood in screening a nearby quarry, the areas of wood used for children's play and the places where orchids grow. Once the information has been lodged in the computer, a query about a parcel of land will reveal the data that has been collected and the plans of different community groups. Good information is the essential foundation for good environmental planning and design.

The GIS cannot of itself say whether the Australian's project should be given the go-ahead. But it can make available the information on which to base a contextually appropriate decision. This may include:

- a long-term agricultural plan to de-emphasize food production on the urban fringe;
- a recreation plan showing an intention to develop the recreation and tourism potential of the area;
- a survey showing that the existing plants and animals in the area are not important for reasons of scarcity or diversity;
- a scenic quality assessment showing that the area has medium to low scenic quality;
- a water management plan showing a need to increase surface water infiltration in the area.

All these factors would tend to support the Australian's application. He would have a better chance of a fair hearing if the planning and development context were defined in a strategic plan and strategic environmental assessment *before* his application was made. Surveys and plans made in response to particular applications tend to be biased.

Conclusion

Conservation is not enough.

One of the great lessons of the twentieth century is that bad planning, like no planning, leads to lack of respect for human rights and the destruction of public goods. Individuals and groups of individuals are often selfish. Without constraints, we destroy nature's bounty of fresh air, clean water, fine scenery, good earth and healthy vegetation. Hence the case for public intervention in private land-use decisions. This chapter has considered when intervention should take place, how it should be done, and what should be achieved. With regard to landscape planning, the following conclusions have been reached:

When? Intervention should take place when there are positive or negative environmental impacts on public goods.

How? Intervention should be guided by a combination of zoning and environmental impact procedures, both statutory and non-statutory.

What? Intervention should achieve better relationships between development and context.

Intervention should be guided by knowledge of the past, an environmental database, alternative visions of the future, environmental controls and theories of context. So much damage has already been done that conservation is not enough. We can and must prepare landscape plans for the renewal of earth, water, vegetation, air and other public goods. But it does not follow that these plans need the force of law. Regulations are ineffective without imaginative leadership.

Part 2

Environmental Impact Design

Introduction

A certain amount of land-use history is contained in the second part of this book. Although it centres on Britain, the stories are uncomfortably similar in other countries. The common pattern struck me after completing the first edition of the book and was outlined in Chapter 1 of this edition. It derives from the universal truths of science and may be common to every land-use in every industrialized country:

1 *Pre-industrial multi-purpose planning* Landowners aimed to achieve as many types of benefit as they could from the land under their control (Fig. 0.2).
2 *Professionalized planning* The professions offered increased efficiency and output through the use of specialized scientific techniques.
3 *Industrialized and single-purpose planning* The output of private goods was maximized and that of public goods ignored (Fig. 0.3).
4 *Public protest* Communities protested at the loss of public goods.
5 *Environmental planning and design* Landusers are moving towards multi-purpose planning.

At present, land-users and professions are at different points on the return to multi-purposism and they have different reputations. In Britain, the high-way engineer may be the most notorious, the water engineer the most enlightened, the park manager the most blinkered, the quarryman the most unimaginative, the nature conservationist the most devious. Architects and planners are the most vilified by the general public. Landscape architects have the widest objectives and the fewest achievements.

In the mid-twentieth century, rivers were planned only for flood control, farmlands for food, forests for timber, military training grounds for war games, roads for vehicular transport, buildings for the benefit of what went on inside their walls. The most scientifically planned of all societies, the

Figure 0.2   The river in Chartres, a delightful product of pre-industrial, old-fashioned, multi-purpose river planning.

Figure 0.3   The river in Bayreuth, an obnoxious consequence of modern, professionalized, single-purpose river planning. Having scrawled graffiti on their walls, the good citizens of Bayreuth should take heart from their cousins in Berlin, and tear them down.

Union of Soviet Socialist Republics (USSR), travelled furthest down this particular road to environmental ruin. Not having visited either place, I feel sure that most of the rivers in Vladivostok and Detroit, like those in London, are open sewers in concrete channels, ugly and dangerous, hostile to fishing, swimming and wildlife. Reclaiming the rivers of Vladivostok, Detroit and London will be expensive. But if the environmental impact of every development project is assessed and designed at the planning stage, the modifications will normally impose a small percentage cost on the developer and yield a large percentage benefit to the community. They will also improve the reputation of land development and speed the process of project authorization. There will even be some golden projects, such as the lake in Redditch New Town (Fig. 11.11), which save developers money while benefiting the community at large. We can plan for both environment and development.

Land-uses should be fitted together with the greatest care and skill. This involves three groups of people: landowners, the public and the professionals. Each must appreciate the potential for multi-objective project design. Landowners and the public have interests to defend. Professionals can work as mediators. Too often, the public interest has been subjugated by professional advisors working in cahoots with landowners. To lift the oppression, questions must be asked and answers given. The lists in Appendix A have been framed for this purpose. With the public breathing fiery questions down their necks, professionals usually do a better job. They can fit land uses together, encourage multi-use planning and make better landscapes.

After zoning land for housing, commerce, transport and so forth, scientific planners used to set aside additional tracts for "open" space or "landscaping". Open it was, landscape it was not. The idea, seemingly praiseworthy, was that vegetated space would freshen the air, improve views and provide for wildlife and recreation. But the patches of open space they created were like photographs on a prison wall. Described as "garks" in Chapter 4, they served as pathetic reminders of what had been lost. When we speak of "our street", "our town", "our country", and "our Earth" we are thinking of rights and duties which extend across property boundaries and transcend the generations. This requires environmental impact design (EID), which may be defined as "the adaptation of a project design with regard to the supply of public goods (social, natural and aesthetic) and the development of multi-objective landscapes".

CHAPTER 4
Public open space

The physical types of open space presently designed are astonishingly limited: the swimming beach, the roadside picnic area, the woodland with "nature trails", the grassed park dotted with trees and shrubbery, comprise the conventional range.

Lynch 1972: 110

Great civilizations allocate open space to public and non-productive uses. Historically, this has included gardens, temple compounds, ceremonial grounds, outdoor markets, social places, gymnasia for exercise and recreation, burial grounds, hunting and wildlife reserves. All this land is now classified by planners as "public open space", because the land is accessible and unbuilt. It is a term which ignores the distinction between parks and greenways. Parks are for protection (Fig. 4.1). Greenways are for movement. The reasons for making public open space are multifarious. Lynch, as quoted above, was right to protest that "the physical types of open space presently designed are astonishingly limited".

Parks take their name from the verb to impark, which means to surround with a hedge, fence or wall. Greenways, as discussed in the second half of this chapter, have characteristics indicated by the two components of the word: the land has environmental quality and it provides a route, for humans, animals or a natural process. Frequently, parks will be patches and greenways will be corridors.

Figure 4.1 Parks are for protection. Greenways are for movement. Both types of space can be public and open.

If badly located, parks and greenways have as little chance of success as stations without railways or railways without stations. The three cardinal principles of property development, location, location and location, apply with additional force to park planning. In the twenty-first century, there is little hope for a large municipal park with tawdry facilities designed for the needs of a previous generation. Park development is a specialized aspect of property development. Some parks need to be re-imparked. Others need to be dis-imparked. The distinction between enclosed and unenclosed land is of greater consequence than that between formal and informal recreation, active and passive recreation, urban and rural recreation.

Public parks

The park is dead. Long live the park.

In "the city of dreadful night", *circa* 1850, acrid smoke belched from every rooftop, and raw sewage flowed in narrow streets. Workers, with their wives and children, toiled from before dawn until after dusk. Zola describes such a life in *Germinal* (Zola 1885). On Sunday, if the hapless workers had free time, most resorted to alcohol. It eased their pains, slaked their sorrows and helped them to dream of strikes and revolution. According to the cynical view of urban history, public gardens were provided by manipulative governments to control the rebellious tendencies of the working class. Ruskin described the public park in 1872 as a place where workers could be "taken in squad" to be "revived by science and art" (Robinson 1872). More charitably, public gardens were provided by public benefactors and enlightened city fathers who wished to improve the lot of the toiling masses. In either case, walls, fences and gates were essential, to discourage licentious behaviour and to make public gardens safe. In an earlier age, chains had been used to make library books safe against thieves.

Imparked greenspace in urban areas became known as parks. Public baths and libraries were also provided. After six days of sordid toil, these facilities enabled workers to rest their limbs, cleanse their bodies and improve their minds. In parks, they could sit on a bench, look at the flowers, listen to brass bands and drive the moths from their Sunday clothes. In the early-twentieth century, when machines took over the really heavy work, city managers espied a new role for parks: the promotion of physical fitness. During the First World War, soldiers proved to be less fit than their nineteenth-century predecessors. After the war came economic depression and an outbreak of juvenile delinquency. The governing authorities hoped that youthful energy could be diverted into organized sport (Fig. 4.2). Again, one can view their motives with cynicism or charity. Galen Cranz's enjoyable

Figure 4.2 After the Second World War the governing authorities hoped that by filling parks with sportsfields they could reduce juvenile delinquency, as shown on the cover of the National Playing Fields Association's first annual report, for 1927. The picture caption reads 'Come and join us'.

book *The politics of the park* takes the cynical line and sees a progressive "decline in the range of social functions performed by parks" and "a practice of elites using parks deliberately as mechanisms for solving urban problems" (Cranz 1982: 225).

Times have changed, somewhat. Library books are no longer chained to desks; houses have piped water and washing machines; private gardens are widespread. Industrial machinery does the physical work, leaving most people in industrialized countries with sedentary jobs. For health and for leisure, sedentary workers require exercise, not rest. Organized sport shows no signs of reducing juvenile delinquency, although municipal authorities keep hoping against hope. Television has opened our eyes to all the different ways of enjoying outdoor life. Sitting in a municipal park, looking at the flowers and listening to the occasional brass band do not feature prominently in surveys reviewing the popularity of leisure-time activities. Rather, people desire access to rich and varied landscapes with scope for many outdoor activities.

Park planners responded to the new age by tearing down park railings and planning webs of interconnected greenspace, originally known as park systems. The diagnosis was correct. The treatment was pathetically oversimplified. Parkland, like most other types of land, should be planned for multiple objectives. New parks and new links should be created by planning recreational and conservation uses in conjunction with other land-uses: urban reservoirs can make splendid waterparks; ornithological habitats and hides should be designed in conjunction with sewage farms; wildlife corridors should be planned beside roads, railways and streams; flood prevention works can yield canoe courses; public gardens can sit on top of office buildings. New uses and new layers of interest should be brought into public open spaces (Fig. 4.3). This requires imaginative EID. Some open spaces could supply firewood and wild food (nuts, berries, herbs); others could infiltrate rainwater back into the ground, instead of allowing the water to accentuate flood peaks; Sunday markets can fit well into parks. Every public open space can have a specialist use, in addition to its general functions. One could be a centre for kite flying (see Fig. 4.4 below); one for tennis; one for lovers of herbaceous plants; one for re-enacting military battles; one for every special recreational interest which has a magazine on your local newsstand. My local newsagent has special-interest magazines for golf, fishing, cycling, skiing, yachting, sail-boards,

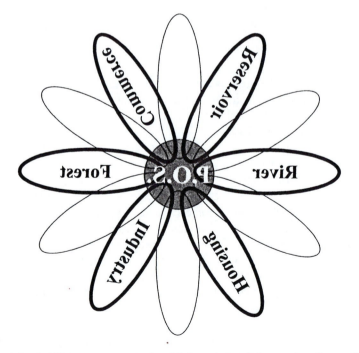

Figure 4.3 Public open space should be planned in conjunction with other land-uses.

fitness, martial arts, boxing, wrestling, horse-riding, climbing, trail walking, athletics, shooting, soccer, rugby, gardening, camping, model boats and model aircraft – but only six of these interests can be pursued in the 185 hectares of public open space near where I live.

In some respects, parks resemble churches. Both were built for idealistic reasons. Both are regarded as essential features of towns. Both can have attendance problems in the age of electronic communications. The world's great historic churches and parks are filled with visitors. But smaller local churches and parks need new roles. People dislike seeing churches turned into shops, or public parks into markets, but a greater range of uses is necessary. The time has come to reinvent and re-engineer the public park. Many of the ancient public open space archetypes continue to have value. But they must be adapted to the conditions of today. Too many planning maps indicate "public open space" with green ink, as though it were all the same, suitable for management in one way by one organization. On a proper open space map, that vapid green ink should be replaced by a harlequin mosaic of disparate hues and shades, reflecting the kaleidoscopic variations of spatial use, management and ownership. To produce such a map, it is necessary to carry out surveys, of ownership, use, values and methods of maintenance.

Towns need a great diversity of public open space types. In addition to the emerald green of public parks, they need spaces that are diamonds, rubies, pearls, ambers, ceramics, lucky charms, holograms and electronic marvels too. The list of open spaces which will be discussed in subsequent sections of this chapter includes commons, municipal parks, sports parks, squares, plazas, public gardens, village greens, national parks, private pleasure grounds and festival parks.

Commons

There always have been public rights in land and there always should be.

When Northern Europe was resettled after the last Ice Age, land belonged to tribes, not individuals. Land was also owned by tribes in America, Africa and Australia before the European settlements. When arable farming became established, it was important for families to till and occupy their own fields. But large areas of land remained. Generally, they belonged to a king, lord or tribal chief, the people having rights to use the land for defined purposes.

Common rights were not something specifically granted by a generous landlord, but were the residue of rights that were once much more extensive, rights that are in all probability older than the modern conception of private property. (Hoskins & Dudley Stamp 1963: 6)

From a planner's viewpoint, the fascinating aspect of commons is that the public owned rights without owning the land itself. Typically, they had rights to gather firewood, catch fish and graze animals, in addition to rights of access. In the surviving commons, there is a right of access but many of the other rights have lapsed or been stolen. In some cases, all the ancient rights should be restored. In other cases, the ancient rights no longer have value, either because society has changed or because the people have moved away. They should be replaced with new rights. Commons continue to be of great social importance, and modern societies have just as much need for rights over privately owned land as did their predecessors. These rights could be subject to compulsory purchase, if need be. America has a great need to revive the notion of common rights. They would benefit modern societies on the urban fringe, in scenic areas, in woods and forests, beside water and in areas that are important for the health of the ecosystem. Greenways, as discussed below (page 137), can be established by creating common rights over private land.

During the eighteenth and nineteenth centuries, surviving areas of common land were looked on with disfavour by the authorities. They were said to be agriculturally unproductive, unsightly, politically dangerous and socially disruptive – as meeting grounds for criminals, drunkards, prostitutes and malcontents. The English political meeting which led to the Peterloo massacre of 1819 was held on common land, and in 1848 the Chartists gathered on Kennington Common. Cattle grazed on Boston Common, in Massachusetts, until the 1830s. Sheep still graze on Lüneburg Heath in Germany. Some commons were saved from extinction by being converted into public parks. John Stow records that Moorfields, in London, "were turned into pleasant walks, set with trees for shade and ornament" during the seventeenth century. By 1720 they were "no mean cause of preserving Health and wholesome Air to the City; and such an eternal Honour thereto, as no Iniquity of Time shall be able to deface" (Stow 1720: 70). His optimism was ill placed: the fields were sold for building development in 1814. Many other commons survived as public parks with restricted use. The Meadows in Edinburgh, the Strays in Harrogate and Clapham Common in London are, to the uninformed visitor, indistinguishable from other municipal parks. No modern poet is likely to write of:

Ye commons left free in the rude rags of nature,
    Ye brown heaths be clothed in furze as ye be,
My wild eye in rapture adores every feature,
    Ye are dear as this heart in my bosom to me.
Hoskins & Dudley Stamp 1963: 63

The injustice done to the people of England does not equal that done to the native peoples of America and Australia, but comparisons can be drawn. According to Hoskins and Stamp, "millions of acres" of common land were enclosed and "in most places this legalised theft was carried through without any active threat from the illiterate and cowed small peasantry, who rarely had a leader in their cause" (ibid. 1963: 60).

J. C. Loudon both defended the commons and argued the case for public parks. In 1835, the year in which he designed England's first public park, Loudon made the following plea for the commons:

> The preservation of some of these chases is as essential to the poorer classes of the metropolis as to the rich. To the former they afford health, exercise and amusement; in the latter they produce and cherish that love of the country, and of rural sports, so important in a constitutional point of view. (Loudon 1835: 562)

Loudon also campaigned to save Hampstead Heath from building development (Simo 1981). It was saved as an open space in the 1870s, but in the 1970s local residents were still fighting – to stop park managers converting land from heath to park (Fig. 4.4) (Davies 1983: 199). Wimbledon Common is owned by trustees and managed as traditional heathland. The natural

Figure 4.4 Hampstead Heath had to be saved first from building development and then from municipal conversion to a public park.

vegetation is maintained at one fifth of the cost of a standard town park and also accommodates a wider range of uses: golf, horse-riding, walking, football, children's play, cricket, model boating, outdoor swimming, gathering firewood, courting and picking blackberries. Common lands should be held in trust, by the people for the people, to be managed with as little expenditure of the people's money as possible.

Municipal parks

The public park, as caricatured at the start of this chapter, has been a happy hunting ground for reformers. The first generation of park planners saw them as a health measure, to allow tired workers access to fresh air and to wean them from liquor (Fig. 4.5). The next group of reformers wished to persuade workers to keep fit, for their country's sake and also for their own good. A 1960s group of reformers wished to shake off the authoritarian mantle of "public health" park management and to open parks up to the easy-going hippie culture of the times. Ironically, this often meant going back to those uses of open space that had been expurgated in the 1860s (e.g. dancing, drinking and fairs). In the 1980s, park reformers had a sense of ecological mission. They wished parks to be havens for nature in the city,

Figure 4.5 A classic and still popular public park – Battersea in London.

full of wild plants and free of exotics, pesticides, herbicides, fertilizers and maintenance by fossil fuels.

Was one group of reformers right and the other groups wrong? In our pluralist age, with society becoming more multi-cultural and multi-faith by the day, it seems right to accord value to each of the historic park management ideas, and to modern ideas as well. Public open spaces should be more diverse (Fig. 4.6). This could be done in several ways. First, we could take a plan of a city, on which all the open spaces are coloured green, and assign different colours to areas where different management objectives would apply. A town with four similar spaces could allocate one to each of the four reform ideas: horticulture, sport, cultural events and nature conservation. Second, we could treat the reform ideas as "overlays", or new ingredients, to be added to the management objectives of each and every space. This is what many park managers have tried to do, with mixed results. Third, we could give each of the reform ideas priority in one of the spaces. Fourth, we could use all three approaches, depending on local circumstances.

The example of Greenwich Park, which is the nearest large park to my home, is a useful illustration. It was enclosed as a royal hunting park in 1433 (Fig. 4.7a) and laid out in 1661 as an aesthetic design in the French manner (Fig. 4.7b). During the eighteenth century (Fig. 4.7c), it was somewhat converted to the style of Capability Brown. During the nineteenth and twentieth centuries, as the public gained progressively freer access, Greenwich came to have the character of a municipal public park (Fig. 4.7d). The new facilities included a flower garden, a boating pond, a tea pavilion, tennis courts, pitches for rugby and cricket. With the new enthusiasm for garden history, dating from the 1960s, there have been proposals for

PUBLIC OPEN SPACE PLANNING CHART						
Ownership	Central govt	Local govt	Trust	Company	Utility	Local people
Colour theme	Red	Yellow	Blue	Green	Brown	White
Mood	Calm	Exciting	Solemn	Sensuous	Sensual	Gloomy
Age group	0–10 yrs	10–20 yrs	20–30 yrs	30–40 yrs	40–60 yrs	60+ yrs
Ethnicity	Anglo-Saxon	Latin	African	Central Asia	SE Asia	East Asian
Culture	Radio 1	Radio 2	Radio 3	Radio 4	Radio 5	World Service
Religion	Christian	Confucian	Jewish	Hindu	Buddhist	Islamic
Landform	Hill	Mountain	Valley	Plateau	Beach	Meadow
Habitat	Marshland	Grassland	Maquis	Forest	Lake	Ocean
Climate	Sunny	Shady	Windy	Humid	Dry	Sheltered
Special use	Fine art	Sport	Swimming	Nature study	Food	Courting

Figure 4.6 Parks should be diversified. This park planning chart shows a range of options. One set of choices has been ringed, for an urban fringe park.

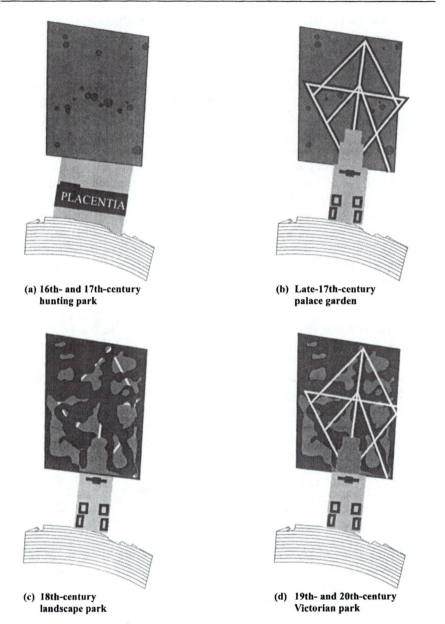

(a) 16th- and 17th-century
hunting park

(b) Late-17th-century
palace garden

(c) 18th-century
landscape park

(d) 19th- and 20th-century
Victorian park

Figure 4.7 Creative conservation is an appropriate policy for Greenwich Park. The historical layers represented by diagrams (a), (b), (c) and (d) should be conserved in a creative unity that looks backwards and forwards in time (e).

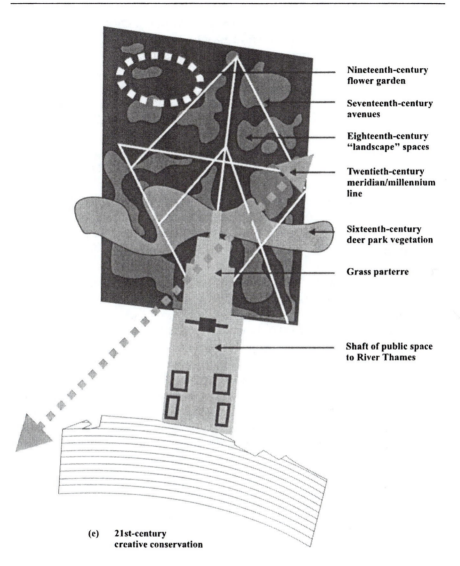

Nineteenth-century
flower garden

Seventeenth-century
avenues

Eighteenth-century
"landscape" spaces

Twentieth-century
meridian/millennium
line

Sixteenth-century
deer park vegetation

Grass parterre

Shaft of public space
to River Thames

(e)   21st-century
      creative conservation

Figure 4.7 (continued)

"restoration", but the great problem is knowing what to restore. Henry VIII's hunting park? Charles II's baroque avenues? The English landscape garden? The Victorian flower garden? The twentieth-century public park? One could make a case for any of them, but one would have to fight off proponents of the alternatives. I believe the best solution is the policy which

Geoffrey Jellicoe described as "creative conservation". Park planners should take the historical layers and weld them into a new harmony (Fig. 4.7e).

The principle of planning-by-layers can be extended to other matters: functions, aesthetics, ecology. There are many keen ornithologists who visit parks. They should plan how to adapt their park for birdlife, as an overlay. Other people like to collect firewood and chestnuts. Others love hedgehogs. These are legitimate activities, which should be catered for. When it snows, Greenwich Park is full of toboggans. The slopes should be made safe and convenient for them, despite the temporary damage caused to the grass, which upsets those who maintain the turf.

Because of its history, location and size, Greenwich Park has to accommodate many things. Other parks could be more specialist. One could become a fully restored Victorian park, with carpet bedding, gates, clocks, cast iron furniture, uniformed park keepers and regular brass band performances. One could become an Athenian gymnasium, for those who wish to exercise their minds and bodies simultaneously. One could become a Spartan sportpark, for those who see exercise as a near-military activity. One could celebrate cycling. One could become a national centre for kite flying.

The historical origins of the public park have led to the present situation where park managers wrestle with the aims of horticultural display, picturesque effect and organized sport. The triumvirate is perused with great determination, but the aims are incompatible. Perhaps the saddest failure is with planting design. Rock gardens of the almond-pudding type have proliferated, grasslands are razored by gang mowers, assorted rhododendrons are bundled together on unsuitable sites, mottled expanses of heather are punctuated with dwarf conifers, herbaceous borders are planted without regard to colour harmony, and rose beds are stocked like vegetable gardens. Even the once-splendid art of carpet-bedding has fallen on hard times. All this despite the fact that a majority of park managers come from a horticultural background. We cannot complain, as Paxton did, that our parks are in the hands of broken-down contractors or retired sea captains (Parliamentary Debates 1859). But we can complain with Cranz that "Like all bureaucracies the park department took on a life of its own and came to be committed first of all to its own maintenance and enhancement" (Cranz 1982: 109).

Squares and plazas

> *Urban squares started as markets, and many should continue to have a commercial role.*

Urban plazas are bounded yet unbound. Since the exchange of goods was one of the primary reasons for creating towns, ancient settlements had a special place for trade in their midst. Often, it was no more than a swelling in the road, to accommodate weekly markets. During the Italian Renaissance, the custom arose of designing such places as formal squares, with dignified proportions and handsome architecture. This changed their appearance but did not stop them operating as markets. Alberti advised that "The squares must be so many different markets, one for gold and silver, another for herbs, another for cattle, another for wood, and so on" (Fig. 4.8) (Rykwert 1955: 173). Palladio also saw squares as markets, but added that

> . . . they afford also a great ornament, when at the head of a street, a beautiful and spacious place is found, from which a prospect of some beautiful fabrick is seen, and especially of some temple. (Palladio 1965: 72)

Ornament is sometimes thought to be the primary purpose of squares and plazas, and an American has suggested that "most of our urban open spaces seem to be designed largely for the convenience of architectural photographers" (Taylor 1981: 11). They are exposed and empty, with uncomfortable seats and a prohibition on street trading. Their managers should remember

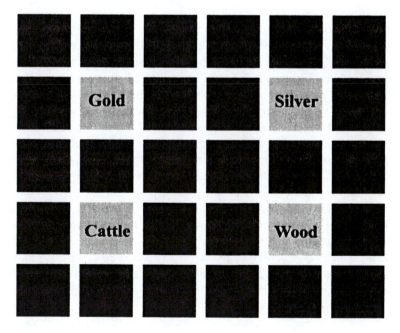

Figure 4.8 Urban "squares" were originally used for outdoor markets.

Figure 4.9 Selling goods remains an excellent use for public open space (Delft).

President Clinton's 1992 campaign slogan: "It's the economy, stupid". Selling goods remains an excellent use for public open space (Fig. 4.9).

Since Alberti's time, the function of urban places has diversified. Many have acquired a recreational function. In England they even became communal gardens belonging to those who lived in the surrounding houses. We call them squares, reserving plaza for busier places. In the modern city we think of the urban plaza as an intensively used "architectural" space for sitting in the sun, eating sandwiches, taking a lunch-time stroll and watching the world go by. These functions, one might think, necessitate planning criteria that differ from those for market places. Such a thought could easily lead the planner astray.

William H. Whyte conducted a brilliant research project on the plazas of New York City (Whyte 1980). Following the logic of the above account, he assumed that the most popular plazas would be those with the best climate and the most beauty. Time-lapse photography was used to test this assumption. Work began in the spring of 1971, and early results confirmed the hypothesis. People were observed to sit in sunny spots and to move around as the sun moved around. Whyte was delighted. But when spring turned to summer this no longer happened. It became clear that some plazas were enormously more popular than others, and that popularity had little or nothing to do with microclimate *or* design. Photography continued for several years and the results were analyzed. Gradually it emerged that the prime factors governing the use of New York plazas were astoundingly similar to those that have led to the creation of urban places throughout history.

Whyte found that in New York plazas are most used at lunch-time – and only if they have good access, food for sale and plentiful seating. The relationship between plaza and street is "the critical design factor". Having been drawn into the plaza "people tend to sit most where there are most places to sit". Quantity and variety of seating have more influence on use than either sun, aesthetics, shape or size. But microclimate can be important. People seek warm places in cold weather and will avoid gusting winds around tall buildings.

Whyte's experimental results confirmed Jane Jacobs' observations in Philadelphia. She examined four urban squares which appeared similar from a map (Fig. 4.10). They were the same size and had the same relationship to the City Hall. But she found only one square to be successful and popular: the one surrounded by a diversity of land-uses. The presence of a

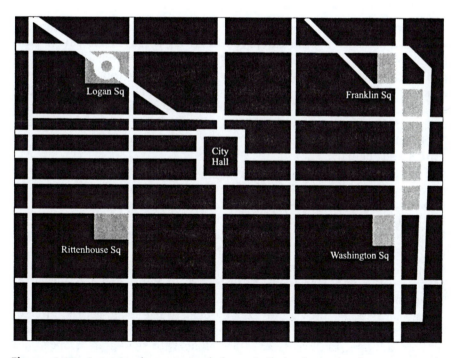

Figure 4.10 Jane Jacobs examined four similarly located urban squares in Philadelphia. She found only one them to be successful. (Rittenhouse Square).

127

major public building, such as an art gallery, can be a great contribution to the success of a plaza. A space without pedestrian generators will have few pedestrians.

An earlier observer, Camillo Sitte, noticed that strong gusts outside medieval cathedrals tended to raise the ladies' skirts (Sitte 1979: 87). But the poor microclimate did not discourage visitors. Le Corbusier, who persuaded so many designers to build towers, was unaware of the effect of high buildings upon microclimate. Sitte believed that squares should have an open centre, an enclosed character, correct dimensions and an irregular shape. He discovered that "the average dimensions of the great squares of the old cities are 142m by 58m" (ibid.: 18). Modern designers should learn from the past. We do not have to reinvent the square, or the wheel. A square needs high accessibility or things to buy if it is to be well used. Little has changed, except that the world's cities have been filled with badly located, odd-looking, under-used places, plazas, piazzas and squares.

Public gardens

Cities need gardens and parks, not "garks".

While "urban park" suggests an area of grass and trees, "public garden" suggests a much more intimate space with loving management. Much harm has been done by confusing gardens with parks. We have made too many gardenesque-parks, or "garks" for short. Their creators imagine they will combine the best of both worlds. More often, they combine the worst. When an actress propositioned the writer Bernard Shaw that they could have children with her looks and his brains, Shaw replied that they might have her brains and his looks. Let us start by considering the gark's parents: the garden and the park.

Town gardens, where they exist, have a wonderfully civilizing influence on cities. For half an hour or half a day, we citizens can luxuriate in a resplendent urban scene, with sweet-scented flowers, comfortable seats, a sparkle of fountains, a bright sun, warmth or deep shade. Birds sing, bees hum, lovers coo. Such a place needs to be secured at night, so that the seats need not be bolted to the ground or the beds filled with tough low-maintenance shrubs. New York's "pocket parks" may be classed as public gardens, as can the Jardin de Luxembourg in Paris, and the garden of Copenhagen's Royal Library (Fig. 4.11).

Parkland should provide an equally delightful but altogether different experience, more like being in the country. Such spaces can liberate the soul. In autumn, one wants to stride along with the wind in one's face and the leaves at one's feet. In winter, the frost should crackle and the mist collect in damp hollows. In spring, woods and meadows should be

Figure 4.11   The public garden of the Royal Library in Copenhagen is beautiful and peaceful. The statue of a philosopher (Kirkegaard) contributes to the calm.

Figure 4.12   This is a gark: an unblessed marriage of garden and park (Blackheath), in south London.

alive with flowers and butterflies. In summer, it is good to laze under a tree overlooking the lake. At all seasons, it is a joy to watch deer or other animals which benefit from the imparkment.

Now consider the poor gark (Fig. 4.12). Mown grass does not change with the seasons. Duck ponds are seriously eutrophic. Clumps of exotic trees are so mixed they resemble shrubberies. There are too many statues of dead politicians. Mass plantings of *Prunus* 'Otto Luyken' (Fig. 4.12), *Rosa* 'Frau Dagmar Hastrup' and *Berberis stenophylla* provide a gardenesque experience, with their evergreen leaves, flowers and berries, but the scale is not domestic. One cannot have an intimate experience with a block of low-maintenance ground cover, any more than one can with a Corbusian residential tower block. GARK can stand for gardenesque arrangement of ruralesque kitsch.

Some garks should be converted to public gardens. This requires walls, lockable gates and a high level of horticultural expertise. If more urban places were maintained in this way, urban dwellers would not need to make such long journeys to find country gardens with beautiful flowers and plant combinations.

Village greens

Good planning is more important than good design.

Some old villages have the most delightful central greens, which act as foci for community life (Fig. 4.13). This has prompted the developers of housing estates to ape their geometry and their nomenclature. But the success of a village green does not depend on its shape, size or name. It depends on location, location and location. A green must be at the heart of a community. Adjoining the green, there should be a pub, a shop, a telephone, a bench, a bus stop. A duck pond and a few ancient trees are desirable extras. So is a cricket pitch, in England.

National parks in towns

Some parks need more-than-local funding.

Cities require some parks that are great works of art. Government stock is safer than other types of stock. Government parks are better resourced than other types of park. Kings and queens used to make royal parks. Substantial resources are needed to create and maintain national works of art (Fig. 4.14). Park-making demands sustained effort, generation after generation. At times, heavy expenditure is required, and the

Figure 4.13 In Finchingfield, Essex, the green is at the heart of the community.

very best designers must be employed. Continued maintenance by thoughtful people with excellent design judgement will then be necessary. Idealism must guide their efforts. Special laws may be required.

After concluding a major study of American parks in the 1970s, Heckscher concluded that

Figure 4.14 As a fine art, parks are most likely to flourish when they are owned and maintained by national governments, as here at Versailles.

. . . the more local a government becomes, the less adequate is the level of maintenance. Where the state is responsible for in-city park development and upkeep (as, for example, in Point State Park in Pittsburgh or the historic park in San Diego's Old Town) high standards prevail. (Heckscher 1977: 9)

Wherever one may stand on the political spectrum, and in whatever country, one can but acknowledge that the parks owned and maintained by monarchs, central governments and capital cities have longer and better lives than those maintained by small communities with insecure tenancies. In Europe, many of the greatest public parks began in the ownership of kings and princes and survive in the ownership of government departments, be they in Berlin, Rome, Paris, Barcelona or London.

Britain's royal parks were originally hunting forests, regulated by forest laws, which gave rights, not unlike common rights, to forest dwellers. Despite the name forest, much of the land was grass and scrub. The Crown had no interest in timber until the close of the Middle Ages (James 1981: 137). Hyde Park was acquired by Henry VIII in 1536 and opened to the general public by Charles I in 1635, entirely "by his

Majesty's free will" (Larwood 1872: 21). No landscape design has ever been prepared for the whole park. It remains in Crown ownership, but the deer were removed in the nineteenth century and the sheep in the twentieth century. Hyde Park now has the appearance of a municipal park, except for the fact that over 250 horses are stabled near the park and exercised on Rotten Row. They are an elegant spectacle. Richmond Park is still managed as a deer park, though not for hunting. Deer, dogs and people have learnt the art of coexistence. It shows an economical, and quite splendid, technique of park management.

London's other royal parks have been designed according to aesthetic criteria, but this tradition comes from Italy and France. Versailles was both a hunting park and a royal garden. Any man was free to enter the gardens, providing he wore a sword. Louis XIV's entourage merely cleared a path through the crowd. Gothein remarks that "from the earliest days of the Renaissance it was customary in Italy for people who owned works of art and gardens to give the public free access to them" (Gothein 1928: 334). Mumford notes that the royal parks were "perhaps the first baroque feature to be opened to the public and duly incorporated in the city" (Mumford 1938: 379). Charles II returned to England from the court of Louis XIV and employed Frenchmen to advise on the design of St James's and Greenwich Parks. Like many European royal parks, they were opened to the public in the seventeenth century. The most important lesson to learn from the royal tradition is that a park can be conceived as a deliberate work of art. Even today royal parks escape the sameness of municipal management.

National parks in the country

Country areas of great importance to a nation should be given the protection of national park status.

National parks in rural areas should be diverse, as should their urban counterparts. Places should be chosen because they contain something of great importance to the nation: a scenic area, a historic area, an area of great species diversity, a natural process area, a recreation area.

True "national parks" are not discussed in this book, but they do illustrate some important principles, which apply to other aspects of park planning. The first national parks, in the USA, were chosen for their scenic splendour and were wholly in public ownership. Their advocates hoped they would give Americans something to rival the historic wonders of Europe. A later generation of national parks, in Europe, was created on land in private ownership. As with urban parks, there is every reason to use both principles. Another interesting point about Europe's national parks is that they have been designated for a variety of different purposes: some for scenic splendour, some for the conservation of plants and animals, some because they are the locus of important ecological processes, some for recreation. Each of these could become a main objective for park planning in and near urban areas.

The Lake District was a remote part of England in 1810, but Wordsworth was concerned that "the Lakes will fall almost entirely into the possession of gentry, either strangers or natives" and expressed the hope that "the author will be joined by persons of pure taste throughout the whole island" in testifying that the Lake District should become "a sort of national property, in which every man has a right and interest who has an eye to perceive and a heart to enjoy" (Wordsworth 1973: 91). In the nineteenth century no public action was taken to protect the Lake District, but national parks were established in America. In 1810, after four years in the Rocky Mountains, John Colter returned with stories of high mountains, deep chasms, spouts of boiling water and terrific waterfalls in a place now known as Colter's Hell. An organized party was sent in 1870 and recommended that the area should be protected. A park bill in 1872 established Yellowstone as the world's first national park (Runte 1979: 33). Since the land had never been settled and already belonged to the Federal Government there was no need to expropriate white-skinned landowners. It was a tract of wilderness; it became a park. By 1962 there were 1,200 national parks in the world.

Britain had no large tracts of land in state ownership which were suited to become national parks, but the desire, first voiced by Wordsworth, to protect areas of outstanding landscape value has been strong. A privately financed National Trust was founded in 1895 to preserve places of historic interest and natural beauty (Lees-Milne 1945). By 1970 it owned over 162,000 hectares of land – a comparatively small area equal to one-fifth of Yellowstone National Park, or the total area occupied by Britain's road verges (Taber 1973: iii). In 1931 the Addison Committee reported in favour of a national parks policy for Britain and the National Parks and Access to the Countryside Act was passed in 1949. Designation as a national park did not change the ownership. It remained private. The idea was to use financial aid and the 1947 Town and Country Planning Act to preserve natural beauty, improve facilities for recreation, protect natural and cultural features and maintain the land in agricultural use. Despite numerous conflicts between the objectives, some lack of finance, and some lack of resolve from local and central government, there can be no doubt that designation as a national park has furthered each of them. Financial subsidy and strict planning control are effective tools. When used in concert, they produce more interesting results than central government ownership-management.

Private pleasure grounds

Private enterprise is good at providing pleasure.

This type of space may be included under the general heading "public open space" because it satisfies the defining criteria. In 1800 too many of Europe's urban public open spaces were privately owned. Royal parks belonged to monarchs. Residential squares belonged to great lords. Tea and beer gardens belonged to private landlords. Private pleasure grounds, like Vauxhall in London, were accessible only to the wealthy. In short, there was a powerful case for creating municipal parks. Unfortunately and unsurprisingly, the movement went too far. There is a direct parallel with the case for taking industrial enterprises into public ownership. From the fact that there is a case for *some* enterprises to be in public ownership it does not follow that there is a case for *all* enterprises to be in public ownership. In many countries, there are some public parks which have far too much in common with 1970s public-sector industries: outdated work practices, lack of investment, high prices, falling consumer appeal, insensitivity to market demand. They deserve a degree of privatization. Industrial organizations tend to flourish when there is a close relationship between ownership and control.

Figure 4.15 The Tivoli Gardens in Copenhagen are the best surviving example of a pleasure ground in private ownership.

Vauxhall, Ranelagh and the other London pleasure gardens of the eighteenth century were "attempts to supply the more lascivious pleasures of the court to the commonalty at a reasonable price per head" (Mumford 1961: 379). The Bal Masque, in France, the German beer gardens and the Tivoli Gardens in Copenhagen are examples of the same tradition. The Tivoli is the best surviving European example of a public garden created and maintained by private enterprise (Fig. 4.15). Its name comes from the town beside the Villa d'Este outside Rome. Vauxall and Ranelagh were laid out in a derivative of the French style of garden design, and offered music, dancing, fireworks and light entertainment, all in the manner of Versailles. They were much frequented by the aristocracy. Horace Walpole wrote of Ranelagh in 1742 that "you can't set your foot without treading on a Prince or Duke of Cumberland" (Wroth 1896: 200). But even this great enthusiast for the English style of garden design did not complain about the layout: patrons must have adopted the sensible view that a different use justified a different style.

Chadwick suggests that private pleasure grounds declined in the nineteenth century as a result of stricter licensing requirements, a new attitude to "amusement" and "a competitor in the shape of gardens provided at public expense for public use" (Chadwick 1966: 42). The greatest Victorian park enterprise was Paxton's venture in setting up a private company to move the Crystal Palace to Sydenham and surrounding it with a pleasure ground. The public paid to see exhibitions and the fabulous water features and floral displays in the gardens. When Hyde Park and Kew Gardens started to compete, with displays of carpet bedding provided by public expenditure, Paxton complained to the House of Commons about unfair competition. He was especially annoyed that the Crystal Palace could not open on Sunday because of Sabbatarianism (Parliamentary Debates 1896).

In the USA the greatest development of the private enterprise park has been Disneyland and its descendants, which have a mixture of fun, excitement, historical reconstruction and technical marvels. These features have precedents in the history of garden design: the concealed jets of water and water games in Italian Renaissance gardens, the giant sculptures at Bomarzo, the hydraulic marvels of Salomon de Caus, the eighteenth-century English re-creations of the landscape of antiquity and the later "Egyptian", "Chinese", "Japanese", "American" and "Alpine" gardens. One Alpine garden, at Friars Park, even contained a miniature Matterhorn. The latest manifestations of the Disneyland idea, at Epcot and many smaller theme parks have developed the scientific and funfair aspects of Disneyland. From a park planning viewpoint it is regrettable that theme parks are not set within open space systems and related to the urban structure. An American critic has suggested that Walt Disney's team achieves a higher standard of urban design than American architects (Taylor 1981: 121). Now the Disney team is producing a residential suburb.

Festival parks

Nations love festivals, especially when they are in parks, but the money will be squandered if an after-use is not planned before the festival-use.

The garden shows held in Germany since 1939 established a tradition which enables the energy of commercial operators to assist in the development of parks. They are sited on existing or proposed parkland and the public are charged an entrance fee during the show. After it closes, the land becomes a public park. Britain held its first garden festival in Liverpool in 1984. It was a means of reclaiming a large area of derelict land. After the festival closed, half the site was designated a public park and riverside promenade. The other half was allocated to industrial development and its theme gardens were destroyed, thus wasting a hefty investment in park design. The promenade forms part of an enlightened open space plan for the city, but the main body of the new park contributed to a level of open space provision that was already overgenerous in that part of Liverpool. Future garden festivals should be part of a citywide strategy. This could be for open space development or it could be for urbanization.

Urbanization, as discussed in the final chapter of this book, is expensive. So is the start of a new family – but there are good reasons to celebrate new settlements and weddings with a ruinously expensive festival. Town developments should have launch parties. If housing is the appropriate after-use, the festival project can put in permanent buildings, roads and trees, as housing infrastructure. This was done for the Dutch Floriade on the edge of Zootermeer New Town. Ideally, the opportunity should be taken to effect innovations in urbanization techniques. Other chapters of this book suggest a need for the imaginative use of vegetated roofs, porous pavements, habitat creation, the after-use of mineral workings and urban forests. Planning an after-use is the key to the long-term success of festival parks.

Greenway function

They should be "green" in the environmental sense and "ways" in many senses.

The best official account of the greenway idea comes from the President's Commission on Americans Outdoors. It called for:

A Living Network of Greenways . . . to provide people with access to open spaces close to where they live, and to link together the rural and urban spaces in the American landscape . . . threading through cities and countrysides like a great circulating system. (President's Commission on Americans Outdoors 1987)

Charles Little's 1990 book *Greenways for America* gave further impetus to the idea, and greenways are now being made in many countries. Little says the five greenway types are:

1 urban riverside,
2 recreational,
3 ecological,
4 scenic and historic,
5 comprehensive. (Little 1990)

In an introduction to a major review of greenways in 1995, Fabos sees the greenway movement as being in its infancy and suggests that at some future point greenway systems "will be as evident on national, state, regional and local maps as our highway or railway networks are today" (Fabos 1995). I look forward to that day. Ahern offers an inclusive definition of greenways:

Greenways are networks of land containing linear elements that are planned, designed and managed for multiple purposes including eco-logical, recreational, cultural, aesthetic or other purposes compatible with the concept of sustainable land-use. (Ahern 1995)

I would prefer to define a greenway as "a route which is good from an environmental point of view". This definition uses green as an environmen-tal term and way in a broad sense to include circulation routes for people, animals, air, water and plants.

The term "greenway" was formed by joining *green*belt to park*way*. It embraces a wide range of concepts drawn from the history of linked open space (Fig. 4.16). The greenway concept may be said to have come of age with the publication of a special issue of *Landscape and Urban Planning* in 1995 (Ahern & Fabos 1995), reprinted as a special book (Ahern & Fabos 1996). Greenways can be planned to serve distinct functions, which are likely to overlap (Fig. 4.17).

Greenway history and typology

The greenway idea is old and rich.

Ceremonial avenues

In the ancient world, avenues were made for religious processions, military parades, coronations and burials. They were found in Babylon and Egypt

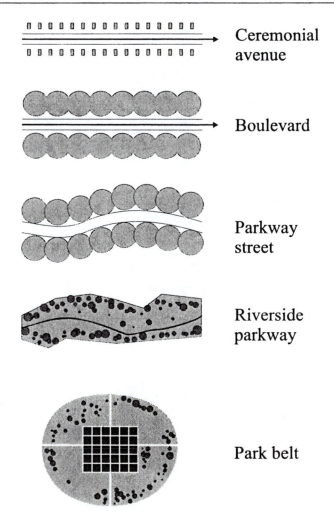

Ceremonial avenue

Boulevard

Parkway street

Riverside parkway

Park belt

Figure 4.16 The greenway concept has a history of at least 3,000 years.

(*c.* 2000 BC). The Temple of Queen Hatshepsut, for example, had a ceremonial avenue which linked it to Thebes. Avenues were used in Imperial Rome and again in Renaissance towns and gardens. In hunting parks they helped horsemen to find and chase the stag. Avenues became a distinguishing feature of baroque cities all over Europe; the boulevards of Paris are the supreme example. Avenues were used as carriage routes in towns and for dramatic effect in baroque gardens. All the old examples were straight lines. They count as greenways because they were green in an environmental sense and they were ways in a transportation sense.

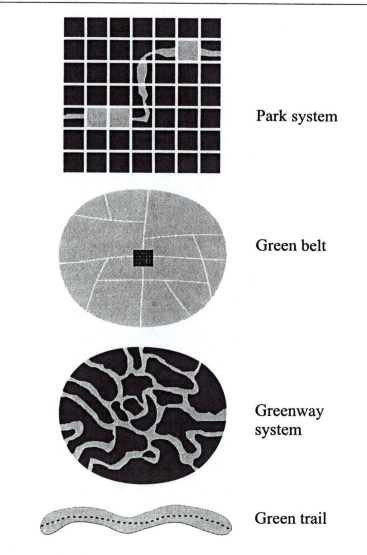

Park system

Green belt

Greenway
system

Green trail

Figure 4.16 (continued)

Boulevards

Boulevards are planned for the pleasure that travellers, rather than spectators, can take in moving along a tree-lined street. They derive from defensive bulwarks used as walks (Fig. 4.18). The first curvaceous urban boulevard was made by John Nash in London, though it was not tree-lined. Regent Street, together with Portland Place, linked St James's Park to the new

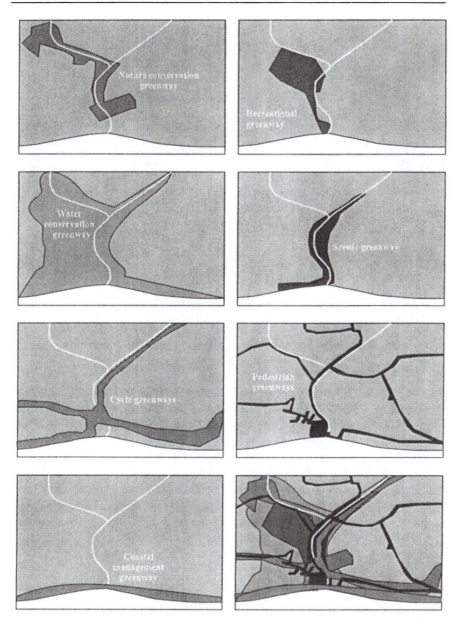

Figure 4.17 Greenways can be planned to serve distinct functions, which are likely to overlap.

Figure 4.18 Boulevards derive from bulwarks used as walks (Montreuil).

Regent's Park, which Nash was building on the edge of London. This was conceived as a pleasurable route from the inner city to what was then the edge of London. St James's Park was also linked to Green Park, Hyde Park and Kensington Gardens.

The plans of Louis Napoleon and Baron Haussmann for the redevelopment of Paris were influenced by London's park-filled West End. Louis Napoleon had spent a period of exile in London from 1846 to 1848 and asked Haussmann to include a London-type network of naturalistic parks in his proposals. The Bois de Boulogne and the Bois de Vincenne were the first to be laid out and were linked up through the heart of Paris by formal tree-lined boulevards. The idea of using tree-lined avenues as connecting links undoubtedly came from Le Nôtre.

Boulevards were made in British and American parks during the nineteenth century. In the twentieth century, the greatest development of the boulevard idea was the American parkway. The design criteria for roads in undulating country led to a boulevard effect.

Parkways

A parkway was originally a tree-lined curvaceous boulevard. Frederick Law Olmsted made a linear park beside the Des Plaines River, for the suburb of Riverside, and proposed a "park way to Chicago" (Newton 1971: 467). In 1870, Olmsted designed Eastern Parkway as an approach to Prospect Park (ibid.: 596). Later, the term "parkway" was used to describe a strip of parkland containing a motor road and planned to give the motorist a pleasurable experience. The Blue Ridge Parkway was designed as a two-lane pleasure drive running for 469 miles along the crest of the Appalachians (Searns 1995). The term parkway was also used by Abercrombie in his 1943-4 plan for London. He defined parkways as "the connecting links of the park system" and distinguished several types: linear parks, riverside walks, footpaths in farmland, bridle tracks, green lanes, bicycle tracks, motorways with a park character (Abercrombie 1943: 107). Many European countries have tree-lined roads in residential areas which are described as parkways.

Park belts

Park belts are rings of recreational open space located on the fringes of urban areas. One of the world's first park belts was planned for the city of Adelaide in Australia. William Light selected the site for Adelaide after a coastal voyage. Before going to Australia he had sailed round the Mediterranean and published a book of picturesque views. Adelaide's site was chosen "because it was on a beautiful and gently rising ground, and formed altogether a better connection with the river than any other place" (Light 1911). Light prepared a plan for Adelaide in 1837. It shows two clusters of urban development, on either side of the River Torre, surrounded by a belt of parkland. The urban area was planned on a grid but contained six urban squares. Light proposed that any future urban growth should be outside the park belt. His plan was adopted, although some encroachments on the park belt have since taken place (Fig. 4.19).

An anonymous book called *The friend of Australia*, published in 1830, has been identified as the source of Light's plan. In a section "On the laying out of towns" the author praises the handsome architecture of London's Regent Street and recommends that

> . . . all the entrances to every town should be through a park, that is to say, a belt of park about a mile or two in diameter, should entirely surround every town, save and excepting such sides as are washed by a river or lake. (Friend of Australia 1836)

At that time Regent's Park lay on the edge of London and was connected to St James's Park and the centre of town by Regent's Street, Nash's cur-

Figure 4.19 The Adelaide park belt.

vaceous boulevard. It seems probable that this precedent and other contemporary books on colonization were the source of William Light's plan for Adelaide, which influenced Ebenezer Howard's and Raymond Unwin's plans for green belts and park belts round London.

Park systems

Park systems differ from park belts in that they run through the middle of urban areas. The first and most famous example was planned and designed by Frederick Law Olmsted, for Boston in the USA. This "Emerald Necklace" has mesmerized park planners since its inception. It linked Boston Common, the Back Bay Fens, Jamaica Pond, the Arnold Arboretum and Franklin Park. The main linking feature was a streamside carriageway (or parkway) in which one could bowl along in a horse-drawn carriage, as in the Bois de Boulogne (Paris) or Hyde Park (London). Tolkien, in *Lord of the Ring*, represented life as a battle of light against dark and good against evil. In these terms, Olmsted's Emerald Necklace was a famous victory for the powers of light over those of darkness. But, as Tolkien would have expected, the forces of darkness struck back. Boston's ring of power was not a complete circle, and after Olmsted's time it became a major traffic artery, even a noose round the city's neck. In recent years, restoration works have been put in hand. After Olmsted had launched the idea, H. W. S Cleveland and G. E. Kessler made park systems in many midwestern cities (Walmsley 1995).

The park system idea then returned to Europe, a gift from the New World to the Old World. At the end of the nineteenth century, many European cities had circular fortifications, which were no longer required for defence and could be made into park systems. The fortifications of Frankfurt and Copenhagen, for example, were made into Olmstedian park systems. London had no fortifications of this type but an English author-planner, Ebenezer Howard, drew inspiration from Olmsted, and from William Light, when proposing a green belt for London in 1898.

Later park systems in American and European cities were intended for walkers, rather than carriage riders. Many of the best park systems were based on watercourses, as in San Antonio's River Walk (Searns 1995). In 1929, Raymond Unwin proposed a "green girdle" for London, a park belt of recreational land at a radius of approximately 56 kilometres from the city centre, with some links into the city. At their best, park systems can have a vital role in "shaping cities by laying out a pattern in advance of urbanisation" (Walmsley 1995).

Patrick Abercrombie used the term "park system" to describe one of the most ambitious open space planning proposals ever made for a capital city. It covered an area with a radius of 70 kilometres, interlacing both the built-up area of London and the surrounding countryside. Abercrombie's park system was never incorporated into London's official planning documents, but it continues to hold planners' imagination in its cool and leafy grip. New sections keep being added and the process is likely to continue so long as London remains an entity. From the standpoint of conceptual clarity, it is regrettable that Abercrombie described his proposal as a park system: it contained an agricultural green belt and agricultural "green wedges", which penetrated the urban area. Only some of it is parkland.

Green belt

The idea of surrounding cities with agricultural belts is very old. The Book of Numbers, for example, records that the Lord commanded Moses to give the Levites both cities and suburbs:

> And the cities shall they have to dwell in; and the suburbs of them shall be for their cattle, and for their goods, and for all their beasts.

> And the suburbs of the cities, which ye shall give unto the Levites, *shall reach* from the wall of the city and outward a thousand cubits round about.

Green belts can have agricultural, recreational and environmental roles in managing urban growth and giving a defined shape to urban areas. They act as buffers, regulating the intense development pressure which is found at the growth points, where town merges into country. London's Metropolitan Green Belt was designated to prevent sprawl, as was Ottawa's National Capital Greenbelt. Most of London's green belt remains in private ownership. Urban growth continues to take place within it, but the process is very much slower than it would be without green-belt designation. Ottawa's green belt was taken into public ownership, largely by the compulsory acquisition of land from private owners. In addition to growth control, it was intended for recreational development and the location of government buildings. Both London's and Ottawa's green belts have suffered from pressure to build and from the neglect of farmland.

Green trails

The easiest way to make trails is along lines of opportunity: old railways, canals, flood-dykes and aqueducts. The USA's National Park Service has been active in making long-distance trails, as has Britain's Countryside Commission. Recreational trails can focus on particular categories of interest or they can be multi-purpose. The interest categories include history, scenery, ecology and recreation. London's Silver Jubilee Walkway is a good example of an urban historic trail. It is a signposted walk through the city. Nature trails are found in urban and country parks. The Appalachian Trail, as proposed by Benton MacKaye in 1921, is the grandfather of recreational trails (Yahner et al. 1995). It runs for 3,300 kilometres from Maine to Georgia in the eastern USA.

Environmental greenways

"Greenway" has come to be used as a generic term for all the kinds of connected green space discussed above. The first use of the term is thought to have been in the name of the Santa Clara Greenway. In *The last landscape*, W. H. Whyte described it as "an 8-mile network of trails, with 'nodules' of open space provided by eighteen school sites" (Whyte 1970: 202). The Platte River Greenway in Denver was named in 1974 (Searns 1995). It includes parks, kayak chutes and a waterfront plaza, linked together with a 160-mile network for walkers and cyclists. Whyte also praised the work of Philip Lewis in planning "quality corridors" for Wisconsin. Lewis said that:

146

The flat, rolling farmlands and expansive forests have their share of beauty. But it is the stream valleys, the bluffs, ridges, roaring and quiet waters, mellow wetlands, and sandy soils that combine in elongated designs, tying the land together in regional and statewide corridors of outstanding landscape qualities. (Whyte 1970: 218)

Whyte's own advocacy of "linkage" undoubtedly influenced the greenway movement. In the final chapter of this brilliant book Whyte wrote:

The best way to enhance the structure of the future metropolis is to save open space now for what it will do now. Later there may be new and unforeseen uses for the land . . . The use does not have to be recreation, though this is of the first importance. In a few cases intensity of use will be low, as with a nature sanctuary. But in almost all cases there should be maximum visual use. Linkage is the key. (ibid.: 398)

Since this was written, many people have advocated greenways as linear zones with a special focus on environmental objectives (Smith & Hellmund 1993). These can include biodiversity, habitat protection, historic preservation, erosion control, flood hazard reduction, water quality improvement, air quality improvement, education and interpretation, scenic protection and recreational provision. The theory of island biogeography (MacArthur & Wilson, 1967) supports the creation of environmental greenways with its claim that the fragmentation of ecosystems into "islands" is a threat to biodiversity (Harris 1984). Since human action is a prime cause of fragmentation, it follows that biological greenways are most necessary in areas of intensive human use (Noss 1993). In order to counter habitat fragmentation, connectivity should be increased and porosity decreased (Formon & Godron 1986).

Greenways can also be places in which cultural diversity is protected and enhanced. The Minute Man National Historic Park in Massachusetts is being managed to recreate a historic landscape at the time of the revolutionary battle of 19 April 1775 (Ahern 1995). Over 175 homes and businesses have been removed from what was becoming a suburban area. Woodlands, farmlands and wetlands are being managed to resemble their condition in 1775. The Cumberland Valley is one of the few lowland sections of the Appalachian Trail. A 26-kilometre corridor of land varying in width from 60 to 520 metres was acquired between 1979 and 1992. It is now being managed both as an ecological and a cultural resource. Old farms are being restored and their buildings given new uses: "For local residents, the historic agrarian landscape within the trail corridor should provide a glimpse into the Cumberland Valley's past" (Yahner et al. 1995).

Greenways can be managed, in and around urban areas, in a similar manner to Britain's national parks, using the following measures:

147

Aquisition of development rights   In Britain, land development rights were effectively nationalized in 1947. In America, development rights can be purchased by public authorities or they can be pooled by groups of private landowners.

Designation of greenway boundary   This should be done on the basis of a wide-ranging landscape inventory and assessment.

Landscape development   Public funds should be used to acquire access easements and to carry out landscape conservation and improvement projects, such as habitat restoration, river channel improvement, footpath and cycle-path construction.

These measures are much less expensive than wholesale land aquisition and produce more diverse results because the energies of land owners are employed. But they need to be supplemented, in places, by the purchase of land. Local communities are suitable owners and individual landscape planners can take the initiative, if they have vision (Fink & Searns 1993).

Greenway character

In terms of character, greenways should have many colours.

The above discussion is mainly about greenway function. It is also necessary to consider greenway character. In a 1996 essay on harlequin space, I argued that cities need parks that are red, blue, yellow, brown, purple, white and green (Turner 1996). Redspace is exciting, bluespace is serene and cool, yellowspace stimulates one's curiosity, orangespace is gay, brownspace is wholesome, greyspace is solemn, whitespace is spiritual, greenspace is calm and relaxing. The colours symbolize characters. As with paint, the primary colours are red, yellow and blue, but they can be mixed. Many combinations are possible (Fig. 4.20). Greenways too can be made in different hues (Fig. 4.21).

Redways appeal to the emotions. They need central locations, which contribute to their bustle and excitement. They should attract land-users with adventurous ideas. Outdoor shopping and eating tend to "redden" space. Street entertainers should be welcomed. Some redways can have a diversity of land-uses. Others can specialize, perhaps in shopping, entertainment or commerce. The period of maximum activity can also vary: morning for food markets, afternoon for restaurants, evening for drinking and entertainment. A redway should be an environmentally pleasant route for as many types of traffic as possible. In a metropolis, this is likely to be pedes-

Figure 4.20 A green incident on a brownway in Duisberg-Nord Landschaftspark.

trian traffic with vehicular access only before opening time. In a village, horses, cycles, dogs and slow-moving cars can be accommodated.

Yelloways appeal to the mind. They are interesting for their own sakes, either for their man-made character or for their natural character. A shopping street with good shopfronts is yellow. A walk through a varied natural habitat is yellow. People seek these spaces for the different interests they provide. Orangeways are intermediate between yelloways and redways. A busy pedestrian greenway from a central station to a shopping centre is likely to be yellow or orange in mood and character.

Blueways appeal to the senses and to the imagination. They will normally run beside water, but it is possible to create sublimity without water. In mood, blueways are cool, sensual, elemental. Water is essential to life on

149

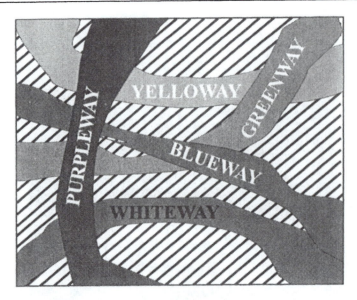

Figure 4.21 Colours can be used to symbolize the character of greenways.

earth and the desire to be near water, in lakes and rivers, has not been diminished by humanity's recent habit of living in cities. Everything should be done to recover and recreate routes that run beside water. They are good places for leisure and exercise.

Greenways, when green in mood, are calming. They appeal to the body and the mind, without being too exciting. The classic way of providing this experience is with rich vegetation. If there is a field layer, herb layer and tree layer, the place is likely to be more satisfying. Greenways can be used as ducts, to bring fresh air into cities. Space for different kinds of exercise is also welcome. This type of greenway could be provided by forests, under forest laws (see Chapter 8).

Brownways have the emotional appeal of redways but they are deeper and meditative. Natural materials can be thought of as brown in mood, like wood and wholemeal bread. In the country and in the town it is possible to have places with a good range of natural materials – wood, stone, earth and gravel.

Purpleways are rare and exotic. They attract visitors, as do redways, but the blueness is a sign of sublimity. Luxury shopping streets and arcades in great cities are purple, as are tracks through ancient woods and rocky clefts. Relative darkness helps to make a place purple, as in a natural gorge or a dark street.

Whiteways are more spiritual than substantial. They tend to be dominated by great extent and by the sky's arc. In the country, this can be

Figure 4.22 The Philosopher's Way in Heidelberg is a whiteway.

because they follow a ridge or run across a great plain. In the town, it is likely to come from size: wide streets fronted by great buildings. The Philosopher's Way in Heidelberg is white because it commands a view over the Neckar to the old town (Fig. 4.22).

Planners need to shake themselves free of the idea that a strip of green joining two points on a map is, of necessity, a good thing. Too often, they become bland strips of grass, which one *can* walk along, but which, because they do not lead from an origin to a destination and do not have any other significant attractions, are not greenways. They are not pleasant and they are not routes. Business parks and housing projects are full of "greenways" that do little and go nowhere, costing much.

Open space management

Greenways can supervene on other land-uses, like happiness on the face of youth.

Many greenway objectives can be achieved by modifying other land-uses. Open space management requires EID. Forest recreation can be provided as a byproduct of wood production, water recreation of water supply, river recreation of flood control, and parkland of mineral workings. These points are argued in subsequent chapters. The public goods that arise from public open space can also be achieved in association with other institutions. A financial centre could have a finance park with time clocks, share shops and screens showing the world's stock markets. An opera house could have an adjacent music park. Libraries could have book parks, with stalls for book-sellers and shelves of books which could be borrowed to read in a cloister-like space. Business parks could have places for sunbathing and waterbathing, to refresh the body for the next half of the day's toil.

Public open space can be owned either by organizations which exist to supply public goods (e.g. a parks service) or by organizations which have other primary roles (e.g. a water company) and supply public goods as a byproduct of their main activities. In both cases there is a need for multiple-use management and user-involvement in EID. Without the involvement of users, open space managers will lack good information, and their actions, however well funded and however well intentioned, will produce an insensitive uniformity. Without participatory democracy, decisions will be based on old information and stale information.

The paramount need is for diversity of ownership, of management, of design and, above all, of use. Many of the historical open space types have a value that is diminished by uniform management. Their strengths and weaknesses have been reviewed in this chapter. The best of them can serve as archetypal patterns or models for the future. We cannot recreate the institutions which laid out open space in former times, or adopt their approaches to art, but we can devise new institutional arrangements, and we should make open spaces which contain the lost virtues and avoid the known vices.

A green web

Public open space should radiate public goods.

In the latter part of the twentieth century, the most appealing approach to the integration of open space types within cities is by means of a green web (Fig. 4.23). Public open spaces can be interlinked with footpaths, bridges, cycleways, bridlepaths, stream valleys, linear parks, waterfront reservations, covered arcades, elegant streets and greenways of every type. The difference between a green web and a park system is that many spaces in the web should be green not in colour, but in the sense that political parties are said to be green (Porritt 1984: 3). Just as "blue" movies are not filmed in blue, so "green space" need not be festooned with greenery. The web should be composed of environmentally delightful open space in which people are free to move without aggravation from noise, pollution, danger or other

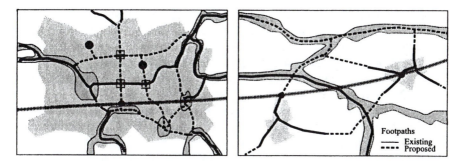

Figure 4.23 The historic approaches to distributing open space in cities can be combined by means of a green web, linking town (left) and country (right).

harmful side-effects. Streets can be included if the traffic flow does not constitute a menace to health and safety.

Linked green space has both philosophical and practical advantages. Lynch outlines the philosophical aspect as follows:

> The open-space system not only makes the city visible, but also the larger natural universe. It can give the observer a sense of the more permanent system of which he and the city are only parts . . . To convey a sense of the web of life, of the intricate interdependent system of living things, will be even more important. (Lynch 1972)

The practical advantages are comparable to those of telephone and transport networks: even if individuals use only short sections of the network, they gain access to the system and know that they *can* use all parts.

An extension of the green web into the countryside will assist in the management of urban fringe land. Parts of the web currently without public access can be made into common land. Its ownership, like all traditional commons, would remain in private hands, but the new commoners would purchase such rights as they wished to own. The most important right is access. Disputes could be dealt with by a modern equivalent of manorial courts. The new commons should extend into urban areas, as green wedges, and into the countryside, as "amenity corridors". Where possible they should follow landscape features, such as hills or valleys, and connect with an international system of long-distance footpaths.

Special maps should be produced, like road or rail maps, but showing the green web and the different kinds of open space to which it gives access. Use of the system for commuting and leisure journeys would provide the visual policing that deters crime. Compared with our ancestors, we travel more and congregate less. For many people movement is a pleasure in itself. It

153

forms the substance of recreational activities – hiking, jogging, horse-riding, cycling, canoeing, sailing etc. These pastimes cannot be accommodated satisfactorily in public gardens or city streets. Nor is there space for them in leafy suburbs, where most of the green space is private, or in small country villages, where the green fields and woods have signs saying "Keep Out. Trespassers will be Prosecuted and Dogs Shot."

The green web should have a great range of specialized facilities for outdoor recreation: an urban wilderness, a town forest, a metropolitan dry-ski centre, public orchards, well-stocked fishing lakes, scrubland in which to gather berries and nuts, a gasworks park, commons on which people can keep grazing animals, camping and caravan sites, an arboretum and botanical garden, a windy ridge for kite-flying and hang-gliding, an athletics centre, swimming lakes, adventure areas, a great bowl for outdoor events, a sumptuous flower garden, outdoor museums for large exhibits, BMX and motorcycle scrambling pits. Less specialized open spaces can be made wherever there is a local demand. People can live beside those areas that best suit their own tastes and preferences in open space. Urban areas would be less monotonous. Green webland should radiate public goods.

CHAPTER 5
Reservoirs

Introduction

Old reservoirs have new capabilities.

The world has a multitude of reservoirs. Usually, and properly, the dams that retain the water were built with immense caution. Their designers were especially worried about dam failures, floods and water pollution. Today, there is less to fear. Hydrological and structural monitoring give advance warning of floods and faults; filtration equipment removes pollution. These changes have made existing reservoirs into potentially rich places for landscape development. Future reservoirs can be developed as multi-functional projects for wildlife, swimming, boating, fishing, waterside building, power generation, irrigation, river regulation, scenic enhancement and, occasionally, great works of art. Existing reservoirs should be assessed and made subject to EID. They are capable of yielding more private and public goods than they do at present.

Reservoir history

Should Hetch Hetchy be submerged for a reservoir, as proposed, not only would it be utterly destroyed, but the sublime canyon way to the heart of the High Sierra would be hopelessly blocked and the great camping ground, as the watershed of a city drinking system, virtually would be closed to the public.

John Muir 1912: 259

Hetch Hetchy Dam, which flooded a valley as wonderful as Yosemite to supply San Francisco, most certainly would not be approved today. It destroyed a valley and led to the above complaint from the founder of America's national parks. In Britain too, the main reason for building dams has been to store water for domestic supply. Public health considerations once provided a reason for restricting other uses, but water can now be purified. Many American dams, although built for flood control, were also built as single-use projects. There is a plaque on a reservoir outside Miami which reminds visitors that "The dams of the Miami Conservancy District are for flood prevention purposes. Their use for power development or for storage would be a menace to the cities below" (Thorn 1966: 265). Britain has had few needs for new reservoirs since the 1980s (Pearce 1981), but it has a great opportunity to convert old single-purpose reservoirs into multi-functional landscapes (Fig. 5.1). Before examining this potential, let us explore the history of reservoir single-purposism and the principles of EID for reservoirs.

Nineteenth-century doctors discovered that the spread of cholera, typhoid and other infectious diseases could be controlled by a supply of clean water and the hygienic disposal of sewage. The public developed a thirst for pure water, and, since the process of water-treatment was imperfectly understood, British suppliers adopted every measure to protect their sources. Where possible, they obtained water from uninhabited uplands. These "gathering grounds" were purchased and fenced to prevent public access. Commoners' rights were extinguished (Hoskins & Dudley Stamp 1963: 84). Suppliers aimed for "a state of neatness and polish . . . beyond what is of direct practical utility (Ministry of Health 1948: 12). Farmers were evicted from gathering grounds. The public often complained about "the depressing influence of ruins", which were once "thriving farmsteads". In 1943 the fifth edition of a textbook on *The examination of waters and*

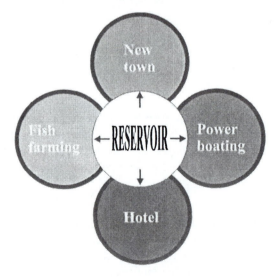

Figure 5.1 Old reservoirs can contribute to new functions.

water supplies stated that "land adjacent to reservoirs, and the banks of feeders, should not be cultivated" and that "Footpaths or highways along the banks of reservoirs are objectionable, since they permit many forms of wilful or accidental pollution" (Suckling 1943: 33).

In fact, the incidence of cholera and typhoid in Europe declined rapidly after the discovery of their causes. Britain had its last cholera outbreak in 1866. Typhoid was more difficult to control but the incidence declined from an average of 320 cases per year between 1871 and 1880 to one case only in the year 1940. There was however a serious outbreak of typhoid at Croydon in 1937–8, which reinforced the authorities' caution (Ministry of Health 1948: 7). The water industry's high standards and automated quality control now offer every prospect that clean water supplies will be scrupulously maintained.

When the risk of serious disease being transmitted in drinking water had vanished, the water undertakers began, with the utmost caution, to consider the possibility that a few clean members of the public might have occasional access. The Bristol Waterworks Company was the most enlightened supplier. It was the first to permit trout fishing, at Blagdon reservoir in 1904. It was the first to permit sailing, at Cheddar reservoir in 1947. It was the first to design a new reservoir with recreational facilities, at Chew Valley in 1956. In 1963 the Durham County Water Board still required "a certificate from applicants who must show that they are not typhoid-carriers before permitting even a small amount of camping on their gathering grounds" (Institution of Water Engineers 1963).

Gathering grounds

Gathering grounds are a historic example of single-purposism.

In Britain, the most important influence on the liberalization of water undertakings was the 1948 Ministry of Health Report of the Committee on Gathering Grounds, known as the Heneage Committee (Ministry of Health 1948: 12). It was set up as a result of the pressures which also led to the enactment of the National Parks and Access to the Countryside Act (1949). Leonard Elmhirst, founder of the Dartington Trust, was a member of this committee and simultaneously of the National Parks Committee and the Footpaths and Access Committee. The Heneage Report is a planning classic, which deserves to be remembered with the Scott, Uthwatt and Hobhouse reports. It greatly encouraged the use of water authorities' land for recreation, afforestation and agriculture.

The Gathering Grounds Committee researched the subject of public health fully, and made the following observations:

1   The Croydon typhoid epidemic of 1937–8 was caused by a contaminated well. It had nothing to do with reservoir water.

2   Of the 21 outbreaks of waterborne disease between 1911 and 1937 that could be traced to water supplies, only one resulted from a polluted reservoir. It was caused by "a typhoid patient who was being nursed in a house whose water-closet drained into a small water-course which communicated with a small reservoir". The water from the reservoir was not purified and the outbreak was not connected with public access.

3   Gulls often cause reservoirs to be contaminated by sewage.

These birds, which are protected by law, frequently develop the habit of spending their days feeding on sewage farms and migrating at night to some convenient stretch of clear water, often enough a reservoir, each with human sewage on its feet and in its gullet.

4   Typhoid germs do not survive in open water and "no case has been mentioned in this country where disease has been transmitted by the pollution of a large reservoir".

5   Military exercises had taken place on gathering grounds and "provided an experiment in large scale human access". There were numerous "instances of insanitary behaviour" on the part of the troops, but only one case of any observed effect upon the quality of the raw water.

6   Many water suppliers extract water from grossly polluted rivers and produce potable water by filtration and sterilization.

7   A number of authorities make "imaginative objections" to the multiple uses of gathering grounds, including "the occasional presence of a defecating cow or dead sheep" and "the presence of fish droppings and dead fish in the reservoir".

The Gathering Grounds Committee concluded that the water industry had "over-developed" its precautions and that the defences "may stifle the life they are designed to protect" by "seriously limiting facilities for healthy exercise and the production of wholesome food". The Committee recommended that: "there is no reason to exclude the public from gathering grounds". The land should be "put to the utmost agricultural use" or, if incapable of agricultural use, "should if possible be afforested, but with due regard to amenity and the requirements of adjacent agriculture". The Committee also recommended safeguards. It said human sewage and farmyard manure should be prevented from entering reservoirs and

the public should be generally excluded from the banks of reservoirs and no bathing should be allowed. Fishing and boating may in some cases be allowed at the water undertaker's discretion but only under rigorous control.

The system of rigorous control for fishing and boating was already practised by the Bristol Waterworks Company, whose club members tended "to display marked hostility to access by other persons and in effect perform the functions of unpaid wardens".

The above recommendations were made for reservoirs from which water is purified, and supplied to customers. The Committee said that for compensation reservoirs, used to maintain river flow in dry weather, no safeguards were necessary: "there is no public health reason why fishing, bathing, boating and camping should not take place on the largest scale". This still does not happen.

The Gathering Grounds Committee also considered the question of deliberate vandalism. It was an occasional problem in 1948 and has become more serious. It advised that water suppliers

> are in much the same position as other landowners and should, in our opinion, be subject to whatever policy regarding access to mountains and moorland may be applicable to landowners in general.

This is an important principle of continuing relevance – which is still unregarded.

Water recreation 1948–1981

Too little and too late.

The report on gathering grounds influenced the management of reservoirs, but most suppliers were reluctant "to withdraw from the position for which they had fought so bitterly in the past" (Institution of Water Engineers 1963). Yet there were still no outbreaks of waterborne disease caused by reservoirs and in 1963 the water engineers set up a committee to review the situation. After taking evidence, the Institution of Water Engineers reported that fishing and sailing could be regarded as fully acceptable uses, providing they were tightly regulated by clubs, but that swimming and water-skiing should not be allowed. No mention was made of sub-aqua diving. The report reminded water engineers of the growing demand for recreation, but its conclusions did not represent any advance on the Gathering Grounds Report.

The Institution was, however, a learned society, and it published the debate which took place following publication of the draft report (ibid.). Many of the comments by members were notably more liberal than those of the report. A. B. Baldwin challenged the terms of reference of the committee because it included only such recreational use as could take place "without detriment to the public water supply". He asserted that Britain had 50 million people living in a small space, and that the community does not expect water engineers to make every other consideration subservient to water supply. He pointed out that water authorities were in severe danger of making themselves ridiculous – some would not allow fishing from boats and others would allow fishing *only* from boats.

G. Delwyn Davies stated that the water engineer's duty was to calculate the risks arising from recreational use and then deal with the risks. He said that a threshold of recreational use must be passed before any increase in pollution becomes evident – and added that if Manchester Corporation provided special trains so that each of its citizens could go and urinate in Haweswater (Fig. 5.2) once a year, then "he doubted whether skilled chemical detection services would discover any increase in pollution at Manchester".

The practice of letting fishing and sailing rights to private clubs was supported in the 1963 report and remains common. It earns money. But it was rightly criticized in the course of a second debate on water recreation, which took place in 1971. G. Little said

Surely, this is merely converting the reservoirs into private stretches of water for the relatively small numbers of members in such clubs. This,

Figure 5.2 In 1963 a water engineer predicted that even if all the citizens of Manchester went to urinate in Haweswater once a year, the increase in pollution would not be measurable.

in turn, defeats the purpose of making recreational facilities available to the public. (Institution of Water Engineers 1963)

A Water Act was passed in 1973 and set up new authorities in England and Wales concerned with all aspects of water, including recreation. Section 20 of the Act imposed the duty to make provision for recreation whenever "reasonably practicable":

> Every water authority and all other statutory water undertakers may take steps to secure the use of water and land associated with water for the purposes of recreation and it shall be the duty of all such undertakers to take such steps as are reasonably practicable for putting their rights to the use of water and of any land associated with water to the best use for those purposes. (Water Act 1973)

It is unfortunate that the phrases "may take steps" and "reasonably practicable" were interpreted by the water industry to mean that the duty was discretionary (Dangerfield 1981: 13). There can, however, be no doubt that Section 20 of the 1973 Water Act led to an expansion in recreational access. A 1977 report (Tanner 1977) said that progress had been made but there was still a long way to go. In 1977, the water industry had 537 reservoirs, occupying 22,885 hectares, with an additional 131,958 hectares of associated land, including reservoir banks, operational areas and gathering grounds. This was a larger area of land than that held by the National Trust, which had 162,600 hectares in 1977. Most of the water industry's land is in areas of high landscape value. It includes one-sixth of the Peak District National Park, one-sixth of the Brecon Beacons National Park, one-tenth of the Lake District National Park, and one-fifth of London's Lea Valley Regional Park. The level of recreation provision at the 537 reservoirs was found to be as follows:

Number with some form of active recreation	344	(64.1%)
with fishing	327	(60.9%)
with no active recreation except fishing	228	(42.5%)
with sailing	84	(15.6%)
with sub-aqua diving	22	(4.1%)
with canoeing	19	(3.5%)
with rowing	9	(1.7%)
with water-skiing	4	(0.7%)
with swimming	1	(0.2%)

These percentages were pitifully low. In total there were only 71 car parks, 21 picnic areas, 13 viewing points, three cafes, two children's play areas and two nature trails. Provision was best at the 54 post-1960 reservoirs designed and built in consultation with planning authorities. The 57 compensation reservoirs had a pattern of use very similar to supply reservoirs – despite the point, made in both 1948 and 1963, that there is no reason whatsoever to restrict their use. In 1976 provision for recreation was better than in 1904, when one water company permitted fishing at one reservoir, but the statistics indicated very considerable scope for improvement.

Water recreation since 1976

The new danger is excessive recreational development.

The British water industry's commitment to supply recreation *and* water was confirmed by the appearance in 1981 of *Recreation: water and land*, published by the Institution of Water Engineers and Scientists (Dangerfield 1981), which has become the Institution of Water and Environmental Management. It was a direct successor to the 1963 pamphlet *Recreational use of waterworks*, but had 336 pages instead of ten. The expansion parallels the growth of water recreation. Membership of the Royal Yachting Association increased from 1,000 in 1950 to 52,000 in 1977 (Fig. 5.3). Membership of canoe clubs has increased seven-fold, of sub-aqua clubs twelve-fold, and of water-ski clubs eighteen-fold. The participation rate for angling reached 8 per cent of the population in 1982 (Tuite 1982). The Institution moved with the times but remained unduly cautious. Fishing and sailing were favoured as revenue-earning activities which could be controlled by private clubs. Ornithology and walking were tolerated. Swimming and the use of motorboats were given serious consideration but rejected (Fig. 5.4). In general, recreation was tolerated to the extent that it could assist the water industry:

> Reservoir exploitation has become of major importance. Not only can it be profitable, and therefore justifiable from the water authorities' point of view, but the amenity and recreational value of reservoirs can be a very significant public relations feature in helping to obtain planning permission for the development of new water resources.
>
> (Dangerfield 1981: 221)

In the USA the problem of obtaining permission for new reservoirs had become so great that by 1981 the Tennessee Valley Authority, even though it had always encouraged recreation, thought its dam-building days would be over when the Columbia dam was finished (Stefan 1981). In 1994, Britain's National Rivers Authority announced that it would concentrate on metering and leakage control, instead of dam-building, to improve water supply (Water Bulletin 1994). To make reservoirs more popular, a few additional land-uses have been tolerated on the water companies' vast landholdings.

Recreational use of waterworks contained a number of fresh ideas. It was suggested that

Figure 5.3 Derwent Reservoir: yachting on reservoirs has become extremely popular.

the typical reservoir environment may well be particularly suitable, for example, for a golf course on the grassed areas not used extensively for agriculture or for a ski slope (grass or nylon) on the back slope of an earth dam; (Dangerfield 1981: 221)

. . . that construction roads could be routed to provide access to future recreation facilities; that contractors services and car parks could be designed with a recreational after-use in mind (ibid.: 90); that construction camps could be designed for conversion into holiday villages (ibid.: 23); that the traditional opposition to power boats might be relaxed:

. . . in some other countries the attitude to the use of mechanically propelled recreation craft on storage reservoirs is more liberal than in the UK. Results of research carried out in the United States of America have indicated that the effect on the chemical quality of the water of conventional outboard petrol motors . . . is insignificant. (ibid.: 59).

163

Figure 5.4 At Kielder, said to be the largest reservoir in Europe, swimming is allowed only from this one steep, sharp, north-facing "beach".

To conservationists the prospect of power boats and uncontrolled recreational development is terrifying.

The Water Act (1989) privatized Britain's water industry. This placed it in a wholly different position with regard to developments at one remove from water supply. Previously, alternative uses had been a nuisance. Now, they became attractive financial opportunities. Planned recreational access is seen as a way of limiting vandalism and of improving public relations (Water Bulletin 1995). Water companies already run cafes, licensed fishing areas, bike hire and holiday homes. If the boards of directors do not realize these opportunities, their companies are likely to be taken over by other companies "to unlock the hidden value" in their immense property holdings.

The "drawdown problem"

It is not a problem.

The so-called "drawdown problem" yields an interesting perspective on reservoir planning. In 1912, John Muir wrote that each summer Hetch Hetchy "would be gradually drained exposing the slimy sides of the basin and the shallower parts of the bottom" (Muir 1912: 261). His criticism of man-made lakes has been echoed by all authors who have written on the landscape of reservoirs (Tandy 1975: 144). When first asked to address the question of reservoir planning, I embarked on a photographic tour to collect illustrations of this terrible problem. It proved impossible to find any atrocities, and after a time it became apparent that the "drawdown problem" is primarily a consequence of conceiving reservoirs as natural lakes. If the viewer is prepared to appreciate the types of scenery found along river estuaries (Fig. 5.5) and sea coasts, then the problem is greatly diminished. It looks worst on clay substrates and when topsoil and vegetation are flooded to a depth which precludes the growth of aquatic and semi-aquatic plants. Water-saturated topsoil does not look or smell pleasant.

Figure 5.5 The exposed beach of Thirlmere Reservoir, in the English Lake District, can be viewed as an ugly "drawdown problem" or as a sublime estuarine shore, depending on one's attitude.

Research has been carried out on the establishment of vegetation on reservoir margins (Gill & Bradshaw 1971). Physical solutions to the problem should be investigated: the performance of artificial sand and gravel beaches, the removal of topsoil to hasten beach formation, the construction of offshore berms to limit wave erosion, the use of quarrying to create steep reservoir margins, and the construction of artificial islands to prevent long views of mud banks. In South-east Asia it is normal to lease the "drawdown" land for intensive agriculture (Stefan 1981: 115). At Ashtabula Lake, in the USA, some $3 million has been spent on stone for bank protection because the demand for water recreation has increased sharply since it was impounded in the early 1950s (ibid.: 18). The solution to the "drawdown problem", as to most aspects of reservoir planning, depends on the location and character of the site.

Reservoir planning

Reservoirs could become urban development zones.

Reservoir planning has entered a third phase. In the first phase, from 1850 to 1950, reservoirs were designed with conifer forests and architectural features to contrast with their surroundings, and the public was excluded (see Fig. 3.1). In the second phase, after 1948, reservoirs were planned to accommodate limited public access and to look as much like natural lakes as possible. In the third phase, reservoirs are likely to become highly intensive recreational areas, surrounded by yacht marinas, restaurants, second homes, holiday villages, golf courses, riding stables and leisure facilities of every kind. This carries a danger. Waterside land has always been valued. It is a commonplace of geography that great cities develop beside rivers, coasts and lakes. Studies of outdoor recreation always show water to be the most powerful magnet for tourists. The cumulative demand for waterfront land may have a severely detrimental impact on the reservoir environment. It requires thoughtful EID.

At present, the level of development beside reservoirs correlates with their age, not with their location or character. Many pre-1948 reservoirs are closed to the public, even in densely populated urban areas. Reservoirs of the 1950s and 1960s have a similar level of development for walking, fishing and sailing, whether they are in towns, such as the Queen Mother Reservoir, or in agricultural areas, such as Grafham Water. Post-1973 reservoirs, such as Rutland, Kielder, and Bewl Bridge, are in open country but have the most extensive recreational development.

Planning principles

Reservoirs should develop in the context of landscape plans.

A general principle, which can be used to guide decisions about the level of development for particular sites, was outlined by Brenda Colvin. She wrote:

> Our landscape is of three main types – wild, agricultural and urban . . . We like the character of each to be strongly marked. The general blurring of outline and loss of individuality that result when a town spreads indiscriminately over open country, or when open space invades a town . . . degrades the quality of any landscape. (Colvin 1973: 227)

This principle (see Fig. 3.11) can be applied to reservoirs in the following manner:

Urban reservoirs should be the most developed. In places, the waterfront can resemble that of a harbour, with close-packed buildings and delightful open space.

Agricultural reservoirs may absorb limited development, but the general aim should be to manage waterside land by agricultural methods. A "playing-field" style of grass-cutting and a "motorway" style of semi-wild grassland are equally inappropriate, because they would mark the reservoir as an industrial intrusion.

Wild reservoirs should be designed with habitat conservation to the fore. The reservoir should be made to resemble a natural lake. The dam should be moulded into adjoining landforms; the vegetation on the dam face should be established by planting turves from surrounding pastures; pump houses should be concealed underground or placed in new structures in vernacular styles; roads should be designed using the informal geometry, widths and materials of local roads; any new tree and shrub planting should be of local species; walls and fences should be in local materials; the management should be that of the surrounding countryside.

Colvin's principle is a good guide, but there are exceptions. Multiple-use policies in and around reservoirs should be governed by contextual appraisal. As discussed in Chapter 3, the EID of a development project can be planned to have a relationship of similarity or difference between the project and its surroundings (Fig. 5.6). Similarity is the best policy in areas of great scenic quality. In a beautiful wilderness, for example, reservoirs should have a wilderness character. But if the scenic quality is low, a reservoir should be different from its surroundings, perhaps as a recreational "honey pot". An urban reservoir might also be different from its

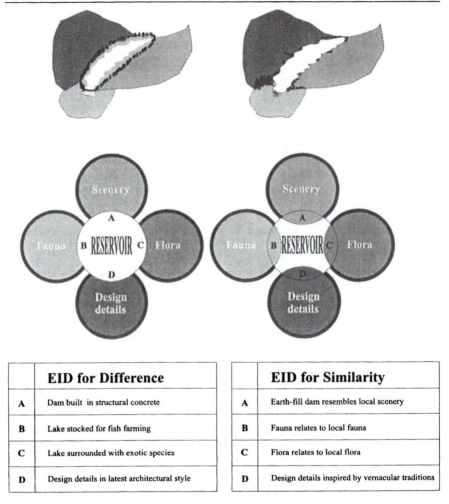

	EID for Difference
A	Dam built in structural concrete
B	Lake stocked for fish farming
C	Lake surrounded with exotic species
D	Design details in latest architectural style

	EID for Similarity
A	Earth-fill dam resembles local scenery
B	Fauna relates to local fauna
C	Flora relates to local flora
D	Design details inspired by vernacular traditions

Figure 5.6 Reservoirs can be similar to or different from their surroundings. Difference is likely to be the best policy in an urban area. Similarity will normally be best in a wild place.

surroundings. Instead of being surrounded with buildings, it can become a dreamlike wildlife reserve, with semi-natural habitats floating above the city. EID rests on contextual analysis.

The present need is for each water supplier to carry out a full assessment of its landholdings, as the Welsh Water Authority attempted in its *Strategic plan for water space recreation and amenity* (Welsh Water Authority 1980). It can then formulate landscape development plans for each reservoir. The plans should make proposals for habitat creation, scenic quality, recreation and the use of waterfront land.

Reservoir archetypes

Archetypes are useful in reservoir planning.

A range of archetypal patterns for the planning of new reservoirs and the redesign of old reservoirs, should be developed. Christopher Alexander, who proposed the use of archetypes in the planning process, suggests that

> we can locate local reservoirs and distribution reservoirs so that people can get at them; we might build them as kinds of shrines, where people can come to get in touch with sources of their water supply. (Alexander et al. 1977: 325)

The following archetypes will be discussed below: wild reservoirs, agricultural reservoirs, urban reservoirs, new town reservoirs, park reservoirs, habitat reservoirs, forestry reservoirs, recreation reservoirs and children's play reservoirs (Fig. 5.7).

Wild reservoirs

Mountains and uplands have a strong attraction for town dwellers. Visitors go to experience the lonely beauty of the wilds and do not wish to find an area dominated by intensive recreation. This widespread aesthetic perception fully justifies the use of a conservation approach to planning the landscape of the water industry. In areas of outstanding natural beauty there is every reason to make reservoirs look like natural lakes. Designers have employed a number of devices to attain this goal.

Brenig Reservoir

Colvin and Moggridge, as landscape architects for Brenig Reservoir in North Wales, reported that "The Planning Policy for Aled Hiraethof envisages that the moorlands, which though outside the National Park are part of the Denbigh Moors Conservation Area, should remain remote and wild" (Colvin & Moggridge 1971). To prevent the straight line of the dam crest disrupting the wild scenery, they recommended "a block of trees on the face of the dam above Bryn-hir". It was planted on a special mount so that tree roots could not penetrate or damage the dam structure. The following landuse proposals were made to secure full integration of dam and landscape:

> Over the face of the dam we recommend various landuses, to enrich its surface just as the land below is enriched. The main structure of the dam will be exposed in parts in screes of fine rocks with occasional tumbles of large rocks, which could be placed if required. Lying against this will be the toe weights, moulded gently into the land

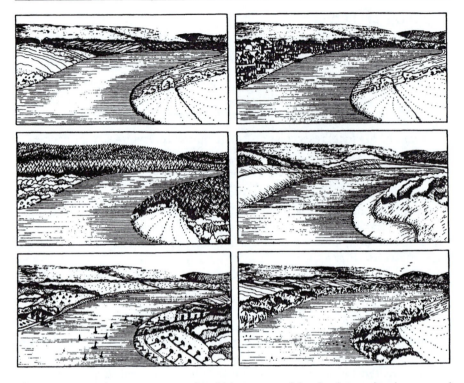

Figure 5.7 Landscape concepts should be prepared for the future development of existing reservoirs. These diagrams show six 'patterns' for land-use around reservoir shores: A agriculture; B a new town; C forestry; D park; E recreation; F wildlife.

below. Where feasible agricultural land will be restored including a large pasture over the toe weight and spoil heap between Elorgarred and Bryn-hir. In other positions vegetation of an indigenous type should be established. We consider that advice should be sought to ensure that grasses and flora suitable for such a position are sown and not an agricultural seed mixture suitable to lowland meadows. (ibid. 1971).

Megget Reservoir
Another upland reservoir was constructed at Megget in southern Scotland between 1978 and 1983; it won a BBC design award. W. J. Cairns and Partners were the landscape architects, and they went to considerable lengths to ameliorate the impact of the reservoir "upon the landscape, agri-

culture, recreation and ecology of the area". The Megget valley supported 5,000 sheep before the flooding. This capacity was maintained "by providing sheltered sheep parks formed by carefully designed shelter-belts high on the valley sides". The new road was planned as a traditional single-track road with passing places. Five new shepherd's houses were built in the vernacular style, and the reservoir control building was concealed underground (McGowan & Miller 1984). The level of provision for recreation is comparable to that on nearby St Mary's Loch: car-parking, walking, boating and fishing. The design of Megget Reservoir makes an interesting comparison with Talla Reservoir which lies 5 kilometres to the west, and was not subject to conservation design.

Talla Reservoir
Talla is a fine example of Victorian water engineering, built between 1897 and 1905 (Fig. 5.8) and designed to have no public access. The structures are faced with Dumfriesshire and Craigleith stone, in the Scots Baronial style. The downstream face of the dam is maintained as a well-kept lawn, and the valley sides have been afforested "to preserve the purity of the water draining into the reservoir" (Institution of Civil Engineers 1907).

Figure 5.8 Talla Reservoir. The drawoff tower and spillway were designed as innovative features to contrast with the existing landscape.

Kielder Reservoir

Kielder Reservoir, the largest in Britain and indeed in Europe, has also been subject to the largest expenditure on objectives other than water supply. The northern arm of the reservoir was impounded by an "amenity dam" at Bakethin, which cost £1.65 million. It protects this part of the reservoir from variations in water level and enhances its value as a nature reserve (Rocke 1980). But it is ugly (Fig. 5.9).

Figure 5.9 Kielder Reservoir. The secondary dam, at Bakethin, was built to retain the water level in one arm of the reservoir, purely for amenity reasons. The principle is excellent; the structure is ugly.

Agricultural reservoirs

Since 1948 Britain has seen a shift of emphasis from upland to lowland sites for reservoir construction. Some have been built in arable farming areas with rolling topography. Since river valleys tend to be well populated, these reservoirs are sited outside the valleys and supplied by pumping. Water is released to maintain river flows and abstracted near to the point of supply. There are no public health restrictions on the use of pump-storage and compensation reservoirs, but planning authorities and local residents have generally opposed intensive recreational development in rural areas. Demand for water recreation is however great, and the permitted recreational facilities, usually fishing, sailing and walking, are used to capacity.

Grafham Water

As in the case of mountain reservoirs, landscape planners have generally adopted a conservation approach to the construction of agricultural reservoirs. The first project of this type was Grafham Water, constructed between 1962 and 1966. At the time of its completion Grafham Water, "with its sailing clubhouse, slipways, and dinghy park, its nature reserve, its provision for anglers, and the three public recreational areas around the perimeter", was considered to be "the most accessible of reservoirs" (Rydz 1971). It was also the first in Britain for which a landscape consultant was appointed – although the scheme's promoters requested a public inquiry to challenge the planning authority's right to impose landscape conditions. The promoters were worried about "endless delays", excessive costs and the possible conflict between ideas about "beautiful structures" and "engineering considerations".

In reality, good EID prevents delays. Adrian Montague, as architect and landscape consultant for the scheme, aimed to "retain the rural character of the scene" and produce the impression of a reservoir surrounded by well-wooded farmland. He also planned the car parks to have good views of the water, but the public has criticized the large exposed rectangles of tarmac (conversation in 1979).

Bough Beech and Bewl Bridge

Bough Beech and Bewl Bridge in Kent are 1970s examples of a similar design philosophy. Sylvia Crowe was the landscape consultant for both schemes. At Bough Beech she proposed the following measures to minimize the impact of the mud bank, which is visible at times of low water: the siting of borrow pits to bring deep water near to the bank, tree planting on promontories to cut off views of exposed mud; the colonization of semi-submerged areas with *Salix caprea*, *Agrostis stolonifera* and other flood-tolerant species (Crowe undated).

At Bewl Bridge, also in Kent and one of the most beautiful modern reservoirs, Crowe's aim was

> to mend the organic structure of the countryside where it has been disrupted by the coming of the reservoir, and to accept the water as a natural feature rather than a recent and unnatural intrusion. (Crowe 1971)

This was achieved by tree planting, by hiding car parks behind curving banks, by designing buildings in local styles, by planting flood-tolerant species on the water margin and by using agricultural fencing instead of the urban fencing that typified pre-1960 reservoirs.

Urban reservoirs

Urban reservoirs have been neglected from a landscape planning point of view. Most of them are not in areas of high scenic quality, and it was thought they could do little visual harm. Their potential for improving the urban landscape has been totally ignored (Fig. 5.10). Many date from the period when engineers prevented all access to all reservoirs because of the imagined pollution risk. But the water is fully treated after being stored, and since it has been abstracted from severely polluted rivers, it is evident that any extra pollution caused by public access can impose little additional load on the treatment plant. When sufficient treatment capacity is available, the prospects for landscape development are dramatic, especially in London. Water supply engineers, as always, are against it.

Figure 5.10 London has over thirty bunded reservoirs that are shut off from the city by steep embankments and high fences.

Queen Mother Reservoir

London has two large concentrations of water supply reservoirs, in the Lea and Colne Valley regional parks. Most of the reservoirs are retained by bunds of earth and enclosed by high security fences so that they are visually and physically severed from their environments. In many cases the bunds resemble railway embankments. Queen Mother Reservoir, near Datchet, is the most recent bunded reservoir. It has public access for sailing, fishing, putting and horse riding. A clubhouse and restaurant on top of the embankment command a delightful view of the water and Windsor Castle. The recreation facilities were designed by the Thames Water Authority's architecture and gardening staff. No specialist landscape advice was obtained and, because the reservoir was constructed under powers given by Act of Parliament, there was no need for planning permission (Thames Water Authority 1978). It is not an unsightly place, but many opportunities have been missed. Most of the other 34 bunded reservoirs in the London area have been less well designed and have less recreational use. Some are completely closed to the public; others are open only to sailors, fishermen, ornithologists or, in some cases, all three groups. Control points are manned when the reservoirs are open.

Walthamstow Reservoirs

The Walthamstow Reservoirs in the Lea Valley demonstrate the visual potential of bunded reservoirs, and should become the most beautiful water park in London (Fig. 5.11). Only registered fishermen and ornithologists are admitted. Children under eight are excluded and children between eight and 16 must be accompanied by an adult. The stylized shapes of the water bodies resemble the great eighteenth-century garden at Studley Royal in Yorkshire. Walthamstow is also a designated Site of Special Scientific Interest and has a large heron population. One of the main reasons for the beauty of the Walthamstow Reservoirs is the fact that the spaces between the reservoirs are filled with soil and planted with trees. This has created an oasis of water and trees raised above the urban area; it yields fine views over the city. Since the soil between the reservoirs is not structural, the trees do not constitute an engineering hazard. In this respect they correspond to the trees which have been planted on the toe weight and mount at Brenig.

Trimpley Reservoirs

Trimpley Reservoirs, near Bewdley in Worcestershire, are also beautiful, and partially bunded, reservoirs. They were designed by Binnie and Partners, with Colvin and Moggridge as landscape consultants. Two small oval reservoirs have been set in a wooded section of the Severn Gorge and appear to float among the trees. A steep grassy bank made of excavated soil extends down to the river. It is grazed by sheep and hides the concrete basins which retain the

Figure 5.11 The Walthamstow Reservoirs could be London's most beautiful water park if they were open to the public.

water. A well-designed dinghy park and a sailing club give visitors the impression that the larger reservoir was designed for recreational use.

Urban opportunities
Trimpley and Walthamstow illustrate an important principle in the design of bunded reservoirs: amenity land should be created at or above water level. Many of the Lea and Colne Valley reservoirs have land in water company ownership that could be used for this purpose. Some of them are also underlain by sand and gravel deposits, which could be exploited. Excavations would increase the volume of stored water and would provide material for the construction of new waterside mounds. It would also be possible to obtain inorganic fill material from the stream of trucks that transport wastes from London to suburban landfill sites. Material of this

type was used in a reclamation scheme for Markfield sewage works in the Lea Valley (Aldous 1972: 131). But even inert fill would have to be handled with the greatest care beside an existing reservoir.

Regent's Park and St James's Park are surrounded by fine buildings. They gain from the view of the park and the park gains a scenic backdrop from the buildings. This principle should be adopted in the design of urban reservoirs. The clubhouse at Queen Mother Reservoir demonstrates the structural feasibility of building on top of reservoir bunds, and there is scope for many other types of building. Since Queen Mother Reservoir is less than three miles from Heathrow Airport it could provide a superb site for a hotel and conference centre. Windsor Castle can be seen over the water. Most of the airport hotels have drab sites and are hardly advertisements for Britain.

The reservoirs and flooded gravel pits around Heathrow should be developed as a gateway waterpark for England. It could be used primarily as a visual amenity and to create sites for prestige buildings. Other urban reservoirs, when free of aircraft noise, could provide housing and hotel sites (Fig. 5.12). It would be possible to design Bakethin-type barriers to preserve

Figure 5.12 Reservoir-side towns could draw inspiration from lakeside towns, like Speiz on Lake Thun in the Bernese Oberland. (Courtesy of the Swiss Tourist Office.)

the water level in the immediate vicinity of the buildings. The water companies could make more money from property development than they do from water. They need imaginative landscape plans.

New-town reservoirs

New urban reservoirs could be planned in conjunction with new towns or town extension schemes, thus helping to save wild lakes from overexploitation. Despite the imposition of rigorous controls, most urban areas continue to expand into open country, creating the hated "urban sprawl". Better suburbs can be designed on better sites. One way of making a dull site an exciting site is by constructing a major water feature: few great gardens or public parks are without a central water feature. Even large commercial developments, such as the National Exhibition Centre in Birmingham, are often furnished with large lakes. It is quite possible that a site could be found for a combined new town and reservoir development project. This might have been done between 1965 and 1985 in the East Midlands. A town expansion scheme took place in Peterborough, and, 25 kilometres away, Rutland Water was built. The five villages which surround Rutland Water have become more prosperous since its completion and are now sought-after residential areas. Houses and gardens overlooking the reservoir are being developed with picture windows, home extensions and viewing areas. The demand is manifest.

In California

> land that sells for a few hundred dollars per acre is worth thousands of dollars per acre if it is near a lake and up to $100,000 per acre if it is a lake-front parcel. (Stefan 1981: 89)

Britain does not have a tradition of building lakeside towns, but they are not so different from seaside towns and new traditions can be launched – as happened with seaside resorts in the eighteenth century. A small start has been made at Brent Reservoir in North London: it is a canal feeder reservoir and not subject to the same restrictions as supply reservoirs are. Some new housing has also been built near water supply reservoirs, such as Grafham Water, when older dwellings have been inundated.

In mountain areas there is a considerable demand for second homes, and sites could be found beside reservoirs. A holiday village could, for example, be sited beside Kielder Reservoir, either near Bakethin Dam or on a peninsula projecting into the water. If well designed it would contribute to the scenery as do Mont Saint Michel in France and Sveti Stefan in Montenegro.

Reservoir parks

Water is inherently beautiful and desirable.

A reservoir can be a spectacular focus for a park design. Islamic tank-reservoirs were always used for recreation. The first English reservoir to be considered from the aesthetic and functional points of view was Wingerworth in Derbyshire. Humphry Repton proposed a multi-purpose lake, which was not built:

> It very rarely happens, that an object of beauty or taste can also be made an object of profit; but, at Wingerworth, the same surface covered by water, may be more profitable than the richest pasture, because it may be so managed as to admit of being occasionally drawn down two or three feet to supply canals, and other circumstances of advantage, in this populous and commercial part of the kingdom; exclusive of the increased supply of fish, where such food is in constant requisition. For this reason, I do not hesitate in recommending the piece of water already mentioned, which forms so striking a feature in the view from the house, and of which the effect will not be less striking, when viewed from the ground near its shores. (Loudon 1840: 464)

The lake was part of a landscape scheme for the whole estate, composed according to principles derived from the great landscape painters. It is obvious that reservoirs should be treated creatively: water is inherently beautiful and desirable.

Forestry reservoirs

Reservoirs and forests can be good neighbours.

Many of the reservoirs built between 1890 and 1940 were surrounded by new forests, because it was thought that the human or agricultural use of gathering grounds would cause pollution. These fears are obsolete. It was also thought that trees would retain water and increase the total volume held in the catchment. This theory was proved wrong by an extensive instrumentation and monitoring exercise in the Plynlimon catchment (Natural Environment Research Council 1976). It is now known that trees consume water and, if they are coniferous, increase the acidity of reservoirs. Afforestation has therefore ceased to be a component of reservoir schemes. From an amenity and multiple-use point of view this is regrettable. A study of the Lake Vrynwy reservoir-forestry project concluded that:

"The combination of visual interest provided by farm, forest and water undertaking attracts more than 100,000 people to the valley each year." The Vrynwy estate "carries several rural industries under one control, has a productive forest with a full spread of age classes earning net income every year, and supports a contented and still developing rural community (Newton & Rivers 1982). It is an example deserving emulation."

Recreation reservoirs

Not all reservoirs need be peaceful.

There is a demand for two different types of recreation reservoir: for quiet and noisy activities. London's urban reservoirs are well suited to this purpose and their development could lessen the flow of weekend visitors into the countryside. Quiet activities should be centred in quiet areas. Sites adjoining bunded reservoirs could be developed with swimming beaches, surfboarding facilities and yacht marinas. In noisy areas, near airports and motorways, a few reservoirs should be developed for intensive use by power boats. High noise levels are incompatible with passive recreation. Speed-boat racing and water-skiing are popular as participant and spectator sports, but are unpopular with other visitors to natural lakes, river estuaries and the seaside.

When reservoirs are intensively used for recreation, water authorities should abstract water only in periods of exceptional drought. In the Wisconsin river basin, where water is drawn from 16 natural lakes and five reservoirs, the authorities aim to confine maximum drawdown to water bodies with the least intensive shoreline usage (Stefan 1981: 11).

Since the medical profession now points to lack of exercise as a primary cause of ill health, there is an opportunity for reservoirs to make their second great contribution to the improvement of public health: by increasing facilities for outdoor recreation (Taylor 1982).

Children's play reservoirs

Like drinking water, children need to be safe.

When water has been abstracted from a supply reservoir and purified to a potable standard, it is stored in service reservoirs before being piped to consumers. They are built to be as secure as possible against all forms of pollution, often in concrete tanks covered with a layer of neatly mown grass and surrounded by childproof fencing. The 1963 report by the Institution of Water Engineers stated that there was no objection to the use of service reservoirs "for sporting or recreational purposes" if the structures were suitably designed (Institution of Water Engineers 1963). It was the only bold recommendation in the report, but caution prevailed and the suggestion was dropped from the second edition. In 1981 *Recreation: water and land* stated that

> Access to some service reservoir roof areas is allowed on a restricted basis but the incidence of vandalism and acts against public property preclude any general relaxation of long prevailing attitudes towards this type of reservoir. (Dangerfield 1981: 48)

One way of providing service reservoirs with a degree of security and yet making use of the neat and clean grass surfaces would be to restrict their recreational use to supervised toddlers and children. Youngsters need to play in a safe and supervised dog-free environment.

Wild life reservoirs

Reservoirs can assist in habitat creation.

There is now a widespread public demand for the conservation of native faunas and floras. Many species are well adapted to coexistence with man, but others require a degree of protection from human interference which can be provided by reservoirs. In recognition of this fact certain parts of new reservoirs have been set aside as nature reserves. All of them are managed and some have been physically adapted in order to increase their value as wildlife habitats. At Rutland Water Sylvia Crowe

> reserved one end of one of the lake's two long "legs" of water as a 142 ha nature reserve, creating a system of bunds and lagoons carefully designed to provide hospitable habitats for a wide range of species. (Aldous & Clouston 1979: 77)

The art of habitat creation is of comparatively recent origin but is likely to become highly developed in societies concerned about the ecological damage that has been done to the natural environment. Habitat creation may, however, cause wildlife reservoirs to have a greater visual impact than conservation reservoirs. I would welcome this.

Some reservoir developments are opposed by wildlife and conservation groups because of the damage they will do to the environment. Cow Green Reservoir, in Upper Teesdale, inundated part of a unique tundra habitat, which once covered large parts of Britain. If such a reservoir must be built then everything possible should be done to create new habitats to compensate for those that are destroyed. This can be achieved by physically manipulating the reservoir margin to create appropriate soil, water and climatic conditions. The construction of a "Bakethin" dam will help to produce stable habitats.

In Britain it is normal practice to clear away trees and shrubs before inundation, to reduce the load on water-treatment facilities, and to guard against the possibility of valves being wedged open by waterlogged driftwood. The practice has a bad effect on the establishment of a fish population, aquatic vegetation and marginal vegetation, because it leads to low nutrient levels in the water. To deal with this problem, at West Point Reservoir in Georgia existing trees were lopped at the lowest planned water level:

> Inundated trees and stumps provide many new areas of cover and the flooding of rich bottomland contributes to the fertility of the water body. Conditions are suited for rapid population expansion into the increased living space, new niches and an abundance of food. (Stefan 1981: 1419)

This policy might increase the cost of operating a water-supply reservoir but it would improve the appearance of its margins and would increase provision for fishing, which is one of the most popular outdoor sports.

Reservoir archaeology

There are few opportunities to preserve a complete village.

Buildings and other existing structures are usually demolished before being immersed beneath a new reservoir. It is recorded that the formation of the Elan Valley reservoirs

> occasioned the destruction of two houses of some pretensions and literary interest . . . the sites of which are situated some forty feet below the top water level of the Caban Coch Reservoir, were associated with the poet Shelley.

Shelley's uncle lived in one of the houses, and Shelley lived in the other with his wife, Harriet. A church, a chapel, a school and 14 cottages were also destroyed (Lees 1908: 6). In a similar manner the village of Mardale was levelled before the Haweswater dam was flooded in 1941. During the drought of 1984 Haweswater fell 21.3 metres (to its lowest level since 1941), and Mardale was exposed. It soon became a tourist attraction and the Haweswater road had to be closed on busy weekends to prevent congestion. Since diving and underwater archaeology have become popular activities, buildings of this type should now be regarded as accessible. Mardale should have been preserved (Fig. 5.13). There are few opportunities to preserve a complete English village. All of them should be seized.

Similarly, Normanton Church was just inside the margin of the area to be flooded by Rutland Water. It could have been demolished, moved, left alone or protected by an artificial island. The latter course of action was chosen, and the church has become "the most popular landmark of Rutland Water" (Anglian Water Authority 1982). The filling has, however, destroyed the classical proportions of the church. In my opinion it would have been better to protect the stonework from erosion and allow the church to appear and disappear as the waters rise and fall. This happened to the Temple of Philae in Egypt before the High Dam was built at Aswan. Philae was "the most romantic tourist attraction in nineteenth century Egypt" (Baines & Malek 1984: 73).

Conclusion

The huge potential of reservoirs should be subject to regular review.

Many people prefer to live, and enjoy their leisure, beside water. An EID approach to reservoir land could provide many opportunities. Rivers and

Figure 5.13 Haweswater Reservoir. The submerged village of Mardale became a popular tourist attraction when it was revealed in the dry summer of 1984.

sea coasts accommodate visitors during holiday periods, but reservoirs are likely to be near urban concentrations, and their potential for uses in addition to water supply should be fully developed. Since only a few of these uses can be anticipated when a reservoir is planned, it is necessary to carry out periodic landscape studies of existing reservoirs. They are a huge man-made resource. The greatest development opportunity in East London is shut away behind the 3-metre concrete fences of the Lea Valley Regional Park. I recommend property investment companies to buy the water companies' stock with a view to stripping out their underused assets.

CHAPTER 6
Mineral working

The past

Old mines can have new uses.

For centuries it has been known that mining produces a range of harmful side-effects – and that they can be ameliorated. The first European textbook on mines and quarries, written by Georgius Agricola in 1550, considered the case against mineral extraction and concluded:

> The strongest argument of the detractors is that the fields are devastated by mining operations, for which reason formerly Italians were warned by law that no one should dig the earth for metals and so injure their very fertile fields, their vineyards, and their olive groves . . . And when the woods and groves are felled, then are exterminated the beasts and birds, very many of which furnish a pleasant and agreeable food for man. Further, when the ores are washed, the water which has been used poisons the brooks and streams, and either destroys the fish or drives them away . . . Thus it is said, it is clear to all that there is greater detriment from mining than the value of the metals which the mining produces. (Agricola 1912: 8)

While mining continues, the environmental side-effects are wholly undesirable. But when working has ceased, beneficial side effects arise. Agricola knew this:

> Moreover, as the miners dig almost exclusively in mountains otherwise unproductive, and in valleys invested in gloom, they do either slight damage to the fields or none at all. Lastly, where woods and glades are cut down, they may be sown with grain after they have been cleared from the roots of shrubs and trees. These new fields soon produce rich crops, so that they repair the losses which the inhabitants suffer from increased cost of timber. (ibid.: 14)

Agricola's book was translated from Latin by Hoover while he was president of America. There are three crucial points:

1 Mineral operations cause great environmental harm.
2 When finished, mining can leave land in a pitiful condition.
3 Mining can create valuable new land characteristics.

The foreword to a book on minerals and the environment, published by the Institution of Mining and Metallurgy, acknowledged with some reluctance that:

> Perhaps the increase in population has forced us to realise that there are now too few pleasant places for us to cover them up with slag heaps or destroy them with sulphur and arsenic; too few fish left in the streams for us to destroy them with toxic effluents; too little fresh air for us to mix it with smoke and dust. Our conscience will no longer allow us to do what our ancestors did without question; and if it did, there are laws to constrain us. (Jones 1975: x)

The name of the world's largest mining corporation stands as a monument to the old times (Fig. 6.1). RTZ, the Rio Tinto Zinc Mining Corporation takes its name from the "tinted river" area of Spain. Copper was mined there by the Romans. This was considered preferable to despoiling the landscape of Italy but

Figure 6.1 The headquarters of the world's largest mining corporation, The RTZ-CRA Group, has no signboard. The initials RTZ come from the Spanish for "tinted river". The tint in the river was pollution.

... in more than a thousand years, the countryside round the Rio Tinto did not recover from the effect of the fumes from the ancient smelters. No vegetation grew and no birds sang amongst the abandoned pit-shafts. (West 1972: 14)

A writer in 1634 described Rio Tinto's "terrorizing aspect, a simple glance at it causing apprehension and dismay to the casual and infrequent visitor" (West 1972: 14). Concern for the welfare of gloomy valleys and unproductive mountains is not such a new phenomenon. Yet the need for care is increasing. The richer a society becomes, the greater its per capita demand for aggregates and other minerals. They are used to make larger houses, longer roads, bigger universities, more airports and other features.

Everyone involved with the planning and environmental aspects of the minerals industry should take note. Unless it adopts an EID approach, the industry's future will be as perilous as a neglected mine shaft. Even in poor countries, minds are no longer closed to environmental despoliation. In rich countries, opposition to mineral working must be expected to grow and grow. In the environs of great cities, it is already intense. To the east of London local deposits of chalk and gravel were used to make concrete. With these extractive industries now subject to severe environmental pressure, the materials are increasingly arriving by sea. Granite aggregates come from the West of Scotland. Cement comes from Southern Europe. To save Europe's mineral industries from extinction, operators must learn:

- to minimize environmental harm while working proceeds;
- to create post-quarrying landscapes which are self-evidently as good as the pre-quarrying landscapes;
- to achieve these goals by imaginative planning and EID, rather than exorbitant expenditure;

It can be done. It must be done. It will be done, some day.

Future practice

The key in reclamation is figuring the eventual landscape and reuse plan before excavation is begun

W. H. Whyte 1970: 355

One area of mineral working in England has recovered so fully that a Broads Authority with the status of a national park was established in 1989 (Fig. 6.2). For several hundred years the area was thought to contain natural water bodies of estuarine origin. In the 1960s it was proved that:

Figure 6.2 The Norfolk Broads: an abandoned mineral working that has become an area of outstanding "natural" beauty.

... the Norfolk Broads, the most used and best-known of British lakes, are literally the handiwork of our ancestors. On the evidence now available they are, beyond reasonable doubt, the flooded sites of former great peat pits, made in the natural fenland in medieval times. At first they must have been ugly sheets of relatively deep water, bounded by sharp margins of undisturbed deposits: but progressive shallowing of the open water by accumulation of mud within their basins, and over-growth of their margins by encroaching vegetation, have combined to soften their contours and produce the generally more natural appearance of the broads we know today. (Ellis 1965: 65)

A comparable area of Holland was quarried for peat, from Roman times until the seventeenth century. Today:

The Friesland lake area is internationally known as a water recreation area. All sorts of activities can be done: sailing, swimming, sunbathing, motorboating, surfboarding, walking and cycling around the lakes ... Especially since the Second World War, tourism has gained an important role in the area. (Moolen 1996)

This is a good principle for future mineral workings, but society cannot be expected to wait three centuries for an acceptable after-use.

Private landowners have often taken care of mineral workings on their own land, for agricultural and other reasons. In the nineteenth century quarries were opened to win building stone – and restored as rock gardens on their owners' estates (Turner 1986: 109). Contemporary legislation for the control of mineral working was concerned with the health and safety of the labour force (Roberts & Shaw 1972: 17). In the twentieth century there has been increasingly comprehensive control over the environmental side-effects of mineral extraction, but in most countries the legislation is still too weak to deal with after-uses.

The Cornish china clay mines began before planning controls existed and will continue indefinitely, because they supply some 40 per cent of the European market. In 1970, a team made up of landscape designers, planners and company representatives was able to agree on reclamation and after-use plans solely because the company needed permission to dump mining wastes on land hitherto unaffected by mineral working (Greengrass 1977: 87). This example emphasizes the importance of phasing when planning the landscape of mines and quarries: it is a means of ensuring that land is cared for.

Australia was one of the first countries to legislate for the restoration of mineral workings. The New South Wales Coal Mines Regulation Act (1912) required topsoil to be replaced and depressions to be drained (Thomas 1978: 143). In 1939 West Virginia became the first American state to control mineral working, but only seven states had required the reclamation of coal workings by 1967 (Cummins 1973). Since the early 1970s mineral workings in North America and Australia have been regulated by laws dealing with particular industries and by general acts concerned with the assessment of environmental impacts. Thus in the USA surface mining of coal is regulated both by the National Environmental Policy Act (NEPA) of 1970, by numerous state laws and by the Surface Mining Control and the Reclamation Act of 1977 (Surface mining 1981). This provides better control over mining than other American land-uses. But avoidance of negative impacts is only half the problem.

The places from which materials are won offer the most stupendous opportunities for land shaping. Occasionally, it can be done purely for artistic purposes. More often, it should be for functional reasons. New lakes can be dug, new mountains formed, old mountains excavated to make special types of enclosed space, new valleys planned, amphitheatres dug. Given the splendour of these possibilities it is puzzling that mineral extraction has for so long been regarded an undesirable land-use which ought to be hidden away behind small mounds and thin belts of sickly trees, necessary though they may be during the operational life of a pit. Multi-purpose planning could reap great benefits for the minerals industry and for society.

When human life has gone, earthworks may be all that survives from man's short occupation of the planet. Largest among the monuments will be the piles of rubble, once cities, and the great pits from which the materials to build them were won. Pits near cities will be found to have been filled with our goods, arranged in neat layers and protected with clay caps. Since the best examples of electric kettles, plastic containers and light bulbs will be found in these pits, visitors from other planets may conclude that we lived in fear of catastrophe. Surely they will never guess at our sheer wastefulness. Nor, unless they find a book on the landscape of minerals in the dump, will they guess at what could have been done with those great pits.

Mineral planning

The alternatives are Similarity, Identity and Difference.

From a landscape planning viewpoint there are three main aspects of a minerals project:

- plant and machinery
- extraction of the mineral
- after-use of the site.

Each can be the dominant landscape planning factor, depending on the nature of the mineral operation and the characteristics of the site. When clay is dug to make bricks, the brick manufacturing plant itself may dominate the local environment. When a shallow surface-mining operation takes place, say for coal or ironstone, the extraction process is likely to dominate – there will be no permanent machinery on site and the land can be restored to its original contours. When minerals are dug from large, deep open pits, as happens for copper and other high-value ores, the most difficult problem is finding an acceptable after-use for the site. Each aspect of mineral planning can assume the proportions of an "industry" in its own right, and may require a separate approach. Certainly each requires EID.

Three alternatives for the relationship between development and context were described, in Chapter 3, as similarity, identity and difference (Fig. 6.3). When planning the landscape of minerals, these can translate into policies for zoning, innovation, conservation or concealment (Fig. 6.4). Each has been applied to mines and quarries. In general it may be said that while zoning and concealment have been used intelligently, if not always effectively, the prejudice in favour of "conservation and restoration" has become so strong that it prevents the creation of new values in places where innovation would be appropriate.

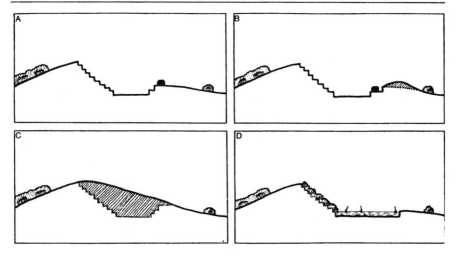

Figure 6.3 A quarry (A) can be hidden (B) during its working life. When exhausted, it can be made similar (C) to its pre-quarrying landform or given a different form (D).

Zoning

Zoning is the oldest approach. Kings and noblemen, who did not wish to be troubled by the negative side-effects of mineral extraction, kept mining areas out of sight, preferably in what Agricola saw as "unproductive mountains". The policy can be used for ubiquitous minerals but not for scarce minerals, which must be dug where they are found. It is applicable to building stones, road metal, limestone and chalk for cement manufacture, clay for brick-making, sand and gravel for building – but not to coal, ironstone, gem-stones, mineral sands, special clays or metalliferous ores generally.

Concealment

Concealment has been favoured by planners because it is the least conten-tious approach: out of sight, out of mind. If an environmentally unpleasant operation must be located in a beautiful place, it is logical that its harmful effects should be minimized by trying to conceal the mine, although noise, dust and traffic may be unconcealed. The Scott Report on Land Utilisation in Rural Areas (1942), which laid the foundation for mineral planning in Britain, explained the policy as follows:

> Extractive industries, almost more than any others, are harmful to agriculture and destructive of the beauty of the countryside: their coming into the countryside cannot be avoided in the national interest

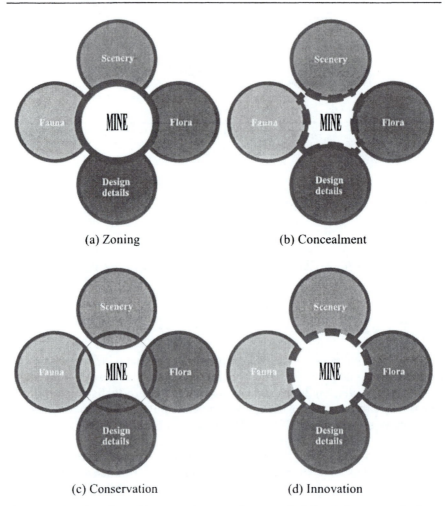

(a) Zoning   (b) Concealment

(c) Conservation   (d) Innovation

Figure 6.4 Mineral workings can be zoned, concealed, treated conservatively or treated innovatively.

and therefore care must be taken to minimise their destructive effects. (Ministry of Works and Planning 1942: 61)

The most characteristic feature of the concealment approach is the use of ridge lines, tree screens and "amenity banks" to hide the mineral operation and mitigate such undesirable side effects as noise and dust (Down & Stocks 1977: 43). In some cases these devices have worked well, but they have also failed through inept or inappropriate application. A line of trees on the rim of a cliff functions more like a flag, signalling the quarry's location, than as an effective screen. The trees become parched because, on a quarry edge, soil conditions tend to be very hot and very dry. Once the extraction phase of a mineral operation has been completed the concealment approach leads to the idea that the land should be restored to its original shape and pre-extraction use. In the USA this is known as the "back-to-contour" restoration philosophy. It can be applied to certain types of surface-mining operation, but strictly speaking the land can never be restored to its original condition: the extraction of minerals always changes something.

Conservation

The conservation approach to minerals planning derives from the correct idea that land is a precious resource which must be conserved by wise use. The Scott Report stated unequivocally:

> We are clear that in principle it is wrong that any body or person should be allowed to work land and leave it in a derelict condition. We therefore recommend that legislation should be passed, imposing an obligation on all those who derive benefit from the working of land for minerals, to restore the land for agricultural or afforestation or other purposes (as may be directed by an appropriate authority) within a short specified period of time after the land has been worked out. (Ministry of Works and Planning 1942: 62)

Although the authors refer explicitly to "other purposes", there has, in Britain, been a strong presumption that if the land was used for agriculture before mineral extraction began, then agriculture is the most appropriate after-use. The Ministry of Agriculture lends powerful support to this view. It is, however, unchallengeable only when one can be certain that the restored land will be beautiful and productive. There are many occasions when massive reclamation costs, soil problems, the post-quarrying landform, proximity to urban areas, adjacent land uses or other factors should lead planners to consider an alternative land-use (Fig. 6.5).

Innovation

The innovative approach to the landscape of minerals is founded on the recognition that there are many occasions on which it is not feasible or appropriate to return land to its initial condition. Highwalls, cliffs and lakes can be appreciated. In the USA a committee of the National Academy of Sciences proposed the not altogether satisfactory word "rehabilitation" to describe the innovative approach. They said that rehabilitation implies "the land will be returned to a form and productivity in

193

Figure 6.5 The men who dug this quarry could never have anticipated its after-use as a regional turnip-washing facility.

conformity with a prior land-use plan including a stable ecological state" (Study Committee on the Potential for Rehabilitating Lands 1974: 11). It is a most important concept.

Many old mineral workings, and especially those that date from the days of the pickaxe and the pack-horse, have created a fascinating landscape which planning authorities now wish to retain. The Lake District National Park Plan states that the public have "indicated a strong concern for most derelict sites to be left alone, as they form part of the landscape character giving interest and variety" (Lake District Special Planning Board 1978: 173). Old quarries are of particular interest to industrial archaeologists and geologists. The Planning Board is, however, "against further large scale aggregate working in the National Park and any new quarry or extension to an existing quarry will be severely restricted" (ibid.: 172). They will not risk the creation of new landscapes because of the grim reputation of modern quarrying. Yet an innovative approach is the only alternative for many types of operation. In 1972 a Commission on Mining and the Environment stated that:

> Where existing landforms have been substantially altered, it would not be sensible to talk of "restoration". Advantage would need to be taken

of the opportunity to create new forms and patterns, and even planning for new land-uses, within the general policy for the area.
(Commission on Mining and the Environment, 1972)

The concept of automatic "back-to-contour" restoration has also been criticized in the USA. Environmentalists have pressed for the Appalachian
strip mines to be restored in this way. They point out that:

. . . where hilly or mountainous land is mined using the contour technique, the result is long sinuous slashes winding around the sides of
hills and valleys. The highwall rises at a steep gradient above the
ruined area, which may contain impounded water, while below lies a
landslide-prone slope of tree stumps and mud. (Coal surface mining
commission 1979: 294)

Back-to-contour restoration is very expensive, unless it is combined with the
mining operation, and the restored land may not have any agricultural
value. A landscape planner has argued that its justification depends "on
emotion, not sound data" (Simpson 1985). He quotes the evidence the
Chairman of the Tennessee Valley Authority gave to a Senate Committee:

One thing Senator, about a highwall, if you leave a highwall, you also
leave a fairly wide, level bench, and in many of these mountain areas
level land is at a premium. It can be used in the future. Haul roads can
be used to get timber out, access for hunting or hiking or fishing, and
in some areas close to a town, of course, it has a higher use, housing
developments, schools, airplane landing strips, and so on.

The erosion and water pollution caused by these old mines is tragic. But as
topographic features they have a visual interest and power equal to the
British waste tips, which have been described as "splendid spoil heaps"
(Barr 1969: 24). The issue of *Landscape Architecture* in which the above
quotation appears also carries an account of a small disused quarry which
has been made into a sculpture garden. The artist worked on the quarry for
over 20 years before he recognized that the quarry itself had become a work
of art. He then "removed all his other works from the quarry" so that its
spatial qualities were displayed (Dalton 1985).

   The four policies for the landscape of industry can also be applied to any
industrial plant that adjoins a mineral operation. Zoning and concealment
are possible when a new works is built in an older quarry. If a large hole is
available, the plant can be hidden. A conservation approach to architectural
design is often chosen as a second best to concealment. The following quotation describes the policy adopted for the tailings plant at Boulby potash
mine on the east coast of England:

The buildings were designed to make use of natural local materials
so that they would become an extension of the existing scene. The

structures have walls of natural stone with slate roofs. The main building houses the shaft headgear, hoist and ventilation fans, but there are
no outward signs of these, the appearance being of a farm building.
(Cleasby 1974: 20)

When buildings cannot be camouflaged the planner must choose
between designing them "as unobtrusively as possible", as was done for
the main treatment plant at Boulby (Cleasby 1974: 17), and an innovative
approach. The manufacturing plant at Hope Cement Works is seen by
Jellicoe as "complex geometry drawing upon the laws of the universe"
(Jellicoe 1979).

Coalition

Sir Geoffrey Jellicoe's plan for the Hope Cement Works uses each of the
four approaches to the landscape of industry: they are not mutually exclusive (Fig. 6.6). The first landscape plan was published in 1943. No legislation
was in force at the time, but the Scott Report had been issued in 1942 and
the owner of the company, an enlightened man, believed the works should
receive special consideration because of their location in the heart of what is
now the Peak District National Park. Jellicoe wrote that:

> It is not recommended that there should be artificial planting inside the
> quarry, nor that the quarry face should be altered from the vertical: for
> the quarry within itself is impressive.

He added that the idea of treating the quarry face like

> . . . the outcrops in the surrounding district . . . would be a mistake
> because the quality of stone is different. Mam Tor, the "shivering
> mountain", is of millstone grit . . . the rock form is therefore dissimilar
> to that of a quarry.

Jellicoe advised that the limestone quarry should be concealed from without

> . . . to give the illusion that the form of the hill is undisturbed . . . the
> mouth of the quarry, therefore should be kept as small as possible, and
> the quarry itself worked fanwise from this.

The quarry is an industrial zone with no environmental control over the
method of working. In 1979, after 50 years of excavation, it was entirely
concealed within the mass of the hill. An older limestone quarry, opened in
1929, was conspicuous in 1943, but has been restored and is now indistinguishable from the mountainside.

For the old clay quarries, which provided the other essential component
of cement, Jellicoe recommended the conservation approach, because

Figure 6.6 Sir Geoffrey Jellicoe and his 1943 model for Hope Cement Works. The site is an example of the successful integration of a minerals project into the landscape. Sir Geoffrey recommended that the limestone quarry should be concealed inside the hill, that the old clay quarries should be restored to "conform" with their surroundings, and that the main structure of the cement works should be accepted as a bold feature in the landscape. An after-use for the limestone quarry will be agreed when the land becomes available for reclamation.

> . . . the first consideration is that they should be brought back to use to conform with their surroundings. A series of lakes with planted banks is suggestive of a landscape even more interesting than existed before.

Jellicoe was also very interested in the creative potential of the mineral operation. When reviewing his plan in 1979 he said that "The limestone quarry with its firm stone carved in radiating terraces is like some giant's amphitheatre among the mountains." It and the new clay quarry

> . . . will be in existence long after the works have vanished (as long, indeed as Win Hill itself) and their ultimate use could be as astonishing

in their benefit to a leisured society as are the Norfolk Broads today with their medieval origins of peat workings.

Hope Cement Works serves to make two important points about the landscape of minerals: it shows that separate policies may be required for each aspect of the operation, and that the treatment of the whole project depends on the character of the site and the timescale of the workings. Since time is a vital factor, the various types of mineral working will, in the following sections, be classified in relation to the expected period of the extraction process. It can range from six months for a surface coal-mining project to a thousand years for a hard-rock quarry.

Mineral workings

Short-life mines and quarries

A large part of the land affected by mineral working is occupied by mines and quarries with a lifespan of under ten years (Fig. 6.7). This is because short-life workings tend to be large in extent and shallow in depth. Concealment is desirable, but the most important planning objective is to secure an imaginative after-use plan *before* workings start.

Surface mining for coal and ironstone caused great devastation in the past. Improvements have been made in temperate countries, but the problem is by no means resolved. The USA has a long history of surface mining and, until the 1960s, a very poor record for land reclamation. From 1930 to 1971, 3.65 million acres were used for mineral workings and only 1.46 million acres reclaimed. The situation changed dramatically when the Surface Mining Control and Reclamation Act was passed in 1977. It is mainly concerned with coal. The Act requires operators to

> . . . restore the land affected to a condition capable of supporting the uses which it was capable of supporting prior to mining, or higher or better uses of which there is a reasonable likelihood. (Committee on soil as a resource in relation to surface mining for coal 1981: 151)

Before opening a new mine a company must obtain a licence and a permit.

The Act also provides for performance bonds, the special protection of scenic areas, water pollution control, backfilling to original contours (unless there is "an economically preferred post-mining land-use"), the separate handling of topsoil and subsoil, revegetation, a period of liability for successful reinstatement of farmland and a levy to raise funds for the reclamation of abandoned mines. It has been estimated that the 1977 Act doubled reclamation costs, but, even with an abandoned mine levy of $0.35 per ton

Figure 6.7 While it is technically possible to restore surface mines for agriculture, they almost always leave the land less productive and less beautiful.

of surface-mined coal, the total mining costs per ton are "only slightly affected" (ibid.: 199).

In Britain, the surface mining of coal and ironstone was regulated by separate Acts of Parliament in the 1950s. The laws are older and less prescriptive than the North American legislation. In 1978 a former director of the National Coal Board's Opencast Executive claimed that its operations had set an example which other industries could well follow (Davison 1978: 167). He considered the Executive's restoration work to be so good that it gave hope for a full reconciliation between industry and the environment. Some coal reclamation has been well done, but few commentators have shared the NCB's opinion. In 1979 the Council for Environmental Conservation (CoEnCo) said:

> We recognise that the Executive has developed technical skill in restoring a three-dimensional surface to opencast areas that fits the surrounding contours in a natural way. But is the result a landscape? We believe that as in the case of soil restoration, the landscape restoration that is being currently achieved is only part of what is needed.

Many restored areas can be picked out in the landscape from considerable distances because the hedgerows, trees and woodlands that were characteristic of the area have been replaced by fencing only, giving a bald, disjointed appearance. (Council for Environmental Conservation 1979: 22)

In 1979 an independent report stated that the agricultural productivity of restored land is low and that ". . . the contours of the opencast workings stand out stark and alien industrial features which dominate the natural character of the countryside over a wide area" (Brocklesby 1979: 17). The Opencast Executive continued to assert that the land was satisfactorily restored (Tomlinson 1982), but there are weaknesses in the regulation of British surface mining.

Surface mining can be controlled in three main ways. The first is to require operators to deposit a bond or contribute to a reclamation fund, as in the USA. This provides a useful incentive but may encourage the idea that reclamation work can be left until completion. It can't. In short-life mines, reclamation work *must* be fully integrated with the extraction process.

The second method of regulation is to set up a system which controls the mineral operator's working practices. This can be done by requiring a mineral company to adopt a defined set of operating techniques before starting a new pit. The Opencast Coal Act (1958) controls the authorization, working methods and restoration of surface-mined coal in Britain (National Coal Board 1974). Over 95 per cent of the land is restored to agriculture, and the remaining land goes to new uses, as at Druridge Bay Country Park (National Coal Board 1967). The Opencast Executive establishes standards for its contractors, but this method of control suffers from the disadvantage that mining regulations are difficult to enforce. Unless a quarry manager is utterly determined to keep subsoil and topsoil apart they will become mixed, and topsoil is prone to compaction in wet weather. An environmental impact statement can also establish a sequence of operations that is difficult to monitor.

The third and most effective method of regulation is to phase the issue of permits to work minerals, and make their issue dependent on the successful reclamation of earlier phases.

These three methods of controlling surface mining have all been tried in Britain. Performance bonds and reclamation funds have been judged most useful for small operators who might go out of business – large companies with substantial resources can, in theory, be forced to reclaim the land (Stevens Report 1976: 107). The system of control which uses a defined method of working has been used extensively for surface mining. Working methods are imposed as planning conditions on sand and gravel workings, and written into leases for coal and ironstone. Sand and gravel working has been subject to local planning control since 1947, and a host of different conditions have been tried by different authorities.

There is no technical problem in reclaiming sand and gravel workings for agriculture, recreation or conservation, but, as with land worked for surface coal, reclamation standards have been regrettably low. With agricultural restoration schemes the question "is the result a landscape?" must be given the same answer as for opencast coal: "usually not". Restoration is not a technical problem. It depends on the motivation and control of the operating company (Street 1984).

Motivation can be dramatically improved by making permission for future phases dependent on satisfactory reclamation in earlier phases. Mineral companies regard this as an unnecessary precaution, but regulatory authorities will find themselves in a vastly stronger position. They can concentrate on undertaking an evaluation of land which has been reclaimed, by whatever techniques the company prefers, instead of having to make frequent and unsatisfactory site visits. To provide a standard of comparison for the evaluation, there must also have been a full assessment before mining began, of soil quality, agricultural yields, visual quality, conservation value and other site characteristics (Street 1985).

Medium-life mines and quarries

A life of from ten to 50 years is of medium length for a mineral operation. Continuous back-to-contour reclamation techniques are sometimes feasible, but the volume of overburden is often insufficient. The longer life of such pits and quarries makes concealment more important during the operational phase, and decisions about an eventual after-use more problematic. One cannot be sure what types of landform and land-use society will desire in 30 or 40 years time. Quarry operators have argued that because of this uncertainty they should be allowed maximum flexibility in planning their operations. Since there may be an unexpected demand for picturesque ravines, holes to accommodate waste products, urban land or agricultural land, they prefer to get on with the digging and plan an after-use at a later date. Since the oldest medium-life quarries of the mineral planning age are only now becoming derelict, there is less experience of medium-life than of short-life quarries. Chalk and clay workings illustrate the problems.

In 1952, five years after Britain's Town and Country Planning Act was passed, the Minister of Housing and Local Government held public inquiries into two major applications for medium-life quarries in Southern England: for clay working in Bedfordshire and chalk working in Essex. Both applications were approved, but, as recommended in the Scott Report, landscape conditions were attached to the planning permissions. They did not work.

In Bedfordshire the Minister wrote that:

> All waste arising from the working or processing of clay shall be
> deposited in the workings in such a manner, and the excavated areas
> shall be further restored by such filling and levelling as may be agreed
> with the local planning authority, having regard in the latter respect to
> the availability of suitable filling materials at suitable times on reason-
> able terms. (Minister of Housing and Local Government July 1952a)

In Essex the Minister wrote that:

> He considers first and foremost that the best possible use should be
> made of all overburden which has any agricultural value so that as
> much land as possible may in due course be returned to food produc-
> tion . . . In general, he thinks that an undulating surface is to be
> preferred to a more or less uniform level and that abrupt breaks in
> levels should, as far as possible, be avoided. Consideration should also
> be given to the possibilities of tree planting. The general object should
> be to leave the workings, after excavation has been completed, as
> pleasant and useful a place as may be practicable within the possibi-
> lities of restoration at reasonable cost. (Minister of Housing and Local
> Government August 1952b)

These opinions, which were obviously well intentioned, became landscape
conditions under which the minerals were worked. Alice Coleman, a famous
geographer, attended a 1952 public inquiry into the chalk working on
Thamesside and was very hopeful that it would result in eventual restoration
(Coleman 1954). She was wrong (Fig. 6.8). In 1996 a considerable number of
abandoned pits in both Essex and Bedfordshire had not been reclaimed. Nor
were they concealed during their operational life. It is very evident that the
conditions imposed on the 1952 planning permissions were ineffective, and
that there are lessons to be learned.

In Essex, the problem arose from the Minister's loose phraseology and
from the use of the word "reasonable" in connection with reclamation costs.
It was taken to mean that the excavations need be reclaimed only when the
company had made a financial gain from the work. In Bedfordshire, the
Deputy Chairman of the brick company announced that "We have always
had in mind that we have had assets in our pits" (Bugler 1975: 142). They
were able to realize some of these assets by charging the Greater London
Council and the Central Electricity Generating Board for the right to dis-
pose of waste material in the old pits. One of the clay pits was made into a
reservoir and leased to a water-sports club.

Some of the chalk quarries are also being filled with shopping centres and
waste materials but it has proved a physical impossibility to backfil! the
quarries to produce "an undulating surface" which can support food production. Since the chalk quarries are on the fringe of London, some have

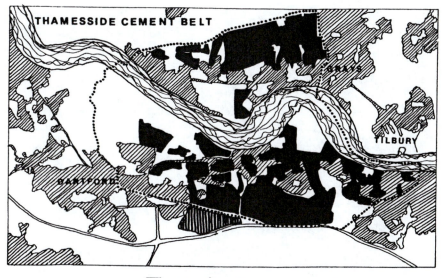

THAMESSIDE CEMENT BELT

GRAYS

TILBURY

DARTFORD

■ AREAS WORKED FOR MINERALS

Figure 6.8 The Thamesside cement belt. Some quarries are still in use, some are dormant, some are derelict, some have been reclaimed. The landscape has been wrecked by mineral working. With foresight and imagination, a remarkable new landscape could have been made.

been profitably reclaimed for industrial buildings, which are conspicuous on the flat quarry floors. No one could think them as beautiful as the rolling agricultural land envisaged by the Minister when he gave permission for the workings.

Chalk extraction has also taken place in North Kent, and some quarries have been backfilled with overburden and refuse. In 1952 it was not known that these materials would become available. The quarries are now agricultural land of low productivity and poor visual quality (Turner 1984). A non-agricultural use would be preferable, if it were visually satisfactory.

The chalk and clay pits illustrate two points. First, as in the case of short-life mines and quarries the safest policy is to phase the issue of excavation permits and plan for "continuous restoration". Second, unanticipated after-use possibilities may arise during the lifetime of a quarry. Restoration to its former use and contours is unimaginative and short-sighted. Even in a simple strip-mining operation it can be disruptive and expensive to re-transport overburden from the first cut, which may have lain in a dump for 30–40 years, and use it to backfill the last cut. A wiser policy is to plan the whole workings to create a new landscape (Fig. 6.9). This can be done on a loose-fit basis to accommodate alternative after-uses. If the final landscape is

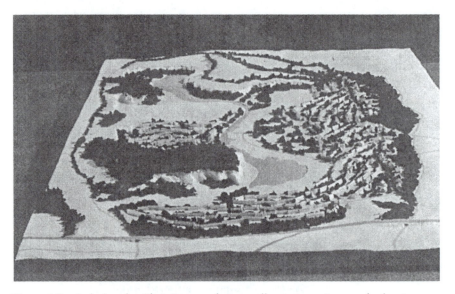

Figure 6.9 A design, by Chris Evason, for a small new town in a worked-out quarry. The landform was shaped to accommodate the housing on a south-facing slope looking over a new lake to a cliff surmounted by an existing woodland.

fertile and visually attractive, and has good access and drainage, it will be found suitable for a wide range of after-uses.

Planning an after-use may result in shallower excavations and a larger land take, but the short-term disturbance will be justified by the long-term after-use potential of the land (Ministry of Housing and Local Government 1960). Deep and dangerous pits should be dug only when a supply of filling material is assured. If quarries are left as cold, badly drained, flat areas surrounded by precipitous and unstable cliffs, they are likely to remain derelict for many decades after workings have ceased.

Continuous restoration is an attractive concept but should not be conceived as a panacea to the reclamation problem. It implies a procedure by which minerals are won and land immediately put back to its pre-mining condition. The planning merits of this procedure are twofold: it gives the local community a high degree of security against land dereliction, and it appears to solve the after-use question. Only a thin band of mineral is uncovered at any one time, and it makes good economic sense to deposit the overburden material in a manner that facilitates an immediate return to the pre-mining use. The deployment of very large excavating machines has increased the scope for strip mining and continuous restoration; the twin techniques are most common for short-life operations but can sometimes be used in medium-life projects.

"Progressive reclamation" is a better name for the procedure as it applies to medium-life projects. "Progressive" implies that each phase of the reclamation work may be of longer duration than justifies the description "continuous". "Reclamation" implies that alternative land-uses will be considered. Since medium-life quarries are likely to be fully screened, the timing of the reclamation work is of less importance than the eventual achievement of a successful result. Over-hasty restoration may limit the scope for innovation and may produce a physically and visually degraded version of the pre-mining land-use. It is better to embrace the opportunity which arises from the vast movement of materials and adapt the land to a new use, be it housing, industry, water storage, recreation or a wholly unanticipated function. Many new uses cannot be established while mining proceeds, and are incompatible with the goal of continuous restoration. The objective should be to reclaim the land for the highest and best land-use it is capable of.

The mining and reclamation of brown coal near Cologne in West Germany is a good example of a mining operation divided into a series of phases, with progressive reclamation of the land to create a new landscape. The brown coal is worked by surface mining at depths of up to 320 metres in seams of up to 100 metres thick. Giant bucket-wheel excavators are able to move 200,000 cubic metres per day (Fig. 6.10). When the Hambach mine was opened, the first cut produced 2.7 billion cubic metres of overburden, which had to be deposited outside the mine. Approximately 1.7 billion cubic metres was used to fill old mines and 1.0 billion to make a new mountain. Since there is no possibility of restoring the land, every effort is made to create a new landscape. Villages, roads and railways are destroyed and rebuilt in new places. This has to be done progressively so that farmers and villagers have somewhere to go when the land beneath their old homes is removed. They consent because the brown-coal authority has proved its ability to create new landscapes. The oldest reclaimed area, near Brühl, has been sculptured into a new landscape, with over 1,200 hectares of forests and lakes (Fig. 6.11). It has considerable charm and attracts large numbers of visitors from Brühl and nearby towns. Mining and planning are regulated by the 1950 Law for Overall Planning in the Rhineland Brown Coal Area (Leuschner 1976).

Long-life mines and quarries

Over 40 years may be regarded as a long life for a mineral operation. It will probably be longer than the period for which any single mining engineer or planner is involved with a project. Some workings can last for a very much longer period: marble has been won from the Carrara Valley since Roman times, and quarrying continues apace. It is common for long-life quarries to

Figure 6.10 A brown-coal mine near Türnich, with a giant bucket-wheel excavator (1996).

Figure 6.11 A restored brown-coal mine near Brühl in Germany. The grass is part of a forest campsite, and the lake is used for swimming and boating (1996).

be deep, open pits of comparatively small lateral extent. They deserve the name quarry (which derives from the Latin *quadrare*, "to square") better than other types of mine. Since they grow larger and deeper as they are worked, progressive reclamation is rarely possible and it may be difficult to find an after-use. Mineral planners should aim to safeguard against harmful side-effects and respect the land so that, as Jellicoe suggested for the Hope Quarries, "their ultimate use could be as astonishing in their benefit to a leisured society as are the Norfolk Broads today".

Sheila Haywood summarized the situation as follows:

> Respect for the land itself is apt to be a surer guide than popular clamour for "instant" results. The land is permanent: even a hundred year operation is transitory in a historical sense, and a fleeting moment in geology. (Haywood 1974: 62)

Some old quarries become tourist attractions during their working lives: the travertine quarries outside Rome, the diamond mines in South Africa, the Rubislaw granite quarry in Aberdeen, "the massive Bingham Canyon open pit copper mine [which] is claimed to be the second largest tourist attraction in the State of Utah" (Down & Stocks 1977: 18). In the aesthetic terminology of the eighteenth century they are, like an Alpine gorge or the Grand Canyon, "sublime" rather than "beautiful". French aestheticians might describe them as a "heoric landscape". The fact that tourists wish to visit such places should not be taken to imply that they wish such features to impinge on their daily lives.

In his Essay on the Sublime and Beautiful, Burke states:

> Whatever therefore is terrible, with regard to sight, is sublime too, whether this cause of terror be endued with greatness of dimensions or not; for it is impossible to look on anything as trifling, or contemptible, that may be dangerous. (Burke 1756: Part II Section II)

> Greatness of dimension is a powerful cause of the sublime . . . A perpendicular has more force in forming the sublime, than an inclined plane; and the effects of a rugged and broken surface seem stronger than where it is smooth and polished. (Burke 1765: Part II Section VII)

Since people do not wish to live with views of terrifyingly sublime quarries, it may be concluded that zoning and concealment will normally be the most appropriate policies. When the quarries are finally abandoned some reclamation expenditure will be necessary to prevent the world's population of "orphan quarries" from growing beyond its present level. If excavations have gone below the water table these pits can, like Rubislaw quarry and the Big Hole of Kimberley (Fig. 6.12), become small versions of Oregon's Crater Lake.

Figure 6.12 The Big Hole of Kimberley is an artificial "crater lake" in a worked-out diamond mine. It is visually spectacular and much visited by tourists, but the visitors' sensations are of sublimity and terror, not beauty. (Courtesy of Satour.)

A few old quarries have been given a very successful after-use. My favourite example is at Dysart (Fig. 6.13) on the coast of Fife. Stone was worked long before canals and railways made long-distance transport from inland quarries feasible. When the quarry was finally abandoned, the town council, proving the virtues of local democracy, converted it into a picturesque harbour, which is now a local tourist attraction. Unfortunately a coal mine discharged colliery waste onto the foreshore and silted-up the harbour (Cunningham 1912: 43). This is one quarry which most certainly should not be backfilled or restored. In the west of Scotland there is a small stone quarry, at Kilsyth, which has been abandoned and made into a country park (Walker 1980). A lake, which occupies the deepest part of the quarry, is enlivened by a small island, built on old mine buildings, and a wooden bridge. In the USA MCQ Industries have established a residential development on the rim of a flooded marble quarry (Committee on Surface Mining and Reclamation 1979: 36).

In 1980 the Scottish Development Department published a report on the potential for a large coastal quarry in Scotland (Dalradian Mineral Services 1980). The idea was to relieve the shortage of aggregates in the south of England by opening a "superquarry" in Scotland and, as in the eighteenth century, transporting the output by sea. A remote site, at Glensanda in the west of Scotland, was found by a mineral operator in 1982. A policy of concealment has been adopted for the life of the quarry. Granite is extracted

Figure 6.13 Dysart Harbour in Fife: the cliff and the inner harbour were produced by quarrying and are now the focus of a picturesque fishing village.

through a glory hole and the "totally enclosed crushing and screening plant will be slotted into specially blasted notches in the hillside to control dust emissions and also obscure them from view outside the site" (*Mine and quarry* 1985). When the quarry is eventually closed there will be an opportunity for innovative development, as at Dysart. Other superquarries have been opened in Wales and Norway. They have a troubling aspect, because puncturing a wilderness cannot be good:

> The southern part of the Isle of Harris is dominated by the grey mountain of Roneval. Eagles nest on its northern corrie, and from the summit there is a glorious panorama east across the Minch to Skye and Wester Ross . . . Roneval is now the focus of a major public inquiry because of a planning application by Redland Aggregates Ltd to turn its eastern slopes into a huge stone quarry (Fig. 6.14) (Johnson 1994).

Imaginative designs have been prepared for Roneval, as they have for the deep open-pit copper mines in Southern Arizona, where "men are creating giant landscapes purely as by-products of their search for mineral deposits"

Figure 6.14 A computer visualization of the proposed superquarry near Lingerbay on the Isle of Harris. (Courtesy of Scottish Natural Heritage.)

(Matter 1977: 203). The designer points out that a major resource is being wasted through a misguided application of the conservation approach. The pits and dumps are being "restored" by revegetation techniques, when they could be developed creatively:

> The builders are scraping off the vegetation of the foothills, paying high premiums for the right to build subdivisions of little plateaux, each one with a picture window view of the valley below. The mining companies are creating foothills with unobscured views of the surrounding areas and then trying their best to disguise their efforts with cosmetic attempts at revegetation. The irony is completed by another set of subdividers developing housing in a floodplain, probably best suited to agricultural purposes, directly below the mining areas thereby setting up the primary source of tension between the inhabitants of the area and the constantly expanding waste dumps above (ibid.: 203).

The disused pits would be flooded, on the "crater lake" principle, and used as reservoirs. It is a most imaginative environmental impact design.

A similar idea has been investigated in Australia. Kerr Quarry was opened in the 1870s to win stone from a scenic area 20 miles east of Melbourne. At that time there were few inhabitants near the quarry and no one was concerned about the landscape. In the 1970s the owners wished to extend the quarry and use the opportunity to tidy up some of the ugly quarry faces that had been formed. By this time the quarry was in the middle of a tourist area; visitors and local residents were concerned about its environmental impact. A landscape designer drew up proposals for housing on the quarry terraces to create "a significant and attractive residential area of unprecedented originality" (Elliott 1976). The proposal was rejected by conservationists, who persuaded the owners to agree to regrading and revegetation. It will be many years before people become experienced in planning long-life quarries. They should remember Agricola.

The economics of after-use

The after-use can yield greater profits than the mineral operation.

An Australian mining textbook contains the observation that: "The obvious place to start a mine, if one was allowed to, is right in the centre of a large city so that one has housing, transport, water, power and market all on the doorstep" (Thomas 1978: 62). Location also has a great influence on the economics of quarry after-use. The subject has not been researched systematically but it is apparent that, while reclamation is certain to impose a financial burden in remote areas, there is a good prospect of its yielding a fat profit if the site is close to a town. Urban quarries, like urban reservoirs, have exceptional development potential. Thorpe Park, near London, is an old gravel pit which has become a theme park. It is well planned and poorly designed.

At Dayton, Ohio, a very large "water supply-park-recreational complex" has been created by mining sand and gravel in the flood plain of a river, near the town. The provisions of the 1977 Surface Mining Control and Reclamation Act would prevent such developments (Committee on Surface Mining and Reclamation 1979: 34).

The relative order of costs in Table 6.1 is representative of the economic situation a mineral operator is likely to face in remote areas. The figures are likely to change, but not the ratios.

The figures do not derive from a single place or project, and in many cases the disparity between reclamation costs and after-use land values will be greater than in the above example. Thus some Australian mineral sand companies spend up to $2500 per hectare on restoring land that will have a value of $12.5 per hectare (Thomas 1978: 66). In such circumstances there is no financial incentive whatsoever for reclamation. It is done solely because governments and operators now accept the Scott Report's argument "that in principle it is wrong that any body or person should be allowed to work land and leave it in a derelict condition".

In prosperous agricultural areas free from urban pressures, the economic position for reclamation work will be very different from that in remote areas. Land will have a higher existing-use value and a higher after-use value. If sufficient overburden is available to restore the land to an agricultural use then the financial position may be as shown in Table 6.2. Once again there is no financial incentive for the company to restore the land. Yet reclamation is economically desirable for society because the agricultural output from the land will produce benefits over a very long period of time.

If a mineral operation is close to an urban area, as often happens for pits and quarries which yield building materials, then the economics of reclamation and after-use are entirely different. The figures in Table 6.3 indicate the economic prospects, but land development companies are as secretive as mineral companies about their costs and profits. It will be assumed that

Table 6.1 The economics of mineral working in a remote area

	£/ha
Value of land in existing use	1,000
Value of land with permission to work minerals	60,000
Cost of back-to-contour restoration (using overburden)	6,000
Cost of reclamation as a nature reserve (with seeding and planting only)	2,000
Value of land after restoration	300

Table 6.2 The economics of mineral working in agricultural areas

	£/ha
Value of land in existing use	6,000
Value of land with permission to work minerals	60,000
Cost of restorating land to agricultural use	10,000
Value of land in agricultural after-use	5,000

Table 6.3 The economics of mineral working near towns

	£/ha
Pre-quarrying land values	
Agricultural land	6,000
Mineral land	60,000
Industrial/residential land	600,000
Reclamation costs	
Seeding and planting of banks	3,000
Back-to-contour restoration (with purchased rubble)	45,000
Reclamation profits	
Hygienic landfill (with domestic refuse)	3,000
Value of land in after-use	
Passive recreation (on unfilled land)	100
Forestry or rough grazing (on landfill)	500
Agricultural land (on rubble)	5,000
Private water sports and angling (on water areas)	10,000
Industrial/residential land	600,000

the hectare of land in question could be used for agriculture, mineral extraction or industrial or residential use, and that it will be partly below the water table after the mineral has been removed. The figures show that different after-uses can have very different financial consequences for mineral companies. In the example an industrial or residential after-use is much the most profitable option for the company. This is followed by the water-sports option. In the London area it has been the case for many years that the rental for sailing and water-skiing is "considerably more than the normal rental for agricultural land" (Jones 1975: x). Hygienic landfill can also yield a profit for the company, although filled land has little after-use value because of problems with subsidence, methane generation (unless this can be sold) and leachate disposal. Passive recreation and nature conservation will not produce a profit for the company, although the costs of preparing the land may be attractively low. Agriculture is normally the least desirable after-use from a short-term financial viewpoint: it requires a high level of expenditure, which cannot normally be recouped from the after-use value of the land.

A 1976 British report on *Planning control over mineral working* took the view that it was entirely reasonable to insist that a company should "restore" the land to its former use but that it would be unreasonable to require expenditure on preparing the land for any other after-use (Stevens Report 1976: 104). This latter expenditure was described as "special treatment for redevelopment". The restoration alternative provides a useful benchmark for the level of expenditure that might be required – but there is no reason why a company should avoid the expenditure when permission is given for a less costly, or more profitable, after-use. If, for example, a quarry is to have a low-cost recreational after-use, it is fair that the company should pay for footpaths, planting and car parking. If, on the other hand, it is developed as a high-profit industrial estate, then the money which would otherwise have been spent on restoration work could be spent on screening, recreation or wildlife conservation.

There is, in principle, no doubt that the proper source of reclamation funds is the mineral operation which created the dereliction, not the after-use, so that external costs are internalized, on the economic principle that the polluter pays (Samuelson 1973: 810). This is an equitable way of apportioning costs, and an efficient way of getting the work done. Excavating plant is often idle during a mineral operation and can be used to prepare for an after-use as part of the mining cycle. Reclamation designs can be tailored to the capabilities of the machines that will be used. In the case of abandoned mines and orphan quarries that were worked before the age of mineral planning, then finance must come from elsewhere: from charity, from public funds, as happens with Britain's derelict coal mines, or from a levy on future workings, as with the USA's derelict strip mines. The last policy can be justified if the consumers who gained from the artificially low price of coal in earlier years approximate to those who consume the output from current mines.

But what should happen to the land itself? Public acquisition should be a "planning gain" providing compensation for any adverse side-effects the public has endured during the operational life of the quarry (Ratcliffe 1976: 86). This happens in Holland:

> Despite the fact that the gravel companies have to hand over the exhausted quarries to the provincial government without payment, the eagerness of several parties to buy and develop this "derelict" or "idle land" clearly demonstrates its intrinsic economic value (Moolen 1996).

Conclusion

With good landscape planning, a better and cheaper after-use can be achieved.

The fundamental principle underlying landscape planning for the minerals industry may be stated as follows. Permission to win and work minerals should not be given unless it can be demonstrated beyond reasonable doubt that, for the community, the post-mining landscape will be at least as useful and/or at least as beautiful as the pre-mining landscape. In order to satisfy this principle, the following measures may be necessary:

- Mining equipment should be used to shape the land for a range of possible after-uses.
- A healthy ecosystem should be established on the land.
- Arrangements should be made for the land to pass into public ownership when mineral operations have ceased and the land has been returned to health.
- The community should decide the after-use and reap the profit.

In some cases it will be appropriate to re-establish the former land-use and conceal the fact that mining has occurred. But, as a US mining engineer argues, ". . . it seldom is economically or physically desirable to restore land exactly to its pre-mining condition" (Cummins 1973: Section 19-3). Everything depends on the location of the mine, on its physical characteristics and on the range of possible after-uses. For fluorspar workings in the Peak District National Park the planning authority aims "to recreate what was there before", but for limestone workings the aim, "is one of creating a new landscape" (Caisley 1980). The latter requires close attention to the aesthetic aspect of quarry design.

Aesthetic issues should never be underestimated: the author of a book on "possibly the longest, most expensive, and most complex environmental dispute in history" believes that

> the Reserve Mining controversy had its genesis in objections to the aesthetic impact of Reserve's operations on the Lake Superior environment, yet few environmentalists were willing to rely primarily on aesthetic arguments in their case against Reserve. (Bartlett 1980: 219)

Since the environmentalists won, chief executive officers should have this observation written into their diaries.

Landscape planners, when working on EID for the minerals industry, have three main roles: first, to advise on which approach to the landscape of industry is most appropriate for each aspect of an operation; second, to be involved in the detailed operation of the mineral workings; third, to plan an after-use for the land. Every author to have investigated the problem has reached the conclusion that a better and cheaper after-use can be achieved if adequate preparations are made during the working life of the mineral operation – however long they may be. It is now common for short-life mineral operations to be pre-planned, although surprisingly few examples are good enough to serve as patterns for future projects. Even fewer medium- and long-life mines and quarries have been successfully reclaimed but the same principle applies. Environmental standards are rising and it is important to phase longer-term operations so that reclamation plans can be revised as circumstances change.

CHAPTER 7
Agriculture

A feast of follies.

Aghast at the absurdities of agricultural policy, I did not include a chapter on the landscape of agriculture in the first edition of this book. Since then (1986) the situation in Europe has worsened, through the introduction of set-aside policies. But there is more debate about reform, and I have sought to apply the principles outlined in Part 1 of this book to the question of landscape planning in rural areas (Fig. 7.1). It may help to think of the task as country planning, rather than as agricultural planning.

Let us begin with the absurdities. After the peace of 1815, British agriculture was protected only for 30 years, until 1846, by the Corn Laws. Fifty years after the peace of 1945, European agriculture continues to be heavily subsidized by town-dwellers. This has mostly led to disbenefits for non-farmers, such as industrialized food and a loss of wildlife habitats. Europe's Common Agricultural Policy became famous for its butter mountains, grain storage silos, wine lakes, BSE and meat stores. After 1992, the storage problem was reduced by equally expensive supply controls. They drive land prices up and food quality down.

In less intensively farmed areas, such as Britain's uplands, subsidies are available either for planting trees on land where they would grow naturally or for keeping sheep which prevent natural regeneration. In the lowlands, subsidies are offered either for intensive farming, which destroys wildlife, or for making nature reserves, which promote wildlife. Towns have more bird species than agricultural land. The set-aside policy, which pays farmers for doing nothing, gives most cash to the great landowners, possibly because they have the most experience of leisure pursuits. Set-aside payments encourage rich farmers to sack poor farmworkers. There would be more sense in subsidizing bureaucrats to write ponderous memos to coal-miners instructing them to excavate coal, stack it in neat piles and wait six weeks before putting it back. Unwanted milk used to be poured into coal-mines, where it polluted water supplies. Under Europe's Common Agricultural Policy, it is given to underdeveloped countries in order to enrich the

Figure 7.1 The South Downs in 1935 and 1995. The area has been preserved by agricultural and planning policies. Without them, the hills would have become woodland and the fields would have become housing estates. Scenic policy should have protected the skyline from electricity pylons.

governing elite, bankrupt local farmers and increase susceptibility to coronary heart disease. The Policy is as stupid as it is wicked.

In the USA there are similar absurdities:

> Conventional agriculture in the United States includes capital-intensive monocultures; continuous cropping; a substantial reliance on manufactured inputs such as fertilizer, pesticides, and machinery; as well as an extensive dependence on credit and government subsidies . . . In addition, soils have become compacted and lost fertility; ground-water has been depleted and polluted with pesticides and fertilizers; wildlife habitats have been lost or damaged due to chemical runoff; and forests, range, and wetlands have been converted to croplands. (Neher 1992)

In the 1960s, it was suggested that British farmers could be subsidized, in part, to maintain the countryside in good condition for the public. This would have included the care of farm walls, hedgerows and ancient grasslands (Fig. 7.2). Their reaction was haughty: "We are farmers – not park-keepers." In the 1990s many farmers were begging to be employed as park-keepers, although not in so many words. Here is a typical comment, from the BBC farming programme on 12 December 1995, about farming on

Figure 7.2 Farmers receive large sums of money for uneconomic food production, but not for repairing their beautiful old farm walls.

Britain's sheep-grazed uplands. "Without farming in the hills we are not going to have the landscape which the public wants. The public must be willing to invest to keep this type of landscape." "The hills" is a romantic name for Britain's great tracts of barren over-grazed peaty moorland with signs reading "Trespassers will be prosecuted and dogs shot." It is odd that the speaker should have used the word "invest" to justify public expenditure on environmental degradation. It means "clothe" in the College of Heralds, "lay siege to" on the field of battle, and "employ money for profit" on Wall Street. In connection with upland farming, the quoted speaker was evidently using "invest" to mean "pour money into drains". He was asking for investment in a type of landscape few want. Public expenditure should be on public goods. Ecological, scenic and recreational assessments and plans are requisite.

The landscape planning principles which will be considered in relation to agriculture may be summarized as follows:

1 Landscapes should be planned from different points of view. These will include those of landowners and different sections of the public, as discussed in Chapter 1.
2 Public landscape planning should focus on public goods, especially recreation, scenic quality and nature conservation, as discussed in Chapter 2.
3 Plans must be adjusted to contexts. This may require zoning plans and EID plans, as discussed in Chapter 3.

Governments have often supported farmers, for strategic, social and political reasons. Since the 1930s, which saw a great agricultural depression, they have also considered support for environmental reasons. The USA led the way. Measures were introduced, as part of Roosevelt's New Deal, to ensure that land subject to severe erosion was not used for agriculture. Although named conservation programmes, "their main objectives were production control and income redistribution for the agricultural population" (Swader 1980). In the 1960s, the USA introduced a programme for withdrawing land from agriculture in order to limit production. A similar programme, known as set-aside, was adopted by the European Community in 1988. As in the USA, it led to less intensive use of some land and more intensive use of other land. One can hardly view this as a conservation measure.

Britain's Wildlife and Countryside Act of 1981 included some "environment friendly" provisions. Farmers who declined a grant to plough up moorland, for example, could obtain financial compensation from the Nature Conservancy Council. This was an odd measure. Should I be paid for not writing books? More positive legislation followed, encouraged by the EU's Environmentally Sensitive Areas (1985) programme. ESAs allow farmers in designated areas to receive an annual payment if they follow beneficial farming practices. In Britain this led to the Farm Woodland Scheme (1988), the Farm and Conservation Grant Scheme (1989) and the Nitrate Sensitive Areas Programme (1990). These programmes allow payments both for positive actions, such as planting woodlands or maintaining stone walls, or for negative actions, such as restricting the use of nitrate fertilizers.

From a public goods perspective, all these programmes are of questionable value. If government payments lead to environmental harm, discontinuing the grants would make more sense than offering compensation for not accepting them. Paying farmers not to use nitrates is like paying smokers not to smoke in public: if the practice is harmful to others, it should be restricted by law. Grants for small woodlands, hedgerows and farm walls seem a better idea, but much depends on contextual circumstances, and there is a need for large-scale plans to precede small-scale decisions.

The agricultural landscape of the late-twentieth century is not a thing which should be eternally "conserved". Some areas undoubtedly are scenically beautiful, rich in wildlife and of great recreational value. They should be protected from agricultural development grants and supported with conservation grants. Other areas are deficient, scenically, recreationally or in wildlife. Here, public funds should be used to remedy deficiencies, where this can be done without damaging existing public goods.

The social, political and economic aspects of agricultural policy will not be discussed in this chapter, except peripherally. These include the historic power of farmers as an organized pressure group, the equity of transferring wealth from poor urbanites to rich farmers, the desirability of maintaining a rural population, the influence of tele-commuting on the demand for rural property, the nutritional value of intensively vs. extensively farmed food, the merits of free trade, international specialization and competitiveness. In the main, this chapter is concerned with the public goods that might be obtained by spending public money in rural areas.

Public goods

All-public and all-private are equally bad.

Agriculture is the predominant human use of the Earth's land surface. It always has been and, one assumes, it always will be. Primitive agriculture may have operated without community involvement. Organized agriculture, to be efficient, requires good access roads, irrigation systems, drainage channels and protective measures against floods and infectious diseases. These are best obtained from a mixture of public and private endeavour. The difficulty is in deciding what is best achieved by public action and what should be left to markets. The 1930s remind us that either an all-public system, such as that used in the Soviet Empire, or an all-private system, such as that used in the USA, can be disastrous. The Soviet system resulted in starvation in the 1930s, while the American system was causing near-starvation and the dust bowl. A mixed economy has significant advantages for both public goods and agricultural goods.

Rivers and roads are useful examples of rural public goods. Both are linear features which confer benefits on the public; both can be privately owned. The distinction is that roads are man-made and rivers are works of nature. Human labour may command a wage, paid from the public purse. Natural assets may command a rent, paid from the public purse. Rural land has characteristics which are part man-made and part natural. Other examples of public goods will be discussed below: a strategic capacity to produce extra food in times of crisis; wildlife conservation; water conservation; scenic conservation; historic conservation; outdoor recreation; a supply of non-farmed food. Two points should be borne in mind:

- In 1995, the European Union spent £95 billion on agricultural support (*Farmers Weekly* 1995).
- The citizens of Europe should demand maximum public benefit from public expenditure on agriculture.

Food production should not be a single-minded, exclusive land-use. Imaginative EID can enable food to be produced in concert with other objectives and other land-uses (Fig. 7.3).

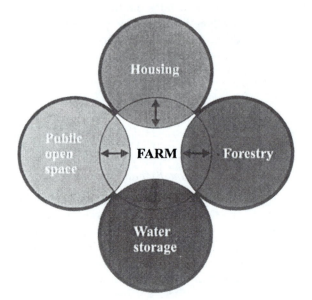

Figure 7.3 Food production can take place with other land-uses.

Strategic reserve

The history of agriculture is characterized by alternating periods of shortage and surplus.

There is a time dimension to the planning of agricultural landscapes, and priorities change. After a war, it is right to turn swords into ploughshares. If food then becomes plentiful, it may be right to turn ploughshares into golf clubs, leisure vehicles, binoculars and fishing tackle. The second half of the twentieth century has been a period of agricultural surplus in the developed world, but we should never forget the historical tendency for "seven fat years" to be followed by "seven lean years". Most of us keep a fire extinguisher, a stock of candles, some spare cash and other insurances against disaster. Likewise, it is normal for wealthy countries to keep an army, stocks of medical supplies, timber and food, in case of war or other disaster. We all feel more secure when such supplies are in existence. They are public goods. In the case of an insurance capacity to produce food, there is no reason why the strategic reserve should be financed by farmers. It is a public good which should be supplied from the public purse. But how?

High-quality agricultural land can be protected against building development, by planning or zoning controls. This needs to be done at national, regional and local levels. The switch from unbuilt land to built land is almost irreversible. Golf courses, community forests and nature reserves, however, can be planned with a view to future reclamation to agriculture (Fig. 7.4). Agricultural landowners need not be compensated for loss of development rights, because other landowners do not receive compensation in similar circumstances. But farmers should be rewarded for such positive acts as maintaining land drains and agricultural equipment. There is a time-scale for bringing land back into production. In one year grassland can be converted to arable. Over a ten-year period, woodland can be cleared, farms built, people trained, drains laid, machinery acquired.

Water conservation

The countryside can play a major role in conserving fresh water.

Fresh water is one of the planet's scarcest resources. Only 0.2 per cent of the earth's water is fresh and of easy access. In arid regions, fresh water is being "quarried", in the sense that underground reservoirs are being drawn down faster than they are being replenished. Agricultural practices can make an

Figure 7.4 The golf course in the foreground could revert to agriculture. The town of Bad Ragaz could not. (Courtesy of Swiss Tourist Office.)

immense contribution to water conservation. The following practices may impose costs on farmers, but will supply the public with a benefit.

Aquifer recharge Since Roman times, European agriculturalists have aimed to "improve drainage" by getting rainwater off the ground and into the sea as swiftly as possible. This is because crops do not flourish when their roots are waterlogged. The process of land drainage must now be reversed, although always with the aim of mitigating adverse effects on agriculture. Where conditions are favourable (e.g. where a permeable soil lies over a porous rock) special measures should be taken to assist surface water infiltration. This will help to maintain river flows.

Farm ponds A great number of new farm ponds are required. Traditionally, farm ponds have been used for fishing, ducks and irrigation water. These uses can continue, but the new generation of ponds will have a special role in the detention and infiltration of surface water runoff.

Riparian land Land on the edge of rivers is especially valuable for the detention and infiltration of floodwater. This land should be allowed to flood and the water kept on the land, rather in the manner of traditional watermeadows.

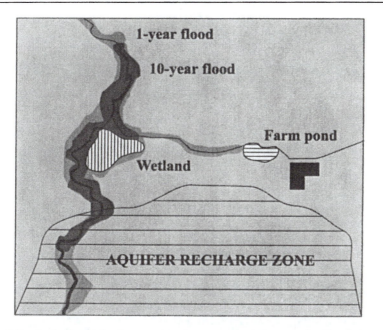

Figure 7.5 Agricultural land can assist in water management, by flood detention and infiltration.

When the above measures have been investigated, a water conservation plan for agricultural land should be prepared (Fig. 7.5). Farmers can be paid to harvest water, as they are to harvest crops.

Habitat creation and conservation

The agricultural landscape should provide a diverse range of habitats for wild plants and animals.

We dream of a countryside rich in wild flowers and wild animals, so much more delightful than the urban desert or concrete jungle (Fig. 7.6). But today's agri-business farms have a narrower range of plant and animal species than a normal town. Pesticides kill insects. Birds have little to eat. Land drainage and water pollution spoil ditches. Frogs, foxes, magpies and hedgehogs are more numerous in suburban gardens than in the countryside. This is not in the public interest. The action which should be taken includes the *conservation* of existing habitats, the *creation* of new habitats and the *interlinking* of habitats to form networks.

225

THE GOLDEN GRAIN.

Figure 7.6 We dream of a countryside rich in wild flowers and animals.

The conservation of existing habitats can be done only when surveys have been carried out. This will require a field survey, a historical investigation and discussions with local naturalists. The creation and enhancement of habitats can often follow on from the water conservation measures discussed in the preceding section. Farm ponds, riparian land and marginal land are well suited to become wildlife habitats. Farmers can be paid a wage for carrying out the capital works and maintenance operations proposed in the habitat creation plan. Public agencies can either purchase the land on which the works are carried out or pay a rent to use the land to obtain public goods.

Historic conservation

Farmland is the result of untold centuries of work.

History used to be conceived as tales of kings, armies and churches. It was studied from documentary records and from old buildings. Increasingly, it is recognized that everything has a history. New methods of investigation are being developed, and historians are diversifying their effort. As a source material for this wide sphere of investigation, the countryside has no rival. It is a vast repository of information about the use of the Earth's surface by man and other animals. But the repository is being destroyed. Oliver Rackham writes that: "The landscape is like a historic library of 50,000 books. Many were written in remote antiquity . . . every year 50 volumes are unavoidably eaten by bookworms . . . a thousand are sold for the value of the parchment . . ." (Rackham 1990: 29). Abercrombie said that "the country is . . . the richest, the most vivid piece of history that we possess" (Abercrombie 1934).

The deliberate destruction of books by a society is a sign of great evil to come. Ignorant destruction is a lesser evil, but still serious. The first step towards protection, as in a library, is to make a catalogue. Historic landscapes must be surveyed. Most countries have catalogued their ancient monuments. The survey process must be extended to hedgerows and walls, cottages and fields, roads and tracks, bridges, woods and forests, banks and dykes, meadows, pastures, pits and ponds. New techniques are available, including air photography, remote sensing and pollen analysis. An army of unpaid amateur surveyors is coming forward to help with the work. Farmers know a great deal about their own land. Much information on industrial archaeology has already been collected. There is a need for general surveys, as part of a full mapping exercise, and for detailed surveys, which are carried out as part of special projects. It will not be possible or desirable to preserve every historic feature, but it is very desirable to have records of any features that are disappearing (Figs 7.7, 7.8).

Scenic conservation and enhancement

The farming landscape should be conserved and improved.

Rural scenery is a resource that is highly valued by urban dwellers. It is normally enjoyed as a public good. The money spent on travel and accommodation does not go to those who own and maintain rural land. Farmers profit only if they run hotels, farm shops, car parks or other facilities

Figure 7.7 This sycamore marks the site of an ancient farmstead. But there are no records, and I may be the only person who is aware of the fact. When the tree goes it is unlikely to be replaced. This photograph should be placed in a library and referenced in a geographical information system.

Figure 7.8 The sheepfold is maintained because it is still used. Were it to fall into disuse, it should be preserved as a historic feature.

(Fig. 7.9). Although people will pay much higher prices for rooms with beautiful, extensive and dramatic views, it does not follow that owners of beautiful and dramatic land should receive public funds, any more than owners of fine buildings have a right to money from passers-by. The distinction between a wage and a rent helps to clarify the position. Farmers deserve a wage for any works they implement on behalf of the public, but they do not have a right to a rent for the public goods they supply.

Farmers think and speak as though every square metre of farmland were equally beautiful. This is not so (Fig. 7.10). Some farms are very beautiful; others are very dull. But scenic beauty is hard to quantify and much depends on location. A woodland in a large city, or on a bare hill (Fig. 7.11), will make an immensely greater contribution to the scenery than the same number of trees in the middle of a forest. Fifty hectares of flat grass can be judged very boring in a city but very beautiful on the floor of a mountain valley. Fifty hectares of peat bog may be beautiful on the shoulder of a mountain, dull when surrounded by 50 square kilometres of similar bog.

The scenic character of agricultural land can change because of a change in farming practice, because the land is put to another use (e.g. a golf course)

Figure 7.9 The car parking levy rewards the farmer for owning a public good. Visitors also pay, through agricultural subsidies and conservation payments, to maintain the landscape.

Figure 7.10 This is agricultural land, but it is not beautiful.

or because the public pay money to improve the scenery. If money is to be made available for the protection or improvement of scenic quality, then a scenic quality assessment should be made, as discussed in Chapter 2. This procedure may be compared to the assessments of an old building that are made from time to time. Building managers tend to improve the worst areas and to leave the best alone. Countryside managers should do likewise.

When a decision has been made to improve the scenic quality of agricultural land, there are several environmental impact design alternatives:

Identity Take action to retain the existing character of the land, by protecting existing vegetation and existing structures (farm walls etc.). This policy is appropriate in areas of high scenic quality.

Similarity Respond to the genius of the existing place, but take steps to enhance the scenic quality. This policy is appropriate in areas where the existing scenic quality is good but not outstanding.

Difference Impose a new aesthetic concept on the existing agricultural landscape. This policy is appropriate when the existing scenic quality is low.

Restoration It may be desirable to restore the land to a previous condition.

Figure 7.11   Alston Moor: scarcity enhances the scenic importance of a small wood.

At the local scale, one can differentiate areas of low, medium or high scenic quality. But an area judged high-quality locally, may be judged low or medium on a national scale. In terms of priorities for improvement, the area would have a low national priority, because it does not attract many tourists.

Context theory, as discussed in Chapter 3, applies as much to rural areas as to urban areas. If change is to take place on agricultural land, the SID index needs to be considered: will the post-development land be similar to, identical with or different from the pre-development land? What Abercrombie called the "local materials solution" is sometimes correct:

> It argues that only old sorts of materials and old methods of building should be used, so that nothing new may appear: at its worst it would go to the length of faking an old appearance and it has given scope to the caricaturist to show Petrol Pumps masked as stumps of old oak trees. (Abercrombie 1934)

Contextual decisions will depend, to a degree, on the existing quality of the land. If the scenic quality is high, there is a good case for resisting change. If it is low, there is a prima-facie case for effecting change. This is similar to the policy many of us follow after moving to a new house: the worst rooms are decorated first.

Conservation farming

Historic farmland can produce high-value "hand-made" food.

Methods that agricultural technologists regard as out-of-date are often the only methods which can conserve the farming landscape. There is a lesson to be learned from the sea, where modern industrial fishing is destroying the world's stock of wild fish. In Chesapeake Bay there is a law which requires oyster-dredging boats to be powered by sail (Safina 1995). They are beautiful, quiet, non-polluting and very good for job creation. The principle can be applied to agriculture. Subsidies could be given to farmers on condition that they maintain farm walls and use traditional farming methods. Simon Jenkins describes a conservative farm in Derbyshire:

> The meadows have never been deep ploughed. Windblown copses shelter a grateful population of voles and sparrows. Farm buildings date from 1700. When the Vesseys arrived to preserve all this in 1960, the soil had not been scarred by a single tractor . . . This is farming with a conscience, farming to make you feel good. (Jenkins 1995)

Jenkins sees this as "a farm of the future . . . a symbol of the New Agriculture". Such farms are likely to produce food with a significantly higher market value than that of industrial food. In Europe, this food comes from low-intensity farming systems: the Alpine pastures of Northern Italy, the grazing marshes on the Atlantic coast, the hay meadows of the Yorkshire Dales, the dryland wood pastures of western Spain (Baldock 1994). Common Agricultural Policy money should be available for agricultural conservation, not intensification.

Recreation

There is a great demand for rural recreation, for which the public is willing to pay.

Western civilization has lived with the dream of rural happiness since ancient times (see Fig. 1.4). Perhaps it is rooted in memories of a time when man lived closer to nature. Horace and Virgil took the idea of "rural retirement" from the Greek poets and passed it on to Renaissance poets and to ourselves. Philosophers, artists, politicians, soldiers, captains of industry, all dream of rural peace and tranquillity. Middle- and upper-income people with the means to pay for it seek to spend their weekends, vacations and retirement years in the countryside. As societies become richer and transport becomes cheaper, the demand for rural recreation grows and will grow. People want beautiful scenery, as discussed above, but they also want physical access to the countryside. Access is a public good. Its supply can be diminished or increased. Historically, it has diminished.

Under the feudal system, land belonged to kings or lords, but individuals had rights of access, grazing, food and fuel gathering over large tracts. These rights were progressively eroded during the agricultural revolution. Common lands were enclosed and "democratic" parliaments, in which only landowners were represented, voted to increase landowners' rights and decrease other common rights. There is every reason for the more democratic parliaments of modern times to reverse the process. In Britain, this has been happening since the 1947 National Parks and Access to the Countryside Act. The process has been slow, because it is seen as a recreational policy, instead of as a policy of diversifying the output from farms to embrace agricultural and non-agricultural goods.

It used to be assumed that people visited public parks for either formal or informal recreation. The former meant organized games. The latter meant walking and sitting. Comparable oversimplifications were applied to countryside recreation. It is assumed that people wish either to walk or to visit attractions, such as museums, castles, picnic sites and golf clubs. In fact, most things can take place in the countryside: sleeping, running, food gathering, courting, digging, planting, car washing, painting, watching wildlife and catching butterflies. Some of them require plans.

Walking is a good example of an activity that needs to be planned. Britain is fortunate to have a network of public footpaths but unfortunate that the network came into existence for a society wholly unlike our own. The footpath routes led from farmsteads to hamlets which have gone out of existence, to churches which are no longer used, to markets which no longer take place. There is no need for the historic rights of way to be extinguished. But there is a great need to plan new routes to serve the needs of our own time (Fig. 7.12). The new network of countryways should run from origins to destinations along lines of opportunity. Routes along hilltops and valleys are very suitable. Links between roads and beaches are very important. The provision of a walkway network, as a public good, need have little effect on the production of private goods from what would remain privately owned land. But rights of access may need to be purchased, and farmers should be rewarded for any work they do to maintain footpaths, gates and stiles.

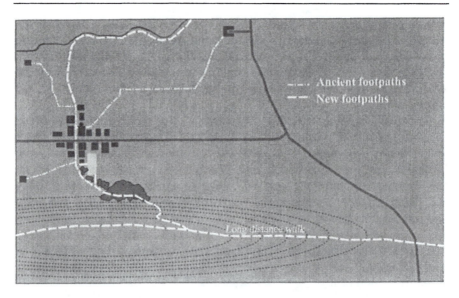

Figure 7.12   New footpaths should be planned, to serve the needs of our own time.

Fallowing

In times of glut, it should be done for non-agricultural reasons.

That land benefits from being fallowed was one of the great discoveries of the eighteenth-century agricultural revolution. This background influenced the adoption of state-funded fallowing policies to deal with the surplus of agricultural produce in the developed countries in the second half of the twentieth century. The policy is described as set-aside in Britain, "land diversion" in the USA and "fallowing" in other countries. British farmers are invited to set aside a proportion of their land for a period of time. Payments are made for *not* farming the land. The set-aside field becomes a source of weeds, while the intensity of production is raised on the remainder of the farm. If the land is fallowed for at least five years, it is described as a non-rotational set-aside and may yield some benefit to wildlife (Firbank 1993).

Because of their history, fallowing policies are applied at the farm level. But there are alternatives (Fig. 7.13). Since fallowing was originally intended to raise agricultural output, it can hardly be the correct policy for countries which now seek to reduce agricultural output. Instead, fallowing should be done, for non-food objectives, at the scale of a watershed, a region, a country or a continent. One could set aside land on the urban fringe, land in

234

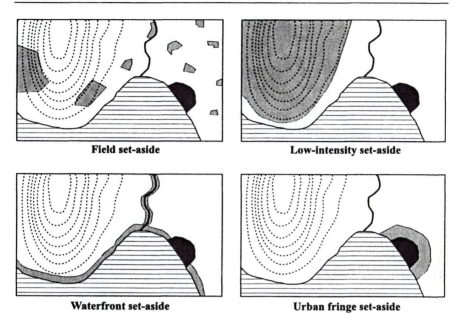

Figure 7.13 In choosing which land to fallow, or set-aside, there are a number of policy alternatives.

stream valleys, low-intensity farming land, greenway land, nature conservation land, forest land, recreation land, coastal land. On the urban fringe, the money being squandered on fallowing could be used to create a wonderful footpath and greenway network. The money would still go to farmers, for strategic or social reasons, but the public would gain something in return. If the only aim is output-reduction, resort could be made to the LRP, the LLS and the UDA: a late riser premium, starting with a payment to those who stay in bed until 9 a.m. and rising to a maximum for those who undertake to lie in until 1 p.m. seven days a week; a liquid lunch supplement, for those who consume three litres of beer at lunchtime; and a useless dog allowance, for those who exchange a sheep dog for a chihuahua (*Farming Programme* 1990).

Wild food

Increasing the production of unfarmed food should become an objective in countryside planning.

Country planners have paid insufficient attention to the variety and quality of food. They have tended to see country planning as a quest for land-use diversification, largely to include recreation and nature conservation on the list of planning objectives. Yet the capacity of rural areas to produce food also needs to be diversified. Fabos remembers how diversification saved his family during the Second World War (Fabos 1985). Here are three arguments in favour of developing wild food production.

First, it is desirable to have a strategic reserve of food which is independent of organized agriculture. Europe rediscovered the value of such a reserve three times in the twentieth century: during the First and Second World Wars and during the break-up of the communist dictatorships in the 1990s. These events are a warning that rich states cannot assume they are safe from famine. Even in peacetime, there are many people who obtain insufficient income from social security and charity and would benefit from a supply of wild food.

Second, wild food has great nutritional value. This point has been made forcefully by Michael Crawford (Crawford & Marsh 1989: 150). He argues that the amazing development of the human brain was coincident with man's ascent to the top of the food chain. Obtaining a wide range of complicated vitamins and proteins made it possible for body and brain to become highly sophisticated. Modern industrial farming is hindering the process by using a more limited range of inputs. Rackham comments that Alpine farmers used to regard hay containing less than a dozen plant species as "unfit for bovine consumption" (Rackham 1990: 340). Diets need to be supplemented with wild foods.

Third, there is great pleasure to be had from collecting what Richard Mabey described as food for free. He gives the reasons for seeking it out as "interest, experience, and even, on a small scale, adventure" (Mabey 1972: 4). It satisfies the "gatherer" strain in man's evolutionary history, just as hunting, physical danger and competitive sports satisfy the "hunter" strain. The range of wild foods is great. Personally, I collect wild strawberries, raspberries, blackberries, mushrooms, nuts and herbs. Supplies of wild food can be greatly enhanced by public action:

- the purchase and planting of small areas of land;
- planting and management grants for privately owned land;
- planting on land already in public ownership (road verges, river banks, public parks);
- research into new management techniques (e.g. for encouraging the growth of wild fungi).

Autumn may become the most popular season of the year for visiting the countryside once stocks of wild food have been restored. In addition to its nutritional merits, wild food carries more social prestige than agricultural crops.

Healthy food

Producing low-quality food produces a low-quality landscape.

Crawford argues that if grazing animals are prevented from eating the dark green leaves of woody plants they will suffer from coronary heart disease, as will humans who eat their flesh (Crawford & Marsh 1989: 223). The BSE (bovine spongiform encephalopathy) scare would not have happened if European producers had concentrated on high-quality food produced by traditional methods. Rich countries should focus their economies on the production of high-value goods. The British-owned sector of the UK car industry died, and the steel-industry nearly died, as a result of aiming to be a volume producer instead of a quality producer.

The geography of public goods

There is a geographical variation in the range of public goods that can and should be obtained from the countryside.

Some land is suited to olives, some to wheat, some to pawpaws, some to cabbages. It is the same with public goods: different regions are geographically suited to the provision of different goods (Fig. 7.14). Yet the existence of a market for public goods depends as much on demand as on supply. Demand is likely to be greatest near population centres and in areas of outstanding scenic quality, such as coasts and mountains. The geography of public goods can be considered at various scales: a farm, a nation state, a continent.

A mixed farm in England (Fig. 7.15) will have a range of farmland types:

Category A   Deep and well-drained land ploughed for arable crops.

Category B   Thinner and stonier soils used for grazing.

Category C   Steeper banks left for woodland and wild animals, some of which are hunted for game.

As the prosperity of farming rises and falls, the proportions of land placed in the three categories will rise and fall for private financial reasons. If a communal agency seeks to purchase public goods from a farmer, then the category of land employed for the purpose will depend on the type of good. Category A land can provide a strategic reserve for food production. Category B land may be important for scenic conservation, and Category C land for nature conservation.

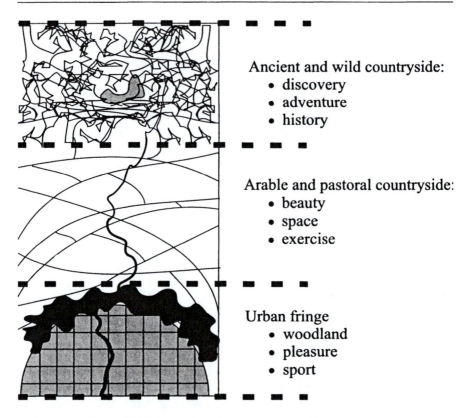

Ancient and wild countryside:
- discovery
- adventure
- history

Arable and pastoral countryside:
- beauty
- space
- exercise

Urban fringe
- woodland
- pleasure
- sport

Figure 7.14 Different types of countryside can supply different types of public good.

Comparable policies can be applied at the scale of a nation-state. There is a marked difference between ancient countryside and planned countryside. Ancient countryside is characterized by mixed hedge species, ancient trees, sunken roads and antiquities (Fig. 7.16). It tends to have a pattern of hamlets and towns. Planned countryside in Britain is "in the main, a mass-produced, drawing-board landscape, hurriedly laid out parish by parish under Enclosure Acts in the eighteenth and nineteenth centuries" (Rackham 1990: 5). It would be possible to use planned countryside as a production zone and ancient countryside as a conservation/recreation zone. Intermediate land could be used as a strategic reserve.

Policies of this type could also be applied to Europe, which has a Common Agricultural Policy (CAP). Three categories of land are shown on the map (Fig. 7.17).

Category A land is an openfield, or former openfield, landscape, well suited to providing a strategic reserve for food production. Its use-intensity can be

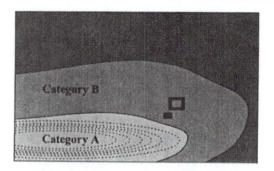

Figure 7.15 Land can be categorized at the farm scale.

Figure 7.16 Ancient countryside is characterized by small fields, walls, hedges, sunken roads and scattered hamlets, as by the Rhine.

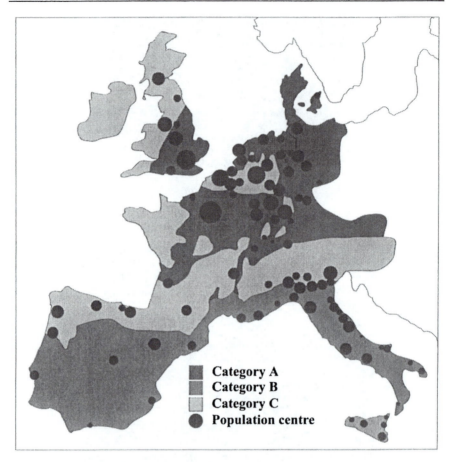

Figure 7.17 Land can be categorized at the European scale.

lowered for decades and raised when required. Public finance should be used to protect productive land from urbanization and afforestation.

Category B land is a predominantly enclosed landscape with stone walls, ancient pastures, field trees, shepherds' huts and other structures of historic interest. Public finance should be used to support the agricultural practices that maintain these features.

Category C land is a Mediterranean openfield landscape with tree crops and horticultural production. Public finance should be used for scenic protection and to maintain a strategic horticultural capability.

At this scale of planning, the consequences of a simplistic policy become apparent. Some regions, and even countries, could cease to have any significant level of agricultural production. This consideration dissuaded Switzerland and Norway from joining the European Union. Other countries, such as France and Germany, would have large concentrations of people surrounded by intensively managed farmland. Decisions about the purchase of countryside public goods need to be taken at each level of decision-making. If a United Nations agency sees particular habitats, artefacts or agricultural practices as part of the world's heritage, it should give them financial support. European, national, regional, local and community bodies can follow the same principle. There is great advantage if different agencies view the problem from different vantage points. But they should all be careful about zoning; in both urban and rural areas, it tends to produce visual monotony and functional inefficiency. And there are innumerable problems of definition and classification. Simplistic zoning means society pays more and receives less.

Mapping

Rural land needs to be mapped in many ways.

Departments of agriculture, as distinct from farmers, have tended to focus on the single objective of agricultural production. So they only collect data related to this objective. In the USA, land capability maps are published by the Soil Conservation Service. Class I soils have few limitations for agriculture, and Class VII soils have severe limitations. One might use this classification to reach the conclusion that Class I soils should be farmed and Class VII soils should be available for non-agricultural uses, including urbanization. This is a crudely simplistic approach to land development. Land with high agricultural value will often have low scenic, recreational, wildlife and urbanization value.

Agricultural land should be mapped in different ways (Fig. 7.18), some of which are listed below:

- arable value
- grazing value
- tree crop value
- horticultural value
- accessibility value
- nature conservation value
- skiing value
- hunting value
- water-sports value
- picnic value

241

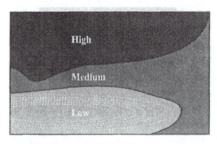

Soil quality

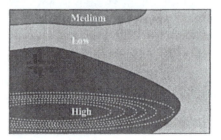

Recreation value

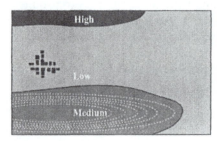

Wildlife value

Scenic quality

Figure 7.18 The countryside can be mapped in different ways.

- hiking value
- scenic value
- historic value
- aquifer recharge value
- flood storage value

Each type of value can be high, medium or low.

The maps can be used to discover where public goods are available, and to make plans. If an area of highly productive agricultural land is near a large town, it is unlikely that food production will be the most beneficial land-use. Money should also be spent to protect and increase the supply of non-agricultural public goods.

Implementation

The supply of public goods from agricultural land can be encouraged by zoning regulations, tax incentives, land reorganization, the acquisition of easements and land purchase.

The developed industrial countries, including the USA, Japan and the countries of Europe, have spent large amounts of money on agricultural support, partly to buy votes but also to secure a strategic capacity for food production. Some of the money has remained with farmers. Most of it has gone to the manufacturers of fertilizers, herbicides and farm machinery. All have become so accustomed to feather-bedding with government funds that they can conceive no other way. In 1957, the *New Statesman*'s "This England" column reported that:

> Sir James Turner gave an assurance that the Farmers' Union are not in principle opposed to the complex operation of turning over from controls to a free economy, but it will take some time to work out the best way of obtaining guaranteed markets and assured prices under the new system. (Hilton 1957: 59)

Farmers worked out a brilliant solution to the problem. In Europe it is known as the Common Agricultural Policy. But a time for change is upon agriculture once more. Underlying the discussion of this chapter is the belief that public funds spent on agriculture should be used to purchase specified public goods, according to the geographical nature of the land. Here are three examples:

Productive agricultural lowlands, remote from towns. Public funds can be used to maintain a strategic capacity for food production. Arable land should be fallowed and maintained by low-intensity grazing. Field drainage systems should be maintained. Farm machinery and farm workers may need to be kept in training, as an "agricultural militia".

Scenic and recreational areas, remote from towns. Public funds can be used for scenic protection and to acquire recreational access. Money can also be used to support the production of high-quality foods by non-industrial methods. The consumption of such products should be part of the recreational experience.

Urban fringe land. Whatever the existing land quality, there is likely to be a future demand for recreation, scenery, water conservation, wild food and firewood. In order to make these goods available, public money may have to be spent on car parks, footpaths, cycleways, bridleways, lakes and forests – "forest" is used in the traditional sense to mean an open area, such as Lüneburg Heath or the New Forest, with some woods, heath, scrub, grazing and open access for the local community and visitors.

The public goods described in these examples can be obtained through a variety of measures:

Payments can be made when there are specific tasks to be carried out, such as the construction of paths and bridges or repairs to farm walls and historic features.

Zoning regulations can be used to encourage one type of development or protect against another type of development. Zoning policies could be used on the urban fringe, to permit low-density residential or industrial development in exchange for the establishment of new forests.

Tax incentives can be used to encourage land-uses, such as tree planting, which produce benefits in the medium or long term.

The acquisition of easements is a good means of establishing new footpaths and cycleways. It is best if the purchase is made on the open market, but it may be necessary to use legal powers, as has always been done for roads, railways and other public utilities. Payment could be made at market prices plus 25 per cent.

Land reorganization The greatest opportunities for the creation of public goods arise with legislation for land reorganization. As in Holland, land can be taken into public ownership, replanned and returned to the private sector. This is an appropriate policy for the urban fringe, where development is taking place and agriculture is declining.

Land purchase by public bodies can be justified if it satisfies a public objective. Waterside land can contribute to nature conservation and recreation objectives. Land at the margin of agricultural profitability will often have a high nature conservation value. Scenic land may attract such large numbers of visitors that agriculture will tend to be unprofitable. New woods tend not to produce economic benefits in the lifetime of the people who carry out the planting. Land that has increased in value because of a public investment can pass through public ownership, to ensure that the rewards from the public expenditure accrue to the public. This should happen, for example, around a new railway station at the urban fringe.

Europe, as noted above, spent £95 billion on agricultural support in 1995. If 30 per cent of this money were invested in environmental public goods, the public would reap a stupendous harvest of benefits.

Conclusion

If public money is spent on agriculture, it should be to obtain specified public goods.

In developed economies, countryside policy needs to be reviewed. Too much money has been wasted on "agricultural support", with public disbenefits, including:

- mass-produced "industrial" food of low quality;
- the destruction of wildlife habitats;
- the loss of scenic quality;
- the loss of tree cover;
- the canalization of rivers.

Rural planning and policies should be revised to produce a range of public goods partly through the use of EID:

- a strategic reserve, for food production;
- greenways;
- high-quality "hand-made food" and wild food;
- the creation of new wildlife habitats;
- recreational opportunities;
- the enhancement of scenery;
- additional tree cover;
- the reclamation of rivers;
- the conservation of farm walls, buildings and other historic features.

These objectives can be achieved with a variety of measures, but only when he land has been mapped and evaluated. A series of overlapping policy plans can then be prepared.

Private ownership of land is a limited right. We may "own" a farm. In time of war, we may be asked to die for *our* country. Belloc wrote that "They died to save their country and they only saved the world." Nothing belongs to us for long. I have use of some air for some time. Water stays with me a little longer. My use of the earth's surface may be for three score years and ten. But all are borrowed and shared. Some land, and some easements, can be owned by the public. Public ownership should be diversified. Rights can belong to local and national governments, local and national trusts, churches and monasteries, charities, groups of local residents, groups with special recreational interests. It is a bad thing for too much land to belong to any one organization or type of organization.

CHAPTER 8

Forests

Introduction

With this, again, comes forestry: no mere tree-cropping, but silviculture, arboriculture too, and park-making at its greatest and best.
                                                    Patrick Geddes (1915: 95).

Woods and forests can be the most wonderful places: beautiful and productive, with sparkling streams, bright pools, dark swamps, open glades, black groves, broad moors and high mountains. They can have fresh seedlings, thrusting saplings, mature trees, ancient trees and rotting trees with fascinating fungi. Animal life should be a great part of the forest: insects, fish, birds, mice, squirrels, badgers, foxes and deer. They need a wide range of habitats with great plant diversity. Fungi transform dead wood into new soil.

In many cultures, forests are the locale of wonder tales (Fig. 8.1). A young man sets off from home, encounters first danger and then mysterious help in the forest, sleeps under a great tree, drinks from a pool, meets a wise old woman in a sunny clearing; she has magical powers, he undertakes acts of bravery, emerges from the forest, marries the king's daughter and lives happily ever after. Across cultures, the structural pattern of wonder tales is remarkably similar. The stories derive from man's past as a forest dweller and reflect a world view, in which life is seen as a pattern of good and evil, light and dark, hope and fear, effort and reward. They have not been forgotten, and many of us wish for more access to woods and forests. Those who clear-fell forests assault the human psyche:

> The global problem of deforestation provokes unlikely reactions of concern these days among city dwellers, not only because of the enormity of the scale but also because in the depths of cultural memory forests remain the correlate of human transcendence. We call it the loss of nature, or the loss of wildlife habitat, or the loss of biodiversity, but underlying the ecological concern is perhaps a much deeper apprehension about the disappearance of boundaries, without which the

Figure 8.1   Forests are the locale of wonder tales. Gustav Doré's "The stag viewing himself in the stream".

human abode loses its grounding . . . Without such outside domains, there is no inside in which to dwell. (Harrison 1992: 247)

Oliver Rackham explains the historic difference between a wood and a forest (Rackham, 1990: 65). A wood is a place where trees grow. A forest is a place where deer can roam, subject to Forest Law. The word forest comes from the language of jurisprudence (Harrison 1992: 69), and a jurist, writing in 1592 explained that:

A forest is a certain territory of woody grounds and fruitful pastures, privileged for wild beasts and fowls of forest, chase, and warren, to rest and abide there in the safe protection of the king . . . And there-fore a forest doth chiefly consist of these four things: of vert and venison; of particular laws and proper officers. (Manwood 1717: 143)

Britain's most famous forest dweller, Robin Hood, lived in Sherwood Forest and broke those forest laws which unduly favoured sheriffs, kings and nobles. Sherwood was not a wood at that time. Most of it was heath-land (Fig. 8.2). Had his merry men dressed in green, it would have been all too easy for the Sheriff of Nottingham to round them up. Wood production is an aspect of forestry, but forest management should never be reduced to wood production, rubber production, meat production or any other single type of production. Forestry should be a broadly based cultural activity conducted on an intergenerational timescale. Since mankind has the power to destroy forests, we must use laws to make and protect forests. This requires institutions with rights of control, or ownership, extending beyond the lifespan of individuals. In the middle ages, kings, great families and monasteries had this power. Today, it could belong to public com-panies, government agencies or non-profit organizations, providing only that their objectives are idealistic, functional and cultural.

Forestry should be conceived as a multi-objective cultural endeavour: no mere tree cropping, timber farming or biomass production. Science helps foresters, but scientific forestry is something of a contradiction: if a wood is

Figure 8.2 Sherwood "Forest" never had many trees, even in the days of Robin Hood, but it did have *ancient* trees.

managed on single-objective scientific principles, it will cease to be a forest. In human terms, it is like treating women as reproductive systems.

Forest clearance tends to accompany economic growth. It was rapid in Europe during the seventeenth and eighteenth centuries, in North America during the nineteenth century, and in the developing countries during the twentieth century. When clearance goes too far, timber supplies become short. Europe began making good the shortfall with imports from North America and Russia. The USA, Europe and Japan now obtain timber from tropical rain forests. When these forests have gone, there will be nowhere to turn. All countries will have to make better use of their own resources.

In Britain there have been reafforestation programmes since the seventeenth century. Some have concentrated on wood production, others have embraced wider objectives. When the government launched its own programme in 1919, the objectives were very narrow. Public protest stirred almost at once, and in the years since 1919 the Forestry Commission's horizons have been gradually prised open. But by 1995 the Commission was not half way to a full multi-objective policy. Between 1919 and 1970, it learned ways of relating plantation forestry to the surrounding landscape. This helped Britain's forest industry to evade the fierce criticism that swept other countries in the 1970s. The internal management of Britain's forests remains blinkered, and there is little functional integration with other land-uses.

The USA began the twentieth century with one-third of its land area in public ownership and a dazzlingly enlightened policy for the management of its public forests. Our modern sense of the word "conservation" to mean "wise use" was first applied in connection with forestry. Pinchot, who set the American Forest Service policy, had a better understanding of sustainability than most modern commentators. But this enlightened regime, known as the Stetson Hat period, came to an end after the Second World War. A Black Hat period followed, in which foresters became commodity-oriented tree farmers. The US public learned to equate foresters with "wood butchers" (Spurr 1976: 41). In 1993, an old-style forester complained to the American Forestry Society that his daughter, with a degree in environmental science, could produce a better forest plan than most trained foresters. Environmental protests led to new legislation.

The USA's Forest and Rangeland Renewable Resources Planning Act of 1974 and the National Forest Management Act of 1976 have made the industry take account of environmental concerns (Hewett & Hamilton 1982: 225). Other countries have faced similar problems. In 1980 an Australian forester lamented that "in most parts of the world foresters are a beleaguered species. Practically everything we do is wrong" (Chervasse 1980). Australia's Softwood Forestry Agreement Act of 1978 led to new controls (Wright 1980). In Sweden "recreational interests were taken into consideration in the Forest Act of 1976–7 despite strong opposition from groups connected with wood production" (Hewett & Hamilton 1982: 77). In the 1990s the critics' fire is concentrated on the tropical rain forests.

The obstacles which lie in the path of good forestry are as follows:

Forest clearance, especially of ancient woods, can yield a financial profit but has many adverse side-effects: soil erosion, nutrient loss, water pollution, landslides, flooding, reduced wildlife habitat, loss of recreational value, loss of species diversity, increased fire hazards, increased risk from insects and disease.

Plantation forestry cannot be commercial in any ordinary sense of the word, because it takes more than one human lifetime for trees to reach maturity. Requiring foresters to be commercial is bound to lead to short-termism and bad practice.

If communities are to invest money in long-term forestry, they have every right to be involved in the decision-making process.

Scientific forestry emphasizes wood production and neglects such public goods as recreation, hunter-gatherer foods, scenic quality, soil conservation and nature conservation. Forest planning requires an appreciation of the natural sciences, the social sciences and the fine arts. Foresters do not often have this knowledge, and they need to remember that science tells us about means, not ends.

Good forestry is most likely to flourish under special management and planning laws that enable a balance to be struck between public and private interests as they affect forestry and other land-uses operating within or adjoining forest lands. These include agriculture, rough grazing, wilderness, water gathering, transport, housing, mineral extraction, recreation and nature conservation.

Forests are best owned by organizations that are both altruistic and immortal. These characteristics, always rare, have sometimes been found in great landowning families, monasteries and governments.

But it is easy to find out when and where forests are well run. An American forester explains:

> You don't have to be a professional forester to recognise bad forestry any more than you need to be a doctor to recognise ill-health. If logging looks bad, it is bad. If a forest appears to be mismanaged, it is mismanaged. But a certain level of expertise is needed if you are going to be effective in doing something about it. (Robinson 1988: ix)

Using Robinson's method on many walks in Britain's state-run forests leads me conclude that they are seriously mismanaged.

Multiple-use forestry

Multiple use has multiple meanings.

Most foresters will agree that forestry should be conducted on a multiple-use basis. But the term can be interpreted in several ways. Let us consider six forest uses: a strategic reserve, a timber supply, a recreation resource, grazing land, scenic quality, nature conservation. Since forests are often managed in compartments, these goals could be achieved in four different ways (Fig. 8.3).

A six uses in one compartment;
B six uses in six non-overlapping compartments;

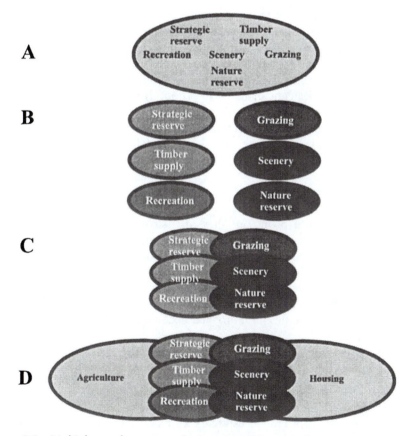

Figure 8.3 Multiple-use forestry can be interpreted in several ways: A   Six uses in one compartment; B   Six uses in six separate compartments; C   Six uses in overlapping compartments; D   Six uses overlapping with uses outside the forest.

C six uses in overlapping compartments;

D six uses overlapping with other uses outside the forest.

The most sophisticated alternative, D, is also the most sustainable – but *each* of the six forest yields should be sustained. British forestry has normally been "one use in one compartment". Instead, there should be EID for each use.

British forestry

Historically, forest management was less single-minded.

There are lessons for Britain to learn from overseas and for other countries to learn from Britain's 60-year dialogue between the forest industry and amenity groups. Britain is in a peculiar position with regard to tree cover and timber production. High forest is the climax vegetation for most of the country but, with only 1 per cent of the world's population, Britain has to buy about 15 per cent of all the timber sold on world markets, because it produces only 15 per cent of its own. About 10 per cent of Britain's land area is under forest, compared with a European and American average of 32 per cent (Crawford 1982). This is what happens to an old industrial country. The figures indicate that there may be a need to enlarge Britain's forest estate – but an overemphasis on wood production continues to arouse public opposition.

In the seventeenth, eighteenth and nineteenth centuries, wood production was one among several objectives. Britain's great landowners certainly hoped for timber and profit but they also strove to improve the scenery, to shelter their farms, to provide cover for game, to make attractive walks and drives and to create value for their descendants. Sir Walter Scott, who was an enthusiastic tree planter and landscape designer on his own estate, wrote that "when ye hae naething else to do, ye may be ay sticking in a tree, it will be growing, Jock, when ye're sleeping" (Scott 1818). The link between forestry and landscape design flourished because most foresters then started out as gardeners.

James Brown, originally a gardener, wrote the most successful nine-teenth-century book on forestry and became first president of the Royal Scottish Forestry Society. Brown believed that

It is admitted by every person of refined taste, that no object is so ornamental upon a landed estate as an extensive healthy plantation, situated upon a well-chosen spot and having a well-defined tastefully bending outline . . . no man ought to attempt the laying out of land for one who is not naturally possessed of good taste for that sort of landscape scenery which is based upon the laws of nature. (Brown 1882: 73)

Brown advised that a man should plant trees

... to give shelter to his farms, to shut out some unpleasant object from his dwelling-house, or to produce ornamental effect to the landscape, but the great and ultimate object is that of being profitable as a crop. (Brown 1882: 73)

Brown's approach now seems wiser than that of his successors, who criticized him.

By 1900 British foresters were looking to France and Germany and seeing that forests could be run on more scientific lines than was customary in Britain. Simpson assailed Brown for aiming at the production of large and beautifully grown trees, instead of the maximum timber crop (Simpson 1900: 37). Others suggested that Brown's method was "simply the gardener's plan of growing trees for ornamental purpose carried to the woods" (ibid.: 199). Simpson himself disagreed with this opinion and said that "The only men fitted to engage in scientific forestry at present are those who have had a gardener's education to begin with" (ibid.: 35). Nisbet was critical of non-timber objectives. He believed that Britain could become self-sufficient in timber if

... our present three million acres of woodlands were trebled in extent, and were all managed on business principles, in place of being under uneconomic management as game coverts and pleasure grounds, as is now mostly the case with British forests. (Nisbet 1900: 83)

The consequences of depending on imported timber became apparent during the First World War. Imports were restricted and there was an acute shortage of wood for pit props, trench-building and other purposes. Between 1913 and 1918, the volume of wood imports fell to 25 per cent of the pre-war level, and the price of wood rose by 400 per cent (Forestry Commission 1920: 21). Britain's private woodlands were ransacked for extra timber. In 1918 a forestry committee, chaired by Sir Francis Acland, identified a need for state forestry. The committee reported that

... the condition of our woods has been greatly influenced, in England and Ireland at least, by sporting and aesthetic considerations. Mixed open woods with good game cover have been preferred to dense clean-grown woods, with consequent loss in the quantity and quality of the timber produced. (Sub-committee on forestry 1918)

The Acland committee therefore recommended a strictly scientific approach to forestry in order to achieve "maximum efficiency of production" –

although he was absolutely correct to predict that "the hope of direct profit is very remote" (ibid.). The government accepted the Acland Report and established the Forestry Commission in 1919. The Commissioners were charged by the Forestry Act with "the general duty of promoting the interests of forestry, the development of afforestation, and the production and supply of timber" (Forestry Act 1919). There was nothing in the Act about aesthetics, sport, wildlife, wild food, rural employment, sheltering farms or recreation. So the Commissioners and their employees were not empowered to take action on these matters.

Criticism of plantation forestry

Plantations have been hated for centuries.

Britain's forestry industry has been subject to public criticism for well over a century. While other countries criticize their foresters for the way they fell trees, the British criticize foresters for the way they plant trees. Since Gilpin published his *Observations on forest scenery* (Gilpin 1791) and Price his *An essay on the picturesque* (Price 1794), British people have believed that forests should look natural (Fig. 8.4). Exotic species and geometrical plantations have been disliked in the countryside. In his *Guide to the Lakes*, first

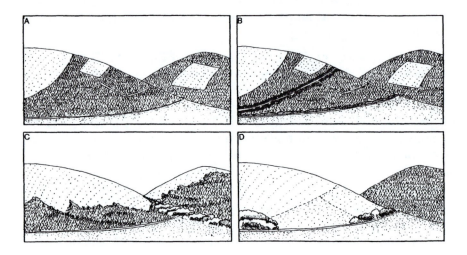

Figure 8.4 Since the end of the eighteenth century, most people have believed that plantations should look "natural", as in diagram C. The alternatives, of zoning, concealment and innovation, are shown in diagrams A, B, and D.

published in 1810, Wordsworth criticizes the planting of "exotic trees among rocks and dashing torrents" and adds that

> . . . this deformity, bad as it is, is not so obtrusive as the small patches and large tracts of larch-plantations that are overrunning the hill-sides. To justify our condemnation of these, let us again recur to Nature. (Wordsworth 1973: 82)

When the Forestry Commission began to establish large conifer plantations, after 1919, a torrent of criticism fell upon the Commissioners' deserving heads from within and without the forestry profession (Fig. 8.5).

In 1928 the then Professor of Forestry at Edinburgh University published a book titled *The forestry question in Great Britain*. Like many British foresters he had worked in the Indian Forest Service and seen a progressive approach to forestry. Stebbing asserted that if one seeks an explanation for "the rigid ideas which have swayed the Forestry Commission" then "one is driven back to the origin of the business, the Acland Report" (Stebbing 1928: 201). He criticized rigid annual targets, and wrote that

> Nor have they [the Forestry Commission], within the writer's knowledge ever shown any serious conviction that a true national forest

Figure 8.5 A larch plantation in the Lake District National Park, overlooking Derwent Water in 1996.

policy should be based on a careful consideration of all the varying demands and reasons for maintaining areas in different parts of the country under these two main types of forest – social, economic, sentimental and aesthetic. (Stebbing 1928: 101)

Stebbing was especially opposed to the policy of replanting the Forest of Dean with conifers instead of broadleaves:

... an opportunity does exist to commence regenerating this forest on the lines nature has ordained for it – as one centre from which the nation should be able to look in a future, distant it will be, for magnificent oak. (Stebbing 1928: 111)

During the Second World War consideration was given to bringing forestry within the scope of town and country planning legislation. In 1944, a famous planning lawyer said:

Now, whilst I love the country and realise that the importance of the good earth as the source of life and wealth cannot be over-estimated, I do not like gardening and I know nothing about the art of planting trees. But I do know that the ranks of coniferous trees planted by the Forestry Commission in pursuance of what are supposed to be the best interests of afforestation are a perfect eyesore wherever I have seen them and are definitely prejudicial to the amenities of the countryside ... and so, as I reflect on planning matters, I often think what a pity it is that some better method of afforestation could not be thought of ... than the setting up of row upon row of coniferous trees. (Heap 1983)

British forestry was excluded from planning control in the 1940s, but the Countryside Commission, and many others, believe the exemption should be discontinued (Countryside Commission 1984: 41). Public criticism of forestry has not abated. In 1983, Prince Charles, after a visit to Dumfries and Galloway, told the Royal Forestry Society that

I get the impression that someone ... has simply attacked a vast acreage with a plough, ploughed up everything, stream sides, frost hollows and so on, planted huge numbers of exactly the same type of tree, slapped a deer fence round the whole lot and then gone off to wait for it all to mature into a cash crop. (Harris 1983) (Fig. 8.6)

In 1996, Simon Jenkins wrote that

... as a boy I watched the Forestry Commission hurl conifer acid at the face of Snowdonia, its triffid spruces killed heather and peat, poisoned streams and obliterated footpaths and views. They marched on, ignorant of contour and horizon. No refinery or chemical works could have done more ecological damage. The pestilential organisa-

Figure 8.6 A forest ride in Dumfries and Galloway. In 1983, Prince Charles had the impression that someone had simply "planted huge numbers of exactly the same type of tree, slapped a deer fence round the whole lot and then gone off to wait for it all to mature into a cash crop".

tion, renamed "Forest Enterprise", to cleanse its name, marches yet across the landscape. What pollution has been wrought in the name of the Great God Tree! (Jenkins 1996)

The Forestry Commission's response to the above line of criticism was astonishingly well developed in the 1930s. Five types of landscape policy were advanced in the 1934 *Annual report*: the sympathetic design of forests; a broadleaf policy; the creation of a new and beautiful conifer-landscape; the establishment of forest parks; and the granting of public access to forests (Forestry Commission 1934: 55). In 1939 a sixth policy was added: the establishment of ecological reserves (Forestry Commission 1938: 22).

Each of the above policies has merit, but it was much easier to state them in annual reports than put them into practice – and the 1919 Forestry Act did not empower the Commissioners to pursue non-timber objectives. It is the 1919 Act, more than the forestry profession, that should be criticized. Many of the pre-1939 annual reports have a section on "amenity", but it disappeared during the Second World War, when the use of home-grown timber increased from 4 to 65 per cent of total consumption (Forestry Commission 1946: 10). The Commission's post-1919 estates were too immature to be felled, but after the war there was a renewed planting drive, again to create a strategic reserve. It continued through the 1950s, but by 1959 the strategic value of forestry was "no longer so strongly emphasised", because of nuclear weapons, and "the social aspects of forestry" therefore "assumed greater prominence" (Forestry Commission 1959: 7). The 1959 *Annual report* reiterated the amenity policies that had been announced 25 years earlier. Some progress had been made, especially with forest parks, but the chief skill developed by the Commission with regard to "amenity" issues was that of saying the right thing while doing the wrong thing. As in the USA, foresters became expert in "considering" multi-objective forestry without taking any significant action (Robinson 1988: 55). Good plans may be prepared for places in the public eye, but the great dank wastes of monoculture remain.

Britain's Forestry Commission was not empowered to consider a multi-objective policy until a ministerial statement on forest policy was made on 24 July 1963. Christopher Soames announced that:

The Commission, in preparing its future programmes, will bear in mind the need, wherever possible, to provide public access and recreation, and will devote more attention to increasing the beauty of the landscape. (*Hansard* 1963).

"Bear in mind" was a weak phrase, but the new policy was a little strengthened when, in 1974, after the appearance of a cost-benefit study on forestry, the Commission published a list of six objectives for the forestry enterprise: wood production, amenity, recreation, rural employment, "a harmonious relationship" with agriculture, and a target rate of return of 3 per cent in real terms (Forestry Commission 1974: 10). The landscape aspects of the forestry industry's progress towards a multi-objective policy will be discussed below.

Sympathetic design

Forest design requires forest designers.

Concealment was the first official landscape policy adopted by the forest industry. "Clinton's rule" (Fig. 8.7), announced in 1927, enjoined that ". . . in all cases where natural hardwood existed alongside public roads, a strip of one chain's width was to be retained as a screen to hide the afforestation work behind it" (Ryle 1969: 258). Hardwood strips were planted, and in 1969 it was said that "from this ancient order of the day has sprung the unhappy 'amenity belt' fetish which persists as the ultimate goal of landscape planning for some unenlightened foresters" (Ryle 1969: 258).

Figure 8.7 Lord Clinton's Rule required a strip of hardwood to conceal conifer plantations (above). The strip was left in place when clear-felling took place (below).

The idea that whole forests might be sympathetically designed first appeared in the 1934 report:

It appears to the Commissioners that by taking a little thought and possibly incurring a little additional expenditure in the utilisation of the land acquired for the new forests it might be possible to provide, for the future, areas as highly prized by the public as is the New Forest today. (Forestry Commission 1934: 49)

They proposed avoiding straight outlines to plantations, laying out roads and rides with more care and varying the species within coniferous plantations. A major obstacle to making "highly prized" forests was that more than "a little thought" was required: they also needed the services of trained designers.

In the 1959 *Annual report* the Commission admitted that

. . . there are examples in their earlier plantations of defects such as straight rides, or fire lines, which unnecessarily ignored natural features. The Commission can have no complaint when criticism is directed to that kind of thing. (Forestry Commission 1959: 8)

In 1972, almost forty years after the 1934 report, the problem had not receded. The interdepartmental cost/benefit study noted that:

Almost all those consulted on this subject were convinced that antagonism to forestry on amenity grounds was largely inspired by the "bad" forestry of the past, and that provided such errors were avoided, the positive contribution of forestry to the visual scene, as enjoyed by walkers and motorists, would be beneficial. (Forestry Commission 1972a: 29)

Annual reports from the Commissioners had sections on education, but the first reference to design training came in 1961 (Forestry Commission 1961: 14). The Commission's first landscape consultant was appointed soon after the Ministerial Statement of July 1963. Sylvia Crowe was asked "to assist them in making their forests as attractive in appearance as they must be efficient in production" (Forestry Commission 1963: 9). In 1963 the Commission owned 708,965 hectares of forest land and oversaw 307,680 hectares of land which had been planted under the dedication scheme. This gave Miss Crowe (later Dame Sylvia Crowe) responsibility for over one million hectares of forest land. It was a large task for a little lady.

Sylvia Crowe conducted a series of visits and then wrote an advisory booklet, *Forestry in the landscape* (Crowe 1966). A second edition was entitled *The landscape of forests and woods* (Crowe 1978). They are excellent publications but could not, on their own, convert scientific foresters into trained visual designers or recreation planners. If these booklets had been available in 1934, and if designers had helped to plan Britain's new forests, then the Forestry Commission might have rivalled the pre-eminence of William Kent, Lancelot Brown and Humphry Repton in the annals of the English landscape. The first opportunity was missed, but, in Sylvia Crowe's opinion, harvesting operations provide a second chance.

In 1973 a single forest officer was sent on a landscape design course at Newcastle University. By 1978 he was "involved in a wide variety of tasks, including the design of an important planting scheme at Beinn Ghuilean in South Kintyre which was featured in the *Sunday Times* colour magazine" (Forestry Commission 1978b: 18). By 1984 the Commission had three staff members with landscape qualifications. Between 1975 and 1982 this team was able to design "about 7,300 hectares of new planting and 7,100 hectares of felling and replanting" (Lucas 1984). The design effort was, rightly, concentrated on the most beautiful and prominent landscapes. In 1986 I calculated that if the rate of progress was maintained, and staffing was kept at the same level, then it would take 468 years to prepare initial designs for the 962,668 hectares of forest land which the Commission owned in 1983 (Forestry Commission 1983). The number of full-time designers has risen to some half dozen, and landscape design is now included in forestry education.

The new conifer landscape

New tree species lead to new styles.

In the USA, where the tree cover has never been removed from 33 per cent of the land area, forest designers have emphasized a conservation approach which borrows "form, line, colour and texture from the characteristic landscape" (Forest Service 1972). In Britain, where tree cover once fell below 4 per cent of the land area, it has been necessary to adopt an innovative approach to forest design, inspired by the scenery of the Alps:

It is also stated, sometimes, that the new British coniferous forests will resemble the great German forests in character by covering the whole landscape in dark green. The comparison, in most cases, is not very apt because the upper limit of economic tree growth in the hill country of Great Britain is relatively low and it is but rarely possible to plant to the skyline. A more accurate comparison would be with alpine forests in which the trees are seen against a background of higher country. (Forestry Commission 1934: 55)

The comparison with Alpine scenery points to the stylistic origins of the new conifer landscape. They lie in the sublime scenery which Englishmen first appreciated on the Grand Tour (Hussey 1927: 4). Towards the end of the eighteenth century a number of English designers, including Price, Knight and Loudon, developed an Irregular Style of landscape design, which drew its inspiration from the Alps and the wilder parts of Britain. The designers who adopted this style became expert in designing man-made landscapes according to the compositional principles of natural landscapes as interpreted by the great landscape painters of Italy (Turner 1986: 101). The Irregular Style was revived by Robinson and Jekyll towards the end of the nineteenth century and has continued to exert an overwhelming influence on designers who work with plants. Robinson was so confident the Commission would adopt his preferred style that he left his estate to the Forestry Commission in 1935 (Forestry Commission 1936: 10). Sadly, it is not managed in the Irregular Style.

The drawings in *The landscape of forests and woods* (Crowe 1978) depict a method of applying the Irregular Style to scientific forestry (Fig. 8.8). It has been further developed by the Commission's landscape architects and is now implemented using overlays on panoramic photographs (Forestry Commission 1980). Landscape designers are trained to think in four dimensions, but the Commission, to its great credit, has pioneered the systematic use of time-lapse sketches as precursors to plans. The sketch designs in the *Landscape of forests and woods* are so convincing that it is tempting to regard the Irregular Style as a kind of visual determinism which will produce the only acceptable style for innovative forest design. This is wrong. In some places there are excellent reasons for basing a design upon straight lines, serpentine lines or other sorts of geometry. Sometimes the landscape has so little existing character that the designer must look to his own imagination

Figure 8.8 Dame Sylvia Crowe helped to convert many plantations to the Irregular Style of landscape design.

Figure 8.9 Tarn Howes, a man-made lake in a man-made forest, shows that it is possible to create new landscapes that are highly valued by tourists.

and the fine arts for inspiration. It should never be forgotten that Tarn Howes, "perhaps the best known and most visited beauty spot in the Lake District National Park" (Brotherton 1977), is a man-made lake in a man-made forest, designed in the Irregular Style (Fig. 8.9).

The broadleaf policy

Broadleaf species have been rooted out.

In 1934 the Forestry Commission described its mission as "the provision of coniferous plantations and the maintenance of existing woodlands" (Forestry Commission 1934: 18). This implied that broadleaved forests would be restocked with broadleaved trees. In a few cases this was

263

done, but it was normal for old oakwoods and beechwoods to be replanted with conifers. The redoubtable Professor Stebbing criticized this policy in 1928 and the Friends of the Lake District and New Forest followed suit. In 1934 the Commission reported that "Directions were given some years ago that in the two largest of the former Crown Woods (New and Dean Forests) broadleaved trees were to be given preference wherever the conditions were suitable" (Forestry Commission 1934: 54). Everything, however, turned on the interpretation of "suitable". Conifer-planting went ahead in the former Crown Woods because broadleaf species would not yield a speedy economic return. If the nation is willing to wait longer until a crop is harvested, or if it is willing to forgo an economic return, on aesthetic or sentimental grounds, then most land becomes suitable for broadleaf planting. It is even possible that in the long run broadleaves will produce a better return than conifers, because the wood is used for luxury goods and because Britain's climate and soils are well suited to hardwoods. About 93 per cent of the Commission's planting was coniferous (Forestry Commission 1949: 56).

In 1980 the Sherfield Report on *Scientific aspects of forestry* recommended more emphasis on broadleaf planting (Select Committee on Science and Technology 1980). This led, in 1984, to a new Forestry Commission consultative paper. It stated, at long last, that "in general there should be a presumption in favour of maintaining broadleaved woodland on suitable sites" (Forestry Commission 1984c). The question of how to assess suitability remained. The Nature Conservancy Council estimates that between 30 and 50 per cent of Britain's lowland broadleaf woods have been lost since the 1940s – either to conifers or to agriculture (Nature Conservancy Council 1984). The new broadleaf policy was adopted in 1985.

Three examples from the Galloway Forest Park may be used to illustrate the Commission's pre-1985 broadleaf policy.

1 The magnificent stand of sessile oak on the west shore of Loch Trool. It is, rightly, being managed as a Site of Special Scientific Interest and as a popular beauty spot (Fig. 8.10).

2 The steep hillside on the east shore of Loch Trool, down which Robert the Bruce rolled boulders onto an English army (Fig. 8.11). It was planted with conifers in the 1960s. They are not growing well and will be difficult to harvest – partly for physical reasons and partly because aesthetic objections will be raised. It would have been better to encourage the oak scrub, which might, in time, have attained a character like the vegetation that survives on islands in the loch. It would be pleasant to walk through, would support a diverse fauna and flora and would emphasize the perils of the route taken by the English army.

3 The stand of sessile oak on the road between Newton Stewart and Bargrennan, beside a lovely reach of the River Cree (Fig. 8.12). It has

Figure 8.10 A magnificent stand of sessile oak on the west shore of Loch Trool is, rightly, being managed for its scenic and scientific interest. Note the Forestry Commission planting in the background.

been underplanted with hemlock to grow on when the oak is harvested. This plan may have had economic merit, but it was fundamentally misconceived on aesthetic and conservation grounds.

Forest parks

Forest parks are duller than they need be.

In 1934 the Forestry Commissioners expressed a hope that "the day will come when, the risk of fire being diminished, it will be possible to admit the public more freely into the plantations" (Forestry Commission 1934: 55). "Admit . . . into the plantations" does not sound very appealing, but at that time the public were excluded from Commission land wherever possible. The Commissioners responded to the 1931 report of the National Park Committee by opening the Argyll National Forest Park, in 1935. By 1949 six forest parks were in existence, and the Commission was able to describe them as "a by-product" of the afforestation programme which had been

265

Figure 8.11 The steep hillside on the east shore of Loch Trool was planted with conifers, which are not flourishing. Instead, natural regeneration of hardwoods, as on the island, should have been encouraged.

obtained "at negligible cost" (Forestry Commission 1949: 7). Forest parks now cover over 180,000 hectares of land, of which less than half is afforested. Where the scenery is spectacular, as in Glen Trool, these parks are fine. Where the scenery is less spectacular, much too little has been done to create new landscape values. The task requires imaginative design.

The Border Forest Park is a case in point. It was taken in the 1934 *Annual report*, as an example of a place that might become "as highly prized by the public as is the New Forest today" (Forestry Commission 1934: 49). Unfortunately, no landscape design was prepared and the forest just expanded until it became "the largest man-made forest in Europe". A further opportunity arose in the 1970s when "the largest man-made lake in Europe" was designed in the middle of the forest. Over a million semi-mature trees had to be felled, but the opportunity for creative forestry was missed, and there were disagreements with the Northumbrian Water

Figure 8.12 This stand of sessile oak was, foolishly, underplanted with hemlock and Douglas fir, in preparation for removing the oak.

Authority over the treatment of the reservoir (Forestry Commission 1979: 14). The forest park and Kielder Water now attract larger numbers of visitors but they come for "active recreation", not to see a landscape of high scenic quality. It is a soulless place. When one recalls what was achieved on less prepossessing sites at Stourhead, Blenheim and Castle Howard, it is evident that a staggering opportunity for creative forest design was fudged.

In 1961 it was reported that: "Both within and outside the Forest Parks it has become the Commission's policy to open their plantations to the public wherever this can be done without undue risk of damage" (Forestry Commission 1961: 41). Footpaths and nature trails have been laid out through existing forests, but a very much better footpath network could have been created if, as in new towns, the footpaths were designed before other developments. Many of the streams that have disappeared beneath the forest canopy would have made excellent footpath routes (Fig. 8.13).

Figure 8.13 Many streams that would have made good habitats or footpath routes were killed by the forest canopy.

The Commission owns over 10,000 miles of private roads, but it was not until 1977 that the first forest drive was opened to the public (Forestry Commission 1977: 15). It was romantically described as the Raiders' Road, in Galloway Forest Park, but was not subject to landscape design. A toll is levied and the road is closed in periods of high fire risk. In 1981 a decision was taken to downgrade some forest roads and to upgrade others to take heavy timber-carrying trucks (Forestry Commission 1982: 25). This decision permitted an increase in the recreational use of forest roads – and an opportunity to attend to their design. Roads are aligned to cause "minimum damage" to the landscape, but should be planned to maximize their value as scenic drives – in the same way that reservoir access roads are designed to give access to the dam site during the construction period and to serve the recreational facilities that will follow at a later date. The detailing of roads should receive careful attention. Most have been cut through the hillside without any attention to grading or the revegetation of embankments.

Conservation and recreation

Forest recreation can be profitable.

In 1938 the Forestry Commission suggested "that typical areas in some of the Commission's forests should be unplanted and reserved for ecological studies" (Forestry Commission 1938: 22). The British Ecological Society agreed, and the Commission's wildlife and conservation policy was launched. It lapsed during the Second World War, but in 1947 it was announced that in the forest parks ". . . attention is given to the conservation of natural resources. . . and throughout the area wild life is protected" (Forestry Commission 1947: 15). In 1964 a new post of Wild Life Officer was established. As in the case of landscape design, an advisory booklet was published, *Wildlife conservation in woodlands* (Forestry Commission 1972b). In 1978 the Nature Conservancy Council and the Natural Environment Research Council published a review of sites of biological importance, which included 6 per cent of all Commission land, most of it already protected by "management plans of one kind or another" (Forestry Commission 1978b: 17). It is good that existing value should be protected, but the Commission should also create new wildlife habitats. They would compensate for the fauna and flora lost when afforestation takes place.

It was estimated that the number of visits by the public to Commission land rose from 15 million to 24 million between 1969 and 1979 (Forestry Commission 1969; 1979). For 1984–5 it was reported that £5.3 million was spent on recreation and £0.8 million was received in income. The money was used to provide for "some 50 different activities" (Forestry Commission 1965: 24, 99).

Since 1970 the Commission has been engaged in developing chalet sites, which are let out for holidays (Fig. 8.14). Forest workers' houses and other surplus buildings have also been converted for recreational use. They earned a 10.8 per cent return on capital, which compares very favourably with the 3

Figure 8.14 It is possible to obtain a better cash return from planting chalets than from planting trees.

per cent target rate of return on forestry itself (Forestry Commission 1983: 102). In future the Commission could encourage the development of second homes, retirement homes, hotels and other types of property development. Buildings, together with water, vegetation and landform, constitute one of the main elements of landscape design. When well designed and well located they make a positive contribution to the scenery – as castles, cottages, farms and country houses have often done in the past. The use of timber is appropriate, but there is no need whatsoever for all forest buildings to resemble log cabins. Nor is there any British design precedent for this style of architecture.

Private forestry

Private forestry is both better and worse than state forestry.

The foregoing discussion has concentrated on the Commission's role in running the state forestry enterprise. It also has a duty to encourage private forestry by grant-aid, research, education and other means. Until recently the private sector of the industry managed to evade the public attention and criticism to which the Commission, as a national agency, is exposed. But criticism grew, and in 1984 the *Listener* reported that:

> The flashpoint at the moment is Craig Meagaidh, a wild mountainside in the middle of the Highlands, where Fountain Forestry, a syndicate of high-rate taxpayers, wants to plant 450 hectares of the lower slopes. The NCC have declared the site one of Special Scientific Interest and are refusing to allow planting to go ahead, at least until – or if – the Secretary of State for Scotland asks them to back down. The Forestry Commission have said they will provide Fountain Forestry with grants despite the NCC's position. (Hutton 1984: 13)

Craig Meagaidh was saved but the private sector's record is in fact both better and worse than that of the Commission. The old family estates have a better record. Many have always carried on forestry as part of a multi-use enterprise and have paid great attention to aesthetics, agriculture, public access, nature conservation and the design of roads and buildings. The new forest estates created by investment companies, with grant-aid and tax incentives, have a bad record. They lag behind the Commission with regard to public access, landscape design, nature conservation and the provision of recreational facilities.

It was not until 1971 that a serious effort was made to resolve the question of ". . . how private woodland owners can at the same time play an effective part in meeting contemporary social and environmental needs" (Forestry Commission 1971: 7). In the following year a new Dedication Scheme was inaugurated to "secure sound forestry practice, effective integration with agriculture and environmental safeguards, together with such opportunities for recreation as may be appropriate" (Forestry Commission 1972a: 9). When the new system was reviewed in 1977, two examples were given of private schemes that had been rejected on environmental grounds. At Haresceugh Fell the Commission "concluded that it would be environmentally unacceptable to permit afforestation of 247 hectares of Pennine upland with the aid of grants because of its special prominence in the landscape". A site on Breckland was rejected because it was one of the last remaining areas of the old Breckland (Forestry Commission 1977: 11). The Commission's guidance note on consultation procedures for forestry grants and felling permissions now makes provision for full consultation with agriculture departments, local planning authorities and the Countryside Commission (Forestry Commission 1984a). Both public and private forestry are now supervised by a Forest Authority.

If the private sector is to match, or better, the environmental standards which are set by the Commission it will be necessary for woodland owners to produce the type of multi-objective plans discussed in the next section. Should the forestry industry become subject to planning control, as proposed by the Countryside Commission, or to environmental assessment, then landscape plans will become necessary for the entire forest estate. They are already required for many land-uses, except agriculture and defence. The RICS argued that the level of grant-aid to private forestry should be raised "to make good landscaping economically feasible" and so that managers "give public access a higher priority" (Royal Institute of Chartered Surveyors 1982).

Silviculture

Selection forestry is best for the environment.

R. S. Troup, who wrote a standard text on silvicultural systems, observed in 1928 that:

> From the aesthetic point of view those systems which maintain a continuous forest cover, and particularly the selection system, are preferable to those in which periodical clearings are made, such as the clear-cutting and simple coppice systems. In Europe a belt of forest treated under the selection system is often maintained round the outskirts of towns and villages. (Troup 1928: 179)

Despite this comment in such an influential book, it remains the case, as Helliwell pointed out in 1982, that:

> In Britain, the subject of visual amenity within the forest seems to have received little attention, with the main emphasis being on the effects of our relatively fragmentary forests in the wider landscape. (Helliwell, 1982)

The effect of different silvicultural systems on the forest interior is a subject of great importance: alternative systems have very different effects on plants, animals and men.

The sharpest contrast, as Troup observes, is between selection forestry and clear-cutting. Under the selection system,

> . . . felling and regeneration are not confined to certain parts of the area but are distributed all over it, the fellings consisting of the removal of single trees or groups of trees scattered throughout the forest. (Troup 1928: 179)

Selection forestry produces a full range of tree sizes and considerable diversity of plant and animal species. Under the clear-cutting system large areas of forest are "clear felled and regenerated, most frequently by artificial means but sometimes naturally" (ibid.: 4). Its modern history starts in Germany at the beginning of the nineteenth century (ibid.: 18). The system became popular because it requires less skill to implement and affords maximum economy in the mechanization of felling and extraction. The disadvantage of clear-cutting is that the forest is devastated, the ecosystem disrupted and the soil exposed to erosion (Fig. 8.15). The new trees look more like an agricultural crop than a forest – until they are ready to be felled. The system has fallen from favour in Germany, the USA and other developed countries. It survives in Britain.

There are a number of variations of the two main silvicultural systems. Helliwell has identified eight separate systems and gives an analysis of their advantages and disadvantages (Table 8.1) (Helliwell 1982: 48). The table reinforces Troup's point that clear-felling is economically best but environmentally worst. For landscape planning the problem is not to choose one or other system for blanket application throughout the country, but to consider which system is best for each location and each forest compartment.

Figure 8.15 This forest and the pond are being devastated by clear-felling.

Table 8.1 Comparison of the main silvicultural systems

	Clear-felling		Shelterwood		Group selection		Selection	
	pure	mixed	pure	mixed	pure	mixed	pure	mixed
Soil	−1		−1		−1		−1	
Flora	−2	−1	−2	−1		+1		+2
Fauna	−2	−1	−1			+2		+2
Amenity	−2	−1	−1			+1		+1
Windthrow		+1	−2	−1	−1	+1		+1
Pathology	−2	−1	−1				−1	
Costs	+2	+2	+1			−1	−1	−2

Source: Helliwell 1982: 48

The *American forest service handbook on timber* provides a useful approach to this problem, by listing five "visual quality objectives", which suggest the adoption of a particular silvicultural system in different zones of the forest:

- Zone 1: preservation
- Zone 2: retention
- Zone 3: partial retention
- Zone 4: modification
- Zone 5: maximum modification (Forest Service 1980)

It is likely that Zone 1 would be managed as nature reserves, Zones 2, 3 and 4 by selection forestry, and Zone 5 by clear-cutting.

An Australian author has pointed out that "visually the most critical areas are those occurring on an 'interface', e.g. sky/land, land/water, trees/grass, forest/national park, or forest/agricultural land" (van Pelt 1980). They should be included within Zones 1, 2 or 3. In the State of Maine, which is 90 per cent forested, a Land Use Regulation Commission controls private timber companies. Maximum modification is permitted in about 70 per cent of the forest land, but the rest comes into one of 11 types of protection zone: wetlands, strips round wetlands, 80-metre strips along rivers, wildlife habitats, high mountains, recreation land, fragile soils, flood-plains, aquifer recharge areas, unusual areas, resource areas (Pidot 1982).

Location must influence visual quality objectives, especially when the wood or forest is near a town, or on a tourist route. Joyden's Wood is a case in point. It is 20 kilometres from Trafalgar Square and 135 hectares in area, partly within the boundary of Greater London. When acquired by the Commission in 1955 it needed restocking. Larch and pine were selected in preference to broadleaves. The Forestry Commission leaflet described the wood as being "surrounded by residential development but surprisingly secluded" (Forestry Commission 1978a). It had a picnic place, which was described as a "grassy landscaped area" and a forest walk "mainly through pine and larch plantations with remnants of old natural birch and oak woods". Since the first edition of this book was published it has been acquired by the Woodland Trust. Priority is now being given to landscape and recreational objectives. It should become an urban forest park from which some timber is extracted – instead of a commercial forest with no car park and minimal provision for recreation.

Visual quality zones have been discussed as protection zones, but in many places there are opportunities for "creative forestry" – a felicitous term devised by the New Zealand Forest Service (New Zealand Forest Service 1983). Visual interest can be created by contrasting light against dark foliage, by forming tunnels through areas of forest, which open onto expansive views, by keeping gnarled old trees as a foil to young trees, by laying out firebreaks as grand avenues centred on important features, by making ponds for recreational use and firefighting water, by making peaceful glades, and by all the other devices available to a designer. In some places trees should be allowed to grow beyond their economic size for visual reasons. Old growth and ancient woods have a magical quality. It is strongest in primeval woods but can also develop in plantations, given time. Coniferous trees are generally regarded as visually inferior to deciduous trees, but they can be very fine when mature. Standing timber is also a strategic reserve. Clawson states that "As an economist, I am shocked at immense inventory value of the standing timber in [American] national forests and at its very slow growth rate" (Clawson 1975: 165). He was shocked because, with 33 per cent of its land area under forest, the USA had sufficient strategic reserves. A country like Britain, with only 9 per cent of its land under forest, should tolerate longer rotations, and lower growth rates, to increase the inventory value of its forest estate.

Community forestry

Land, money and laws are necessary.

Many countries have become interested in "community forestry", and a group of Canadian foresters has suggested the following definition: "a tree-dominated ecosystem managed for multiple community values and benefits by the community" (Duinker et al. 1994). It is a local, rather than a national, approach to forestry. In principle:

- Costs should be met by communities.
- Ownership should be local and public.
- Management policies should be set locally.
- Benefits should accrue locally.

The Menominee Indian Reservation is a "superb example of a successful community forest in the US" and an example of "the land ethic in practice"

(Pecore 1992). The reserve was established in 1854 and the tribe leaders used selection forestry to balance annual yield with timber growth. Income from the forest pays for social services, medical services, education and law enforcement. As a European example, we can take the city of Hameenlinna in Finland, which owns some 10,000 hectares of forest land. It is zoned as follows: economic forest, for timber production; landscape forest, for multiple use, sports and recreation forest; special forest, for education and nurseries. The city employs a professional forester, a forest technician and about twenty staff. It makes money by selling timber and fishing licenses and by letting the public hunt small game (Duinker et al. 1994).

Britain launched a policy for community forestry in 1987 (Countryside Commission, 1987b). The strength of the policy was that a forest was conceived not merely as a dense woodland. It embraced farmland, water bodies and recreational land. The weakness of the policy was the lack of any intention to take a significant proportion of the designated forest into community ownership, or to allow local communities to make policy or management decisions. With these drawbacks, community forests have been shown on maps but can be detected on the ground only from the occasional country park and the thin strips of grant-aided trees planted on private land. The lesson of history remains to be learned: effective forestry requires land, money, laws and wise management over many years.

Forest landscape plans

Forests need multi-objective landscape plans.

The chief success of British forestry, apart from wood production, has been the *visual* integration of forestry with other land-uses. The chief weakness of British forestry has been the internal management of plantations for multiple objectives. In this, there is much to be learned from the USA. Gifford Pinchot's objective, of 1905, should head every forest plan, to obtain "the greatest good for the greatest number in the long run". Within forests, the principles of excellent forestry, as described by Gordon Robinson, should be followed:

> Excellent forestry consists of limiting the cutting of timber to that which can be removed annually in perpetuity. It consists of growing timber on long rotations, generally from one to two hundred years, depending on the species of trees and the quality of soil, but in any case allowing trees to reach full maturity before being cut. It consists of practising a selection system of cutting whenever this is consistent with the biological requirements of the species involved and, except in

emergency situations, keeping the openings no larger than is necessary to meet those requirements. It consists of retaining whatever growth is needed for the comfort and prosperity of all the native plants and animals. Finally, it consists of taking extreme precautions to protect the soil, our all-important basic resource. (Robinson 1988: 1)

In Britain, critics of plantation forestry should re-focus their attention on the internal management of forests. When they look badly managed, they are badly managed. To improve matters, comprehensive landscape plans of the type recommended by Sylvia Crowe in 1978 should be prepared for each and every forest:

Since each forest is a complex multi-purpose landscape a comprehensive landscape plan is needed to make the best use of all resources, to ensure that no one use will conflict with another, and to bring all uses together into a landscape which will both function well and look well. An analysis of the character of the landscape should be made, and a plan prepared. The plan should be based on contoured surveys, showing natural features, outstanding views, points of public access and areas of particular attraction to visitors. It should also record any fragile areas needing protection from over-use, and soil conditions relating to wear capacity. It should cover enough of the surrounding land to put the forest into context, including the footpath and bridleway links to the countryside and villages outside the forest. (Crowe 1978)

Her recommendation was included in a Forestry Commission publication but never acted upon. In 1992 the Commission began to produce ambitious forest design plans (Forestry Commission 1993). Though somewhat influenced by amenity and conservation objectives, they are essentially plans for tree-felling and restocking. For forests in the public eye, better forest design plans are produced.

Forest landscape plans (Fig. 8.16) should be set forth in public documents, with simplified versions displayed in visitors' centres and similar places. This would make the public aware of the forest industry's respect for the landscape. A plan should explain how the design has been related to existing features and how the design concept for the forest was generated. It should show visual quality objectives; areas of broadleaf retention and planting; silvicultural systems; conservation areas; areas that will become old-growth woodland; habitat creation areas; wildlife networks; recreational networks; art trails; story trails; the provision for hunter-gathering; historic trails; the provision of footpaths, bridleways, cycle-paths and other recreation facilities; integration with agriculture and other nearby land-uses. Even if the Commission continues to be exempt from planning control, the landscape plan and its accompanying report should be made available to

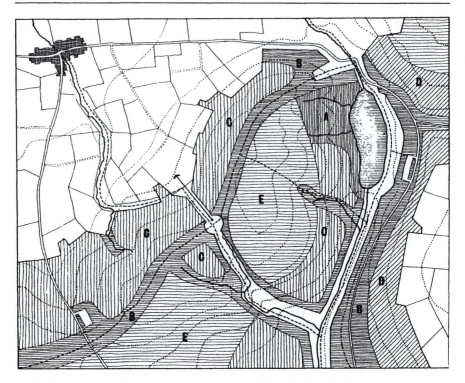

Figure 8.16 It is necessary for forest landscape plans to deal with visual amenity, recreation, nature conservation and timber production. This can be done by developing landscape management objectives for defined zones within the forest. For example, Zone A – preservation and nature conservation; Zone B – retention, recreation and nature conservation; Zone C – partial retention and recreation; Zone D – modification; Zone E – maximum modification for timber production.

the local authority and deposited in local libraries. This is normal practice for large quarries, reservoirs, power stations and other major projects, where the industrialists must demonstrate their good-neighbourliness.

The principal objective of the Forestry Commission is "the efficient production of wood for industry" (Forestry Commission 1984b), but this cannot be the principal objective in every part of every forest. Some forests should be managed as woods, others as wilderness. In many places the duty "to protect and enhance the environment" or "to provide recreational facilities" will take precedence over the principal objective. Decisions about priorities will be based on an environmental assessment of forest location and site characteristics. Nature reserves are already mapped and protected. The Nature Conservancy has asked for conservation to be included in the written plan of operations prepared for every forest (Kirby 1984). Similar attention should be given to areas of high scenic and recreation value.

There is a great need for foresters to consider the wider context and to become expert in EID. They can help to create a national web of greenspace open to the public. Wherever possible lake shores, ridge lines, viewpoints, streams, recreational facilities, long-distance footpaths and scenic areas should be incorporated. Forestry has an important role in and around urban areas. In rural areas the "web land" should be subject to retention policies so that it stands between zones of "maximum modification" in the same way that hedgerows and farm woodlands make compartments in the agricultural landscape.

Forests require special legal and planning regimes. Those who frame them should study forest history and learn from the successes and failures of the industrialized countries. A forest should not be merely a large wood: it should be a place where special laws apply. Originally, the laws were framed to benefit kings and nobles. In Britain, the 1919 law was framed to provide a national strategic reserve of timber: it was almost an act of war. Today, forest laws should aim to create public goods, including a strategic reserve of timber and wild food.

CHAPTER 9
Rivers and floods

Where are the streams of yesteryear? Underground.

Whyte 1970: 362

Those streams of yesteryear will have to be reclaimed. They lie imprisoned in underground culverts or restrained by concrete walls and artificial embankments. Because wild nature is everywhere under threat, we want our rivers back. Drainage works and impermeable surfacing continue apace. Unless drastic action is taken, all the rivers in all the urban regions of all the industrialized countries will be lost. A river engineer once drew a comparison between river works and road works:

> Proper arterial drainage is as necessary to any country as its system of trunk roads – it is a vital service to the nation and should be so regarded. The question which really should be asked – "Is this work necessary?" – is one well within the competence of an experienced land drainage engineer to answer. (Nixon 1966a)

Since 1966 trunk roads and "proper arterial drainage" have been criticized by environmentalists who, when asked, "Is the work necessary?", scream "No!" The city of Paris posed the question about a trunk-road system in 1966. Planners calculated that to meet the demand for road space it would be necessary to provide 50 four-lane roads and a 500-metre belt of car parking around the centre. "*C'était impensable*" (Les Guides Bleus 1979). Parisians decided that the extra cars should be kept out of their city for environmental reasons. Now, the world's municipal authorities must inaugurate massive river reclamation programmes. In so doing, they need to remember the reasons for treating rivers so badly: flood prevention, urbanization, forest clearance and agricultural drainage. The disease cannot be cured without removing its causes. For river catchment planning to be sustainable (Gardiner 1994) other land-uses will have to be planned in conjunction with river works. Gardiner argues that catchment planning must be linked to land-use planning, so that we can have "prevention rather than cure". Farming, forestry and urbanization have great environmental impacts on rivers. Planning authorities must act if rivers are to be reclaimed. River engineers and river authorities do not and should not have the necessary powers.

Flood prevention

Floods induce fear – and high expenditure.

Men have always been frightened of floods. They are the subject of many legends and remain the chief cause of natural disasters (Parker & Harding 1978: 234). In The Bible we read that:

> In the six hundredth year of Noah's life . . . were all the fountains of the great deep broken up, and the windows of heaven were opened. And the rain was upon the earth forty days and forty nights . . . And all flesh died that moved upon the earth, both of fowl, and of cattle, and of beast, and of every creeping thing that creepeth upon the earth, and every man . . .. (Genesis 7: 11–21)

Most floods are caused by heavy rain or high seas. Other occasional causes include earthquakes, snowmelt, landslides and dam failures. The worst UK floods in recent times have been the Dale Dyke dam failure of 1864, the Lynn river flood of 1952 and the East Coast floods of 1953. They claimed 244, 28 and 300 lives respectively. The language in which these events were described by contemporary observers reveals the fear they engendered. This is what happened at Dale Dyke:

> On Friday, March 11, 1864, exactly at midnight, a calamity, appalling and almost unparalleled, occurred along the course of the river Loxley, and the banks of the Don, where it passes through the town of Sheffield. An overwhelming Flood swept down from an enormous reservoir at Bradfield, carrying away houses, mills, bridges, and manufactories, destroying property estimated at half a million sterling in value, and causing the loss of about two hundred and forty human lives. (Harrison 1864)

Authorities respond to the fear of floods by spending munificently on flood protection measures. Simultaneously, societies take many actions, often for good reasons, which increase the flood risk: forest clearance, agricultural drainage, urban drainage and river "improvement" (Fig. 9.1).

Figure 9.1 The confluence of two "improved" rivers in South London: top, as illustrated in the 1986 edition of this book, and bottom, after further "improvement". For the poor river things get worse and worse.

Forest clearance

Forest clearance aggravates flooding.

A forest can absorb rainwater, like a great sponge, and help it run into the ground. This benefit is removed when the forest is removed. The current plight of Bangladesh is a tragic example (Khalis 1993). At one time there were great swamps and forests in the foothills of the Himalayas. Malaria kept humans out. After the introduction of anti-malarial drugs, the forest was cleared and the rate of runoff greatly accelerated. Periodically, this causes terrible floods and loss of life in Bangladesh (Fig. 9.2). The developed countries that have removed their forests have also increased their liability to flooding. Axemen have no interest in EID.

Agricultural drainage

Farm drainage aggravates flooding.

When agricultural land becomes waterlogged, air is unable to reach the root zone, soil remains cold, germination is slow, cultivation is difficult, plants do not flourish. An appreciation of these simple truths has led European

Figure 9.2 Forest clearance is the prime cause of the floods which ravage Bangladesh. (Courtesy of Bangladesh High Commission.)

farmers to undertake drainage works at least since Roman times. In periods of agricultural prosperity the works have proceeded apace; in periods of depression they have been neglected. The periods of great activity, 1840–80 and 1940–85 for England, were when technical developments occurred and government finance was available.

The antiquity of land drainage has resulted in a legacy of special laws to help farmers and engineers undertake the work. Britain's 1833 Sewers Act enabled commissioners, who had to be landowning farmers, to define drainage districts and levy a financial charge. Comparable legislation established Water Management Districts in Holland and Drainage Districts in the USA (Smedema & Rycroft 1983: 111). British farmers retain their dominance over the authorities responsible for the administration of land drainage. An article in *Political Studies* described a successful rearguard action fought in 1973 by the National Farmers Union, in cahoots with the Ministry of Agriculture, Fisheries, and Food (MAFF), to prevent the new Water Act from giving the control of farm drainage to the Department of the Environment. It reports that MAFF "shared the distaste of the mainstream land drainage lobby for the proposed large multi-purpose authorities" (Richardson et al. 1978). Multi-purposism is anathema to the beneficiaries of single-purposism.

During the 1981 debate on the Wildlife and Countryside Act, Lord Buxton declared the old laws entirely obsolete, although the Ministry "appears to operate in blinkers labelled 'increased agricultural production' and to pursue blindly that objective":

> The Government, surely, cannot possibly condone individual citizens, however worthy, levying rates on other citizens without any official pattern or objective scrutiny, . . . entering people's property without any notice; spending huge sums of taxpayers' money without any proper supervision or assessment of the consequences; and finally, declining to reveal any of their statistics, documentation or calculations. (Parliamentary Debates 1981).

Conservationists generally oppose agricultural drainage because of the adverse side-effects on fauna and flora. Increased soil fertility enables agricultural plants to flourish but reduces wildlife diversity. In 1984, a book published by the Institute for European Environmental Policy confirmed "the widespread view that wetlands are amongst the most threatened of European habitats and that drainage is one of the prime causes of this" (Baldock 1984). In 1993 the International Union for the Conservation of Nature (IUCN) commented that "Wetlands have been treated with such hostility by many human societies over so many years that their conservation seems almost counter-cultural" (Dugan 1993: 8). In the USA, after catastrophic losses, wetland destruction has been halted and new wetlands are being created (Kusler & Kentula 1990). Wetlands are rich in wildlife and have a vital role in flow regulation.

British water authorities were first advised to take account of conservation in 1963. It became a passive duty "to have regard", in 1973, and "to further the conservation and enhancement of natural beauty and the conservation of flora, fauna and geological or physiographical features of special interest" in 1981 (Wildlife and Countryside Act 1981). The public inquiry into the drainage of Amberley Wild Brooks caused all authorities to take the subject seriously. It is a most beautiful area, especially when part-flooded (Fig. 9.3). In 1977 the Southern Water Authority submitted a pump-drainage scheme to the Ministry (MAFF). It was based on an estimate of the financial cost of the scheme and an economic appraisal of the benefits that might accrue to farmers. No attempt had been made to assess the environmental damage which the scheme might cause (Penning-Rowsell 1978). Local residents and conservation groups protested against the scheme, and the result was Britain's first public inquiry into a land-drainage scheme. The inspector, who was a town planner and engineer, recommended that the scheme should not be grant-aided. His advice was accepted and Amberley Wild Brooks has not been drained. A research group at Middlesex Polytechnic, which carried out the benefit assessment of the drainage scheme, observed that "high but inexplicit economic value was put on the conservation significance of Amberley Wild Brooks" (Parker & Penning-Rowsell 1980). The Amberley Inquiry was a landmark. Using public funds to destroy public goods for private gain was, at last, judged improper, if not wicked.

Figure 9.3 Amberley Wild Brooks is beautiful when flooded and valuable for wildlife. In 1977 the Southern Water Authority was prevented from using public funds to drain the Brooks.

285

Urban drainage

Urban drainage aggravates flooding.

Urbanization aggravates the flood problem. It is obvious that when land is covered with an impermeable material used to make roofs or pavements then more water runs off the land, and less seeps into the ground. Accurate calculations can be done for small areas, but it is difficult to predict, or measure, the consequences of large-scale urbanization. Dunne and Leopold, using American data, predict that the urbanization of a one-square-mile drainage basin will increase the peak discharge by a factor of between 1.5 and 6, depending on soil conditions, the extent of the storm-water drainage system and the proportion of the area rendered impermeable. They take "complete urbanisation" as approximately equal to 50 per cent of the area being impermeable (Dunne & Leopold 1978). In Britain, the *Flood studies report* reached similar conclusions and stressed the difficulty of making accurate predictions (Packman 1981).

The traditional method of dealing with storm runoff from impermeable surfaces is to install an underground drainage system. This led Geddes to exclaim that "drains are for cities, not cities for drains" (Geddes 1917: 3). Engineering and landscape students are taught how to predict the volume of runoff and how to size drainage pipes to accommodate the flow. They forget that because the water-courses into which the drains discharge are rendered more liable to erosion and flooding, they will have to be turned into concrete channels, as described in the previous section.

River works in Britain

River improvement aggravates flooding.

River works were brought under special legislation at an early date, because they affect all riparian landowners. In Britain the legal principles applied to Romney Marsh in the thirteenth century were extended to the whole country by the 1531 Bill of Sewers. It remains "the basis of all drainage legislation" (Royal Commission on land drainage in England and Wales 1927) and established the principle that every landowner who benefits from a river improvement can be required to contribute to the cost of the works. The Sewers Act of 1833 gave commissioners powers to define drainage districts, levy a rate and spend the money on drainage. This Act resulted in considerable land-drainage activity but did not provide sufficient funds for improvements to main rivers, because the people who benefited from the scheme were taken to be those with land below, or just above, the highest known flood level. Upstream drainage without downstream river widening caused severe flooding. In 1877 a Select Committee of the House of Lords reported that:

> It is evident to the Committee, from the information which has been laid before them, that considerable damage has been caused in various parts of England by the prevalence of floods during the last winter, and that such floods have been more frequent and of longer duration in recent times than formerly. Among the causes which have been assigned for this state of things, the Committee find that prominence is given to the very general adoption of the system of subsoil drainage, owing to which a greatly augmented quantity of water is rapidly carried into rivers, and to the deterioration which is constantly taking place in the channels of the rivers themselves whereby they are rendered inadequate to carry off the water of their respective watersheds. (Report of the Select Committee 1887)

No action was taken until a Royal Commission on Land Drainage reached the same conclusion in 1927. It reported that owners of higher land were thought to have ". . . a natural right to discharge their water into the lower levels", where owners then had "to expend vast additional sums on protective measures in the shape of barrier banks and on increased outfall facilities" (Report of the Royal Commission on land drainage in England and Wales 1927). The 1927 report was followed by a Land Drainage Act in 1930. New authorities, known as Catchment Boards, were given powers to levy rates on whole catchments and to spend the money on improvements to main rivers. The use of the term "catchment" instead of "watershed" indicates a human-centred approach. Upland landowners, with property above the highest flood level, had to contribute towards the cost of improving rivers in lowland areas. The 1930 Act led to a great increase in the number of river improvement schemes. Catchment Boards began work at river estuaries and progressed upstream. Their work was continued by the River Boards after 1948 and by the Water Authorities after 1973. Authority for river work was passed to the National Rivers Authority in 1989 and to the Environment Agency in 1996. These agencies have a wider brief and a more enlightened approach.

From 1930 to 1940 "so much tree clearance was done" that in 1954 E. A. G. Johnson, the Ministry of Agriculture's chief engineer, said it was ". . . difficult to get a complete picture of the *derelict* state of the rivers before the passing of the Land Drainage Act of 1930" (my italics). Tree clearance also removed shade and, in Johnson's opinion, led to the growth of water weeds, ". . . which could form an even greater obstruction than much of the tree growth" (Johnson 1966: 44). Since the 1960s waterweeds have been controlled by herbicides, but the policy has been very unpopular with conservation and wildlife groups. In 1954 Johnson said that ". . . . great care is now taken to remove only those trees which form a definite obstruction to flow", but in 1969, still most unhappy about the effect of engineering work on rivers, Johnson wrote that

> . . . in far too many places developments have had little regard either to the existing or potential amenity value of rivers. Indeed, in far too many places rivers and streams have been regarded as nuisances, something to be culverted, enclosed between factory walls or between the fenced-in back gardens of houses. (Johnson 1969)

Johnson's views were a welcome contrast to the traditional engineering approach. Nixon, as Chief Engineer to the Trent River Authority in 1966, used that remarkable old term "training" in an article on his authority's approach to rivers (Nixon 1966b). He illustrates the approach with photographs of "trained" rivers. They are encased in concrete or confined between parallel berms, like the unfortunate River Crouch at Wickford (Fig. 9.4). Nixon described it as a River Improvement Scheme, but one can see that, whatever else may have been improved, most certainly it was *not* the river. His visual insensitivity is further revealed by the technocratic judgement that precast concrete blocks look "more pleasing than natural stone pitching".

Figure 9.4 The River Crouch in Wickford, as "trained" by Nixon's engineers. The road bridge, a later embellishment, did not appear in Nixon's photograph.

Seeing plants as weeds and animals as pests, he is a fine example of blinkered single-purposism.

Throughout Europe and North America river "improvement" schemes have followed the same pattern (Fig. 9.5), so that ". . . the vast majority of rivers and streams have been regulated, straightened, misused, polluted, canalised or even piped" (*Garten & Landschaft* 1983). The US Council on Environmental Quality, in a 1973 report on riverworks, estimated that the Corps of Engineers, the Bureau of Reclamation and the Tennessee Valley

Figure 9.5 The drainage may have been "improved" by this 1985 publicly financed scheme, but the Mouse Water was despoiled.

Authority had constructed 13,358 kilometres of flood defences and 8,047 kilometres of "channel improvements" on main rivers, while the Soil Conservation Service and the Corps of Engineers had "channelized" 55,104 kilometres of streams (Dunne & Leopold 1978). Dunne and Leopold state that the works tend to cause channel instability, downstream bank erosion, bed degradation or aggradation, aesthetic despoliation and damage to fauna and flora. They suggest an alternative approach:

> Channel changes in urban streams cause costly construction and maintenance and unsightly, dangerous conditions. Many a small stream though an urban area will be seen encased in concrete, lined with a high, strong wire fence to keep children from falling into the fast-moving water during storm flow. An alternative design might well have been a stream-side park with bicycle paths, picnic places, attractive vegetation, and hydrologically desirable flood capacity that will tend to decrease rather than increase flooding downstream. Where this latter alternative is chosen, the urban creek can be an aesthetic amenity and a social asset. (Dunne & Leopold 1978)

Channelized watercourses must now be reclaimed as "rivers". Dunne and Leopold use the Sammamish Slough to illustrate the point. The channel was graded to engineering profiles, sown with grass seed, and sprayed with herbicides to keep down trees and shrubs. After a decade of this treatment a firm of landscape architects was hired ". . . to plant trees along its banks, halt the spraying, grade the banks to a shallower angle, and encourage the development of wildlife habitat and public access". It was done without reducing the conveyance capacity of the channel. Another reclamation project, which I love, is described in a special streams issue of *Garten & Landschaft* (1983). The River Wandse, where it runs through a nature reserve, was reclaimed from a ruler-straight engineered channel and restored to its old meandering course, which was plotted from old maps and by searching the ground for moisture, indicating plants (Fig. 9.6). Truncated sections of the linear channel were retained as wetland habitats (Glitz 1983).

In Denmark, the Watercourse Act of 1949 stated that ". . . drainage shall have priority over any other use" (Brookes 1988: 17). The government agency responsible for land drainage worked with great efficiency, and by 1997 98 per cent of Danish watercourses had been straightened (Brookes & Douglas Shields 1996:2). This was a higher proportion than in any other European country (Fig. 9.7). Eventually, after a campaign by conservationists, the process was put into reverse, the same government agency having responsibility for the work. Straight rivers (||) are being reconverted to serpentine rivers (S) and a dollar sign ($) is used, by wits, to summarize the situation.

The history of British river engineering practice in the second half of the twentieth century is illustrated by London's rivers, with the River Lea a

Figure 9.6 The River Wandse, in Germany, previously straightened by river engineers, was restored to its old meandering course in the 1980s. (Photo courtesy of Freie und Hansestadt Hamburg.)

good example. It was once Izaak Walton's favourite fishing river. A downstream channel enlargement project, started in 1948, was seen as ". . . the first instalment of a comprehensive concept for the *improvement* of the River Lea" [my italics] (Association of River Authorities 1965). The second instalment, below Chalk Bridge, was a grim concrete flood relief channel lined by chainlink fences (Fig. 9.8). It could persuade the most determined sceptic of the need for Environmental Impact Design. The third instalment, from Chalk Bridge to Ware, looks like a canal, because weirs and sluices retain the water at top-of-bank level, and had a detrimental impact on wildlife. One part of a fourth instalment, on a tributary of the Lea, was carried out with more care for wildlife, but further work was blocked by pressure from conservation groups and the Nature Conservancy Council. Comprehensive

291

Figure 9.7 An "improved" river in a Copenhagen park.

landscape improvement schemes are needed for the work carried out on the Lea from 1948 to 1976, and for all London's rivers – especially the Roding, the Cray, the Ravensbourne, the Wandle (Fig. 9.9), Beverly Brook, the Quaggy and, of course, the Thames itself. Gone are the days when a poet could pen a river stanza for the Chronicle of London:

Figure 9.8 The amazing thing about this flood relief channel on the River Lea is its treatment as an industrial zone fenced with chainlink. The dull public park beyond the fencing would benefit enormously from a well-designed water feature.

Figure 9.9 A manhole marking the route of the River Wandle, beloved by John Ruskin, as it passes through Wandle Park. Some day, it *will* be reclaimed.

Above all rivers thy river hath renown
Whose beryl streames, pleasant and preclare
Under thy lusty walles runneth down;
Where many a swan doth swim with winges fair,
Where many a barge doth sail, and row with oar,
Where many a ship doth rest woth top-royal.
O town of townes, patron and not compare,
London, thou art the flower of Cities all.

(William Dunbar, 1465–1530)

At some happy point in the future, it may become possible to follow the melancholy book *The lost rivers of London* (Barton 1962) with a triumphalist sequel: *How we won them back.*

Present conditions

The flood problem has been aggravated.

Let us review what has happened in the industrialized countries (Fig. 9.10). Forest clearance took place on the hills, in the valleys and on the plains. This accelerated water runoff. Ploughing and drainage took place in agricultural areas. This accelerated water runoff. River channels were deepened, widened, straightened and fixed. This accelerated water runoff. Large new urban areas were rendered partially impervious, with roofing and paving materials. This accelerated water runoff. The capacity of washlands and floodplains to accommodate peak volumes was diminished by building upon them. Accelerated water runoff raised flood peaks. It then became necessary to put urban rivers into underground culverts or concrete canals, or to supplement their capacity with "flood relief channels". The net effect of all the changes was a dramatic increase in peak storm discharge. Embankments had to be built to prevent overtopping by floodwater. When these works are viewed together it is clear that they do not constitute a good use of public or private funds.

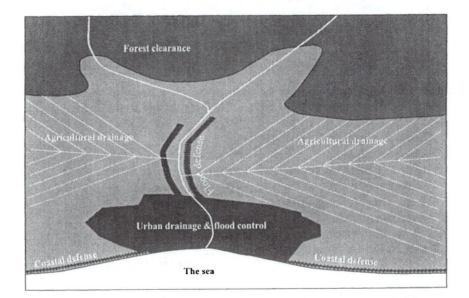

Figure 9.10 In all the industrial countries, rivers have suffered from forest clearance in the uplands, farm drainage in the lowlands and water-proofing in urban areas.

River reclamation

And he shewed me a pure river of water of life, clear as crystal, proceeding out of the throne of God and of the Lamb.

(Revelation 22:1)

In the past, "improving" rivers meant increasing their flow capacity. In future it should refer to multi-purpose schemes designed to improve the capacity of each river valley to function as a visual amenity, a recreation area, a fishery, a nature reserve, a water supply, a storm detention area, a drainage network and a movement corridor for boats, walkers, cyclists and equestrians. We are fortunate that the means have become available:

- multi-purpose planning
- managed flooding
- storm detention basins
- infiltration facilities
- vegetated roofs
- porous pavements
- natural riverworks.

As discussed below, these measures should be used to increase the base flow in rivers, to reduce flood peaks and to improve the physical design of river channels.

Multi-purpose planning

Rivers can do more than carry water.

The 1969–79 Reuss Valley Improvement Scheme is a good example of a multi-purpose river planning project. It is in Switzerland, which, compared with many countries, has more democracy and less technocracy. The Reuss Valley lies outside Zurich between the Jura and the Alps. In 1953 a new dam was thought necessary to deal with the ancient flood problem, but the project was delayed by a clash of interests between agriculture, flood protection and nature conservation. No scheme was agreed until 1969. The Reuss Act provided that

> Consideration shall be given to the requirements of landscape protection, the water system, hunting and fishing. The scenic character of the area shall be conserved as much as possible. The cantonal executive shall issue landscape design plans after hearing the communal

councils, the committees of the land improvement co-operatives and the nature and landscape conservation agencies.

Plans were produced for farming, reafforestation, nature conservation, building and recreation. By 1979 the following sums had been spent: 80 million francs on agriculture, 62 million francs on a power station, 44 million francs on flood protection, and 10 million francs on landscape and nature conservation (Executive Council of the Canton of Aargau 1979). It is significant that a wide range of community groups and design professions were involved in the scheme. Local democracy works. The Reuss scheme illustrates the principle of multi-purpose planning.

The widest possible range of public goods should be obtained for a given level of public expenditure. McHarg described this principle as that of obtaining "the maximum social benefit and the minimum social cost" (McHarg 1971: 32). This requires the integration of professional disciplines under local democratic control. It contrasts with the normal situation where a "lead profession" has responsibility for interpreting unnecessarily centralized government regulations, producing a paucity of public goods.

The change from single-purpose to multi-purpose river management requires the preparation of landscape plans. Some reaches of a river may be fully multi-purpose; in other reaches, there is likely to be an emphasis on habitat creation or scenic quality or fishing or water quality or something else. As with open-space planning (page 148) colours can be used to symbolize the intended character of different reaches of a river (Fig. 9.11).

Managed flooding

Flood risk can be managed.

Normal rainfall maintains the flow in streams and rivers. Exceptional rainfall causes floods of different sizes. Engineers classify the size of floods by the probable period within which they are likely to return. A one-year event is the largest flood that is likely to return every year, and a 100-year event is the largest flood that is likely to return within a century. Contours can be drawn to show the geographical flood extent for each return period. In a natural landscape, larger volumes of water will cause more land to be flooded (Fig. 9.12). In a developed landscape, there will be less variation. Normally, anything up to a five-year flood will be confined to the river channel or to a wider flood-channel. When a ten-year or 100-year flood event occurs, buildings and roads will be flooded. Users and residents do not like this, but their inconvenience has to be set against other considerations. Not only are flood defence works extremely expensive, financially

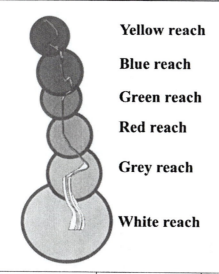

Yellow reach

Blue reach

Green reach

Red reach

Grey reach

White reach

	Land use	Character
Yellow reach	Nature reserve	Ecological and scenically diverse
Blue reach	Agriculture	Serene, calm and stately
Green reach	Forestry	Cool, relaxing, and interesting
Red reach	Town centre	Gay, exciting and unexpected
Grey reach	Commerce	Sculptural, solemn and memorable
White reach	Recreation	Expansive, open and awe-inspiring

Figure 9.11 Colours can be used to symbolize proposed riparian character.

and environmentally; they tend merely to exacerbate the downstream flood problem.

One solution is to incorporate managed flooding into the land-use planning system. Each town can draw existing and proposed contours for each flood event:

- half-year: nature reserves, playing fields, parks, gardens;
- one-year: non-essential car parks, lightly trafficked roads, flood-tolerant buildings;
- 25-year: most roads and car-parks, the ground floors of non-essential buildings;
- 100-year: sizeable urban areas, but not hospitals or other essential services.

297

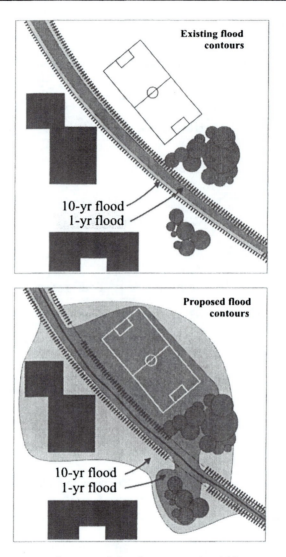

Figure 9.12 Existing and proposed flood contours should be mapped.

In order to lessen flood damage to valuable property, as large an area as possible should be included within the half-year and one-year flood zones. Some buildings can be placed within the frequent-flood zone, with measures to make them flood-proof or flood-tolerant (Fig. 9.13): electrical services can be sealed or routed above the flood-level; water-sealed doors can be made, as on ships; furnishings can be resistant to water-damage; pedestrian access routes can be provided above the flood-level; drainage flaps and bilge-

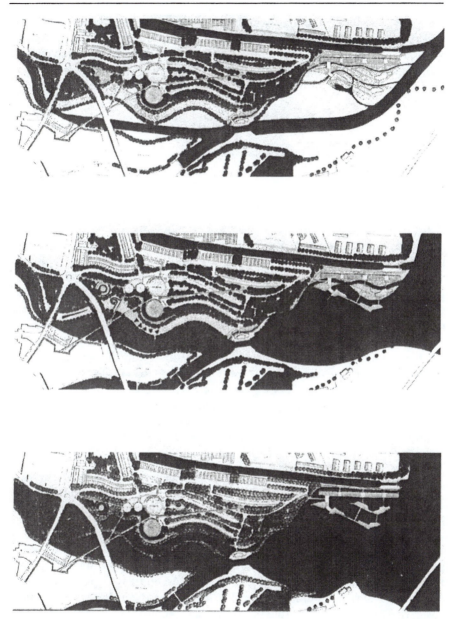

Figure 9.13 Buildings can be designed so that they are usable during occasional periods of flooding. In this design by Martin Wallace and Ray Hole, the top diagram shows the normal flow situation, the middle diagram shows a medium flood, and the lower diagram shows the building (on the right) surrounded by the water it is designed to resist.

299

pumps can be fitted; buildings can be raised on stilts above the flood level; waterproof concrete can be used for walls; extra foundations can be used to resist erosion by floodwaters. If landowners do not wish to incur the cost or inconvenience of these measures, they should not build in floodplains and they should have no claim on public expenditure for flood defence.

Storm detention

Storm water should be detained.

After centuries of accelerated surface water runoff, it is now accepted that rainwater should be controlled "at source". Runoff should be detained where it falls and discharged from the area as slowly as possible. This will attenuate the flood hydrograph. Water authorities, if they have the power, can insist that when new development takes place the volume of storm water discharge must not increase. This policy is sometimes known as "zero runoff". They can also impose a drainage levy on landowners who discharge rainwater into public sewers. Any developer who installs paving, roofing or drainage that will cause an increase in the rate of runoff can be required either to pay compensation or to carry out works which detain water and prevent it from causing flooding in downstream areas. This technique is known as "urban stormwater management" (Hall 1984). When significant volumes of water are detained on the land, flood levels and flood peaks will diminish. The practice has many advantages but should be more than an engineering exercise:

> The preferred approach should be to regard urban runoff as a resource for potential re-use rather than an inconvenience, and to undertake stormwater flow management design in a catchment context. (CIRIA 1992a: 5)

Water can be used to recharge aquifers, to irrigate vegetation, to create ponds, wetlands and water features. From a nature conservation standpoint, these features are highly desirable. The CIRIA report also points out that "controlled surface flooding" leads to significant economies in drainage costs (ibid.: 55). This is the point McHarg made in 1975 (page 375). Another CIRIA report observes that ". . . some planning authorities have accepted storage ponds as part of open space provision while others have rejected even landscape flood areas" (CIRIA 1992b: 11). The problem results from a petty dispute between drainage authorities and parks departments over the responsibility for the maintenance of vegetated flood storage areas. Would they be parks or drains?

The principle of storm detention has been considered "increasingly neces-sary" in Britain (Institute of Civil Engineers 1981: 2). One of the chief reasons for the massive flood relief programme in the Lea Valley was urbanization. Its catchment of 1,500 square kilometres has an average pop-ulation density of 1,667 per square kilometre. When the first instalment of the river improvement scheme was nearing completion, in 1958, it was believed that urban growth in the Lea Valley and the construction of new towns at Stevenage and Welwyn Garden City ". . . made the extension of the Flood Alleviation Scheme up the valley into Hertfordshire even more necessary". It was thought that ". . . new towns with their large areas of impermeable road, roof tops and shopping areas pose a major threat to hitherto natural streams" (Wyllie 1958). Since much of the urbanization took place on permeable chalk and sand, the paved surfaces caused dramatic changes in the rate of runoff and needlessly prevented rainwater from recharging the aquifer. By 1982, ten dry basins had been built in Stevenage, and a 0.78-hectare wet basin, known as the Black Fen Valley Lagoon, was used for storm detention (and model boating) in Welwyn Garden City. They have been planned as central features in the French new towns (Secrétariat Général du Groupe Central des Villes Nouvelles 1977). At Reston in Virginia, which is a planned community with a target population of 35,000, three detention ponds were included in the layout. Since lake-front property sells for three times the price of other land in Reston, the detention ponds are seen as an excellent commercial proposition (Robbins et al. 1981).

There are two wet basins and one dry basin in the Cray Valley, which were treated as single-purpose engineering projects (Thompson 1966: 135). The dry basin, at Hall Place, is a soggy area in a public park (Fig. 9.14). If it had been designed as a wildlife habitat, it would have improved the appear-ance of a vacant expanse of grass. The wet basins look marvellous when the flood waters gather to remind us of the swamps that once characterized the winter landscape of northern Europe. Most swamps have been drained, and it is a tragedy that the principle of storm detention was not adopted at an earlier date. In the first edition of this book I commented that the Cray wet basins, at Ruxley, are cut off from the surrounding urban area by fences, and that only licensed fishermen were allowed to enter. Members of the Kent Trust for Nature Conservation are now allowed in, but there is no public access.

Detention basins can also be used to improve water quality, by filtration, sedimentation and biological assimilation (Startin & Lansdown, 1994). Reedbed systems have been shown to reduce oxygen demand and to remove phosphates, nitrates, suspended solids and bacterial loading. These advan-tages, which are considerable, are best achieved by integrating water man-agement into the town and country planning system.

Figure 9.14 Storm detention basins on the River Cray in south-east London. The wet basin (above) is beautiful in time of flood, reminding one of the swamps that used to characterize the winter landscape of northern Europe. The dry basin (below) is a soggy area in an otherwise dull expanse of public park: it should be re-designed as a wetland habitat.

Rainwater infiltration

Storm water should be infiltrated.

Wherever possible, rainfall should be infiltrated into the ground where it falls. It should not be ducted into pipes, conduits, ditches or rivers. This ensures that the volume of peak discharge is not increased, and the interval between the start of a storm and the time of peak discharge is not reduced. Infiltration has a number of advantages (CIRIA 1992b: 15):

- Soil moisture levels are enhanced.
- The base flow in streams can be regenerated.
- Water quality is improved, and the discharge of pollutants into the drainage network is restricted.

Conducting water in vegetated swales helps evaporation, transpiration and infiltration. Vegetation also keeps the soil structure open. But swales should not be designed as geometrical ditches. They should be integrated with the landform design. More water will be infiltrated when soils and rocks are porous, but infiltration is also advantageous in less permeable substrates. Research in Sweden has shown that the use of soakaways, porous drains and infiltration basins can prevent dieback in trees and the structural damage to buildings which occurs when shrinkable clays become too dry (Holmstrand 1984).

In 1981 two American engineers reported on the results of a survey into methods of storm-water management (Peortner & Reindl 1981). They found that "temporarily storing, or detaining, excess stormwater runoff and then releasing it at a regulated rate" had become "a fundamental principle in stormwater management". A total of 325 public authorities in the USA and Canada responded to a questionnaire, and 219 authorities reported that storm detention facilities had been installed. Details of the 12,683 facilities were analyzed, and it was found that 47.5 per cent were dry basins, 24.7 per cent were car parks, 18.8 per cent were ponds, 5.5 per cent were rooftop storage areas, and the remaining 3.3 per cent were underground tanks, oversized sewers, tunnels and other special facilities.

The authorities gave the following reasons, listed in decreasing order of importance, for installing storm detention areas:

1 to reduce downstream flooding;
2 to reduce the cost of the drainage system;
3 to reduce on-site flooding;
4 to reduce soil erosion;
5 to capture silt;
6 to improve on-site drainage;
7 to reduce pollution;

8 to improve aesthetic quality;
9 to enhance recreational opportunities;
10 to replenish groundwater supplies;
11 to supplement domestic water supplies;
12 to catch water for irrigation.

There are few technical innovations that can so completely transform a single-purpose design into an opportunity for multi-objective design. Vegetated roofs, roof gardens, storage ponds, streams and reinforced-grass carparks bring multiple benefits. Collectively, they are known as source control.

Vegetated roofs

Vegetated roofs reduce flooding.

Because they are smooth and steeply inclined, unvegetated roofs tend to have the fastest rainwater discharge rates of any surfaces in urban areas. Vegetated roofs (Fig. 9.15) discharge less water, and the rate of discharge is reduced:

- Roof water is transpired by plants and used in metabolic processes.
- Roof water is retained as soil moisture.
- Flat roofs have additional detention capacity.
- Roof water is returned to the atmosphere by evaporation.

Roof surfaces have higher evaporation rates than ground surfaces, because they are more exposed to sun and wind. Vegetation increases the area from which evaporation can take place.

Cumulatively, these effects are significant. From a light shower, there will be no runoff. From a moderate shower, only half the precipitation may be discharged from the roof. With a heavy shower, there may be a delay of an hour or more before there is any discharge from a previously dry roof. The total annual discharge may be halved.

Porous pavements

Porous pavements reduce flooding.

In old towns, most streets were surfaced with gravel. Stone pavements were a luxury for use in grand towns, so that ladies' and gentlemen's clothes were

Figure 9.15 Vegetated roofs are interesting, beautiful, good for thermal insulation and of value as wildlife habitats. Above, London. Below, Cologne.

305

Figure 9.16 Paved sidewalks were originally a means of protecting gentlefolks' clothes from mud.

not soiled (Fig. 9.16). When the volume of wheeled traffic increased, moving within and between towns, sealed pavements became necessary. The sealant acts as a "roof" to stop water entering road foundations and behaving as a lubricant in the substructure. Sealed pavements have greater strength than porous roads. This led people to think they are better. But sealed pavements are only necessary when traffic loadings or traffic volumes are high. For light traffic it is much better to have a porous "green lane". If necessary, the surface can be protected from abrasion by a matrix of concrete or geotextile. Natural surface roughness helps to calm traffic speeds (Fig. 9.17).

Pedestrians can be provided with smooth porous pavements, because they do not like walking on a rough surface. A good-quality self-binding gravel forms an excellent surface. Modern materials are also available. These include porous concrete blocks, bricks and stone with porous joints (Fig. 9.18). Bitumen-macadam can also be porous if it is made with a no-fines aggregate. In time, the effectiveness of porous pavements diminishes, as silt accumulates.

Natural riverworks

Bio-engineering is better.

Figure 9.17 Unsealed "green lanes" allow rain to percolate into the soil, instead of discharging into drains. This lane is in a densely populated part of Greenwich, London.

In the heyday of single-objective river engineering, say the century from 1880 to 1980, riverworks were designed according to the principles of structural engineering. The design of embankments, walls and other structures was based on estimates of loads, flows and pressures. Since then, the behaviour of natural rivers has been studied and engineers have become interested in designs which behave more like natural water-courses. Brookes sees these techniques as "design with nature", as advocated by McHarg, and as "reverence for rivers", as advocated by Leopold (Brookes 1988: 189). Bio-engineering techniques are used to retain soil and protect against erosion. Particular attention is given to pools, riffles, point bars, floodplains and bank vegetation. Co-operation with ecologists has developed the habitat potential of riverworks (Royal Society for the Protection of Birds 1994). The results of this approach are aesthetically better, but the works can still lack the romantic beauty which inspired Robert Louis Stevenson to write:

> Dark brown is the river,
>   Golden is the sand.
> It flows along for ever,
>   With trees on either hand

(R. L. Stevenson, Where go the boats)

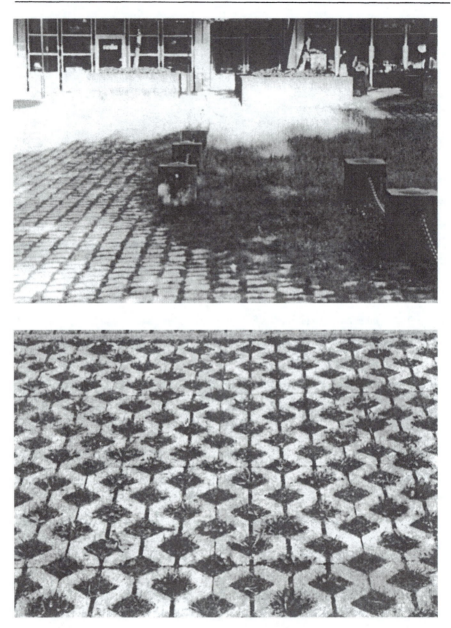

Figure 9.18 Hard surfaces can be made porous, using concrete blocks (below) or granite sets (above).

River control structures

River structures should serve many objectives.

Structures are used to control the flow of rivers for a number of purposes, including bank stabilization, water storage, flood protection, depth regulation, aeration, flow measurement and storm detention. They also affect fisheries, wildlife, swimming, boating and the visual appearance of our towns and countryside. Structures can be designed with either single or multiple objectives in view.

It is only in exceptional circumstances that multi-objective designs have been attempted (Fig. 9.19). The best examples are in semi-arid countries where water is scarce and highly valued for economic, aesthetic and religious purposes. The stepped tank wells of India were conceived as multi-purpose projects and admired by Patrick Geddes. He tried to halt the European practice of filling in the tanks to control malaria. Geddes pointed out that tanks cool the air, help to control flooding and can be stocked with fish (Geddes 1917).

In Iran there is a long history of designing structures which serve as dams, weirs, bridges and pavilions. The most famous surviving example is the Khaju Bridge outside Isfahan (Fig. 9.20), which carries traffic and feeds

Figure 9.19 A weir designed by the artist Victor Passmore in Peterlee New Town. He wrote that "the function of this feature is not only optical, but also environmental and pedestrian".

Figure 9.20 Kajhu Bridge, in Iran, could be the best multi-purpose water-retaining structure ever made. (Courtesy of Shilla Tabrizi.)

irrigation canals. Its superstructure was part of the original design, unlike the adventitious buildings on Old London Bridge and the Ponte Vecchio:

> From the steps on the lower side of the bridge the people wash their linen or play in the cool water, and interior stairways lead thence up to the second story of the bridge . . . Poets in contemplation, mullahs and philosophers in argument, families in reunion, gossiping women and friends at various amusements, all may enjoy the beauties of the scene in isolation and comfort. (Pope 1939: 1237)

Britain also has examples of river control structures that are "more than engineering". They occur either in important city-centre locations or as the product of an enlightened attitude to the landscape of industry. In London, the Victoria Embankment is a historic example of a multi-purpose project, although it spoiled the riverbank. Joseph Paxton was instrumental in its promotion. The embankment serves for river protection, as a promenade, and as the route for an underground railway and a trunk sewer (Chadwick 1961: 216). There are handsome sections of river embankment at Greenwich, Hammersmith and Strand-on-the-Green, but many opportunities were squandered during the period 1972–84.

When construction work began on the Woolwich Flood Barrier in 1972 it became necessary to launch a massive programme of downstream flood protection works, largely funded by MAFF. The opportunity for creative riverside design was taken up in some places. MAFF part-funded the architectural design of the barrier, and the GLC laid out viewing gardens on the adjoining banks. Elsewhere the flood walls and embankments were built in a crude and unsightly manner. Even at Thamesmead, the site of a major GLC housing project, the flood wall was designed by engineers and then "decorated" by landscape architects. The Otterspool Promenade, designed as part of the 1984 Liverpool Garden Festival, is a very much better example of joint design by landscape and engineering specialists (Turner & Lancaster 1984). Similarly, the Rhine embankment in Cologne is both a flood protection measure and a fine park.

Other British cities have also considered the amenity aspects of river engineering. In Bath:

> Alternative forms of sluice were suggested, one being a radial gate and two vertical lifting gates. These were submitted to the Royal Fine Arts Commission who recommended the radial gate in principle, but requested that the services of a landscape architect be obtained to produce the most aesthetically pleasing overall scheme. Mr Conder, of Casson, Conder and Partners, was appointed and he has produced a scheme which does not derogate from the hydraulic requirements, is aesthetically pleasing and fits in with future proposals of Bath Corporation in the area. (Greenhalgh 1968)

The Pulteney Weir is beautiful (Fig. 9.21). Equal care should be given to other structures, even when they are not in the middle of historic cities.

Weirs and sluices can also be designed for active recreation. Canoeists are often seen paddling into the white water generated by river control structures. In 1972 a group of Bedfordshire canoeists asked the Anglian Water Authority to find a site for a canoe slalom course in a very flat part of England (Anglian Water Authority 1982). The Authority took up the idea and in 1981–2 built a slalom course at Cardington Lock 2.5 kilometres east of Bedford. The course has a dual function, acting primarily as a river flood control structure and at other times as a canoe slalom course. There is a control sluice at the head of a concrete-lined channel, which connects the upper reach of the river to the lower. Immediately downstream of the control sluice is the canoeists' launching pool, leading directly to the slalom channel. The cost of the structure was £273,000 of which 50 per cent came from the Great Ouse Local Land Drainage Account (with grant-aid from MAFF), 24.5 per cent from the Anglian Water Authority's Recreation and Navigation Account, 18.3 per cent from the Sports Council and 7.2 per cent from a group of eight local councils.

311

Figure 9.21 The weir below Pulteney Bridge in Bath is calm and graceful.

From a landscape planning viewpoint the Cardington slalom is a notable achievement, and superior to any river control structure in the Lea Valley Regional Park. But as a landscape design it is only a moderate success. The Teesside Whitewater Course on the River Tees, near Stockton, also succeeds as a landscape design (Fig. 9.22). It was made possible by Teesside Development Corporation's construction of the Tees River Barrage. The white-water course is on land previously operated as a tip for construction industry material. It was shaped to form a bowl. The scheme incorporates a navigation lock, a fish pass, a warm-up lake, a caravan and camping park. It also makes an addition to the local network of wildlife corridors. It is an admirable example of a multi-purpose river control structure (Davis 1995).

Coastal defence

Coasts need landscape plans.

Coastal "defence", like river "improvement", has too often been regarded solely as an "engineering problem". The US Army Corps of Engineers gave a classic statement of this attitude in 1964: "Our campaign against the sea must be waged with the same care that we would take against any other

Figure 9.22 The Tees Barrage and Teesside Whitewater Course Flagship Schemes of Teesside Development Corporation is an excellent modern example of a multi-purpose river control structure. (Courtesy of SGS Environmental and Teesside Development Corporation.)

enemy threatening our boundaries" (Clark 1982). Like British engineers they ignored natural processes and social factors. As a consequence of this approach many coastal areas suffered damage to their ecology and amenities. The exceptions are sandy coasts, where the protective value of dune vegetation has been recognized, and resort towns, where some effort has been made to adapt sea walls for amenity use.

The oldest method of sea defence is the construction of earth embankments. It was used in Egypt and Mesopotamia and remains in widespread use. Sea embankments normally cause either erosion or deposition. When they are positioned to gain extra land, wave energy tends to be concentrated in a physically smaller zone, and erosion is increased. Littoral vegetation is lost and the shoreline available for recreational use is diminished. If the erosion problem is severe, earth embankments are surfaced with stone, concrete and bitumen to give additional protection. Such works are rarely pleasing to the human eye, or to wildlife, although they can give convenient road access to beaches. Extensive works of this kind are found on the coast of Holland. Since more than half of Holland owes its existence to sea defence, it is understandable that priority should have been given to engineering considerations. It is possible to enhance the amenity value of an embanked coast by introducing more variation into the design of the bank profiles, by adjusting the alignment to create new wildlife habitats and by recharging the foreshore with sand and gravel.

The nineteenth-century development of seaside resorts introduced a new consideration into the design of sea walls. Visitors who came for sea air and good views did not wish to be cut off from the sea by embankments. Engineers responded by constructing vertical sea walls with promenades on top. It is now known that these walls had a deleterious effect on beach erosion. They deflect part of the wave energy downwards and cause the water to erode the foreshore. Many authorities responded by constructing groynes, which look like military defences against a seaborne invasion. They have some effect in diminishing longshore drift but are more effective on gravel than sandy beaches. If groynes do succeed in trapping beach material they will cause increased erosion on adjacent downdrift beaches. As with river improvements, a "solution" in one place causes problems in another – and a need for more engineering work. In Britain this problem has been aggravated by the fact that the "coastal protection" of urban areas comes under the Department of the Environment, while "sea defence" of agricultural land comes under the Ministry of Agriculture, Fisheries, and Food (Trafford & Braybrooks 1982).

In 1982, the Deputy Director of the Hydraulics Research Station endorsed an American account of coastal defence work:

> For more than a century in the USA jetties, groins, seawalls and other structures have been built in a futile effort to trap sand and to protect beaches. These structures, designed to alter the sediment flow and to interfere with the natural equilibrium of the beach, have in most cases caused further problems. Engineers and planners in the United States now believe that the best method for beach restoration should not alter the natural processes – rebuilding beaches artificially (beach nourishment) by replacing sand lost to the system permits the natural process to continue unhampered. (Price 1982)

Small-scale beach recharge has been practised in Britain for many years. The first major project was the "renourishment" of Bournemouth beach as a pilot project in 1970. It was followed by a 1.6-kilometre scheme at Portobello, outside Edinburgh, in 1972, and an 8.5-kilometre scheme at Bournemouth in 1974–5. These projects have been very successful both in protecting the old sea walls from further erosion and in improving the recreational value of beaches. They are also cheaper than concrete walls (Thorn & Roberts 1981).

The town of Sheerness, which has always been prone to flooding, exhibits four different approaches to the design of sea defences. The old sea wall was an earth embankment surfaced with stonepitching. When the town began to flourish as a holiday resort, a new amenity sea wall was built east of the old town. It is a fine Edwardian seaside structure with a stepped wall and semicircular platforms surmounted by elegant pavilion shelters (Fig. 9.23). During the 1970s a third type of sea wall was built in Sheerness. It is a plain concrete bank surmounted by a walkway and a curved wall designed to reflect wave energy outwards. The wall was kept low, to preserve views from seafront houses, and the landward side was designed by an architect (ibid.). A fourth type of sea defence was also constructed during the 1970s and has a better environmental impact. It is a beach recharge scheme using gravel instead of sand. The gravel was dredged from the sea and pumped ashore from barges. Beach recharge is the most natural method of sea defence but, as with other types of barrier, its environmental impact must be designed. The opportunity should be taken to establish new plant communities and to create recreational facilities. At Sheerness the beach is used by a catamaran club and by windsurfers. They are able to use an old ramp to gain access to the shore, but the roadway is steep, narrow and without a proper turning area at the top or bottom of the slope. If the access road had been properly designed, and vegetation established on the landward slope of the bank, the impact of the gravel bank on the environment would be better.

The planning of sand-dune coasts is relatively advanced. Ian McHarg carried out a coastal landscape planning project in New Jersey after a great storm in 1962. He observed the damage which was done because

Figure 9.23 The Edwardian seawall at Sheerness, unlike its modernist successors, was designed as a visual and recreational amenity.

holiday homes had been built among the dunes without regard to the planning principles that had been known to the Dutch for centuries:

> Forty-foot waves pounded the shore, breached the dunes and filled the bay, which spilled across the islands back to the ocean. When the storm subsided, the extent of the disaster was clear. Three days of storm had produced eighty million dollars worth of damage, twenty-four hundred houses destroyed or damaged beyond repair, eighty-three hundred houses partially damaged, several people killed and many injured in New Jersey alone. (McHarg 1971: 16)

McHarg recommended the adoption of measures to preserve "the dune grass, hero of Holland", and other vegetation. Plant roots bind the sand and create a flexible, permeable barrier with great capacity to absorb water and wave energy without giving way. Pedestrian access erodes dune vegetation. In by far his most convincing example of "ecological planning", McHarg recommended unlimited recreational use of the beach, a denial of access to the primary dune, some recreational use of the trough behind the primary dune, and no building development on the secondary dune. He said that building development should be confined to the comparatively stable and "more permissive" environment of the backdune.

In 1972, the USA passed a Coastal Zone Management Act, which has led to many reforms and encouraged coastal states to consider sea defence in a broad landscape planning context. Multi-disciplinary design teams are now responsible for multi-objective projects. The design objectives include the protection of life and property, energy production, recreation, transport, food production, wood production, national defence and the conservation of ecological, cultural and aesthetic values. The Act, which led to a major shift in emphasis from wetland drainage and macro-engineering to the more natural technology of beach recharge, habitat conservation and biological engineering, is discussed in a special issue of the *Journal of the American Planning Association* (1985). With agricultural land becoming less valuable, there is now discussion of "managed retreat". Embankments are breached or allowed to decay. Old fields become new marshlands.

In 1993 and 1995, the UK government published a review and policies for coastal planning (MAFF 1993a; 1993b; 1995). The government confessed that earlier policies had ignored natural and social factors but, in its statement of aims, reasserted the primacy of defence:

> To reduce risks to people and the developed and natural environment from flooding and coastal erosion by encouraging the provision of technically, environmentally and economically sound and sustainable defence measures. (MAFF 1993a)

Risk reduction and defence are wholly inadequate as goals for any land-scape planning exercise. But the MAFF reports did call for a series of "voluntary strategy plans" for coasts. They suggested:

- shoreline management plans: for the defence of the shoreline;
- coastal zone management plans: to help resolve competing pressures in the coastal zone;
- catchment management plans: to help resolve competing pressures in river catchments.

Voluntary plans can be useful – if their objectives are sufficiently broad. Human evolution took place at the water margin, and coasts remain the most vital places (Crawford & Marsh 1989). They should be treated as special landscape planning zones with a great emphasis on conserving and creating public goods. As beside rivers, we require public access, nature conservation, habitat creation, scenic conservation and scenic restoration. If agriculture and forestry are to receive financial subsidies, coastal fields and forests should be subsidized in very special ways. If building is to be allowed, it should be a special type of building. Coasts have beauty, magic and power. Reverence is the approach of choice.

Conclusions

We must win our rivers back.

After centuries of "improving" rivers and "defending" coasts against floods, the developed countries have given their waterfronts a military aspect, domi-nated by embankments, retaining walls and concrete ditches. A major recla-mation programme is necessary to reclaim our channels, water-courses, culverts and coastal defences (Brookes & Douglas 1996). Their dignity must be restored, as streams, brooks, rivers and shores. Landscape character plans should be formulated. Rainwater should be infiltrated near where it falls – or else it should be detained near where it falls, and discharged slowly. Rivers and coasts should be planned, designed and managed. In places, this will require no human intervention: the coast should be as natural as pos-sible. In other places, their scenic and recreational potential should be devel-oped. Rivers and coasts have exceptional scope for contributing to a green web of public open space. Engineering is not enough. Negative environmen-tal impacts should be mitigated. Positive environmental impacts should be planned and designed. Engineers have an important role but, working under local democratic control, they must learn to co-operate with community groups, landscape planners, scientists, ecologists, geologists, landscape designers and architects. Waterfront land is our most valuable land.

CHAPTER 10
Transport

Introduction

Transport planning has been dominated by single-purpose planners and designers.

To civilize means to "reclaim from barbarism". This requires transport. Without it we would have no cities, no mass production, no specialization, no journeys to work, no tourism, no modern conveniences. Hilaire Belloc was clear on this point:

> The Road is one of the great fundamental institutions of mankind . . . It is the Road which determines the sites of many cities and the growth and nourishment of all. It is the Road which controls the development of strategies and fixes the sites of battles. It is the Road that gives its frame-work to all economic development. It is the Road which is the channel of all trade and, what is more important, of all ideas . . . the Road moves and controls all history. (Belloc 1924)

But the planning and design of roads, like other modes of transport, tends to become the preserve of blinkered specialists infatuated with the dream of maximizing the transport mode for which they assume responsibility. They ignore other public goods. They neglect EID. With regard to highways Ian McHarg, the son of a preacher, observed that:

> If one seeks a single example of an assertion of simple-minded single purpose, the analytical rather than the synthetic view and indifference to natural process – indeed an anti-ecological view – then the highway creators leap to mind. There are other aspirants who vie to deface shrines and desecrate sacred cows, but surely it is the highway commissioner and engineer who most passionately embrace insensitivity and philistinism as a way of life and profession. . . . There they go, laden with money, offering the enormous bribe of ninety per cent of the cost of realising their narrow purposes. Give us your beautiful rivers and valleys and we will destroy them . . . Give us your cities,

their historic areas and buildings, their precious parks, cohesive neighbourhoods, and we will rend them – in New Orleans, and Boston, San
Francisco and Memphis. (McHarg 1971)

Fortunately, dynasties do not last and sinners can repent. Writers, community groups, environmentalists, planners, landscape architects and others
have been pouring their fire into the bastions of the highwaymen. Piles of
bodies have accumulated in the moat. They are the bodies of those who died
with their lungs and limbs damaged by the injurious side-effects of road
transport. Now, the bastions can be breached. We will have a more pluralistic approach to transport planning.

Word derivation yields useful information on the history of transport
routes (Tolley 1990: 162). "Way" comes from the Latin *via*. "Highway" is
a contraction of king's highway: it meant a public road, created and protected by sovereign power. "Street" comes from the Latin *strata* (= paved)
but now tends to mean a road bounded by contiguous buildings. "Road"
comes from the Old English *ridan* (= ride), which reminds us that a road's
original purpose was to carry horse traffic (Fig. 10.1). "Lanes" are routes
contained within boundaries; "tracks" are not contained. "Autoroutes" are
for automobiles, which are self-powered. Rackham identifies three reasons

"HE RODE AWAY IN THE DIRECTION OF BRISTOL."

Figure 10.1 Our word "road" comes from the Old English *ridan*. Roads were for
riding horses.

for making a highway: to reach a destination, to provide a durable surface, to provide boundaries that prevent conflicts between travellers and residents. Regrettably, the rich history of different route types has been collapsed into a hierarchy of standard products: the intercity autoroute, the local distributor and the residential access road. Cycleways and footways are made as "baby roads" (Fig. 10.2), forgetting the significant differences between car tyres, narrow-tyre bikes, wide-tyre bikes, feet city-shod, feet country-shod and feet in high-heeled shoes. Railways, canals, pedestrianization schemes and park roads also suffer from single-purposism.

Old roads had many functions. As routes, they accommodated pedestrian, wheeled and animal traffic. As public outdoor space, they accommodated markets, public festivals, children's play and social interaction (Fig. 10.3). Travellers could sleep under trees, while their animals grazed on wide verges. Some roads were spatial designs and works of art (Fig. 11.19). But at some point in history, an analytical mind asked itself the fatal question: "what are roads *for*?" "Transport" boomed the inevitable reply, meaning "assisted movement" (Ramsey 1990). From this, it apparently followed that the "best" roads were those that carried the largest number of motor

Figure 10.2 Cycleways can be made as "baby roads", ignoring the preferences of cyclists, pedestrians and toddlers.

Figure 10.3 A street used to be a multi-functional space fronted by buildings and used for transport, markets, public festivals, children's play and social intercourse of every kind (St Mary's Wynd in Edinburgh).

vehicles in the greatest safety at the highest speeds. All other considerations could be merrily jettisoned. Traffic planning became an applied science: applied to the single objective of facilitating motor transport. Roads ceased to be pluralistic and public open space.

Donald Appleyard relates that when Californians tried to introduce techniques of calming motorized traffic in the 1970s, the action was ruled to be illegal because it was not described in the highway engineer's manual (Appleyard 1987). Furthermore, the public had no representation on the only committee which could make changes to the manual: it was composed entirely of highway engineers. Northern California had the same rules as Southern California. This was more social engineering than highway engineering, and a sad instance of Adam Smith's observation that when several members of a trade meet together it is to conspire against the public interest.

Highway engineering design manuals define a limited number of road-types (e.g. for various traffic flow levels) and then specify criteria for each. The criteria lead to geometrical "standards", such as curve diameters and the geometry of road junctions. This produces standard products, which disregard contextual factors and the judgements of local communities. It is not that we need 300 types of road, instead of three, but that every single road should be adapted to local circumstances. Highway engineers oppose diversification, but they can be subject to democratic control.

Remembering the etymology of "road" from "ride", one of our first principles in planning a family of routeways should be to pay attention to non-motorized transport. Each transport mode produces a distinctive pattern of positive and negative side-effects. Each should be designed with respect to that pattern.

Pavements, for foot and wheeled traffic, create the essential public space in every city, with the possible exception of some modern American towns. Kunstler gives the following description of his hometown:

> Saratoga, like virtually every other town in America, has become one big automobile storage depot that incidentally contains other things . . . This part of town is not friendly to pedestrians. Not that it's against the law to walk here, only that no one would have much reason to walk here unless his car broke down. . . There are no sidewalks out here on South Broadway, just strings of parking lots punctuated by curb cuts. (Kunstler 1993: 135)

Pavements should be the places where people meet for the social and business functions that make cities worth while. Most social relationships are difficult; pavement planning is very difficult. In our lives, we want to be socially close, socially apart and mixed in all sorts of ways. On the public pavements of our cities, we want traffic modes to be close, apart and mixed in all sorts of ways. Streets should have different characters and, as with open-space planning (page 148), colours can be used to symbolize intended street character (Fig. 10.4).

There may be a few places where it is necessary to have a dozen separate surfaces for pedestrians, joggers, child cyclists, adult cyclists, motor cyclists, wheelchairs, horse-riders, skaters, private cars, delivery vehicles, through traffic, buses and taxis (Fig. 10.5). And there may be places where 12 transport modes can share one pavement. But normally we should use great ingenuity. The aim is to make pavements which can be shared in different ways. There needs to be greater respect for the past, a greater sensitivity to context and a greater diversity of transport route types. We need experts in each route type and we need experts in EID who can integrate them with each other and with the environment.

Historic conservation

Historic roads are as deserving of conservation as ancient buildings, woodlands and other landscape features.

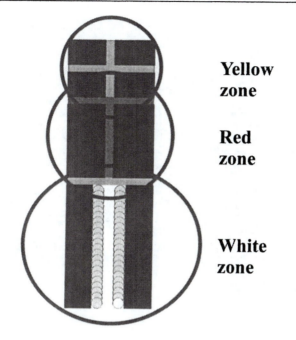

	Land-uses	**Character**
Yellow street	Shopping, walking, taxis, buses, cycling	Busy and diverse
Red street	Walking, cycling, shopping, street theatre, restaurants	Gay, exciting and unexpected
White street	Driving, walking, offices, residential	Expansive, open and awe-inspiring

Figure 10.4 Colours can be used to symbolize intended street character.

The tracks, lanes and streets which were the enablers of civilization have been destroyed like slum housing and old clothes. Most of the world's ancient tracks, lanes, streets and ways have been, or are being, overlaid with modern engineered pavements (Fig. 10.6). Little can be done about those that have gone. Those which survive should be researched, photographed, surveyed, catalogued and treasured, remembering that civilization never could have developed without them. The best old roads from each historical period should be conserved, as Grade I ancient monuments (Fig. 10.7). They would allow modern man to know transport as it was experienced by our forebears. One day there will be guidebooks specializing in ancient roads, like those specializing in historic houses, castles and gardens.

323

Figure 10.5 Since it would be crazy to have separate tracks for each transport mode, we have to plan ways of sharing paved surfaces.

Adaptation to context

Road design must relate to its context, as must the design of buildings and other prominent structures.

One can see clear differences between roads designed in Ireland, Italy and the USA, but within each country new roads are standard products, like electricity sockets. This approach derives from our technocratic overlords and is, I believe, misconceived. Roads should be designed in relation to contexts.

Take the example of a long-distance highway being built through a varied landscape. The engineer's first step will be to establish "design criteria" for the horizontal and vertical curves, probably in a published manual. A standard bridge design may follow. Bank profiles will be defined for earth slopes. A topsoiling specification will be agreed with the horticultural specialist. Standard details will be worked out for kerbs, fences, drainage, crash barriers, lighting, retaining walls and all other details. Hardly any of this stan-

Figure 10.6 Ancient tracks should be conserved as ancient monuments. They should not be "modernized".

dardization is necessary; most of it is thoroughly undesirable. The road may pass through:

- limestone hills with thin soil and a drystone wall vernacular;
- a clay vale with rich soils and a tradition of oak paling and sand-stone walls;
- a sandy plain with scrub vegetation and unfenced roads.

To anyone who has not been taught otherwise, it is obvious that the detailing of the road should vary according to the patterns of the existing landscape (Fig. 10.8). Roads are very significant landscape features. Geometrical design criteria, and design speeds, may need to change in mountainous country. Fence and wall details should normally be characteristic of the area through which the road passes. Bank profiles, soil and vegetation characteristics should reflect those of the locality. If the road is to be different from its context, then, as discussed in Chapter 3, a well-argued case must be prepared and presented to the planning or environmental authority. An identity index should be specified and calculated for each section of the route. EID is necessary.

The techniques for establishing vegetation on the margins of new roads was for too long regarded as a branch of agriculture. It is now coming to be

Figure 10.7 Old tracks should be conserved. Honister Pass in 1935 (above) and 1996 (below).

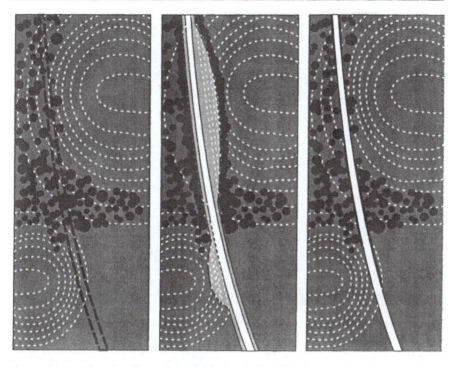

Figure 10.8 The detailing of roadside land should relate to the patterns of the existing landscape – not to the drawings in a road-engineer's manual. Left, road alignment; centre, engineered road; right, contextualized road.

seen as a branch of nature conservation. A landscape manager, noting that it will take time to discover how best to manage ecosystems for amenity, writes that:

> In the meantime, if the amenity land manager is ever in doubt as to his best course of action, he has merely to think of what a modern farmer or forester would do, and do the opposite. His objective is to make one blade of grass grow where two grew before. (Green, 1986)

Modern roads render the land over which they pass impervious to water. It is collected in drains and discharged into streams, rivers, soakaways or specially constructed storm detention basins. Regrettably, the water is not clean when it has run off a vehicular surface. It is polluted by hydrocarbons and heavy metals. But this is no excuse for the ugliness of detention basins (Fig. 10.9). Instead of being standard products, they should relate to local climatic, geological and hydrological conditions. Filtration can remove pollutants.

327

Figure 10.9 There can be no excuse for the ugly and anti-ecological character of most detention basins.

Road alignments should relate to contexts. Modern roads fit most comfortably into the landscape when the relief undulates gently. The "flowing alignment" (McLusky 1979: 9), which is preferred by engineers, fits with flowing contours. Approaches to dealing with the visual problems which arise are dealt with in *The good roads guide* (Department of Transport 1992). The flowing alignment is much less successful in mountains, on flat land and in urban areas. British mountains are not high, and the expansive scale of the flowing alignment tends to erode landscape character. This is especially apparent in the Lake District, which merits a historicist approach to highway design. In urban areas the flowing alignment is often disastrous: it breaks the continuity of the urban fabric and converts towns into suburbs. It would be better to adopt a creative approach.

Multi-mode transport

We can have a far greater range of route types than at present, and better links between transport modes.

If vehicle speeds or traffic volumes are high, routeways may have to be designed for the exclusive use of motor vehicles. But if speeds and volumes can be kept low to moderate, it is possible for cars, walkers, riders and cyclists to share a route. For example, lightly trafficked country lanes work well when infrequently used by all transport modes: cars, trucks, cyclists, horses, pedestrians and herds of animals. Also, in shopping streets where speeds and the number of vehicle movements are low, cars and pedestrians can share a paved surface without hazard. Where special provision is made for pedestrians, cyclists or horses, it is usually for the special convenience of car drivers.

What traffic volume counts as low depends on local circumstances. Roads should be contextualized, for the reasons set out above, and diversified, as discussed below, to give users a wide choice of transport modes, journeys and experiences. There is a need to invent new routeway types – and to reinvent some historic types. Also, there is a need for better junctions between transport modes. When the modes are the responsibilities of competing experts, junctions are neglected. Yet they are of supreme importance. Alexander's Pattern Language began with the observation that the meeting point of a footpath with a bus route is a pivotal node in a town, which should be marked with a newsagent, a coffee shop and a sitting place (Turner 1996: 22). Similarly, railway stations should be hubs for footpath, bus, cycle and skate routes.

Bridleways

Roads were made for horses.

Le Corbusier, a pioneer of modernist planning, derided wobbly old paths as "the way of the pack-donkey":

> The pack-donkey meanders along, meditates a little in his scatter-brained and distracted fashion, he zigzags in order to avoid the larger stones, or to ease the climb, or to gain a little shade; he takes the line of least resistance. But man governs his feelings by his reason. . . . The Pack-Donkey's Way is responsible for the plan of every continental city; including Paris, unfortunately (Corbusier 1977: 11).

Corbusier was right to see the horse as a major historical influence on road alignment (Fig. 10.10). He was wrong to criticize the beast of burden for meditation, wrong to lament the influence of horse transport upon cities, wrong to see the age of horse transport as having ended. Britain is said to have had more horses in the 1990s than it did in the 1890s, because of the rise in population and in leisure expenditure. Yet horses have been unfairly

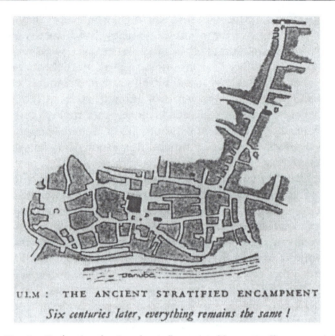

ULM : THE ANCIENT STRATIFIED ENCAMPMENT

Six centuries later, everything remains the same !

Figure 10.10 Le Corbusier, hating the influence of horse traffic upon cities, reproduced this plan of Ulm in *The city of tomorrow* and, as a caption, wrote: "Six centuries later, everything remains the same!".

displaced from their historic routes by motor vehicles. Surviving bridleways are overused and unpleasant, with sharp branches overhead and deep mud underhoof.

The solution is to plan a revitalized network of bridleways. This is particularly important in towns, where most people now live. Parkways, linking parks, should incorporate bridleways. In areas with large populations of horse-owners, there could be stables and paddocks near railway stations. This would allow some people to ride to and from stations. The high cost of the service would be borne by horse-owners and could well be less than the cost of keeping a second car for driving to and from the railway station, as so many people do. On reaching their offices, horse-riders could use the same changing facilities as cyclists.

Green residential roads

Houses can front onto green roads.

Roads in housing areas are usually designed as scaled-down versions of distributor roads: they are impervious to water and excessively pervious to vehicular traffic. One alternative is to make lightly trafficked earth-bound roads or porous pavements (Fig. 9.17). They should be safe for pedestrians and cyclists but difficult to drive along at speeds above 10 kilometres per hour. This can be achieved by designing a large bumpy footpath, over which cars are able to pass, instead of a small road. Motorists should feel they are on a drive in a private garden (Hass-Klau 1990). The surface treatment of such roads will depend on geological conditions in the locality. In sandy, gravelly and rocky areas, it may well be possible to do without a binder, to use uneven stone pitching, or to use a vegetated geotextile. Where there is a silt or clay substrate, it may be necessary to improve the local drainage and to raise the road surface above the general level. If vehicle speeds are too high, the residents association could sponsor a speed camera.

Urban avenues

Cities can have new avenues.

Avenues were a central feature of baroque city planning (see Fig. 2.23). Rome, Paris, Berlin and Washington DC have magnificent avenues. They were designed for aesthetic, transport, ceremonial and military purposes. As design features, they resemble the dramatic entrances to important buildings. Avenues help travellers to find their way and give them a theatrical sense of occasion.

Yet the avenue was jettisoned by modernist highway planners. They saw it as a functional irrelevance with no justification. To the science of highway engineering, avenues are a waste of money. But the transport planners' true clients are citizens, not government regulations or members of local transport committees. What the good citizens want is good cities. It is, therefore, time to reinvent the broad, straight tree-lined road. Avenues can intensify the majesty of a metropolis and give dignity to a small town.

No functional, modern road can stand comparison with the grand avenues of Paris or Washington, with the Ringstrasse in Vienna, or with Princes Street, the Mound and Moray Place in Edinburgh. Nor have we made any dignified high streets, winding roads or country lanes of the type that attract visitors to English villages. In Bracknell New Town, the old village high street was demolished and rebuilt, at great cost, as a windswept shopping mall fronted by modern buildings (Parris & Parris 1981: 32). Rassmussen was amazed at the waste of land on road space in Harlow New Town and questioned the design team about it in the 1950s:

One of the planners apologetically said to me that it was caused by the road engineers' exorbitant demands . . . I must confess that it shocked me that when planning eight new towns there was no time to discuss such fundamental principles. (Rassmussen 1982: 439)

Panoramic roads

Driving can be a pleasure.

The panoramic road can be seen as a picturesque counterpart to the avenue. It can be awesome to view a city in panoramic view. Roads are more usually seen to destroy peace, quiet and the natural environment. In a few places, these problems can be met head-on by setting out to design an expensive road which will be as exciting to navigate as a great bridge. Dramatic effects can be achieved by making a road pass, in quick succession, underground, beside water, over high land, through a dark wood. Tunnels, fences, walls, mounds and other types of defence can be used to limit the spread of noise and air pollution. In Newcastle upon Tyne a long, high block of flats known as the Byker Wall shelters a housing scheme from a road and a railway to the north. This creates a favourable microclimate to the south. Where barriers are not required, every effort should be made to open up distant views of a city. Panoramic roads give the motorized traveller a sense of a city's layout, scenery and character, and provide a useful traffic artery.

Leisure roads

Many journeys, but few roads, are planned for leisure.

Functionalist doctrine has produced too many roads on which the only pleasure is to reach one's destination in the shortest possible time. This runs against Robert Louis Stevenson's remark that "To travel hopefully is a better thing than to arrive, and the true success is to labour" (Stevenson 1881). A new road type should be planned, like the original American parkways, primarily for the pleasure of bowling along at 50 kilometres per hour looking at beautiful scenery and stopping for the occasional walk, swim or outdoor meal; the road surface should be porous, and quiet at slower speeds.

Off-roads

Off-road driving is enjoyable but can be damaging.

People enjoy adventure and like taking their vehicles off roads (Fig. 10.11). For the liberal environmentalist, this taste poses problems. Uncontrolled vehicular use will erode soils and destroy habitats. Normally, it is best to keep vehicles away from wilderness. But the world may have a few land-scapes where off-road driving does not cause harm: deserts. In arid deserts, ice-deserts and other ecological deserts (e.g. industrial farmland) with low-intensity use by animals and man it is possible to designate zones for off-road driving. In areas of higher use, off-road vehicles can be allowed to travel on the leisure equivalents of farm and forest tracks.

Speed roads

Speeding may be allowed in some places.

People enjoy fast driving, but should not be allowed to enjoy themselves by driving at speed on ordinary roads or in populated areas. Considerations of safety, noise and pollution mean that speed causes too much detriment to public goods. One possibility would be to create a new category of high-speed leisure roads in scenically dull and unpopulated areas. They could be owned and supervised by private operators in large forests, deserts and

Figure 10.11 People enjoy driving off-road vehicles. (Courtesy of Land Rover.)

333

agricultural zones, where vehicles travelling at 200 kilometres per hour would not be a nuisance. On occasion the roads could be closed for leisure use and put to a functional or military purpose, such as timber extraction or a troop movement exercise. Some countries, such as Switzerland, might have no space for speed roads. Others, like Russia, might find them popular tourist attractions. In smaller-scale landscapes, speed roads could be for 2-wheeled vehicles only.

Park roads

They were designed for horses and should carry horses.

When first laid out in the nineteenth century, park roads were designed for horse-drawn vehicles (Fig. 10.12). Carriages were an ornament to Regent's Park in London and to Central Park in New York. So long as carriages were horsed, park roads continued to fulfil their function. But as traffic became

Figure 10.12 Victorian parks had roads for horse-drawn traffic. They should be returned to horse-drawn vehicles.

motorized, the balance of side-effects shifted from positive to negative. Motor vehicles were excluded from Central Park but remain a great environmental hazard in Regent's Park, as they do in Boston's park system. The trouble with excluding all vehicles from park roads is that the roads become vacant spaces. The best solution is to restore park roads to their original purpose: horse-drawn vehicles. They could belong to private people, or they could be available for hire. Carriage rides are popular in Central Park, New York, and at Beamish North of England Open Air Museum.

Railways

Railways require environmental impact design.

In Britain, all types of railway line are subject to safety precautions, which require their separation from pedestrians by fences, walls, bridges and level crossings. This applies even to miniature railways in parks and garden festivals. The regulations date from an era when steam trains dropped lumps of coal, emitted sparks and were little understood by the public. Railway authorities seem never to have forgotten that a former president of the Board of Trade, no less, was killed at the opening of the world's first steam railway service in 1830. Safety regulations should be retained for high-speed intercity trains, but greatly relaxed for slow commuter trains, which are more predictable and therefore safer than buses. A slow-speed train has a pattern of side-effects which resemble those of a tram. This permits an intimate relationship with the urban landscape. Special slow-speed loops should be added to high-speed lines, to allow for frequent stopping without the impedimenta of railway stations.

Cycleways

Cycleways can be beautiful, safe and luxurious.

Good design for cycling is significantly more difficult than good design for motor vehicles. This is because the bicycle is a delicate instrument requiring muscular exertion. In favourable conditions, cycling is a sublime pleasure: one can bowl along with a silent grace unattainable by any other means. Even in bad conditions, it can be as enjoyable as swimming or sailing in a rough sea. But this only applies if one's struggle is against the forces of nature. A cyclist's joy is too easily destroyed by motor vehicles. Not only are they noisy and smelly, they cause severe turbulence and threaten to crush the unlucky pedaller. If one is being deafened by internal combustion engines, bored by a featureless landscape, poisoned by diesel fumes or forced to take diversions through back streets, one's enthusiasm for cycling can dim. Personal recollection provides the following examples of good cycle routes:

- beside a river, canal or lake
- along a quiet residential street
- in a group of fellow cyclists
- fast, down a steep hill
- slowly, down a busy shopping street
- under shady trees on a hot day
- on a foot-wide ribbon of smooth macadam in a dark wood
- on a farm track across heathland
- on a sheep track along a high ridge
- on a narrow, high bridge
- through an (empty) roofed pedestrian overpass
- on a track with a panoramic view of a town.

Although their interests sometimes coincide, there is a sharp difference between the needs of commuter cyclists and those of leisure cyclists. Commuter cyclists require the most direct possible route from A to B. Leisure cyclists require pleasure and are quite likely to drive to the place where they will ride. Unless the distinction between leisure and commuter traffic is respected, both groups will resort to mechanized transport. It is not a question of making an accommodation for cyclists: they need to be flattered, encouraged, cajoled and cosseted. When launching a National Cycling Strategy, Britain's Department of Transport stated that ". . . it is crystal clear that the bicycle has been underrated and underused in the United Kingdom for many years" (Department of Transport 1996).

Decision-makers should never forget that cyclists' behaviour is environment-friendly in the highest degree. It is also good for personal health. No expense should be spared in the planning and design of utterly superb cycleways (Fig. 10.13). Society should invest in facilities which persuade citizens to become "green commuters". There are many opportunities and few standard solutions. Much depends on the speeds and volumes of cars, trucks and cyclists. If 35 per cent of journeys are to be made by cycle, then substantial expenditure is necessary. It can be reduced to 35 per cent of the transport budget when the basic infrastructure is in place.

Cycle-paths and separate cycle-lanes are the obvious solution – but one of the best books on cycle planning contains a well-researched and destructive analysis of these ideas (Fig. 10.14). Nobody should plan or build a cycle-path without reading Forester's *Bicycle transportation* (Forester 1994). The author is a life-long cycling enthusiast with a dispassionate commitment to the principles of transport planning. His arguments are as follows:

Figure 10.13 Who could resist the charm of cycling on such an attractive cycleway (in Utrecht).

Figure 10.14 A modern guillotine in Dartford designed for cyclists.

- Cycle-paths are promoted by
  - people who want roads without cyclists;
  - cyclists who do not understand traffic engineering.
- Cycle-paths have a higher accident rate than shared bike–car roads. The accidents result from hitting obstacles, other cyclists, pedestrians (especially children) and dogs.
- Accidents also occur where cycle-paths join roads.
- A mixture of slow and fast cyclists on a narrow cycle-path is dangerous.
- Cycle-paths work in Northern Europe only because they are used by cyclists travelling short distances at speeds below 12 mph. American cycle-commuters travel at higher speeds for greater distances.
- Motorists are good at seeing what is in front of them, and only a small proportion of cycle accidents are caused by cars hitting cyclists from the rear.
- Most car–bike collisions that occur at junctions can be avoided if cyclists behave as vehicles and occupy a full car space.
- Many cycle accidents happen to unskilled cyclists.
- Cyclists cannot be accommodated on high-volume, high-speed free-ways, motorways and autoroutes.
- Motor roads achieve their highest flow-rates at 22 mph. This speed is within the capability of cyclists.

- The maximum number of journeys made by cyclists on a cycle-path will be lower than that made by motorists on roads of the same width. But cycle storage takes up less space than car storage.
- Cycle-paths will not be used if they result in longer journeys or longer waits at intersections.

The validity of Forester's arguments was demonstrated in Britain's new towns. At Milton Keynes, the combined leisure and commuting cycleway system, known as the Redway, was reviewed unfavourably by the Milton Keynes Cycle Users Group soon after its completion. They reported that over half the adult commuter cyclists in Milton Keynes prefer the grid roads, in spite of their dangerous roundabouts, because they are less hilly, more direct and easier to use. Furthermore, the accident rate on the Redway is greater than on the grid roads. It has steep gradients, sharp corners, planting boxes, pedestrians and other obstacles. The likelihood of a serious accident on the Redway is greater than on roads in Central London (Milton Keynes Cycle Users Group 1984).

Forester's arguments are persuasive, but they need to be read with some caution. As an engineer, he tends to see cycle-paths as right or wrong, rather than as sometimes right and sometimes wrong. Also, his points have less application in Europe, where he disparages cyclists for behaving as "wheeled pedestrians" who only travel at 12 mph. American cities have low densities and wide roads, which both enable and require cyclists to travel long distances at high speeds. European cities often have high densities and narrow roads, which are a pleasure for the slow cyclist. Having been engaged in debate for many years, Forester may also have learned to exaggerate his case. He enjoys cycle-racing and underrates the vileness of cycling amid fast, noisy vehicles emitting lung and eye irritants from their exhaust pipes. Furthermore, as his title suggests, his interest lies more in "transportation" than in leisure cycling. Forester concludes that the best provision for cyclists is an extra-wide inside lane on a mixed car–bike road. But he does acknowledge significant exceptions:

- A leisure cycleway can be separate from roads if it passes through delightful scenery.
- Cyclists are pleased to use less hilly routes, or short cuts that connect two sections of "real" road.
- If it is faster, cyclists will use a special path at busy junctions. If this is a bridge it may need a wind shield and a roof.
- For a very high volume of cycle traffic, it may be worth building a cycle freeway or "veloway". This will require two 1.2-metre lanes in each direction and a design speed of 40 kilometres per hour (25 mph) on the level and 53 kilometres per hour (40 mph) on hills. There is a veloway beside the river Rhine.

Building upon these exceptions, we can identify a number of different ways of making provision for cyclists.

Leisure cyclists should be in close contact with the landscape. A narrow ribbon of macadam can twist, laze and dash through the countryside. For the lone cyclist in unfrequented country, a 300-millimetre-wide strip is adequate – and falling on grass is nicer than falling on macadam. Twin strips, of the same width but 1.5 metres apart, will cater for larger flows. These strips will allow either for cycling two-abreast or for cyclists passing in opposite directions. Cyclists can cross the central reservation. In a forest or over a hill, the two paths might diverge, although this would prevent the occasional use of farm or forest vehicles, which could improve the financial justification for such a road. Verges and passing places allow still greater volumes – cycling on grass requires more effort but is not unpleasant for short distances.

In Britain, Sustrans is having considerable success in making cycle routes. The name is an abbreviation of Sustainable Transport. Sustrans began with the conversion of disused railway lines into cycleways. These have the advantage of being long and straight, with shallow gradients and good bridges, but they are dull as routeways. In many respects, their best use is for commuter traffic. Sustrans also makes use of low-volume roads through beautiful scenery.

Old roads that have not become heavily used are well suited to the needs of both leisure and commuter cyclists. When the vehicular traffic on an old road exceeds a certain level, a new road should be built on a new alignment. This allows the old road to be made available for low-speed vehicles and for cycling.

If a city wishes to experiment with the construction of a high-volume cycle freeway, it should be started as a short cut in a location where the volume of cycle traffic is already high. Catering for an existing demand makes better use of resources than building a cycleway to create a demand.

Universities are special places for cycle-planning. Students and staff have a much greater propensity to cycle than most. Campuses should always be planned with good accommodation for cyclists and with safe routes reaching into the wider community (Fig. 10.15). If flow-volumes are high, cyclists must have real roads, separated from pedestrians by kerbs.

Short cuts have a great appeal for cyclists, but they must connect to roads. They save effort, they save time and they give one a pleasant feeling of superiority over the pathetic motorists, who waste time and money, bumper to bumper, in environmentally unfriendly queues. Here are some examples of desirable short cuts:

Figure 10.15 If cycle routes and storage are provided, university campuses will be places of intensive cycle-use.

- lightweight bridges over railways, busy roads and busy intersections;
- routes across town centres and residential areas from which motorized through traffic has been excluded;
- paths through parks and greenways.

Child cyclists have special needs, which should be met if they are to grow up with the cycling habit. Below the age of ten, it is unwise for parents to allow children to mix with motor vehicles or fast-moving cyclists. Zones with a special surface are desirable, so that parents can say, for example: "You must stay on the red route." These safe zones can extend outwards from junior schools and may provide links to shopping, leisure and residential areas.

The above points about the character of cycleways may seem obvious to readers, but they are not put into effect by the planners and designers of cycleways. Too often the cycleway is treated as a child of the road, tagging along beside its parent or sharing its dull characteristics: parallelism, constancy, kerbing, junction-waits and a lack of shelter. Off-road "mountain" cyclists have shown their disdain for these characteristics. Cycleways should be mapped and star-graded for convenience, beauty, safety, gradients and climatic exposure. This would provide useful information for cyclists and display the miserable quality of most designed cycleways.

Skateways

Skating is fun.

The advent of efficient in-line roller skates has opened up new opportunities in transport planning. The usual principles apply:

- If volumes are low and travellers well disciplined, modes can be mixed.
- If volumes are high, exclusive routes are a necessity.
- Different criteria apply to leisure routes and commuter routes.
- Routes must be contextualized.

Track requirements for skating are similar to those for cycling (Fig. 10.16). For commuting, skaters require the most direct route possible. For leisure, they prefer good scenery. In parks and beside holiday beaches, skaters want a stagy route on which they can see and be seen, displaying their bronzed and beautiful limbs.

Commuters could use skates as a way of getting from their homes to rail stations, and from rail stations to their workplaces. Leisure skaters would like to have long-distance routes – a trans-continental skateway would be an attractive proposition. In part, it could run beside rivers and canals.

Figure 10.16   Do cyclists and skaters require segregated lanes?

Canals

Canals should not belong to transport agencies.

At one time, canals were a cause of negative side-effects. Their use in transporting coal, iron ore and other heavy materials made them into industrial zones, where it was unsafe for children to play and where adults had no desire to walk. Canals were the autoroutes of their time. Since heavy traffic has moved to roads and railways, small canals have become redundant as commercial waterways and are used mainly for leisure. The Canal San Martin in Paris is unusual in that it was built at the end of the canal age and treated from the start as an aesthetic amenity in the city. Subsequent changes have made it into an amenity park. Most waterway authorities have welcomed the twentieth-century growth of leisure traffic, as a new source of revenue, but they have been unwilling to find new ways of relating canals to the environment. Canals should be a focus for urban renewal projects. Except for lock gates, they are safer than either rivers or the sea. In 1938 Mumford suggested that "... they should, in fact, become the backbone of a regional park system" (Mumford 1938: 332), as many of them have become. But to play this role, they should not belong to profit-oriented transport authorities, such as the British Waterways Board.

Birmingham, which has a greater length of canal within its boundary than either Venice or Amsterdam, was a pioneer of canalside reclamation in the 1960s. At first, it was able to redevelop only the non-towpath side of a few parts of its canal system. The first major project, James Brindley Walk, overlooked a marvellous canal basin but did not make any use of British Waterways Board's "operational" land. A report on the city centre canals, in 1972, recommended using the towpaths to form a pedestrian "inner ringwalk", which would complement the city's "inner ringroad" (Bayliss & Turner 1972). No action was taken for a decade. When the first edition of this book was published, the canal, on which the proposed ringwalk was based, remained hidden behind high fences and grim buildings – because canals were still conceived as transport arteries and places of danger. Now the canal has been transformed into a great urban amenity, which allows walkers to see the Farmers Bridge flight of locks – surely the most remarkable scenic feature in Birmingham. It is very difficult for a canal transport authority to convert itself into a leisure provider and real-estate developer. In the USA, the problem was tackled by making 296 kilometres of the Chesapeake and Ohio Canal into a National Historical Park, managed for recreation.

Footways

Pedestrians should be pampered.

Walking requires even more muscular exertion than cycling. Therefore pedestrians deserve even more consideration than cyclists. Standard practice, for the last century, has been to make a raised sidewalk or pavement alongside the vehicle route (Fig. 11.19). It is a good arrangement, but it is very far from being the only good arrangement. As always, much depends on context and on the volume and speed of traffic. Since vehicular traffic is rising in every town, more redesign will have to be carried out in the interests of pedestrians.

Nobody likes to walk near a 100-kilometre-per-hour freeway or motorway. If vehicle flows or speeds are high, footways cannot run beside roads; they must be routed through greenspace, residential or shopping areas. If vehicle speeds and flows are low, a paved surface can be shared with pedestrians. Drivers are made to feel like intruders on pedestrian space, which makes them take extra care. Footways can also be shared with cyclists, providing the flow of neither group is excessive and the cyclists behave like "wheeled pedestrians". On non-essential routes, there is no need for a 2-metre-wide pavement. It is boring and it jars one's feet. Here, a genuine footpath is the best solution: it should be one or two feet wide and surfaced with bound gravel, so that it becomes smoothly uneven, like the sole of a human foot (Fig. 10.17).

Figure 10.17 Footpaths can be made by feet for feet.

But why shouldn't pedestrians have a space that is totally vehicle-free? The primary reason is that pedestrians are also vehicle-users. Unless they live within a few minutes walk of their destination, they will want to arrive by bus, bicycle or car, and they will not be content with a drop-off point where "vehicle zone" meets "pedestrian zone". A second reason is that if the total volume of pedestrian traffic is low, walkers must worry about their personal security. Passing vehicles offer safety, providing there are not too many of them.

Pedestrianization schemes

If they are to succeed, knowledge, imagination and design judgement must be employed.

The practice of excluding all vehicles to deal with their negative side-effects has been applied to shopping streets with high pedestrian flows. It has often been successful, although a surprisingly low level of design effort goes into most pedestrianization schemes. Too often, "paving patterns" are rolled out like cheap carpets, without serious concern for functional, aesthetic or archetypal considerations, or for the local vernacular. Pedestrianization thus becomes an excuse for "substituting street furniture clutter for vehicular clutter" (Toulson 1984). The better schemes have been the result either of using traditional patterns and materials or of holding competitions to produce a unique design solution. A design choice has to be made at the outset of a pedestrianization project. Rouen was the first French city to adopt the idea of pedestrianization. Germany has a great many successful schemes (Fig. 10.18) and has often used design competitions. Isezaki Mall in Yokohama also has a very elaborate paving pattern. The worst approach to pedestrianization, often used in Britain, is to send the scheme down to a junior employee in the planning or highways department to experiment with the latest range of concrete paving products. The results are tacky.

Town centres require a special type of street, one which functions like a gracious pedestrian mall but is accessible to permitted vehicles. If ways can be found to permit buses, taxis, pedestrians and cyclists, they will contribute to the convenience of users, and to the life, bustle and variety of a town. Delivery vehicles can use the space out of hours. It can be called a BaTaPaC road (for Buses and Taxis and Pedestrians and Cyclists). The mixture is desirable, because excitement and communication are two of the most attractive features of towns. Permits, either electronic or physical, can be issued on a short- or long-term basis to specified categories of vehicle travelling at less than 10 kilometres per hour. At very busy times, all wheeled

345

Figure 10.18 Pedestrianization schemes in Bayreuth (above) and Frankfurt (below).

access may be stopped. The design criteria for town-centre streets should be related to social, aesthetic and environmental considerations.

Traffic calming

Traffic calming is a bad name for a good idea.

Outside town centres, it is also necessary to place limits on the free flow of vehicles. But they should not be vindictive (Fig. 10.19). We are all pedestrians and we are all vehicle-users. The policy of traffic calming derives from Jane Jacobs' observation that the objective of transport planning should be the attrition *of* cars *by* cities. The typical weapons of attrition are speed humps, chicanes, width restrictions and diversions. All are designed to calm vehicles – although their effect on drivers, cyclists, horse-riders and others is quite opposite: the driven need sedation. Chicanery is not calming. One of the earliest schemes, in Cologne, was planned well and has matured well (Fig. 10.20).

There is a pleasant irony in the current discussion about traffic calming. After a century of designing roads exclusively to facilitate traffic movement, vehicles have become overexcited, and must be calmed. The danger is that

Figure 10.19 Traffic-calming schemes should not be vindictive.

Figure 10.20 Functional traffic calming in Cologne.

traffic calming will be treated, once again, as a bald engineering exercise.
Vehicular traffic is but one consideration; thought must be given to many
other issues. When my local municipality embarked on a traffic-calming
programme, I wrote to ask for a copy of their policy document. They sent
me a construction detail for a speed hump, with a note on the spacing
interval required by the Department of Transport. Like the mumps, they
have burst out everywhere, causing pain to travellers and disrupting both
visual and wheeled harmony. Traffic-calming measures should be treated as
an exercise in environmental design (Fig. 10.21). Any structures built must
also serve other purposes: car parking, bus shelters, children's play, spatial
enclosure, public art, climatic improvement, cycle routes, street lighting,
urban forestry.

Carmen Hass-Klau has made a comparative study of traffic calming in
Britain and Germany (Hass-Klau 1990: 212). Both countries were influenced
by the Buchanan Report of 1963. Colin Buchanan was a multi-disciplinary
person (architect, planner and engineer) with an unusually broad view of
transport planning. He recommended the idea of pedestrian precincts and,
to make them possible, proposed the construction of new roads (Buchanan
1963). His report was read by a British Minister of Transport, who just
happened to head a major construction company, primarily as an argument
for building new roads. In Germany, where the need for new roads had

Figure 10.21 Environmental traffic calming in Utrecht.

never been doubted, the Buchanan Report was read as a case for making environmental areas in which pedestrians could walk and shop without being harassed by vehicular traffic. Buchanan was regarded in Germany as the father of traffic calming. At first,

> Although there were many urban planners who wanted more pedestrianisation, they were opposed by hard-core traffic engineers who were of the opinion that without motor traffic the traffic-free areas would become slums. (Hass-Klau 1990)

Munich's city centre was pedestrianized in 1972, in preparation for the Olympic Games. Concrete slabs and planters were used, but they were later replaced with natural stone slabs. The scheme has been a notable success and gave great impetus to other schemes. An early lesson was that if calming measures are installed in one street then traffic will switch to the nearest adjoining street. This makes it essential to have an area-wide traffic-calming policy. Another criticism of German calming schemes was that "when you have seen one pedestrian area you have seen them all". Uniformity destroys the character of historic cities and makes new urban areas as homogeneous as multiple retail shops. Nor should pedestrian zones be planned as islands in a sea of traffic. There must be a pedestrian network at least as comprehensive as the vehicular network.

349

Britain also became disenchanted with motor traffic in the 1970s but did not adopt any alternative transport policy. Traffic calming did not become popular until about 1990, and, in Hass-Klau's view, British towns then set about making the mistakes German towns had made in the 1970s. Individual schemes were launched without ". . . an area-wide concept which has also to include major roads, public transport, cycle facilities and other car-restraining policies". Uniform design details were adopted, no comprehensive pedestrian networks were planned, and no post-construction studies were initiated.

Streets

Bring back the street.

In the eighteenth and early-nineteenth centuries, towns were developed by laying out streets and then allocating building plots to developers. This was done with Craig's plan for Edinburgh New Town, Nash's plan for Regent's Park and William Light's plan for Adelaide. Nash also designed the elevation of the buildings beside Regent's Park – but not the internal house plans. In each of these examples the public streets and squares were designed *before* the architecture. This method of town development has been largely forgotten, because roads are seen as "transport infrastructure" instead of "public open space".

The design of streets, fronted by coherent architecture, could still be used in town expansion and new-town schemes. Aesthetic criteria should be developed for the layout of minor roads, footpaths, cycleways and parks *before* the buildings are designed. To some extent this is done in business parks and related developments. A considerable advantage of applying the principle to town development is that it enables land-uses, and buildings of different ages, to be mixed. Developers can come forward with proposals for single houses, groups of houses, workshops, offices, bars, schools, shops and other land-uses.

Transport planning

Transport modes have to be integrated, with each other and with the environment.

Cities need experts in planning for each transport mode (train, car, bus, cycle, pedestrian, horse, skates etc.) and experts in the integration of transport modes. When it comes to integration, there are bound to be conflicts. Experts can go some way towards their resolution, but they must take advice from user groups, democratic bodies and landscape planners.

Transport modes have flexibility in different degrees. Trains run in straight lines and need high passenger volumes if they are to be economic. In a high-density city, such as Hong Kong, this is no problem. In medium- and low-density cities, stations must be planned to attract passengers who arrive by foot, bicycle, bus and private car. Roads have more flexibility in their planning than railway lines, but they too are expensive structures. Pedestrians and cyclists can make do with cheaper pathways and more diversions, but any inconveniences inflicted upon self-powered travellers will persuade them to use mechanized transport instead.

In town development, transport planning requires an evolutionary approach. One could start by making two-lane roads with sidewalks, which differ from ordinary roads in four respects:

- The pedestrian surfacing should be of best quality natural stone or hard clay bricks, so that it will last for ages.
- The two vehicular lanes should each be 5 metres wide, instead of the standard 3.6 metres, so that they can accommodate cyclists and buses.
- The vehicular surfacing should discourage vehicles from travelling above 60 kilometres per hour.
- Roads should be designed according to aesthetic and environmental criteria, as well as to vehicle-flow criteria.

Such a road can evolve. In the short term, it can be used like a standard road. In the medium term, it can become a mostly pedestrian street with a path for buses, taxis and cyclists. In the long term, if it turns out to be a nodal space, it could become a pedestrian-only shopping mall with delivery vehicles permitted only before opening hours. Or it could become a feeder mall to a covered shopping centre. Or it could become a high-density residential street, fronted by town houses. Or it could become the central mall of a business park. Providing only that it is well made, it will have a future value as durable as that of an antique table. Towns are bound to change but should always be of good quality.

I dream of a town where citizens have access to public transport via environmentally pleasant "green" routes, for walking, cycling, riding, skating or canoeing. While waiting for a bus or train, it should be possible to sit in comfort, sometimes in the sun and among flowers. Coffee and newspapers should be on sale. There should be a shelter with seats. The young, the old, the poor and the dispossessed should have access to public transport or green transport. Well-used walks should enjoy the benefit of visual policing and should be safe from the dangers of drunk drivers, so-called joy-riders and runaway trucks.

Towns must provide for private cars. Because cars are so mobile, roads can be circuitous. Busy loop roads are better than busy main streets. From the loops, cars should be able to penetrate urban areas rather than traverse them. The degree of permeability to various transport modes will depend on the predominant land-use: universities should be extremely permeable to bicycles and public transport; low-density residential areas need to be permeable to all transport modes; busy shopping centres need every possible type of transport; food superstores must be accessible to private cars.

Road planning should not be separated from other aspects of planning. So road designers must think about pedestrians, nature reserves, water management, recreation, architecture and the noble art of bridge design. They can learn from their medieval predecessors, who understood engineering to be the exercise of ingenuity:

> The great bridges had a spiritual and not merely a utilitarian significance: they were works of charity and of piety, the gift of benefactors or subscribed by the public through indulgences. Many of them had chapels or even resident hermits. (Rackham 1990: 268)

Some ways should please by their pure functionality. Others should be the yield of art and devotion, to provide for the many types of traffic which now exist.

For the soul, to travel hopefully is better than to arrive.

CHAPTER 11
Urbanization

Urbanization requires planning.

Urbanization happens (Figs 11.1, 11.2). Old settlements expand and new settlements are founded. It can be a consequence of increased wealth, population growth or smaller households. This chapter considers the need for new settlements, EID for the urbanization process, how urban land-uses should be fitted together, and how new settlements should be fitted into the landscape.

Buildings have rooms and corridors. Towns have land-uses and streets. The comparison (Fig. 11.3) might lead one to think that urban design is simply architecture on a heroic scale. That would be an error. Towns are organic and buildings inorganic. Where life processes are involved, planning differs. Many of us have houses and families. Both require planning, but only one of them can be strictly controlled, as stern parents will always discover. Architecture or engineering can rest on a single controlling vision; good urbanization requires attention to many visions and many processes. Final designs are not possible.

As discussed earlier, many professional designers, including architects, engineers and landscape architects, have caused aesthetic and ecological chaos by neglecting EID and focusing their attention on the interests of the land-user who commissioned their services, or the professional skill in which they were originally trained. In Geddes's words:

> Each of the various specialists remains too closely concentrated upon his single specialism, too little awake to those of others. Each sees clearly and seizes firmly one petal of the six-lobed flower of life and tears it apart from the whole. (Tyrwitt 1947)

Among the petals which have been seized by overzealous planners and designers are hills, valleys, rivers, parks, lakes (Fig. 11.4), footpaths, roads, housing, commerce and industry. One by one, they have been ripped off and "planned", regardless of the wider landscape. Urbanization works best when builtform is related to landform and land-uses to each other.

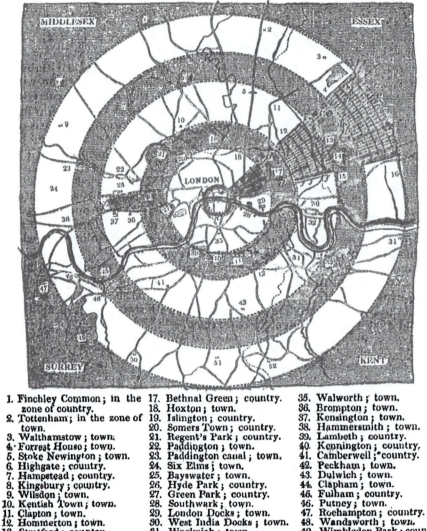

1. Finchley Common; in the zone of country.
2. Tottenham; in the zone of town.
3. Walthamstow; town.
4. Forrest House; town.
5. Stoke Newington; town.
6. Highgate; country.
7. Hampstead; country.
8. Kingsbury; country.
9. Wilsdon; town.
10. Kentish Town; town.
11. Clapton; town.
12. Hommerton; town.
13. Stratford; country.
14. West Ham; country.
15. West Ham Abbey; country.
16. East Ham; town.
17. Bethnal Green; country.
18. Hoxton; town.
19. Islington; country.
20. Somers Town; country.
21. Regent's Park; country.
22. Paddington; town.
23. Paddington canal; town.
24. Six Elms; town.
25. Bayswater; town.
26. Hyde Park; country.
27. Green Park; country.
28. Southwark; town.
29. London Docks; town.
30. West India Docks; town.
31. Woolwich; town.
32. Isle of Dogs; town.
33. Greenwich Park; country.
34. Deptford; town.
35. Walworth; town.
36. Brompton; town.
37. Kensington; town.
38. Hammersmith; town.
39. Lambeth; country.
40. Kennington; country.
41. Camberwell; country.
42. Peckham; town.
43. Dulwich; town.
44. Clapham; town.
45. Fulham; country.
46. Putney; town.
47. Roehampton; country.
48. Wandsworth; town.
49. Wimbledon Park; count
50. Tooting; town.
51. Norwood, town.
52. Sydenham; town.

Figure 11.1 Loudon, in 1829, said we should plan for the continued expansion of London ". . . in alternate zones of buildings, with half mile zones of country of gardens, till one of the zones touched the sea" (Loudon 1829: 687). His foresight was commendable, although his plan was simplistic.

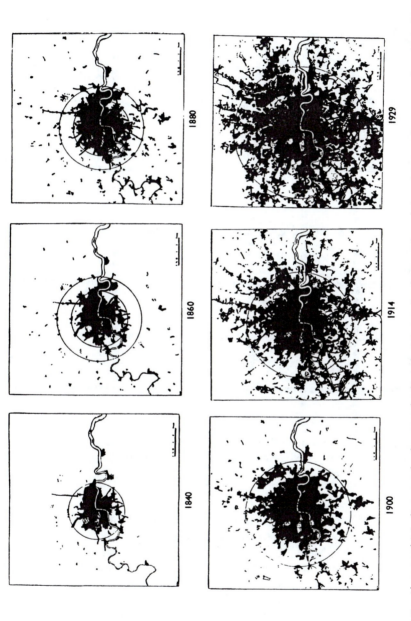

1840   1860   1880

1900   1914   1929

Figure 11.2 Abercrombie's diagrams for the growth of London. Expansion has continued since 1929, as he expected, and it behoves us to make contingency plans for the future expansion of cities.

355

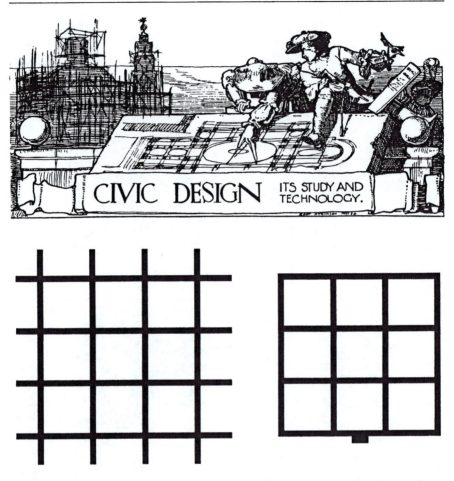

Figure 11.3 Thomas Mawson's view of civic design (above). Planning land-uses and roads can be conceived, mistakenly, as similar to planning rooms and corridors in a building (below).

The first edition of this book contained a chapter titled "The landscape of new towns". They are an interesting category of design, but why should we make new towns? Most of the world's great cities began as villages. If a village succeeds, one can always enlarge it to make a town, a city, an "edge city" or a mega-metropolis. In the old days, there were locational reasons for making fishing villages and agricultural villages. Some of them grew into cathedral towns, fortress towns, university towns, industrial towns and capital cities. With improved communications, most urban functions can be performed from existing settlements. But there are still reasons for starting afresh.

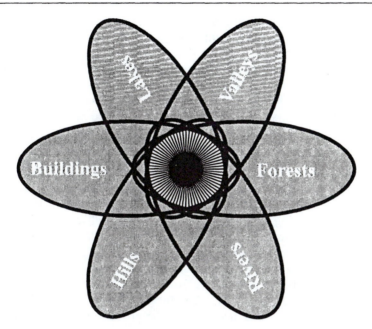

Figure 11.4 *The six-lobed flower of life.*

Higher urban quality People choose to live in proximity for social and economic reasons, but they complain about environmental conditions: the city is a concrete jungle; it is ugly; it is unsafe; the air is polluted; there is insufficient contact with nature. Thinking in this way soon leads one to dream of new settlements with the advantages of the town combined with the advantages of the country. Ebenezer Howard used the term "garden city" to name this dream. There were contradictions in the idea, but it led to improvements in residential design.

Attractive location A settlement may be required in a place that is attractive for residential use or because it has special job opportunities (e.g. a mining town). Economic trends may cause people to spend their working lives in or near a metropolis. But in vacation time they go elsewhere. Tourism continues to provide a resource-based reason for settlement location in areas of high scenic and environmental quality. The demand is for villages rather than towns.

Innovative design Starting afresh presents opportunities to create settlements that respond to the technical, social, environmental and aesthetic ideas of our own times. We wish, for example, to have settlements that are sustainable, good for parents who have jobs, good for old folk who wish to live near their children, good for families who want both community

357

and privacy. The classic twentieth-century "single" housing area does not possess these characteristics. A single use, housing, causes long journeys to work, shops and schools. A single dwelling size, for 2.4 children, causes families to move as they grow and change. A single transport mode, the car, causes low residential densities and excessive use of non-renewable energy. So we need models for new settlements. This requires investment in innovation, as do new models of aeroplanes and computers.

Variety of settlement size   The present trend towards the extinction of the small village is sure to continue, unless new settlements are started. Increases in population lead to larger settlements, as do increases in wealth. Wealth creates a desire for more space: bigger shops, schools, museums, houses, parks, gardens and everything. If we allow existing settlements to grow and grow, without starting new settlements, everyone will end up living in a metropolis, which is not what everyone wants. The planning system is far from neutral as a determinant of settlement size. In Japan, it has led to the protection of agricultural and forest lands, so that cities have become extremely large and extremely dense. In the USA, zoning laws have led to large low-density cities. In Britain, planning laws led to the establishment of 35 new towns after 1945 but then stopped the process of new town creation. Existing settlements have been allowed to expand instead. Villages are becoming towns; small towns are becoming large towns; large towns are becoming conurbations. This is regrettable. Whether or not large towns are desirable, one can hardly dispute that villages and small towns are also desired, and that any planned growth should be located with regard to existing landscape features (Fig. 11.5).

A respectable case can be made for a society to adopt a "no growth" policy. But if populations do grow, which is sufficiently certain to necessitate contingency planning, we should make plans for new settlements. In Britain, the 1946 New Towns Act should be reactivated. Other countries should use other legislation to facilitate the selection, assessment and acquisition of the most suitable land for urbanization.

Site selection

Finding a good site is the hardest task.

Scenically, should one choose the best land or the worst land for a major building project? It depends on the settlement type. If starting a great city, it is desirable, as instanced by Athens, Istanbul, Sydney and San Francisco, to have a spectacular site. But there are difficulties in obtaining society's agree-

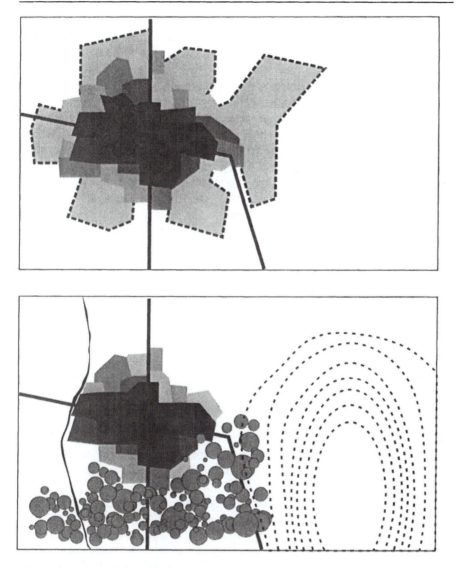

Figure 11.5 If villages keep growing (above), they will become large towns. Their boundaries should be related to landscape considerations (below). This is not done for "village envelopes" in the UK.

ment to new construction, especially in areas of beautiful scenery. In 1995, Britain's chief planning inspector commented that: ". . . if ANYBODY suggests a new settlement ANYWHERE, they can expect a ton of bricks – whether it is a logical well-supported proposal or a piece of facile opportunism" (Shepley 1995).

For this reason, it is wise to conserve the "best" land as a public good and select the "worst" land for new construction. We can then rely on the skill of planners and designers to create good new settlements. But worst and best are relative terms. Sandy lowlands may be best for agriculture, aquifer recharge and road construction. Rocky uplands may be worst for these purposes but best for scenery, recreation and nature conservation. The hard choices which have to be made should be based on a McHargian set of descriptive and evaluative maps (Fig. 11.6). They can guide decision-making but they cannot take decisions. Sometimes it will be right to build in the most beautiful places. More often, beautiful land should be conserved and new settlements placed on less important land or on land that has been degraded by human use. Since everyone's attitude to urbanization is "not-in-my-back yard", societies must resort to the democratic process. A referendum may be necessary.

Site acquisition

Settlements need parents.

Settlements require land. Roads can be built on private land, but a genuine highway, which interconnects a community, cannot be made without the compulsory acquisition of land. Nor can towns. Regrettably and inevitably, it follows that some injustice must be done to existing landowners when a new highway, or a settlement, is built. They should be compensated with a generous premium. It could be 25 to 100 per cent above the value of the land in its existing use. Since the value of land may rise 1,000 per cent on conversion from rural to urban, the premium is not excessive from the community's point of view.

Who then should provide the development capital for making a new village? An answer can be reached by considering the nature of a "settlement". To settle is to "become established in more or less permanent abode". The etymology is from *setl*, "a place to sit". Settlement is a most ancient procedure, as humanity has spread across the globe. If the aim is to establish a community, community action is required. Parents make gifts to their children, and existing communities should make gifts to new communities. It is good to have a group of city parents. In the old days, they were known as city fathers and entrusted with the task of representing the interests of future inhabitants. City parents should act as a client body for the design team and behave in a manner distinct from the board of directors of an industrial company or a new-town development corporation. Short-term profit matters – but so do education, conservation, recreation and many other types of value.

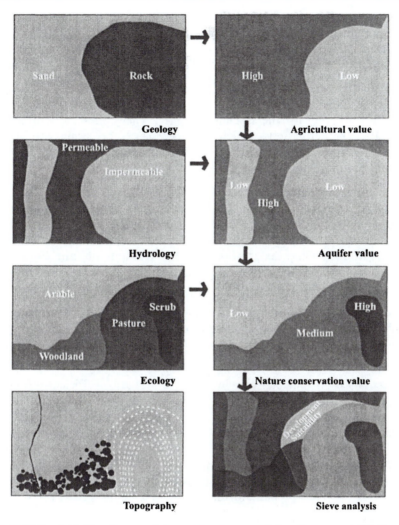

Figure 11.6 A McHargian set of sieve maps can reveal sites that are suitable for new settlements.

Site appraisal

Good decisions rely on good information.

Vitruvius recounts that our ancestors checked on-site characteristics by sacrificing cattle and examining their livers. A modern technique is to live on-site, preferably at intervals spread over four seasons, preparing surveys, studying local history, talking to those who know the area, sketching, photographing, studying the existing fauna and flora, talking to local inhabitants. Patrick Geddes made use of this method when working on the town expansion competition for Dunfermline, in 1903–4, and again when preparing plans for Indian cities between 1914 and 1922. He wrote that:

> It is a great day for the student of a city, when, after the long and repeated peregrinations which are necessary, he begins to feel acquainted with the general and detailed aspect of the great town throughout its many quarters. (Geddes 1918: 1)

Geddes agreed with Humphry Repton, who wrote that ". . . the plan must be made not only to fit the spot, it ought actually to be made upon the spot" (Loudon 1840: 500). If one considers the capital invested in a new settlement, the cost of employing planners to live on-site for a year is utterly trivial. A thorough knowledge of the site should help to prevent the production of standardized plans. Whyte complains that, for new towns all over the world,

> There is really only one plan. The kind of geometrics favoured may differ, but whether linear or concentric or molecular, the plans end up looking so alike it is a wonder such large staffs are deemed necessary to draft them. (Whyte 1970: 259)

They are based on vehicular circulation plans and are insufficiently adapted to site characteristics.

To make better towns, we need many plans instead of one plan; they should be based on many appraisals and prepared from many points of view, including those of topography, morphology, climate, public open space, earthmoving, rivers, lakes, vegetation and communications. All are important, and there is no particular order in which the data should be gathered or the plans prepared. Motor vehicles should not take precedence.

Topographic plan

Topography comes first.

A settlement requires a plan for its relationship with the existing topography. If the relief is varied, there are a number of traditional alternatives:

- Build in the valleys and leave the hills as open space.
- Build on the hills and leave the valleys as open space.
- Build on the plain, avoiding hills and valleys.

362

If the settlement is beside a large body of water, there are other alternatives:

- Place buildings along the water's edge (e.g. Venice).
- Locate public open space on the waterfront (e.g. Chicago).
- Build a corniche on the waterfront (e.g. Cairo).
- Use a blend of the above policies (e.g. London and Paris).

When decisions have been taken about the relationship between builtform and landform, one can think about the disposition of other land-uses. It is particularly important to find good topographic positions for a town centre and town park.

A study of the post-war British new towns will show that where town centres have been given significant topographic positions, such as the valleys at Hemel Hempstead and Livingston, or the hilltops at Harlow, Redditch, and Cumbernauld, it is much easier to appreciate the form of the town and to find one's way about. Where a town centre does not have a topographically significant site, as at Bracknell, Crawley, Cramlington and Newton Aycliffe, the visitor is often confused. On flat sites, a skyline and landmark policy can aid orientation.

The location of a town centre should be an aspect of a broad concept for the relationship between built and open land. At Harlow, the town centre and all the neighbourhoods are located on hills, which are separated by "green wedges" in the valleys of the River Stort and the Todd Brook. At Hemel Hempstead the town centre is in a valley, but other urban areas are on plateau tops separated from one another by a park system in the valleys of the Rivers Gade and Bulborne. The plan works better at Hemel Hempstead than at Harlow, because tree belts on the crests of the valley sides cut off views of the armadillo-like urbanized hills. Redditch town centre is on a central ridge, and the other urban areas are located in valley bottoms separated by wooded ridges. Most of the housing areas have a pleasant rural character, which is emphasized by the backdrop of trees. Redditch has no extensive views of housing carpeting the land into the far distance. In Livingston the town centre and town park face each other across a valley, which is good, but the ridge lines have not been secured with planting.

In the USA ecological considerations have been used to generate similar plans, for preserving valley land and confining urban development to the higher land. The Green Springs-Worthington area outside Baltimore is a good example. It is known as the "Plan for the Valleys" and described in Chapter 8 of *Design with nature* (McHarg 1971). Green Springs-Worthington was not designated as a new town, but in the 1960s it was evident that rapid urbanization was probable. The population was expected to grow from 17,000 to 110–150,000 between 1962 and 1992. McHarg's concern was that if ". . . subdivision after subdivision was laid down, irrespective of scenic beauty or physiographic phenomena" then ". . . a

363

wallpaper of development" would be unrolled on the landscape and the ecosystem destroyed. That is how most cities conduct their urbanization.

A study of the Green Springs-Worthington topography, geology, surface water, ground water, floodplains, slopes, woodlands and aquifer recharge areas revealed that ". . . the valleys should be prohibited to development save by such land-uses as are compatible with the present pastoral scene" and that ". . . development should be largely concentrated on the open plateau". The valley land has higher ecological value than the plateaux. In order to realize the plan, landowners set up a Real Estate Syndicate to acquire development rights and compensate owners whose land was not planned for development. Various public authorities assisted by zoning for building density, natural-resource protection and floodplain preservation. They also agreed to lay sewers on the plateaux but not in the valleys.

Cergy-Pontoise in France is an example of a new town founded on a strong topographic concept. In age and size it compares with Milton Keynes, which has a less dramatic site and a less obvious topographic concept. Cergy-Pontoise is 27 kilometres north-west of Paris and was planned between 1966 and 1969. Milton Keynes is 65 kilometres north of London and was planned between 1967 and 1969. Both towns had a population of over 100,000 by 1980. The first difference to strike a visitor is that it is very easy to find one's way about Cergy-Pontoise, and to get lost in Milton Keynes. Cergy-Pontoise is built on sloping ground, which surrounds the last meander of the River Oise before its confluence with the Seine. In time it will form a vast urban amphitheatre. Sand and gravel are being dug from inside the meander, and the land is being made into a great water park and leisure centre, which can be seen from most parts of the town. The park sparkles with light, water and vegetation.

Milton Keynes has an undulating topography but only a 60-metre difference in level between its lowest and highest points. Peter Youngman, as landscape consultant to the master-plan team, endeavoured to make the most of the landform. He advised that the natural features of the site

> . . . could easily be over-ridden and lost sight of; but they are strong enough, if their qualities are fully exploited, to contribute towards the city's uniqueness of character as a whole and towards the individual identity for its different parts.

Youngman stated a preference for:

> . . . concentrating tall blocks and dense building on the high ground, keeping the low land open; for a very strong form of development, to a single coherent scheme, expressing the steep slope west of the canal; for the city centre in linear form along the central plateau; for development in the area of the Shenleys to be fragmented and varied; and

for building to be kept below the skyline of the western boundary. (Youngman 1968)

This policy is similar to the landscape plan for Harlow: in each town the centre is on high ground and the open space in valleys, which are, in any case, prone to flooding. Milton Keynes is a less comprehensible town because of its larger size and because the policy of tipping waste material alongside the grid roads caused the natural features of the site to be lost.

Urban morphology and climate

Heed the wisdom of the ancients!

The physical shape of a settlement can have a pronounced effect on its climate. Palladio explained the relationship as follows:

> The more the city, therefore, is in a cold place, and hath a subtile air, and where the edifices are made very high, so much the wider the streets ought to be made, that they may, in each of their parts, be visited by the sun. . . . But the city being in a hot country its streets ought to be made narrow, and the houses high, that by their shade, and by the narrowness of the streets, the heat of the site may be tempered, by which means it will be more healthy. (Palladio 1965: 59)

Palladio followed Vitruvius in recommending that streets should not be aligned with the prevailing wind (ibid.: 60). Their advice went unheeded at Milton Keynes, and the main street in the town centre was laid out on a south-west to north-east axis. It aligns with sunrise in midsummer but funnels the prevailing south-westerly wind. Cumbernauld in Scotland, with equal disregard for the wisdom of the ancients, was placed on a hilltop site with the aim of creating a strong urban image, like an Italian hilltown (Fig. 11.7). A very large shopping centre was built on top of a ridge, causing severe microclimatic problems. Cumbernauld is one of the most exposed towns in one of the most windswept urban regions in the world. Ian McHarg, having advised against the site for this reason, left Scotland for ever. Cumbernauld lies directly in the path of incoming gales from the North Atlantic.

In 1803 Repton cautioned against the error of sacrificing aspect for prospect:

> There is no circumstance connected with my profession, in which I find more error of judgement, than in selecting the situation for a house . . . Not only visitors and men of taste fall into this error . . . No sooner has he discovered a spot commanding an extensive prospect, than he

Figure 11.7 In imitation of Italian hill-towns, Cumbernauld was planned on an exposed ridge (above), with roads on the ridge top (below) in one of the windiest urban regions in the world. This decision caused Ian McHarg to emigrate.

immediately pronounces that spot the true situation for a house; as if the only use of a mansion, like that of a prospect-tower, was to look out of the windows. After long experiencing the many inconveniences to which lofty situations are exposed . . . after vainly looking forward to the effect of future groves, I am convinced that it is better to decide the situation of a house when the weather is unfavourable to distant prospects. (Loudon 1840: 273)

There have been microclimatic problems in the planned centres of other new towns. At East Kilbride they have been ameliorated by roofing the 1950s pedestrian streets to form enclosed shopping malls with full climatic control. At Skelmersdale the main footpath system was set into existing cloughs to establish a sheltered footpath network (Skelmersdale Development Corporation 1964: 42).

Mistakes have also been made in planning "standard" Western town developments for tropical climates. The post-1945 plans for Kuwait City, by British consultants (Al-Yawer 1982: 111), for Chung Hisn in Taiwan, by American consultants (Gibson 1972: 208), for Chandigarh in Pakistan, by an international team (Ashihara 1983: 151) and for Tsukuba Academic Town in Japan (Ashihara 1983: 152) were all planned to create wide open spaces for roads and parks. In each of these towns the designers should have paid attention to Palladio's advice on the relationship between urban morphology and climate. Warm, humid climates need well-ventilated streets; cold climates need sunny streets; windy climates need sheltered streets; wet climates need roofed streets; harsh climates need indoor streets; hot, arid climates need shady streets.

Parks

Parks rely on contexts.

Making new parks and greenway systems is difficult in an existing town. Once it has been built upon, land is unlikely to have fertile soil, vegetation, surface water or other topographic features. It is also difficult to find land that is accessible to potential users and encircled by land-uses that benefit from the existence of a park. In a new settlement these constraints are lifted. Land for parks should be selected at an early stage in the planning process. Establishing a park is faster, and enormously cheaper, if the site is well endowed with natural features. It was normal practice in the British new towns to establish an interconnected park system, based on stream valleys, and to locate an important park near the town centre (Fig. 11.8). The deep valleys at Peterlee were well suited to this policy and have made excellent parks and nature reserves.

As discussed in Chapter 4, parks should be enriched by the inclusion and juxtaposition of other land-uses. Howard's diagram no. 2 (Fig. 11.9) shows a keen awareness of the recreational potential of peri-urban land-uses. River control structures can be used to impound water and feed canoe courses. Storm water detention basins can be used as wetland habitats, playing fields, or seasonal ice-skating rinks. Cycleways can be routed through parks. Sand and gravel can be dug from the park for construction purposes, thus, at the same time, creating boating lakes, nature reserves or fish ponds. Waste material from construction projects can be tipped to form artificial hills and ski slopes. Good sites can be made in a park for museums, art galleries, swimming pools, riding stables, solariums, cafes, beer gardens and restaurants. Town forests can be planted to provide shelter and a supply of firewood. Significant buildings can be sited beside the park to profit from the view and contribute to the park's scenery. The mixture of uses could, of course, create an unseemly jumble; it is essential to start with good plans and to keep modifying them as new opportunities arise (Fig. 11.10).

Examples of the above ideas can be found in many new towns. Cergy-Pontoise has lakes that result from gravel extraction and which are used for swimming and other water sports. Reston, in Virginia, has used balancing ponds as features in parks and housing areas. Stevenage and Welwyn Garden City have storm detention areas in their parks. Basildon has a large central hill made from waste material, and a swimming pool beside a lake in the central park. Milton Keynes has a "bowl", for outdoor events, and a belvedere, made of surplus earth. Stevenage, Cumbernauld, Washington, Telford, Warrington and Milton Keynes have extensive urban forestry programmes. Hemel Hempstead has a beautiful water garden, planned and designed by Sir Geoffrey Jellicoe, with town-centre

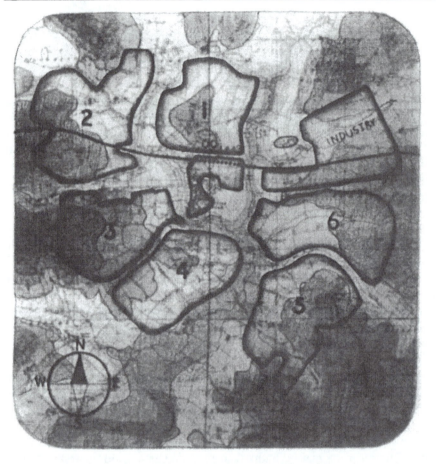

Figure 11.8 This diagram, drawn by Peter Shepherd working as an assistant to Patrick Abercrombie, made it standard practice for the British new towns to have park systems based on stream valleys.

buildings on its south and east boundaries. However, some of the new towns have failed to achieve the maximum benefit from the juxtaposition of land-uses because the park design was given to a separate agency and entirely divorced from the town design (Turner 1982). The landscape consultant to Basildon New Town resigned over this policy.

Earthmoving

Earthmoving provides great opportunities.

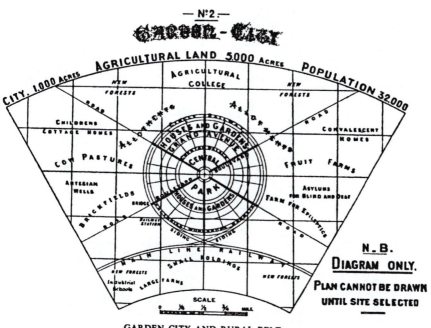

GARDEN CITY AND RURAL BELT

Figure 11.9 Howard was interested in the recreational potential of urban fringe land.

The construction of a new town is bound to necessitate the excavation and deposition of very large quantities of earth. Since landform is one of the main aspects of landscape design, it is surprising that the subject has not received more attention in master plans. Milton Keynes has been criticized for its spoil disposal policy, but the 1970 master plan for the town is exceptional in having a section on earthmoving, written by Youngman:

> Much may be disposable locally, within the range of scrapers and graders, for specific uses or for scenic purposes in re-shaping the existing topography. Provided designs are ready at the time the soil is to be shifted, this would be the most economical way of disposing of it. But in some areas (factory sites and the city centre for example) this will not be so easy; and there will be considerable quantities of soil to be carted from development sites. Ideally this should be put to positive use . . . here is a landscape material as useful as vegetation and it should not be squandered. A long term programme of organised tipping is needed. (Milton Keynes Development Corporation 1970: 326)

When Walter Bor came to reappraise the master plan for Milton Keynes in 1979, he criticized the ". . . well-intentioned but mistaken landscape policy

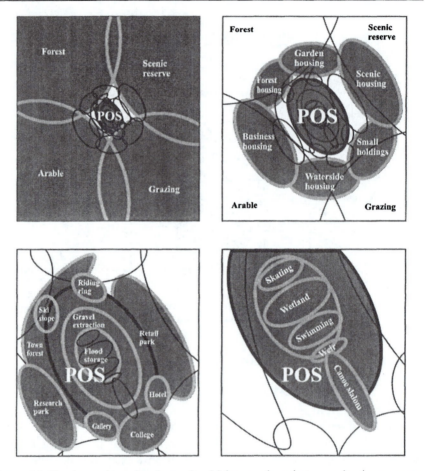

Figure 11.10 At each scale, there should be overlaps between land-use zones. Overlaps invigorate each land-use and produce good public open spaces. Often public open spaces (POSs) should be areas of overlap.

[of] making more generous road reservations than envisaged in the original plan", which tend to ". . . accentuate the fragmented overall appearance of Milton Keynes" (Bor 1979: 243). In a similar vein, Reyner Banham wrote that ". . . substantial earth banks, put there with the laudable intention of containing traffic noise" have turned the roads into ". . . a private landscape world, without contact with the real landscape beyond the banks" (Banham 1976: 359). The problem arose because the Development Corporation did not prepare a "long term programme of organised tipping". Large quantities of surplus material were simply tipped beside the grid roads and transformed too many of them into what appear as deep cuttings. They may be

370

splendid when the trees reach maturity, but their character will be rural, not urban (Bor 1979: 243). There are so few views of the town that the roads have had to be numbered and prefixed with the letters H or V so that visitors know whether they are traversing the grid horizontally or vertically. Only long-term residents become familiar with the road system.

The supply of construction materials is another aspect of earthmoving. It includes crushed rock for roadstone, sand and gravel for concrete, structural fill for foundations and non-structural fill for other types of embankment. If these materials can be quarried from the new-town site there will be significant savings in transport costs. Careful site selection for quarries will also enable the land to be shaped for a particular after-use. At Redditch, the road engineers planned to destroy three attractive hills to build an embankment. This policy was opposed on landscape grounds, and a study of the drift geology revealed that an alternative supply could be obtained by excavating what is now the Arrow Lake, a considerable amenity for the town (Fig. 11.11). It was obtained "free", as a side-effect of the road construction programme (Turner 1974).

Advance planning of earthmoving operations saves money. There is a great risk of double-handling if the excavation components of different building contracts are not considered at the outset. It is all too easy for contractors to make arrangements so that the same item of work is paid for

Figure 11.11 The lake in Redditch New Town was obtained "free" as a byproduct of road construction.

in one contract as "removal of excavated material from site" and then paid for in another contract as "supply of approved filling material". If 25 million cubic metres of earth are being moved at a cost of £5 per cubic metre it is evident that inadequate landscape planning can lead to waste on a large scale. Earthmoving plans must be produced before urbanization (Fig. 11.12). They have enormous creative potential.

Streams

Streams should be treasured.

Urbanization changes the pattern of surface-water drainage. Figure 11.13 shows the pattern of streams and ditches in Bracknell before and after the construction of the new town. It can be seen that many water-courses have been filled, or culverted, in order to improve their flow capacity and prevent children from playing in the water. This was the standard method of dealing with surface-water runoff in the early days of the new towns. The 1952 Master Plan Report on Bracknell has the following section on surface-water drainage:

> For all practical purposes no surface water sewers exist in the area at present, and it is therefore necessary to construct considerable lengths of trunk sewers to deal with the great increase in the quantity of surface water which will run off from the area when all the new roads, buildings and other paved areas have been constructed. At present much of the rainwater drains away into the ground.

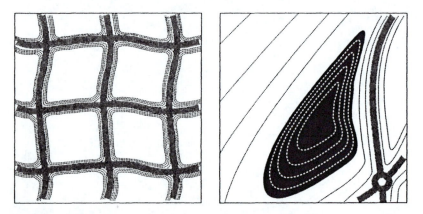

Figure 11.12 The earthmoving policy for Milton Keynes New Town (left) resulted in a fragmented landscape. The earthmoving policy for Redditch New Town (right) saved a hill and created a lake.

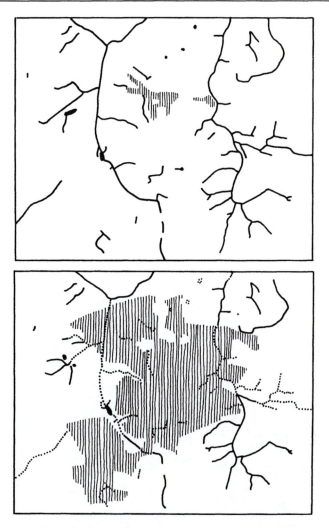

Figure 11.13 Bracknell had a dendritic stream pattern in 1949, although a number of water-courses had been culverted (top). By 1977, urbanization had resulted in most of the streams being culverted (bottom). They should be reclaimed.

The question of whether the Down Mill Stream and the Bull Brook should be culverted or widened to take this additional discharge has been very carefully considered, and the Corporation decided to culvert the former on the length north of the railway to make provision for the future widening of the Designated Area. The present flow in The Cut below the confluence of the two streams in times of storm has been estimated to reach a rate of 5,300,000 gallons per hour; it has been estimated that when the town has been built the rate of flow will rise to 18,400,000 gallons per hour. (Bracknell Development Corporation 1952: 11)

Although the new towns' record for culverting streams is bad, they have a better record for storm detention than most urban areas in Britain (Hall & Hockin 1980). In 1985 Bracknell had 11 storm detention facilities, and six of them were wet basins.

As discussed in Chapter 9, the practice of reducing the number of streams and accelerating the rate of runoff by installing paving and drainage has greatly aggravated the downstream flood problem. Redditch was one of the first of the British new towns to experiment with the retention of streams in housing areas. In Matchborough the stream was kept as a basis for the main open-space provision in the housing area. It is a delightful feature and very popular with children (Fig. 11.14). A hydrological survey revealed that sufficient water would remain in the stream despite the fact that ". . . much

Figure 11.14 The retained stream in Redditch New Town is popular with children.

374

of its catchment area would be cut off by the new development" and removed in underground pipes. At one point the stream is piped beneath an estate road and a ford has been built, over which the water flows in times of peak discharge.

The idea of using natural streams and ditches for urban storm-water drainage has been developed to a greater degree in the USA. At Woodlands, 35 miles north of Houston in Texas, a new community is being built on a site of over 8,300 hectares. The developer wished to create "a more satisfactory suburban living environment" and appointed Wallace, McHarg, Roberts and Todd to prepare a master plan (Juneja & Veltman 1979). Since the site was flat and badly drained it was necessary to keep the soil wet enough to preserve the woodland, yet dry enough to permit residential development. These objectives were achieved by using a "natural" drainage system instead of storm-water sewers.

All the drainage water at Woodlands is retained on site using storm detention basins and, wherever possible, existing streams and ditches. Building development is clustered on impervious soils which were occupied by vegetation of low diversity. The more permeable soils, with denser and more diverse vegetation, are protected so that surface water can seep downwards and recharge the aquifer. Roads and golf fairways direct surface water towards the recharge areas. It is anticipated that when the site is fully developed 15 million gallons of water per day will be withdrawn from the aquifer. The developer, Woodlands Development Corporation, estimated that a natural drainage system for the whole site would cost $4,200,400 as against $18,679,300 for a conventional underground storm-water drainage system. McHarg comments that "Such figures accelerate conversion to ecological principles. There is no better union than virtue and profit" (McHarg & Sutton 1975). The system also works well: on 18 April 1979 ". . . no house within the Woodlands flooded while all adjacent subdivisions were awash" (Juneja & Veltman 1979). Careful treatment of wetlands and waterspace is an excellent way of generating landscape character on flat sites.

In Europe, it would be worth initiating a new settlement purely for the purpose of developing and testing new methods of urban storm-water management. It would be lush, soft, squelchy, quiet and rich in wildlife.

Lakes

Towns need lakes.

Water-based recreation has become extremely popular. If the demand can be met in new towns it helps them to compete with older urban areas.

Opinion polls in France have shown that the proximity of facilities for swimming, water sports and other leisure activities is the reason given by most families for moving to the new towns in the Paris region (Rubenstein 1978: 139). Cergy-Pontoise and Saint-Quentin-en-Yvelines are the sites of new towns and of regional leisure centres. Their planners were inspired by Tapiola and Stockholm to find town sites where it would be possible to create good facilities for outdoor water and woodland recreation. Tapiola means "the realm of the kingdom of the woods". At Cergy-Pontoise and le Vaudreuil the water bodies are the result of sand and gravel extraction. At Melun-Senart and Evry the lakes have central positions and function as *bassins regulateurs*. They are estimated to have produced a 60 per cent saving when compared with a conventional storm-water disposal system using culverts and canalized streams (Secrétariat Général du Groupe Central des Villes Nouvelles 1977: 24).

Lakes have also been used as a focus for new towns in other countries. One of the most important examples is Canberra. Australia's new capital was planned by Walter Burley Griffen, an American who admired Olmsted and Howard. Griffen won an international competition for the capital in 1911 with a radial plan. It has some resemblance to the plan for Letchworth Garden City, but the grand avenues span an artificial lake. One of Canberra's satellite new towns, at Belconnen, is also centred on a lake which is retained by a road embankment (National Capital Development Commission 1970). Lake Havasu City is a leisure and retirement town in Arizona; it owes its existence to the reservoir known as Lake Havasu. A peninsula which once projected into the lake has been made into an island and linked to the mainland by the old London Bridge (Bailey 1973: 93). At Reston, in Virginia, there are seven artificial lakes, which serve for erosion control, storm-water management and recreation. The developers estimate that lake-front property commands a 300 per cent premium over other categories of residential land (Robbins 1981). In Britain, water engineers have opposed residential development beside supply reservoirs, on health grounds, and have usually designed storm detention basins in an austere utilitarian manner. The lakes at Peterborough (Fig. 11.15) and Milton Keynes are pleasant features but are not fronted by urban development. We should integrate towns with reservoirs (page 178).

Tree planting

Towns need community forests.

Tree planting is one of the cheapest and most effective methods of giving coherence to building development. It is for this reason that all the British

Figure 11.15 The lake in Peterborough could have been a focus for town development.

new towns have carried out extensive planting programmes. Telford and Milton Keynes both describe themselves as "forest" new towns (Aldous 1979: 25–7). The planting programmes undoubtedly have a beneficial effect, and the resulting "verdure" is one of the main reasons given by foreign visitors for liking the British new towns. The planting could, however, have been more effective. Many trees were planted on small patches of left-over land, instead of forming part of a wider landscape strategy – and too many trees died because of careless soil management before planting. Subsoil has often been over-compacted by earthmoving plant, and large quantities of topsoil have been lost during the operations.

Tree-planting has been most successful, both horticulturally and aesthetically, when it has been used to achieve broad landscape objectives, such as the visual reinforcement of ridge lines, valley sides and water-courses, or the formation of avenues, shelter belts and parks. It has been less successful when treated as a cosmetic. The Chairman of Bracknell Development Corporation, Sir Lancelot Keay, said that ". . . a new town should not be seen without trees, 'just as a woman should not be seen without her make-up'" (Parris & Parris 1981: 34). He lacked chivalry and Bracknell lacks a coherent landscape structure.

All the British new towns have taken advantage of existing woodlands and hedgerows, but it is disappointing that few of them have carried out tree-planting schemes before building development. Cumbernauld was one of the first new towns to undertake a serious forestry programme. Youngman advised the Development Corporation to adopt "a vigorous forest policy" in order to achieve "shelter and mass planting within the town; an economic use for such land as is unsuitable for building and yet cannot be fitted into the farming pattern" (Youngman 1957). He recommended that the new woodlands should be managed on the selection system, but with amenity, not timber production, as the primary goal. Stevenage has an urban forestry policy which has created a network of town woods. By 1966 it had 112 hectares of woodland planted and managed under the Forestry Commission's dedication scheme (Balchin 1980: 207). They should be run as community forests.

Advance planting was done in the outlying areas of Redditch (Turner 1974), and at Warrington tree belts were established three years in advance of building contracts. The Oakwood district of Warrington ". . . is an attempt to put Nan Fairbrother's vision into practice" (Tregay & Gustavsson 1983: 19). She said: ". . . we should surround our towns and cities with trees" (Fairbrother 1970: 324). Trees established before building takes place grow better because the soil has not been disturbed. Earthworks cause compaction and destroy the crumb structure of topsoil. When building does take place it is a great advantage to have a framework of existing planting. This fact has been demonstrated by the Scandinavian new towns and by those British new towns, including the southern parts of Crawley and New Ash Green, that have expanded into existing woodland (Fig. 11.16).

Communications

Roads can spoil towns.

An American transport consultant wrote that ". . . the planning of new towns must start with the pedestrian, from the point of view of both transportation and livability. All other transportation elements must conform to that framework" (Bailey 1973: 79). Otherwise the town will be dominated by vehicles. The predominance of road transport was the greatest weakness of the British new towns.

The problem is exemplified by Runcorn. It has a dramatic site and is based on a sound landscape concept, but:

> Without a good map and an alert eye for road signs, frustration and disorientation are inevitable. Expressways are generally placed in wide

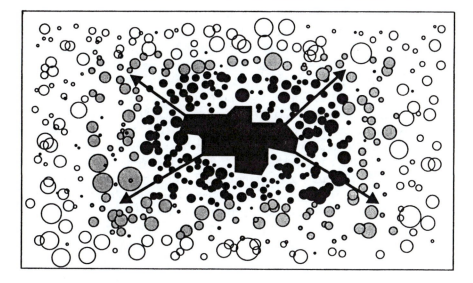

Figure 11.16 Settlements can expand into woodland.

parkland strips, fenced off from pedestrians, and crossed only by walkway-bridges at limited places. The busways are also fenced, as they pass through the middle of the residential neighbourhoods, which are thus effectively cut in two. Roads and busways therefore become barriers rather than links. The excessive emphasis on segregating them is the result of what now appears to be an almost neurotic reaction to the danger of the motor vehicle, and tends to dominate the town. (Opher & Bird 1980: 4)

Lavish expenditure on vehicular circulation has been wasteful of resources and, if the roads and busways were not underused, fast-moving traffic would be a serious cause of noise and air pollution. The footpaths in Cumbernauld are dwarfed by the road system. Walking distances from inner housing areas to the ridge-top shopping centre are short and unpleasant, except in midsummer. Pedestrians must walk uphill and cross narrow bridges over wide, underused roads. From outer housing areas the journey is arduous. One suspects that only unemployment and low car ownership keep the footpaths in use (Opher & Bird 1981: 2–4). At Washington New Town the main road looks like an airport runway and is designed to carry more traffic than many sections of the A1 London to Edinburgh trunk road. Even Thamesmead, which is inside Greater London, has been over-provided with roads to a surprising degree; the highways to the town centre could be mistaken for a major regional artery. Future new towns should be designed to facilitate internal journeys by foot or bicycle.

If footpaths and cycleways are to be attractive they must be direct and should be laid out before roads or buildings are positioned. Initially they should run alongside streams, hedgerows, ponds and other landscape features. Pedestrian routes can then form a starting point for the layout of buildings, as did the roads and tracks that predated building in the old towns. Each architect's response to the presence of a footpath will reinforce the importance and significance of the route. The Gilbey's Gin building in Harlow is a good example of how this can work (Fig. 11.17). It sits astride one of the main footpaths like a gate to a medieval town. A similar effect was achieved in the Seafar scheme at Cumbernauld (Fig. 11.18). The best cycleways in Harlow are the old lanes, from which motorized vehicles are now excluded. The first roads in Tapiola turned out to be too narrow when the town expanded, and have been converted into pedestrian paths. This is better than providing too much road space in the early years.

Many new towns have cycleway systems that did not receive priority in planning and are unsuccessful as commuter routes. In Harlow, Stevenage and East Kilbride the cycleways are wide enough to be single-track roads, and too often they run alongside main roads. Cyclists in these towns find it

Figure 11.17 The Gilbey's Gin building at Harlow was designed *after* the footpath.

Figure 11.18 In the Seafar estate, Cumbernauld, more effort went into designing the footpaths than into the roads. A landscape architect (William Gillespie) worked on site, designing the path as it was built.

simpler to ride either on the roads, which can be followed at intersections, or on footpaths, which are sufficiently direct to be attractive as cycleways and give direct access to houses and schools, without their having to bump over 150-millimetre kerbs. In London's Hyde Park the use of a kerb to separate cyclists from pedestrians has been found unnecessary, because cycle speeds are low. Some cyclepaths, such as those that run along old country lanes in Harlow, or streams elsewhere, are very pretty. The combined leisure and commuting cycleway system in Milton Keynes was discussed in the preceding chapter (page 339). It is a reminder of the complexities of planning and of the need to involve a wide range of specialist groups.

Most roads in Britain's post-war new towns are aesthetically dull. There are few new streets that can stand comparison with the elegant avenues in the pre-war garden cities of Letchworth and Welwyn. Nor do purely-functional roads compare with the avenues of Paris or Washington DC, with the Ringstrasse in Vienna or with Princes Street, Moray Place and The Mound in Edinburgh (Fig. 11.19). Nor are there any dignified high streets, winding roads or country lanes of the type that attract visitors to English villages. In Bracknell New Town, the old village high street was demolished and rebuilt, at great cost, as a wind-swept shopping mall fronted by modern buildings (Parris & Parris 1981: 32).

Figure 11.19 Streets are most successful when they are designed *before* the buildings (The Mound in Edinburgh).

Good streets could not be made in the British new towns because the roads were designed, as explained in the previous chapter, according to rigid functional criteria and arbitrary rules. Rassmussen was amazed at the waste of land on road space at Harlow and questioned the design team about it in the 1950s:

> One of the planners apologetically said to me that it was caused by the road engineers' exorbitant demands. . . . I must confess that it shocked me that when planning eight new towns there was no time to discuss such fundamental principles. (Rassmussen 1982: 439)

Wastage of land on roads became even worse in the new towns of the 1960s. But if over-capacity or wide verges are the result of a deliberate aesthetic policy, perhaps to make an avenue, they may create a sense of grandeur. Likewise, deliberate under-capacity can produce a sense of intimacy and charm, as in narrow lanes and medieval towns (Fig. 11.20). Highway design criteria should therefore be relaxed, for spatial and aesthetic reasons, and roads integrated with buildings, mounding and planting. It is desirable to have one street which yields a synoptic view of the town's character.

Figure 11.20 The under-capacity of medieval streets (York), by our standards, gives them an intimacy and charm modern streets lack.

Land

"All public" is just as bad as "all private".

New settlements require land. Yet the capital cost is high and the payback period long. Public developers are driven to high taxation; private developers are driven to bankruptcy; only the speculators reap profits. The best solution is a blend of public and private ownership. Land should be taken into public ownership, at 25 per cent above existing-use prices, provided with a public infrastructure and then sold to private people and public companies as urbanization proceeds. The British New Towns Act of 1946

383

used this principle, but too much land was kept in public ownership, and the parcels of land released for private development were too large. In the USA the Housing and Urban Development Acts of 1968 and 1970 offered financial support to large private developers so that they could create planned communities. Loans were guaranteed, under Title VII of the Act, and supplementary grants made available for water, sewerage, open-space provision and beautification. Front-end investment of this type is very important in new-town development, but land is more important than money.

In Britain, the parcels of land released for development were known as housing estates or industrial estates and were allocated to individual developers and their design teams. This policy had a profound effect on urban form (see Fig. 1.14). It produced large areas dominated by units of housing or industry, in uniform and often eccentric architectural styles. Patrick Nuttgens described the "monumental repetition of units" in mass housing as "the most serious intellectual and moral mistake architects have ever made" (Nuttgens 1981). The aesthetic reason for giving housing estates to different design teams was to create architectural variety, as in unplanned towns, combined with stylistic unity, as in the planned aristocratic quarters of eighteenth-century towns. The policy failed because, at the town scale, the housing estates were visually unrelated, and within each estate the units were similar but unconnected. Nor were houses placed to make good outdoor spaces. Roads, gardens and communal green spaces were badly designed. There was too much uniformity within estates and too much disunity between estates. Typically, they are of similar-sized dwellings, because of zoning regulations, but with a hotchpotch of architectural styles. One may or may not prefer the visual effect of uniformity but it is monoculture with all the associated diseconomies and disecologies.

There were also two economic reasons for parcelling land into housing estates. It was thought that building a large number of housing units in one place and at one time would produce economies of scale. This has not been proved (Lynch & Hack 1984: 283), and studies of other industries have not revealed a linear relationship between the size of an enterprise and unit production costs. The arguments Schumacher produced to support his "small is beautiful" hypothesis may apply to house construction (Schumacher 1973). A second economic justification for housing estates concerns cash flow. It is thought that money spent on estate roads and services should produce an early return. This consideration is valid but goes against the principle of investing for the long-term benefit of the community. Public authorities and large private developers should justify their involvement in private housing by a willingness to look ahead and to make front-end investments in roads and other infrastructure projects. Land should not be developed in large blocks for administrative convenience. The concept of a street can be extended to provide an alternative to housing and industrial estates, as discussed in the previous chapter (page 350).

Roads, footpaths, cycleways and cycle-paths should be laid out before any buildings are designed. This enables land-uses, and buildings of different ages, to be mixed. Developers can come forward with proposals for single houses, groups of houses, workshops, offices, bars, schools, shops and other uses.

Some of Britain's new towns have so much surplus roadspace, pathspace (Fig. 11.21) and parkland that land could be found to implement the policy even now. Nan Fairbrother wrote that ". . . the early New Towns, for all their merits, would feel far better places to live in if one town were superimposed on another and shuffled together to fill up the gaps" (Fairbrother 1970: 325). Some gaps are already being filled on "open-plan" estates at Peterlee, and elsewhere. No plans are immutable, and it is time to produce new landscape plans for the new towns of the past fifty years.

Figure 11.21   There is so much surplus pathspace and vergespace in the new towns that Nan Fairbrother believed a second new town could be superimposed (East Kilbride).

Housing

Planning housing areas for a single aspect of the public good tends to produce an unacceptable degree of uniformity.

The history of housing layout shows many instances of well-intentioned specialists grabbing petals from the six-lobed flower of life. Measures taken for the public good have been pushed to the point where they have damaged the public interest. When too many petals have gone, housing estates have died and the dwellings have had to be demolished.

In Britain, the story has been one of problems followed by panaceas, as shown in Figure 11.22. Each of the panaceas was based on a limited design theory, concerned mainly with one petal. And each became a "problem". Warren Housing, reviled by Engles, was succeeded by Byelaw Housing. Unwin and his friends attacked Byelaw Housing, arguing the case for housing on garden-city lines. Reformers from Clough Williams Ellis to Ian Nairn then slammed the sprawling uniformity of suburbia and sub-topia. Corbusian planners argued for the superficially attractive solution of stacking dwellings and allowing the "landscape" to flow underneath. Mixed development was the next solution, to be followed by "design guide housing".

A shocking feature of this progression is the fervour with which each group of reformers decried the work of its predecessors. When we look back, each of the panaceas has real merit and suits certain groups of the population. Warren housing, where it survives in olde worlde villages, is treasured. Garden suburbs have always been loved by residents. Stefan Muthesius, Oscar Newman and many young couples have sung the praises of the English terraced house. Others love the cell-like isolation and superb views from tower blocks. The most serious criticism of the theories which generated these schemes is that each has been too dominant and has ruled exclusively in that dreaded ghetto, the housing estate.

Commerce

Planning commercial projects in isolation disregards the public good.

Modern commercial projects are planned by property specialists for the near-exclusive benefit of their landowners. Too often, developments in what Joel Garreau has dubbed Edge City tend to be on the fried egg pattern: each gleaming structure rises from a flabby skin of car rooftops (Fig. 11.23). At the start, each egg appears as an isolated phenomenon, set in a wooded

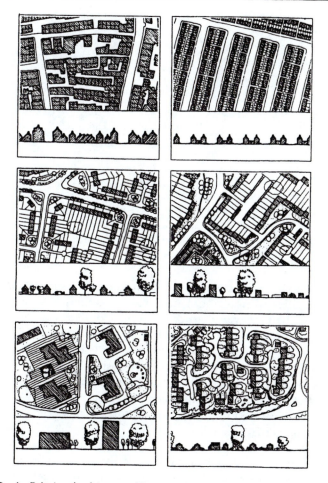

Figure 11.22 In Britain, the history of housing layout has been a story of problems and panaceas.

or agricultural landscape. Later on, more eggs are fried and the car parks coalesce. The aesthetic and ecological disadvantages to the firstcomer may well be offset by the advantages of better local services and an increased pool of skilled labour.

Planners see Edge Cities as chaotic places. They are in fact the consequence of powerful economic and social factors: the location of executive houses, schools, educational institutions, power lines, airports, railway stations and, above all, roads. You cannot have an edge city without a good infrastructure, and the way to make edge cities even better is to improve the infrastructure. This requires planning.

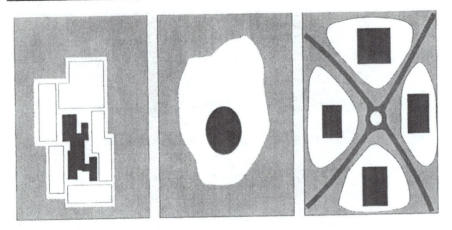

Figure 11.23   Edge cities are characterized by "fried egg" site planning.

When a major new highway is built through undeveloped land, we must expect edge cities to mushroom near road junctions. The land has to be planned, and the best way is to draw up proposals for a variety of greenways. In the short term, they may not be as important as roads. In the long term, they are more important, because they provide for the evolution of the area into a higher-density town. Greenways should be planned for all the separate reasons discussed in Chapter 4: pedestrian and cycle circulation, surface water drainage, wildlife corridors, recreation, visual amenity. Historic cities developed around roads. Future cities should develop around greenways (Fig. 11.24).

Garreau believes that the developers of edge cities are opposed to public open space for security reasons. If this is really the case, it may not be possible to have greenways open to the public, but they should still be planned at the start of the urbanization process. Some can have restricted access. Some can provide benefits other than recreation. Some can be opened to the public when there is sufficient visual policing to make the space safe. The principle is clear: "greenways first in urban development".

Industry

Noxious industries require special zones. Other types of industry do not.

Industry used to be considered one of the grand avenues to human progress. "To be happy and prosperous", my great-grandfather used to say, "one must be busy and industrious". But in modern cities ". . . industry gets

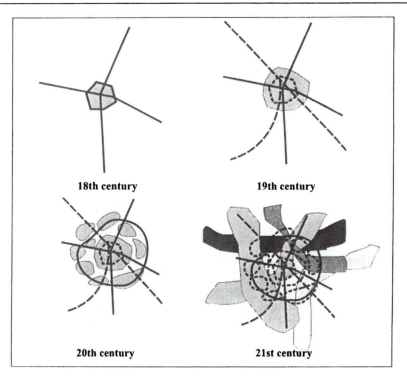

18th century

19th century

20th century

21st century

Figure 11.24 In the twenty-first century, city development should be preceded by the designation of various types of greenway, as shown in the lower left diagram.

treated like a disease" (Alexander et al. 1977: 228) and set apart from other land-uses, like the fever hospitals of my grandfather's time.

There are few industrial parallels to the songs, paintings and poetry which celebrate the farmer's life of honest toil in pastoral surroundings. Sir Uvedale Price, whose *Essays on the picturesque* were read avidly throughout the nineteenth century, had a surprisingly modern attitude to the effects of industry on the landscape. He wrote of cotton mills that ". . . nothing can equal them for the purpose of disbeautifying an enchanting piece of scenery" (Hoskins 1955: 170). Other nineteenth-century industries were nastier and more dangerous. Iron works, chemical manufactures and coal mines were extremely hazardous places, both for their employees and for neighbouring land-users. Some observers were fascinated by the demonic spectacle, as their ancestors had been by battlefields, but these industries were not seen as a source of aesthetic pleasure or spiritual uplift. In some parts of Britain the noxious new industries gathered together to create "a sort of pandemonium on earth", as in the following description of the Black Country, written in 1850:

> From Birmingham to Wolverhampton, a distance of thirteen miles, the country . . . seemed a sort of pandemonium on earth – a region of smoke and fire filling the whole area between earth and heaven; amongst which certain figures of human shape – if shape they had – were occasionally to glide from one cauldron of curling flame to another. The eye could not descry any form or colour indicative of country – of the hues and aspect of nature, or anything human or divine. Although nearly mid-day, in Summer, the sun and sky were obscured and discoloured; something like horses, men women and children seemed to move in the midst of the black and yellow smoke and flashes of fire; but were again lost in obscurity. (Tandy 1975: 25)

The Black Country was dominated by industry, but, now the smoke has cleared, we can see that "the region of smoke and fire" also contained houses for the working people. Even today, when most of the old smoke-stack industries have gone, the area is remarkable for its close mixture of industry, housing and agriculture. W. G. Hoskins wrote that life in the Black Country reached ". . . the rock bottom of filth and ugliness, and of human degradation", and that industrialists ". . . were completely and grotesquely insensitive. No scruples weakened their lust for money; they made their money and left behind their muck" (Hoskins 1955: 176). Those who could afford it moved away and left what became, in effect, an industrial zone. It will take a long time to efface the memory of smoke-stack industries.

The first true industrial zones, without inhabitants, were the docks of the eighteenth and nineteenth centuries. They were enclosed by high walls to prevent theft (Pudney 1975: 34). In the twentieth century the docks were followed by industrial estates in which bad-neighbour industries could be concentrated. Trafford Park, in Manchester, was started in 1896 and was followed by similar estates in Chicago, in 1902, and elsewhere. In Britain, the major nineteenth-century public health problems had been solved by 1945, but, according to Desmond Heap, ". . . there was still (to put the matter quite shortly) the problem of the dwelling-house built in the shadow of the factory and of the factory erected in the midst of the garden suburb" (Heap 1969: 4). This problem was dealt with by the Town and Country Planning Act of 1947. Industrial zones were set aside in the new towns, and land was "zoned for industry" on development plans for old towns. Industry became a single-purpose land-use. The trend towards concentration, regardless of the specific side-effects an industry might produce, has increased commuting distances and caused the peak flows of workers' cars to become ". . . the principal conflict between adjacent residential and industrial uses, surpassing the traditional nuisances of noise, smoke and dirt" (Lynch & Hack 1984: 306).

Many industries do not produce unpleasant side-effects, and this has led to the establishment of another kind of industrial zone: one designed to provide a good environment for the workers and a prestige location for the companies. Such zones are known as business parks, science parks, technology parks, food parks etc. The Team Valley Trading Estate, planned by Lord Holford in 1936, was one of the first to be designed for this purpose. Its name reminds us that the original idea was to create opportunities for trade as well as a better environment. Sadly, the Team Valley Trading Estate is only a moderate success in landscape terms. The open space takes the form of large, vacant expanses of "empty land made decent with grass" (Holford 1937). The River Team, which could have graced this land, was encased in a concrete box culvert. The effort devoted to the industrial buildings has merely given them a quiet, suburban respectability: they do not reveal the dynamism and excitement of productive industry. Modern business parks, like Aztec West, have a well-designed landscape setting, but one that still appears desolate because industrial workers do not wish to spend their leisure time on their employers' doorsteps. They must leave the estate to shop or eat. The problem can be solved by mixing industry with other land-users, who will use the open space and "benefit from the offshoots of the industrial activity" (Alexander et al. 1977: 230).

A trend towards multi-purpose land-use is under way, although there is more talk than action (Blacksell & Glig, 1981: 62). Planners favour the idea of "clean" industry in towns but remain preoccupied with the harmful side-effects produced by a few industries: chemical works, sewage treatment works, steel works, slaughterhouses, oil refineries and some mineral workings. For these industries the only reasonable landscape policy is to designate a zone and surround it with a buffer. There will be a continuing need for well-buffered zones for this type of industry. Other types should be freely mixed with housing, offices, shops and parks, depending on the range of side-effects they will generate, and from which they could benefit.

Conclusion

The fallacy of the undistributed middle.

Manifestly, we want access to clean air, sunshine, beautiful cities, sparkling rivers, ancient woods, gathering places in which to encounter other people. In Part 1 of this book, I argued that landscape planners ought to focus on public goods and EID. We should be plural in spirit and forward-looking in practice. This requires knowledge and information. Then, with clear objectives to guide us, as beacons guide ships, we can respond to contexts and prepare plans that reflect the diverse wishes of diverse groups.

With imagination and skill, land-uses can be integrated. In Part 2, I argued that single-use planning is generally bad planning. It causes side-effects and public goods to be neglected, so that the land-uses fall into disfavour and then decay. In this chapter, I have taken a long view of the urbanization process. While it proceeds, communities should found new settlements which conserve the existing landscape and create new public goods. Planning is required – but not too much of it.

At the start of the twentieth century, when optimistic reformers first argued the case for planning, they were confident that state control would produce a better world, with social justice, green parks, housing set apart from industry, towns ringed by fields, sunny streets, dung-free roads and the hygienic disposal of other waste products. By the end of the twentieth century, some of the dreams have been realized and others have become nightmares. The new cities have dirty rivers, polluting roads, dreary parks, ugly scenery and dangerous footpaths. The City of Dreadful Night has become the City of Dreadful Day.

Planning was part of the problem. In the Soviet Union, government planning produced grim totalitarian cities dominated by wide roads and high blocks, set far apart. In the USA, government planning took the form of over-investment in roads, rigid land-use zoning and under-investment in public space. Western Europe compromised between these extremes, keeping its ancient town centres but surrounding them with a mixture of Soviet and American planned development.

The author of London's best plan, Patrick Abercrombie, argued that:

> When two or three buildings are gathered together, there arises the question of their relationship to each other; when a road cuts across an open stretch of country, there is its relation to the landscape; when a piece of land is enclosed, the question of the boundary lines occurs, and the decision as to the use to which it is put or the manner in which it is divided up. All these are examples of Town and Country Planning (Abercrombie 1934: 11).

Like other modernist planners, he was too hasty in arguing from *some* to *all*. Twentieth-century planning rested on an invalid argument form:

Some actions by land-users affect other land-users.
All actions which affect other land-users require planning.
Therefore all actions by land-users require planning.

To logicians this is known as the fallacy of the undistributed middle. I prefer the following, valid, argument:

Some actions by land-users affect public goods.
All actions which affect public goods require planning.
Therefore some actions by landowners require planning.

Landscape planning can produce settlements that are rich in public goods. We should, as Nan Fairbrother said, make new landscapes for our new lives.

Appendix: Environmental impact questions

Single-purposism, as we have seen, tends to create projects that harm the environment. Instead, we should design projects with as favourable an environmental impact as possible. This is the objective of environmental impact design.

The questions about impact in this appendix have been grouped, as general and sectoral questions, similarly to their discussion in the book. Clearly, they overlap and the list is incomplete. It needs to be elaborated. As land-users, we tend to take an interest in the environmental consequences of our neighbours' activities and to resent questions about our own. We are aggrieved when public goods are damaged and delighted when the supply is augmented. If damage is unavoidable, we expect compensatory measures. Environmental compensation, delivered at the point of impact, is economically more efficient than financial compensation. It goes to the people who have suffered a loss. We should, by asking questions, audit *the impact of development projects on public goods*

- when a landowner applies for planning permission, a building licence or authorization from an environmental quality regulator;
- when public money is to be spent on a project, so that society can obtain the maximum social benefit at the minimum social cost.

The questions can be used to carry out a public goods audit of proposed development projects.

PART 1: General questions

Objectives   Is it a single-objective project or a multi-objective project?

Planning process   Have the affected landowners and land-users helped to generate the plan?

Impact on public goods   Will the existing stock of public goods be increased or decreased?

Compensation   If existing public goods will be damaged, what environmental compensation is proposed?

Relationship to local plans   Does the project design contribute to local plan objectives for improving the stock of environmental public goods (natural, social and visual)?

Urban design   How does the project design relate to local urban design objectives?

Sustainability   Does the project design contribute to sustainability objectives?

Transport   How will the project encourage the use of self-powered transport and public transport?

Vegetation   Will the project design increase or reduce the quantity and diversity of plant life?

Surface water   Will the surface-water runoff from the site be increased or reduced?

Landform   How does the project design respond to the existing landform and to local plans to develop it?

Habitats   How does the planting design relate to the habitat potential plan for the locality?

Greenspace   Is the project design compatible with the objectives of the local greenspace plan?

Recreation   Is the project design compatible with local recreation objectives?

Air   How does the project design relate to air quality objectives?

Scenic plan   Is the project set in an area of low, medium or high scenic quality? How will the scenic quality be affected by the project design?

Spatial quality   How does the project design relate to the local plan for spatial quality?

Skyline   How will the local skyline be affected by the project design?

Zoning   What landscape character zones overlap the site?

General character   How does the development project respond to the Genius of the Place? Is the proposed character designed to be identical to, similar to or different from that of its surroundings? What is the value of the SID Index for the project?

Detailed character   How does the development project respond, in detail, to the character of its surroundings (e.g. architectural style, plant materials, construction materials etc.). Are the design details intended to be identical, similar or different?

Nature   Has the project been designed *with* nature or *against* nature?

Language   What does the project 'say', in the language of the environment?

Archetypal patterns   What extensions will be made to larger-scale Alexander patterns? What provision will be made for smaller-scale Alexander patterns?

Material colour   Will the colour relationship with local construction and plant materials be one of similarity, identity or contrast?

Planning information system   Has the project design been checked against the historical records and development plans in the local planning information system?

PART 2: Sectoral questions

PUBLIC OPEN SPACE

Access   Is the open space designed to be bounded or unbounded?

Character   Will the predominant character be that of a man-made or a natural area?

Use   What provision will be made for specialist activities in the public open space?

Colour   What is the most appropriate colour to symbolize the intended character of the public open space?

Planning   How will the public open space relate to adjacent land-uses?

Historic conservation   How does the present design reflect previous designs for the site?

Nature conservation   How does the public open space contribute to wildlife, water and air-quality objectives?

Markets   Will there be a provision for the sale of goods in the public open space?

Management   Will the management of the open space be funded with national, regional, local or community finance, by a public–private partnership or by a private organization? Has the creation of a non-profit community trust been evaluated?

Ownership Will there be a direct relationship between the ownership and the control of the public open space?

Greenways In what sense will the open space be "green"? For what types of traffic will it be a "way"?

RESERVOIRS

SID index Is the reservoir designed to be similar to or different from its surroundings?

Reservoir fringe land Will the waterfront land be urban, agricultural, estuarine, recreational or natural?

Urbanization Is it appropriate to design the reservoir in conjunction with a new settlement?

Reservoir margin What physical and biological works will be carried out before the land is inundated (e.g. to create beaches at water level and habitats beneath water level)?

Recreation How will the reservoir improve opportunities for outdoor recreation?

Swimming What provision will be made for outdoor swimming?

Habitat creation How will the reservoir contribute to the creation of new habitats?

Scenery How will the reservoir improve the scenery?

Archaeology Has the land to be flooded been considered as an underwater archaeological reserve?

MINERAL WORKINGS

Quality Will the landscape be at least as useful and as beautiful after mining as before?

Plant and machinery How will adverse side-effects be mitigated? What beneficial side-effects are planned?

Mineral operation What harm will be done? How will the landform be adapted to produce a beneficial end-result?

Phasing Is there a phasing plan for the completion of the mineral workings and the establishment of after-uses?

Character At surface level, will the post-mining and pre-mining landscapes be similar, identical or different?

After-use Has full consideration been given to planning for a range of possible after-uses?

Landownership Should the community help with land aquisition? Will the land pass into public ownership when the extraction process is complete?

AGRICULTURE

Character Should the existing character of the agricultural land be conserved, or should a different character be developed?

Public goods What public goods are produced? What public goods could be produced? Who will pay for the public goods? Should the landowner receive a wage or a rent for the public goods provided?

Mapping From which points of view has the agricultural land been mapped?

Strategic reserve Will the farm provide a strategic reserve capacity for food production? If land goes out of production, how long would it take to bring it back into production?

Conservation Will the farm contribute to water conservation, historic conservation and scenic conservation objectives?

Recreation Will access to the countryside be improved?

Food Will the supply of wild food and non-industrial food be improved?

Geography Has the supply of public goods been considered in relation to their local, regional, national and international availability?

Implementation What arrangements have been made to implement a farm landscape plan?

Ownership Will any easements or common rights be purchased or pass into public ownership for another reason?

Finance Will the public benefit from money spent on agricultural production subsidies?

FORESTRY

Character Will the forest be beautiful and productive? Will it have sparkling streams, bright pools, dark swamps, open glades, black groves and many animals?

Internal land-use relationships How many land-use objectives have been incorporated into the forest design plan?

External land-use relationships   How has the forest design been integrated with the pattern of surrounding land-uses?

Myth   Have any myths or stories been incorporated into the forest design?

Land cover   Which parts of the forest will be wooded and which will be open land?

Food   What wild food will be produced within the forest?

Wildlife   How will wildlife benefit from the forestry operations?

Ancient woods   What areas have been set aside to become ancient woods?

Roads   Have recreational, aesthetic and conservation objectives been considered in the design of forest roads, rides and fire breaks?

Public participation   How will the local community help to design and manage the forest?

Silviculture   Which silvicultural systems will be used? Will any of the forest land be clear-felled or managed by selection forestry?

Management   Will forestry objectives receive different priorities in different compartments of the forest?

Landscape plan   Will the forest landscape plan be published, discussed with community groups, deposited in local libraries and exhibited on notice boards?

RIVERS AND FLOODS

Drainage   Will the volume and rate of surface-water runoff from the site be increased or reduced?

Flooding   Which areas of town and country will be allowed to flood, and with what frequency?

Detention   Will any special measures be taken to detain surface water within the development site boundary?

Infiltration   Will surface-water infiltration be increased or reduced? What special techniques will be employed?

Roof vegetation   Will the roofs of new buildings be vegetated? If not, why not?

Pavements   Will porous paving be used in the development? If so, will there be an adverse impact on water quality?

Riverworks   What is the intended use and character of the reach where the works will take place?

Recreation What provision will be made for outdoor swimming, boating and other recreational activities?

Coastal works What is the intended use and character of the coastal area where the works will take place? Is the project design single-purpose or multi-purpose? Are the works designed in the context of a coastal landscape plan?

TRANSPORT

Colour What is the most appropriate colour to symbolize the intended character of the routeway?

Names Will the proposed route be a road, a ride, a highway, a lane, a track, a footpath, a speedway, a bridleway, a street, an avenue or an autoroute?

Multi-mode sharing To what extent will traffic modes share the paved surface? To what extent will traffic modes be segregated?

Cycling Will a provision be made for cycling and cycle storage? Will the use of cycles and the safety of cyclists be monitored?

Transport interchanges Have modal interchange points been integrated with other land-uses? Do they make provision for cycle storage? Have they been designed as attractive multi-functional spaces?

Conservation Will historic transport routes be conserved?

Alignment Has the route alignment been adapted to its context? Was it produced using standard criteria from a design manual?

Phasing What provision has been made for future changes in the route's use and character?

Margin details Does the treatment of walls, fences, banks, drains and vegetation relate to local traditions, or to an innovatory landscape plan?

URBANIZATION

Location Where will planned urbanization do the least harm and the most good? Can it be designed in conjunction with other land-uses?

Size Will the eventual settlement size be small, medium or large?

New settlements What is the best location for the new settlement from the point of view of the local community? Should a local referendum be held to choose sites for urbanization?

Community involvement How will the future community be represented in the planning and design process?

Topography   How will the urbanization relate to the existing topography?

Regional identity   How will the settlement respond to the character of the local climate, local design tradition and local materials?

Public open space   Which land is best suited for designation as public open space?

Earthmoving   Is there an earthmoving plan for the urbanization process?

Water   How will the pattern of surface-water drainage be affected? Will new water bodies be created?

Trees   Will the urbanization have an advance tree-planting programme?

Circulation   What will be done to contribute to a sustainable transport network?

Finance   If the urbanization benefits from public infrastructure investment, how will the public gain a return from this investment?

References

Abercrombie, P. 1934. *Country planning and landscape design*. London: Hodder & Stoughton.

Agricola, G. (trans. H. C. Hoover & L. H. Hoover) 1912. *De re metallica*. London: Mining Magazine.

Ahern, J. 1995. Greenways as a planning strategy. *Landscape and Urban Planning* **33** (1–3), 131–55.

Ahern, J. & J. Gy. Fabos 1996. *Greenways: the beginning of an international movement*. Amsterdam: Elsevier.

Aldous, T. 1972. *Battle for the environment*. Glasgow: Fontana.

Aldous, T. & C. Clouston 1979. *Landscape by design*. London: Heinemann.

Alexander, C. et al. 1977. *A pattern language*. New York: Oxford University Press.

Al-Yawer H. 1982. Urban space in the Islamic city. In *The Arab City*, I. Serageldin (ed.), 111–19. Riyadh: Arab Urban Development.

Anglian Water Authority 1982. *Cardington canoe slalom course*. Bedford: Anglian Water Authority.

Anglian Water Authority und. *The world of Rutland Water*, no. 1 *General information*, promotional leaflet. Huntingdon: Oundle Division of the Anglian Water Authority.

Appleyard, D. 1987. Foreword. In *Public streets for public use*, A. V. Moudon (ed.) New York: Van Nostrand Reinhold.

Ashihara, Y. 1983. *The aesthetic townscape*. Cambridge, Mass.: MIT Press.

Association of River Authorities Year Book. 1965. London: ARA.

Attoe, W. 1981. *Skylines: understanding and molding urban silhouettes*. Chichester: John Wiley.

Bacon, E. N. 1967. *Design of cities*. London: Thames and Hudson.

Bailey, J. (ed.) 1973. *New towns in America*. New York: John Wiley.

Baines, J. & J. Malek 1984. *Atlas of Ancient Egypt*. Oxford: Phaidon.

Balchin, J. 1980. *First new town: an autobiography of the Stevenage Development Corporation*. Stevenage: Stevenage Development Corporation.

Baldock, D. 1984. *Wetland drainage in Europe*. London: Institute for European Environmental Policy, p. 158.

Baldock, D. (ed.) 1994. *The nature of farming: low intensity farming in nine European countries*. London: Institute for European Environmental Policy.

Banham, R. 1976. The open city and its enemies. *Listener* (23 September), 359–60.

Barr, J. 1969. *Derelict Britain*. Harmondsworth: Penguin.

Bartlett, R. V. 1980. *The Reseve Mining controversy*. Bloomington: Indiana University Press.

Barton, N. 1962. *The lost rivers of London*. London: Phoenix House.

Bayliss, M. & T. Turner 1972. *Towpath walk: Ladywood Middleway to Farmer's Bridge Junction*. Birmingham: Birmingham City Architects Department.

Betsky, A. 1995. *Building sex: men, women, architecture and the construction of sexuality*. New York: William Morrow.

Blacksell, M. & A. Glig 1981. *The countryside, planning and change*. London: Allen and Unwin.

Bor, W. 1979. Milton Keynes New City – ten years on. *Ekistics* no. 277 (July/ August), 243.

Bracknell Development Corporation 1952. *Master plan report*. Bracknell: Bracknell Development Corporation.

Brett, L. 1970. *Parameters and images*. London: Weidenfeld and Nicolson.

Brocklesby, M. 1979. *A reassessment of opencast coalmining*. London: Opencast Mining Intelligence Group.

Brookes, A. 1988. *Channelized rivers: perspectives for environmental management*. Chichester: John Wiley.

Brookes, A. & F. Douglas Sheilds 1996. *River channel restoration: guiding principles for sustainable projects*. Chichester: John Wiley.

Brotherton, I. 1977. *Tarn Hows: an approach to the management of a popular beauty spot*, CCR 106. Cheltenham: Countryside Commission.

Brown, J. 1882. *The Forester*. Edinburgh.

Brundtland Commission. 1987. *Our common future*. New York: World Commission on Environment and Development.

Buchanan, C. D. 1963. *Traffic in towns*. London: HMSO.

Bugler, J. 1975. Bedfordshire brick. In *The politics of physical resources*, P. J. Smith (ed.). Harmondsworth: Penguin/Oxford University Press.

Burchfield, R. W. (ed.) 1976. Entry for "Landscape". In *A supplement to the Oxford English Dictionary*. Oxford: Oxford University Press.

Burke, E. 1756. *A philosophical inquiry into the origin of our ideas of the sublime and beautiful*, Part II. London.

Caisley, R. 1980. The planning authority's role in the restoration of limestone and fluorspar extraction sites. *Reclamation Review* 3 (4), 223–8.

Chadwick, G. F. 1961. *The works of Sir Joseph Paxton 1803–1865*. London: Architectural Press.

Chadwick, G. F. 1966. *The park and the town*. London: Architectural Press.

Chadwick, G. F. 1978. *A systems view of planning*, 2nd edn. Oxford: Pergamon.

Charles, HRH Prince of Wales. 1989. *A vision of Britain*. London: Doubleday.

Chervasse, C. R. R. 1980. The opportunities before us. *Australian Forestry* 43, (3), 156–9.

CIRIA 1992a. *Report 124: Scope for control of urban runoff*, vol. 2: A review of present methods and practice. London: Construction Industry Research and Information Service.

CIRIA 1992b. *Report 124: Scope for control of urban runoff*, vol. 3: Guidelines. London: Construction Industry Research and Information Service.

City of Bristol, City Docks Joint Study Team 1977. *Bristol City Docks Local Plan, Topic Studies, Townscape and Environment*. Bristol: City Planning Department.

Clark, M. J. 1982. Coastal management and protection in the United States of America. In *Shoreline protection: proceedings of a conference organised by the Institution of Civil Engineers*, 49–54. London: Thomas Telford.

Clawson, M. 1975. *Forests for whom and for what?* Baltimore, Md.: Johns Hopkins University Press; Resources for the Future Inc.

Cleasby, J. V. 1974. Environmental aspects of Boulby mine, Cleveland Potash Ltd. Paper 9. In *Minerals and the environmment*. London: Institution of Mining and Metallurgy.

Coal surface mining commission 1979. *Coal surface mining: impacts of reclamation*. Boulder, Colo.: Westview Press.

Coleman, A. 1954. Landscape and planning in relation to the cement industry of Thames-side. *Town Planning Review* **25**, 216–30.

Colvin & Moggridge, 1971. *Brennig Reservoir Scheme: landscape report*. Dee and Clwyd River Authority.

Colvin, B. 1973. *Land and landscape*. London: Murray.

Commission of the European Communities 1985. Council directive on the assessment of the effects of certain private and public projects (85/337/EEC). *Official Journal of the European Communities* L175/40, 5 July.

Commission on Mining and the Environment 1972. Chairman Professor Lord Zuckerman: *Report of the Commission on Mining and the Environment*. London: Commission on Mining and the Environment.

Committee on Soil as a Resource in Relation to Surface Mining for Coal 1981. *Surface mining: soil, coal, and society*. Washington, DC: National Academy Press.

Committee on Surface Mining and Reclamation 1979. *Surface mining of non-coal minerals*, Appendix 1. Washington, DC: National Academy of Sciences.

Council for Environmental Conservation 1979. *Scar on the landscape: a report on opencast coal mining and the environment*. London: CoEnCo.

Countryside Commission 1984. *A better future for the uplands*. Cheltenham: Countryside Commission.

Countryside Commission 1987. *Landscape assessment: a Countryside Commission approach*, CD18. Cheltenham: Countryside Commission.

Countryside Commission 1987b. *Forestry in the countryside*. Cheltenham: Countryside Commission.

Cranz, G. 1982. *The politics of park design: a history of urban parks in America*. Cambridge, Mass.: MIT Press.

Crawford, D. B. 1982. Land use planning – the problems of conflicting interests. *Journal of the Royal Scottish Forestry Society* **36** (2), 91–101.

Crawford, M. & D. Marsh 1989. *The driving force*. London: Heinemann.

Crowe, S. 1966. *Forestry in the landscape*, Forestry Commission booklet no. 18. London: HMSO.

Crowe, S. 1971. Bewl Bridge. *Landscape Design*, November (96).

Crowe, S. 1978. *The landscape of forests and woods*, Forestry Commission booklet no. 44. London: HMSO.

Crowe, S. undated. Bough Beech Reservoir: proof of evidence. Unpublished paper.

Cullen, G. 1961. *Townscape*. London: Architectural Press.

Cummins, A. B. (ed.) 1973. *SME mining engineering handbook*, vol. 2. New York: Society of Mining Engineers of the American Institute of Mining, Metallurgical, and Petroleum Engineers.

Cunningham, A. S. 1912. *Dysart: past and present*. Leven: Russell.

Dalradian Mineral Services 1980. *Potential for a large coastal quarry in Scotland*. Edinburgh: Scottish Development Department.

Dalton, D. W. 1985. Still life in quarry. *Landscape Architecture* **75** (3), 66–9.

Dangerfield, B. J. 1981. *Recreation: water and land*. London: Institution of Water Engineers and Scientists.

Davies, H. 1983. *A walk around London's parks*. London: Hamilton.

Davis, C. 1995. A bowl of white water. *Landscape Design* (244) 26–8.

Davison, D. J. 1978. *The environmental factor: an approach for managers*. London: Associated Business Programmes.

Department of Environment 1989. *Planning control in Western Europe*. London: HMSO.

Department of Transport 1992. *The good roads guide: environmental design for inter-urban roads*. London: Department of Transport.

Department of Transport 1996. *The national cycling strategy*. London: Department of Transport.

Down, C. G. & J. Stocks 1977. *Environmental impact of mining*. London: Applied Science Publishers.

Dugan, P. 1993. *Wetlands in danger*. London: Mitchell Beazley.

Duinker, P. N. et al. 1994. Community forests in Canada: an overview. *Forestry chronicle* **70** (6), 711–20.

Dunne, T. & L.B. Leopold 1978. *Water in environmental planning*. San Francisco, Cal.: W. H. Freeman.

Elliott, R. J. 1976. *Landscaping and land use planning as related to mining operations*. Adelaide: Australian Institute of Mining and Metallurgy.

Ellis, E. A. 1965. *The Broads*. London: Collins.

Elton, C. 1966a. *Animal ecology*. London: Methuen.

Elton, C. 1966b. *The pattern of animal communities*. London: Methuen.

Executive Council of the Canton of Aargau 1979. *Improvement of the Reuss Valley*. Aargau, Switzerland: Executive Council of the Canton of Aargau.

Fabos, J. Gy. 1995. Introduction and overview: the greenway movement, uses and potentials of greenways. *Landscape and Urban Planning* **33** (1–3), 1–13.

Fabos, J. Gy. 1985. *Land use planning: from global to local challenge*. New York: Chapman and Hall.

Fabos, J. Gy. & J. Ahern 1995. Special issue: Greenways. *Landscape and Urban Planning* **33** (1-3).

Fairbrother, N. 1970. *New lives, new landscapes*. London: Architectural Press.

Farmers Weekly. 17 November.

Farming Programme. BBC Radio 4. 15 December.

Fink, C. A. & R. M. Searns 1993. *Greenways: a guide to planning, design and development*. Washington, DC: Island Press, The Conservation Fund.

Firbank, L. G. 1993. *Managing set-aside land for wildlife*. London: HMSO.

Forest Service 1972. *National forest landscape management*, vol. 1, Agriculture Handbook no. 434, 19. Washington, DC: Forest Service/U.S. Department of Agriculture.

Forest Service 1974. *Report of the Chief Forester*. Washington, DC: USDA.

Forester, J. 1994. *Bicycle transportation*, 2nd edn. Harvard, Mass.: MIT Press.

Forestry Act 1919.

Forestry Commission 1920. *First annual report of the Forestry Commissioners*.

Forestry Commission 1934. *Fifteenth annual report of the Forestry Commissioners*.

Forestry Commission 1936. *Seventeenth annual report of the Forestry Commissioners*.

Forestry Commission 1938. *Nineteenth annual report of the Forestry Commissioners*.

Forestry Commission 1946. *Twenty-seventh annual report of the Forestry Commissioners*.

Forestry Commission 1947. *Annual report of the Forestry Commissioners*.

Forestry Commission 1949. *Thirtieth annual report of the Forestry Commissioners*.

Forestry Commission 1959. *Fortieth annual report of the Forestry Commissioners*.

Forestry Commission 1961. *Forty-second annual report of the Forestry Commissioners.*

Forestry Commission 1963. *Forty-fourth annual report of the Forestry Commissioners.*

Forestry Commission 1965. *Forty-fifth Annual report of the Forestry Commissioners.*

Forestry Commission 1969. *Fiftieth Annual Report of the Forestry Commissioners.*

Forestry Commission 1971. *Fifty-second annual report of the Forestry Commissioners.*

Forestry Commission 1972a. *Fifty-third annual report of the Forestry Commissioners.*

Forestry Commission 1972b. *Wildlife conservation in woodlands,* Forestry Commission booklet no. 29.

Forestry Commission 1974. *Fifty-fourth annual report of the Forestry Commissioners.*

Forestry Commission 1977. *Fifty-seventh annual report of the Forestry Commissioners.*

Forestry Commission 1978a. *See your forests: South England.*

Forestry Commission 1978b. *Fifty-eighth annual report of the Forestry Commissioners.*

Forestry Commission 1979. *Fifty-ninth annual report of the Forestry Commissioners.*

Forestry Commission 1980. *Sixtieth annual report of the Forestry Commissioners.*

Forestry Commission 1982. *Sixty-second annual report of the Forestry Commissioners.*

Forestry Commission 1983. *Sixty-third annual report of the Forestry Commissioners.*

Forestry Commission 1984a. *Consultation procedures for forestry grants and felling permissions.* Forestry Commission.

Forestry Commission 1984b. *The Forestry Commission's objectives.* Forestry Commission.

Forestry Commission 1984c. *Broadleaves in Britain: a consultative paper.*

Forestry Commission 1985. *Sixty-fifth annual report of the Forestry Commissioners*

Forestry Commission 1993. *Seventy-third annual report and accounts.*

Forestry in Great Britain: an interdepartmental cost/benefit study 1972. HMSO.

Frampton, K. 1987. Towards a critical regionalism: six points for an architecture of resistance. In *Postmodern culture,* H. Foster (ed.), 16–30. London: Pluto Press.

Fukuyama, F. 1992. *The end of history and the last man.* London: Hamish Hamilton.

Gardiner, J. L. 1994. Sustainable development for river catchments. *Water and Environmental Management* **8** (3).

Garreau, J. 1991. *Edge City: life on the new frontier.* New York: Doubleday.

Garten & Landschaft 1983. Special issue on rivers, February.

Geddes, P. 1904. *City development.* Bourneville: St George Press.

Geddes, P. 1915. *Cities in evolution.* London.

Geddes, P. 1917. *Town planning in Balrampur.* Lucknow.

Geddes, P. 1918. *Town planning towards city development: a report to the Durbar of Indore,* vol. 1, 1. Indore.

Gibson, J. E. 1972. *Designing the new city: a systematic approach.* John Wiley: New York.

Gill, C. J. & A. D. Bradshaw 1971. The landscaping of reservoir margins. *Landscape Design* (95), 31–4.

Gilpin, W. 1791. *Observations on forest scenery . . . illustrated by scenes in the New Forest.* London: Blamie.

Glasson, J., R. Therivel & A. Chadwick 1994. *Introduction to environmental impact assessment.* London: UCL Press.

Glig, A. W. (ed.) 1980. *Countryside planning yearbook,* vol. 1. Norwich: Geo Books.

Glitz, D. 1983. Artificial channels – the "ox-bow" lakes of tomorrow. *Garten & Landschaft*, February, 109–11.

Goldsmith, O. 1770. *The deserted village*. London.

Goodey, B. 1995. Landscape. In *Methods of environmental impact assessment*, P. Morris & R. Therivel (eds), 78–95. London: UCL Press.

Gothein, M.-L. 1928 edn. *A history of garden art*. London: Dent.

Greater London Development Plan, section 9. London: Greater London Council.

Green, B. H. 1986. Controlling ecosystems. In *Ecology and design in landscape*, A. D. Bradshaw et al. (eds), 195–209. Oxford: Blackwell Scientific.

Greengrass, D. 1977. *Pollution and environment*. Milton Keynes: Open University Press.

Greenhalgh, F. 1968. Land drainage and water conservation problems in Bristol Avon River Authority Area. In *Association of River Authorities Year Book*, pp. 161–78. London: ARA.

Hall, M. J. 1984. *Urban hydrology*. Amsterdam: Elsevier.

Hall, M. J. & D. L. Hockin, 1980. *Guide to the design of storage ponds for flood control in partly urbanised catchment areas*. Technical Note 100. London: CIRIA.

Hall, P. 1988. *Cities of tomorrow*. Oxford: Blackwell.

Hansard 1963. Statement by the Minister of Agriculture, Fisheries, and Food, Mr Christopher Soames. 24 July.

Harris, B. 1985. Rationality and its enemies. In *Rationality in Planning*, M. Breheny & A. Hooper (eds), 60–76. London: Pion.

Harris, E. M. H. 1983. *Forestry and conservation*. Royal Forestry Society.

Harris, L. D. 1984. *The fragmented forest: island biogeography theory and the preservation of biotic diversity*. Chicago, Ill.: University of Chicago Press.

Harrison, R. P. 1992. *Forests, the shadow of civilization*. Chicago, Ill.: University of Chicago Press.

Harrison, S. A. 1864. *A complete history of the great flood at Sheffield on March 11 and 12 1864*. Sheffield: Harrison.

Hart, L. 1936. *"T E Lawrence" in Arabia and after*. London: Cape.

Hass-Klau, C. 1990. *The pedestrian and city traffic*. London: Belhaven Press.

Hayek, F. A. 1979 edn. *The road to serfdom*. London: Routledge and Kegan Paul.

Haywood, S. H. 1974. *Quarries and the landscape*. London: British Quarrying and Slag Federation.

Heap, D. 1969. *An outline of planning law*. London: Sweet and Maxwell.

Heap, D. 1983. Planning – a lawyer's reflections. *Journal of Planning and Environment Law*, Special issue, November, 9. (The address was originally delivered in Leeds in February 1944.)

Heckscher, A. 1977. *Open spaces: the life of American cities*. New York: Harper & Row.

Helliwell, D. R. 1982. *Options in forestry*. Chichester: Packard Publishing.

Hewett, C. E. & T. E. Hamilton 1982. *Forests in demand: conflicts and solutions*. Boston, Mass.: Auburn House Publishing.

Hilton, A. (ed.) 1957. *This England*. London: *New Statesman*.

Hobbes, T. 1651, 1919 edn. *Leviathan*. London: George Routledge and Sons.

Holford, Lord 1937. Team Valley Trading Estate. *Journal of the Royal Institute of British Architects*, 20 February, 396–400.

Holmstrand, O. 1984. Infiltration of stormwater. In *Planning and control of urban storm drainage*, vol. 3 of *Proceedings of the Third International Conference on Urban Storm Drainage*, P. Balmer et al. (eds), 1803–91. Göteborg: Chalmers University of Technology.

Hoskins, W. G. 1955. *The making of the English landscape*. London: Hodder & Stoughton.

Hoskins, W. G. & L. Dudley Stamp 1963. *The common lands of England and Wales*. London: Collins.

Hough, M. 1990. *Out of place*. Newhaven, Conn.: Yale University Press.

Hume, D. 1974 edn. *Treatise on human nature*, ed. P. H. Nidditch. Oxford: Clarendon Press.

Hussey, C. 1927. *The Picturesque*. London: Putnam.

Hutton, W. 1984. Forestry in Britain: money can grow on trees. *Listener*, 8 March, 13.

Institute of Civil Engineers 1981. *I.C.E. flood studies report – five years on*. London: Thomas Telford.

Institution of Civil Engineers 1907. The Talla water-supply of the Edinburgh and District Waterworks. In *Proceedings of the Institution of Civil Engineers*, vol. CLXVII, 102–52.

Institution of Water Engineers 1963. Draft report of the council on the recreational use of waterworks. *Journal of the Institution of Water Engineers* 17 (2), 71–114.

Institution of Water Engineers 1971. The recreational use of water. *Journal of the Institution of Water Engineers* 25, 87–127.

James, N. D. G. 1981. *A history of English forestry*. Oxford: Blackwell.

Jellicoe, G. A. 1979. *Blue Circle Cement, Hope Works, Derbyshire: a progress report on a landscape plan 1943–93*. London: Blue Circle Cement.

Jenkins, S. 1995. Farmer, preserve that farm. *The Times*, 21 January.

Jenkins, S. 1996. A chance to touch eternity. *The Times*, 26 October.

Johnson, A. 1994. What's super about big quarries? *ECOS* 15 (3/4), 35–41.

Johnson, E. A. G. 1966. Land drainage in England and Wales. In *River engineering and water conservation*, R. B. Thorn (ed.). London: Butterworth.

Johnson, E. A. G. 1969. Land drainage. In *Association of River Authorities Year Book*. London: ARA.

Jones, M. J. 1975. *Minerals and the environment*. London: Institute of Mining and Metallurgy.

Journal of the American Planning Association 51 (3).

Juneja, N. & J. Veltman, J. 1979. Naural drainage in the woodlands. *Environmental Comment*, November, 7–12.

Khalis, G. Md. 1993, Flood in Bangladesh: a challenge to socio-economic development. *Bangladesh Quarterly* 12 (8), 3–16.

Kirby, K. J. 1984. *Forestry operations and broadleaf woodland conservation*. Peterborough: Nature Conservancy Council.

Krier, R. 1979. *Urban space*. London: Academy Editions.

Kunstler, J. H. 1993. The geography of nowhere. New York: Simon & Schuster.

Kusler, J. & M. Kentula 1990. *Wetland creation and restoration*. Covelo, Cal.: Island Press.

Lake District Special Planning Board 1978. *Lake District National Park Plan*. Kendal: Lake District Special Planning Board.

Landscape Design 1971. Current Work: 3. *Landscape Design* no. 96, 32–3.

Landscape Institute & Institute of Environmental Assessment 1995. *Guidelines for landscape and visual impact assessment*. London: E&FN Spon.

Larwood, J. 1872. *The story of the London parks*. London.

Le Corbusier (trans. F. Etchells) 1977 edn. *The city of tomorrow*. London: Architectural Press.

Lees, E. A. 1908. *Elan supply*. Birmingham: City of Birmingham.

Lees-Milne, J. (ed.) 1945. *The National Trust: a record of fifty years' achievement*. London: Batsford.

Leopold, A. 1970. *A Sand County almanac*. San Francisco, Cal.: Sierra Club.

Les Guides Bleus 1979. *Les Villes nouvelles en Île-de-France*. Paris: Hachette.

Leuschner, H.-J. 1976. The opencast mine of Hambach – a synthesis of raw material, mining and landscaping. *Braunkohle* **28** (5).

Lewis, P. 1964. Quality corridors in Wisconsin. *Landscape Architecture*, January.

Light, W. 1911. Col. William Light: a brief journal. In *A biographical sketch of Col. William Light*, T. Gill (ed.). Adelaide.

Little, C. 1990. *Greenways for America*. Baltimore, Md.: Johns Hopkins University Press.

Loudon, J. C. (ed.) 1829. *Gardener's Magazine*, **5**, 686.

Loudon, J. C. 1835. *Encyclopaedia of agriculture*. London: Longman.

Loudon, J. C. (ed.) 1840. *The landscape gardening and landscape architecture of the late Humphry Repton, Esq*. London: Black.

Lucas, O. 1984. The Forestry Commission. *Landscape Design* (150), 10.

Lynch, K. 1960. *The image of the city*. Cambridge, Mass.: MIT Press.

Lynch, K. 1972. The openness of open space. In *Arts of the environment*, G. Kepes (ed.), 108–34. New York: Braziller.

Lynch, K. & G. Hack 1984. *Site planning*. Cambridge, Mass.: MIT Press.

MacArthur, R. H. & E. O. Wilson 1967. *The theory of island biogeography*. Princeton, NJ: Princeton University Press.

McClusky, J. 1979. *Road form and townscape*. London: Architectural Press.

McGowan, P. & J. Miller 1984. Environmental impact assessments. *Landscape Design* (150), 57–9.

McHarg, I. 1971. *Design with nature*. New York: Doubleday.

McHarg, I. L. & J. Sutton 1975. Ecological plumbing for the Texas coastal plain. *Landscape Architecture Quarterly* **65** (1), 78–89.

McLoughlin, J. B. 1970. *Urban and regional planning: a systems approach*. London: Faber and Faber.

MAFF 1993a. *Strategy for flood and coastal defence in England and Wales*. London: Ministry of Agriculture, Fisheries, and Food.

MAFF 1993b. *Coastal defense and the environment*. London: Ministry of Agriculture, Fisheries, and Food.

MAFF 1995. *Shoreline management plans: a guide for coastal defence authorities*. London: Ministry of Agriculture, Fisheries and Food.

Manwood, J. 1717. *Manwood's treatise of the forest laws*, 4th edn, ed. W. Nelson. London: E. Nutt.

Marshall, A. 1961 edn. *Principles of economics*. London: Macmillan.

Matter, F. S. 1977. Balancing resource extraction and creative land development. In *Reclamation and use of disturbed land in the southwest*. Arizona: University of Arizona Press.

Milton Keynes Cycle Users Group 1984. *Cycling in Milton Keynes: a user's view*. Milton Keynes: Milton Keynes Cycle Users Group.

Mine and quarry 1985. Glensanda: Scotland's new super quarry. *Mine and quarry*. **14** (9), 19–21; **10**, 14–19.

Minister of Housing and Local Government 1952a. Letter to the London Brick Company, 17 July.

Minister of Housing and Local Government 1952b. Letter to the Thurrock Chalk and Whiting Company, 2 August.

Ministry of Health 1948. *Gathering grounds: report of the Gathering Grounds Sub-committee of the Central Advisory Water Committee* (the Heneage Report). London: HMSO.

Ministry of Housing and Local Government 1960. *The control of mineral working*: "Green Book". London: HMSO.

Ministry of Works and Planning 1942. *Report of the* [Scott] *Committee on Land Utilisation in Rural Areas.* London: HMSO.

Moolen, B. van der 1996. Public acceptance of mineral workings. *Mineral Planning*, 10–13.

Moro, P. 1958. Elevational control. *Architects Journal* **127**, 203.

Morris, P. & R. Therivel 1995. *Methods of environmental impact assessment.* London: UCL Press.

Muir, J. 1912. *The Yosemite.* New York: Century.

Mumford, L. 1938. *The culture of cities.* London: Secker & Warburg.

Mumford, L. 1961. *The city in history.* London: Secker & Warburg.

National Capital Development Commission 1970. *Tomorrow's Canberra.* Canberra: Australian National University Press.

National Coal Board 1967. *Opencast coal: a tool for landscape renewal.* London: National Coal Board.

National Coal Board 1974. *Opencast operations.* London: National Coal Board Opencast Executive.

National Forest Landscape Management, vol. 2, *Agriculture Handbook* no. 559, 5. Washington, DC: Forest Service/US Department of Agriculture.

Natural Environment Research Council 1976. *Water balance of the headwater catchment of the Wye and Severn 1970–75.* Wallingford: Institute of Hydrology/NERC.

Nature Conservancy Council 1984. *Nature conservation in Great Britain: summary of objectives and strategy.* Peterborough: Nature Conservancy Council.

Nature Conservancy Council 1990. *Handbook for phase 1 habitat survey: a technique for environmental audit.* Peterborough: Nature Conservancy Council.

Neher, D. 1992. Ecological sustainability in agricultural systems: definition and measurement. In *Integrating sustainable agriculture, ecology and environmental policy*, R. K. Olson (ed.), 51–61. Binghampton, New York: Haworth Press.

Newton, J. P. & M. J. Rivers 1982. Vrynwy Estate: an example of the multiple use of rural land. *Quarterly Journal of Forestry* **LXXVI**.

Newton, N. T. 1971. *Design on the land.* Harvard, Mass.: Belknap Press.

New Zealand Forest Service 1983. *Creative forestry.* Wellington, NZ: Forest Service.

Nisbet, J. 1900. *Our forests and woodlands.* London: Dent.

Nixon, M. 1966a. Economic evaluation of land drainage works. In *River engineering and water conservation works*, R. B. Thorn (ed.), London: Butterworth

Nixon, M. 1966b. Flood regulation and river training. In *River engineering and water conservation works*, R. B. Thorn (ed.), London: Butterworth.

Noss, R. F. 1993. Wildlife corridors. In *Ecology of greenways*, D. S. Smith and P. Cawood Hellmund (eds), 43–68. Minneapolis, Minn.: University of Minnesota Press.

Olson, D. J. 1986. *City as a work of art.* Newhaven, Conn.: Yale University Press.

Opher, P. & C. Bird 1980. *British new towns: Runcorn and Warrington.* Oxford: Oxford Polytechnic.

Opher, P. & C. Bird 1981. *British new towns: Cumbernauld, Irvine, East Kilbride.* Oxford: Oxford Polytechnic.

Packman, J. C. 1981. Effects of catchment urbanisation on flood flows. In *I.C.E. flood studies report – five years on*, Institute of Civil Engineers (ed.), London: Thomas Telford.

Paley, W. 1970 edn. *Natural theology.* Farnborough: Greg International.

Palladio, A. 1965 edn. *The four books of architecture.* New York: Dover Publications.

Parker, D. J. & D. M. Harding 1978. Planning for urban floods. *Disasters* 2 (1).

Parker, D. J. & E. C. Penning-Rowsell 1980. *Water planning in Britain.* London: Allen & Unwin.

Parliamentary debates 1859. 18 July. London: House of Commons.

Parliamentary Debates 1981. Lords, vol. 425, 1981–82, 17 November.

Parris, H. & J. Parris 1981. *Bracknell: the making of our new town.* Bracknell: Bracknell Development Corporation.

Patrick Nuttgens 1981. *Architects' Journal*, 4 November, 881.

Pearce, F. 1981. Water, water everywhere . . . *New Scientist*, 8 October, 90–3.

Pecore, M. 1992. Menominee sustained-yield management: a successful land ethic in practice. *Journal of Forestry*, **90** (7), 12–16.

Penning-Rowsell, E. C. 1978. *Proposed drainage scheme for Amberley Wild Brooks, Sussex: benefit assessment.* London: Middlesex Polytechnic.

Peortner, H. G. & J. Reindl 1981. United States practices in detention of urban runoff. In *Proceedings of the symposium on surface water impoundments*, vol. 2, H. G. Stefan (ed.), 945–54. New York: American Society of Civil Engineers.

Pidot, J. R. 1982. Maine's land-use regulation commission. *Journal of Forestry* (Society of American Foresters) **80** (9) 591–3.

Pope, A. U. 1939. *A survey of Persian art*, vol. 2. Oxford: Oxford University Press.

Popper, K. 1945 edn. *The open society and its enemies.* London: Routledge & Kegan Paul.

Porritt, J. 1984. *Seeing green: the politics of ecology explained.* Oxford: Blackwell.

President's Commission on Americans Outdoors 1987. Report and recommendations. Reprinted as *Americans outdoors: the legacy, the challenge.* Washington, DC: US Government Printing Office.

Price, U. 1794. *An essay on the picturesque as compared with the sublime and the beautiful; and on the use of studying pictures, for the purpose of improving real landscape.* London.

Price, W. A. 1982. Closing address: *Shoreline protection: proceedings of a conference organised by the Institution of Civil Engineers*, 247. London: Thomas Telford.

Pudney, J. 1975. *London's docks.* London: Thames and Hudson.

Punter, J. V. 1990. *Design control in Bristol 1940–1990.* Bristol: Redcliffe Press.

Rackham, O. 1990 edn. *The history of the countryside.* London: Dent

Ramsey, A. 1990. Planning urban networks for walking. In *The greening of urban transport: planning for walking and cycling in western cities*, R. Tolley (ed.). London: Belhaven Press.

Rassmussen, S. E. 1982 edn. *London: the unique city.* Cambridge, Mass.: MIT Press.

Ratcliffe, J. 1976. *Land policy.* London: Hutchinson.

Relph, E. 1987. *The modern urban landscape.* Beckenham, Kent: Croom Helm.

Rendel, S. 1997. A new technique. *Landscape Design* (257) February, 17–18.

Richardson, J. J., A. G. Jordan & R. H. Kimber 1978. Lobbying, administrative reform and policy styles: the case of land drainage. *Political Studies* **26**, 47–64.

411

Robbins, J. C. 1981. Feasibility of multi-purpose lakes: a case study in Reston, Virginia. In *Proceedings of the symposium on surface water impoundments*, H. G. Stefan (ed.), 1022–30. New York: American Society of Civil Engineers.

Robbins, J. C., D. L. Rifenberg & J. D. Stokely. 1981. Feasibility of multi-purpose lakes, a case study in Reston, Virginia. In H. G. Stefan (ed.) *Proceedings of the Symposium in Surface Water Impoundments*. vol. II. American Society of Civil Engineers pp. 1022–30.

Roberts, P. W. & T. Shaw 1982. *Mineral resources and strategic planning*. Aldershot: Gower.

Robinson, G. 1988. *The forest and the trees*. Washington, DC: Island Press.

Robinson, W. (ed.) 1872. *The Garden*, vol. 1.

Rocke, G. 1980. The design and construction of Bakethin Dam, Kielder Water Scheme. *Journal of the Institution of Water Engineers and Scientists*, **34** (6), 493–516.

Royal Commission on Land Drainage in England and Wales 1927. Report of the Select Committee 24 July: *The operation of the existing statutes in regard to the formation and proceedings by Commissioners of Sewers*. London: House of Lords.

Royal Commission on land drainage in England and Wales 1927. Chairman Lord Bledisloe, Report. Cmd 2993.

Royal Institute of Chartered Surveyors 1982. *Forestry and land use*, 6. London: Royal Institute of Chartered Surveyors.

Royal Society for the Protection of Birds 1994. *New rivers and wildlife handbook*. Sandy: RSPB.

Rubenstein, J. M. 1978. *The French new towns*. Baltimore, Md.: Johns Hopkins University Press.

Runte, A. 1979. *National parks: the American experience*. Nebraska: University of Nebraska Press.

Rydz, D. L. 1971. The formation of the Great Ouse Water Authority. *Public Administration*, Summer, 245–68.

Rykwert, J. (ed.) 1955. *Ten books on architecture by L. B. Alberti*. London: Tiranti.

Ryle, G. 1969. *Forest service*. Newton Abbot: David and Charles.

Safina, C. 1995. The world's imperilled fish. *Scientific American*, November, 30–7.

Samuelson, P. A. 1973 edn. *Principles of economics*, 10th edn. New York: McGraw-Hill.

Schmid, A. 1989. Landscape planning in the Federal Republic of Germany. *International Federation of Landscape Architects: Yearbook*. Versailles: IFLA.

Schumacher, E. F. 1973. *Small is beautiful*. London: Blond & Briggs.

Scott, W. 1818. *The heart of Midlothian* (Chapter 8). Edinburgh.

Searns, R. M. 1995. The evolution of greenways as an adaptive urban landscape form. *Landscape and Urban Planning* **33** (1–3), 65–80.

Secrétariat Général du Groupe Central des Villes Nouvelles 1977. *Cadre de vie en villes nouvelles*. Paris: Secrétariat Général du Groupe Central des Villes Nouvelles.

Select Committee on Science and Technology 1980. *Scientific aspects of forestry* (House of Lords Report, vol. 1). London: HMSO.

Shepley, S. 1995. Still life in planning? In *Town and Country Planning Summer School*, 6-8. London: Royal Town Planning Institute.

Simo, M. 1981. John Claudius Loudon: on planning and design for the garden metropolis. *Garden History*, 184–201.

Simpson, J. 1900. *The new forestry*. Sheffield: Pawson & Brailsford.

Simpson, J. W. 1985. The emotional landscape and public law 95–87. *Landscape Architecture* **75** (3), 60–3.

Sitte, C. (trans. C. T. Stewart) 1979 edn. *The art of building cities*. New York: Reinhold.

Skelmersdale Development Corporation 1964. *Skelmersdale New Town planning proposals report on basic plan*. Skelmersdale: Skelmersdale Development Corporation.

Smedema, L. K. & D. W. Rycroft 1983. *Land drainage*. London: Batsford.

Smith, D. S. & P. C. Hellmund 1993. *Ecology of greenways*. Minneapolis, Minn.: University of Minnesota Press.

Soja, E. J. 1989. *Postmodern geographies: the reassertion of space in critical social theory*. London and New York: Verso.

Spirn, A. W. 1984. *The granite garden*. New York: Basic Books.

Spurr, S. H. 1976. *American forest policy in development*. Seattle, Wis.: University of Wisconsin Press.

Startin, J. and R. V. Lansdown 1994. Drainage from highways and other paved areas: methods of collection, disposal and treatment. *Water and Environmental Management* **8** (5), 518–26.

Stebbing, E. P. 1928. *The forestry question in Great Britain*. London: John Lane.

Stefan, H. G. (ed.) 1981. *Proceedings of the symposium on surface water impoundments*. New York: American Society of Civil Engineers.

Steiner, G. 1971. *In Bluebeard's Castle*. London: Faber and Faber.

Stevens Report 1976. *Planning control over mineral working*. London: HMSO.

Stevenson, R. L. 1881. *Virginibus Puerisque* VI El Dorado. London: Kegan Paul.

Stow, J. 1720. *Survey of London*, ed. J. Strype. Book 3, London.

Street, E. A. 1984. An investigation into those factors which are significant in the restoration of agricultural land after sand and gravel extraction. Unpublished doctoral thesis, University of London.

Street, E. A. 1985. Evaluation procedures for restored land. *Environmental Geochemistry and Health* **7** (2), 56–63.

Study Committee on the Potential for Rehabilitating Lands 1974. *Surface mined for coal in the Western United States* (Environmental Studies Board: National Academy of Sciences). Cambridge, Mass.: Ballinger Publishing.

Sub-committee on Forestry 1918. *Reconstruction committee*, report of the sub-committee on forestry.

Suckling, E. V. 1943. *The examination of waters and water supplies*. London: Churchill.

Surface Mining 1981. *Surface mining: soil, coal, and society*. Washington, DC: National Academy Press.

Swader, F. N. 1980. Soil productivity and the future of American agriculture. In *The future of American agriculture as a strategic resource*, B. S. Batie & O. E. Heady (eds). Washington, DC: Conservation Foundation. (Quoted in Bowler, I. R. 253.)

Taber, R. K. 1973. *Motorways and the biologist*. London: North East London Polytechnic.

Tandy, C. R. V. 1975. *Landscape of industry*. London: Leonard Hill Books.

Tanner, M. F. 1977. The recreational use of water supply reservoirs in England and Wales, *Research Report 3*. London: Water Space Amenity Commission.

Taylor, D. J. W. 1982. Health aspects of recreation at reservoirs. *Journal of the Institution of Water Engineers and Scientists* (5), 388–98.

Taylor, L. (ed.) 1981. *Urban open spaces*. London: Smithsonian Institution/Academy Editions.

Thames Water Authority 1978. Conversation with Metropolitan Water Division, 5 September.

The Friend of Australia 1836.

Thomas, L. J. 1978. *An introduction to mining*, 2nd edn. Sydney: Methuen of Australia.

Thompson, G. 1966. The use of balancing reservoirs and flow reservoirs in dealing with run-offs from urban areas. In *River Engineering and Water Conservation Works*, R. B. Thorn (ed.). London: Butterworth.

Thorn, R. B. 1966. *River engineering and water conservation works*. London: Butterworth.

Thorn, R. B. & A. G. Roberts 1981. *Sea defence and coast protection works: a guide to design*. London: Thomas Telford.

Tolley, R. (ed.) 1990. *The greening of urban transport: planning for walking and cycling in western cities*. London: Belhaven Press.

Tomlinson, P. 1982. The environmental impact of opencast coal mining. *Town Planning Review* **53** (1), 5–28.

Toulson, D. 1984. A decade of pedestrian streets in West Yorkshire. *Landscape Design*, December, (152), 25.

Trafford, B. D. & R. J. E. Braybrooks 1982. The background to shoreline protection in Great Britain. In *Shoreline protection: proceedings of a conference organised by the Institution of Civil Engineers*, 1–8. London: Thomas Telford.

Trancik, R. 1986. *Finding lost space*. New York: Van Nostrand.

Tregay, R. & R. Gustavsson 1983. *Oakwood's new landscape: designing for nature in the residential environment*. Warrington: Warrington and Runcorn Development Corporation.

Troup, R. S. 1928. *Silvicultural systems*. Oxford: Clarendon Press.

Tuite, C. H. 1982. *The impact of water-based recreation on the waterfowl of enclosed inland waters in Britain*. Slimbridge: Wildfowl Trust.

Tunnard, C. 1953. *The city of man*. New York: Scribner.

Turner, T. 1974. Redditch New Town. *Landscape Architecture Quarterly*, April, 159–63.

Turner, T. 1982. Planning the landscape for a new town. *Town and Country Planning* **51** (10), 267–71.

Turner, T. 1984. Does the cement industry have a future in South East England? *Mineral Planning*, (21).

Turner, T. 1986. *English garden design: history and styles since 1650*. Woodbridge: Antique Collectors Club.

Turner, T. 1992. Open space planning in London from standards per 1000 to green strategy. *Town Planning Review* **63** (4), 365–86.

Turner, T. 1996. *City as landscape: a post-postmodern view of design and planning*. London: E. & F. Spon.

Turner, T. & M. Lancaster 1984. The sun rises over Liverpool. *Landscape Design*, April, (148), 33–6.

Tyrwitt, J. 1947. *Patrick Geddes in India*. London: Lund Humphries.

van Pelt, J. 1980. Landscape analysis and design for conifer plantations. *Australian Forestry* **43** (3), 178–88.

Walker, A. 1980. Auchinstarry Quarry, Kilsyth, Scotland. *Landscape Design* (129), 17–19.

Walmsley, A. 1995. Greenways and the making of Urban Form. *Landscape and Urban Planning* **33** (1–3), 81–127.

Water Act 1973. S.20.

Water Bulletin, 1994. No more reservoirs are needed, says NRA. No. 600, 3.

Water Bulletin, 1995. Land access: no picnic. No. 671, 8–9.2.

Weddle, A. 1967. *Techniques of landscape architecture*. London: Heinemann.

Wells, H. G., J. Huxley & G. P. Wells 1931. *The science of life*, Book 6, part 2. London: Cassell.

Welsh Water Authority 1980. *A strategic plan for water-space and amenity*. Brecon, Powys: Welsh Water Authority.

West, R. 1972. *River of tears*. London: Earth Island.

Whyte, W. H. 1970 edn. *The last landscape*. New York: Doubleday Anchor.

Whyte, W. H. 1980. *The social life of small urban spaces*. Washington, DC: Conservation Foundation.

Wildlife and Countryside Act 1981. Section 48.

Wordsworth, W. 1835 edn. *Guide to the Lakes*. Kendal: Hudson and Nicholson.

Wordsworth, W. 1973 edn. *Guide to the Lakes*. Oxford: Oxford University Press.

Wright, P. 1980. The trouble with pines. *Australian Forestry* **43** (3), 189–94.

Wroth, W. 1896. *The London pleasure grounds of the eighteenth century*. London: Macmillan.

Wyllie, P. J. L. 1958. Flood control in the River Lee Valley. Unpublished paper, Thames Water Authority, London.

Yahner, T. G. et al. 1995. Cultural landscapes and landscape ecology in contemporary greenway planning, design and management: a case study. *Landscape and Urban Planning* **33** (1–3), 295–316.

Youngman, P. 1957. Cumbernauld New Town: preliminary landscape report. Unpublished report, 5, 28 May.

Youngman, P. 1968. Memorandum No. 5. Unpublished manuscript, 22 April.

Zola, E. 1885. *Germinal*. Paris.

Index

Abercrombie, P. 68, 71, 143, 145, 227, 231, 355, 368, 392
Acland Committee 253
adaptation to context
 Alexander patterns 101
 and the identity index 104
 buildings 83, 94, 97, 99, 391
 forestry 277, 279
 mineral workings 190
 parks 367
 pavements 322
 reservoirs 167
 roads 324, 342, 400
 sea defenses 316
 theories of 1, 72, 89
 using GIS 104
Adelaide 143, 144, 350
Age of Science 6
Agricola G. 185, 191, 211
agriculture
 absurdities 217
 conservation farming 232
 EID 245
 fallowing 217, 234
 habitat creation 225
 healthy food 237
 historic conservation 227
 mapping 241
 planning principles 220
 public goods 221, 237, 243
 scenic conservation 227
 scenic quality 230
 strategic reserve 223
 water conservation 223
 wild food 236
Ahern J. 79
air plans 36, 44
Alberti 125
Alexander C. 99, 169, 389
Alexander plans 36, 47

Amberley Wild Brooks 285
American Institute of Planners 10
American Society of Landscape
 Architects 10
ancient countryside 238, 239
Appalachian Trail 143, 146, 147
Appleyard D. 321
archaeology 61, 104, 182, 397
architecture writ large 10, 11
Areas of Outstanding Natural Beauty
 (AONB) 92
Aristotle 60
Ashihara Y. 65
Aswan High Dam 183
asthma 44
Attoe W. 67
avenues 14, 65, 66, 121, 138, 275, 331, 376, 381, 382
Aztec West 391

Bacon E. 65
Bakethin Dam 178
Bangladesh 283
Barton N. 293
Basildon New Town 368
Battersea Park 120
Bayreuth 110, 346
Beamish North of England Open Air
 Museum 335
Belloc H., 245, 318
Berlin Wall 3, 27
Bewl Bridge Reservoir 173
Big Hole of Kimberley 208
Bingham Canyon 207
biodiversity 42, 52, 147, 246
bio-engineering 306
Birmingham 37, 343
Black Country 389
Blackheath 129
"blue" movies 152

Bluebeard's Castle 6
Bomarzo 136
Bor W. 369
Border Forest Park 266
Boston Common 118, 144
Bough Beech Reservoir 173
boulevards 139
Bovine Spongiform Encephalopy (BSE), 217, 237
Bracknell New Town 331, 372, 377, 381
Bracknell streams 373
Brenig Reservoir 169
bridges 73, 352
Bristol 83, 84, 85, 86, 87, 88
British New Towns Act 1946, 383
British Waterways Board 343
Brookes A. 290, 317
Brown J. 252
Brown Lancelot 91, 121, 261
brown-coal mines 206
Bruntland Commission 53
Buchannan Report 348
Byker Wall 332

canals 43, 146, 179, 209, 294, 320, 342, 343
Canberra 376
canoeing 42, 54, 116, 153, 161, 311, 351, 367
Central Park 334, 335
Cergy-Pontoise 364
Chadwick G. F., 12, 13, 136
Charles II 133
Chartres 110
Chesapeake Bay 232
Chicago 142, 363, 390
china clay mines 189
cholera and typhoid 156
churches 30, 32, 96, 233, 245
   and parks 117
CIRIA 300, 303
city fathers 360
"city of dreadful night" 114, 392
civic design 356
Clawson M. 275
Cleveland H.W.S. 144
coast management 59, 316, 400
Coleman A. 202
Cologne 347, 348
colour planning 84, 396
coloured space 121, 148, 296, 322
Colvin and Moggridge 169, 175

Colvin B. 167
Common Agricultural Policy 217, 222, 232, 238, 243
common rights 117–18, 153
community forestry 275, 276
community groups x 20, 30, 107, 296, 317, 319, 399, 400
compensation 51, 214, 220, 223, 394, 395
conservation of roads 323
context theory 73, 89
Copenhagen 96, 128, 129, 135, 145
Countryside Commission 58, 146, 256, 271, 272, 276
Cranz, G. 114, 124
Crawford M. 236, 237
creative conservation 122, 123
critical regionalism 95
Crowe Dame Sylvia 181, 260, 262, 277
Crystal Palace 136
Cullen G. 65
Cumbernauld New Town 365, 366, 367, 378, 379, 380
cycleways 36, 95, 152, 244, 320, 335, 367, 380, 385
   planning 338
   Redway in Milton Keynes 338
cycling 54, 55, 84

deconstruction 17, 99
Delft market 126
Derrida J. 17
design control x, 83
design with nature 94, 307, 363, 396
Detroit 111
development control x, 83
Disneyland 136
drawdown problem 165
Duisberg-Nord Landschaftspark 149
Dunfermline 362
Dysart Harbour Fife 209

East Kilbride New Town 366
ecology 43
ecology and economics 30
"edge city" 356, 386–8
Edinburgh 75, 118, 320, 331, 350, 381, 382
Egypt 138, 183, 313
Elton C. 30
Engles F. 386
English Nature 42
environmental assessment (EA) 80, 102

and GIS 105
and zoning 78
environmental impact assessment (EIA)
    82
    European Community Directive 82
environmental impact design (EID) viii
    x, 168, 230, 245, 279, 391
    definition 111
    for agriculture 220
    for forestry 252
    for minerals 187, 190, 215
    for public open space 116, 151–2
    for reservoirs 155, 166, 184
    for roads 325
    for urbanization 353
    impact questions 394
    rivers 283, 318
    transport 322
Environmental Impact Statement (EIS)
    32, 80, 200
environmental planning database (EPD)
    104, 108
environmental public goods 35
Environmentally Sensitive Areas 220
Eurodisney 79
external effects 34
Exxon Valdez 4

Fabos J. Gy. 138, 236
Fairbrother N. 385, 393
fallacy of the undistributed middle 391
fallowing 217, 234
farm ponds 224
festival parks 136
financial appraisal viii
finance parks 151
Finchingfield green 131
Florence 68
Florida Power and Light Company 82
Forest of Dean 256
forestry 246
    afforestation 249, 254, 259
    broadleaf policy 263
    Clinton's rule 259, 260
    community forestry 275
    conservation and recreation 269
    cost/benefit study 260
    Crowe Dame Sylvia 260, 262, 277
    deforestation 246
    EID 252, 279
    excellent 276
    forest design plans 277

Forest Law 247
Forest Laws 279
forest parks 265
Irregular Style 262
landscape design 261, 262
landscape plans 276
landscape policy 257, 259
multi-objective 258
multiple-use 251, 277
private forestry 270
Sherfield Report 264
sylviculture 272
sympathetic design 258
UK Forestry Commission 249, 255,
    257, 278
US Forest Service 274
wonder tales 246
Frampton K. 95
France 133, 135, 241, 253, 345, 364, 376
Frankfurt 346
Friends of the Earth 39
Friesland Holland 188
Fukuyama F. ix

garden design 65, 92, 136
garden shows 137
Gardiner J.L. 280
garks 128-9, 130
Garreau, J. 388
gathering grounds 157, 159
Geddes P. 8, 28, 65, 90, 246, 286, 309,
    362
    six-lobed flower of life 353, 357, 386
gender and planning 4
General Motors 54
Genius Loci 89-90
geographical information systems (GIS)
    3, 20, 22, 23, 59, 104, 106, 107
geography and planning 3, 7
German Federal Nature Conservation
    Act (1976) 35
Germany 10, 35, 37, 79, 137, 205, 241,
    253, 261, 273, 345, 346
Gilpin W. 254
GIS-based planning 20, 27
Glasson J. 82
Glensanda Superquarry 209
Golden Section 61
Goldsmith O. vii
Goodey B. 57
Grafham Water 173, 178
Grand Canyon 207

green belt 14, 79, 92, 138, 143, 145
green commuting 54, 336
Green Springs-Worthington 363, 364
green trails 146
green web 48, 70, 115, 152, 154, 279, 317
Green B. H. 327
greenspace plans 36, 48
greenways 118, 139, 245, 367, 388, 397
  and parks 113
  definition 137, 138
  environmental 146
  functions 141
  harlequin 148
  in edge cities 388
  in urbanization 388
  objectives 151
  types 137, 138
Greenwich Park 121–4, 133
Griffen W.B. 376

habitat creation 80, 104, 137, 168, 181,
  225, 226, 277, 296, 317, 397
habitat plans 36, 42–4, 71
habitat potential 43
Hall P. 3
Hameenlinna Finland 276
Hampstead Heath 119
Harlow New Town 331, 363, 380, 381,
  382
Hass-Klau C. 331, 348, 349, 350
Haussmann Baron 65, 142
Haweswater Reservoir 160, 183
Haywood S. 207
Heap, D. 256, 390
Heathrow Gateway Waterpark 177
hedgehogs 25, 27, 28, 107, 124, 225
Heidelberg 151
Helliwell D.R. 273
Hemel Hempstead New Town 363, 367
Heneage Report 157
Hetch Hetchy Dam 155
Hobbes T. ix
Holland 188, 214, 244, 284, 314, 316
Hong Kong 68, 351
Honister Pass 326
Hope Cement Works 196, 197
Hough M. 90, 95
Howard E. 143, 145, 357, 369
Hume D. 5
Hyde Park 132, 136, 140

identity index, 101

image maps 66, 67
impact questions 394
  agriculture 398
  forestry 398
  general 394
  mineral workings 397
  public open space 396
  reservoirs 397
  rivers and floods 399
  transport 400
  urbanization 400
Institute of Environmental Asssessment
  58
Institution of Water Engineers 159
interaction matrix, 80–81
International Union for the
  Conservation of Nature (IUCN),
  284
Italy 133, 186, 232,

Jacobs J. 127, 347
Japan 58, 90, 243, 249, 345, 358, 366
Jellicoe G.A. 123, 196–97, 367
Jencks C. 96
Jenkins S. 232, 256
Joyden's Wood 274

Kajhu Bridge 310
Kames Lord 4
Kansas City 37
Kassel 46
Keilder Reservoir 164
Kennington Common 118
Kessler G.E. 144
Khaju Bridge 309
Kielder Reservoir 166, 172, 267
Kimberley Big Hole 207
Knight R. P. 92, 262
Krier R. 65
Kunstler J. R. 322

La Défense 103
Lake District 78, 133, 134, 161, 194, 263,
  264, 328
Lake Vrynwy 74, 180
land drainage 284
landform plans 36
landscape 27, 28, 58
  artist's use of word 9
  definition 8
  designer's use of word 9
  geographer's use of word 8

landscape assessment 58
landscape ecology 43
Landscape Institute 58
landscape plans 35, 68, 108, 167, 220, 276, 312
landscape units 59
landscaping 56
Lao Tzu 66
Lawrence T.E. 15
layering 20, 21, 104, 107, 116, 123
Le Corbusier 45, 65, 93, 127, 329, 386
Le Nôtre Andre 65, 142
Lea Valley Regional Park 184, 312
Leopold A. 4
Levi-Strauss. C. 96–7
Lewis P. 146
Light W. 145, 350
lighthouse plans 28–30, 70, 89
Lingerbay superquarry 210
Little C. 137
Loch Trool 264
London 69, 118, 132, 133, 143, 363
    Abercrombie Plan 392
    cycling 339
    forestry 274
    green belt 145, 146
    green girdle 145
    Hyde Park 381
    Isle of Dogs 103
    London Bridge 310, 376
    open space plan 42, 68, 70, 143
    parks 142
    Regent's Park 334
    reservoirs 175, 178, 180, 184
    river reclamation 293
    rivers 111, 290, 292
    skyline 68, 97
    St James's Park 140
London Docklands 69, 103
long-distance footpaths 153
Loudon J.C. 119, 262, 354, 366
Lynch K, 65, 66, 152, 384, 390

Mabey R. 236
managed flooding 296
Mardale 182, 183
Marne La Valée 79
Marshall A. 31, 33
Mawson T, 356
maximum social benefit 222, 394
McHarg I. 95, 101, 296, 300, 307, 315, 318, 360, 361, 363, 365, 375

McLoughlin J.B. 12
McLuhan M. 20
McLusky J. 328
Megget Reservoir 170
Menominee Indian Reservation 275
Michelangelo 37
Milton Keynes New Town 339, 364, 365, 369, 376
mineral working 190
    "back-to-contour" restoration 195
    coalition approach 196
    concealment approach 191
    conservation approach 193
    economics of after-use 211
    EID 190
    innovative approach 193
    long-life mines 205
    medium-life mines 201
    planning 190
    reclamation 187
    Scott Report 193, 201
    side effects 185
    Stevens Report 214
    superquarries 209
    zoning 191
Minute Man National Historic Park 147
mitigation viii, x
mixed economy viii
modernism 14, 93, 95
monoculture x, 80, 219, 258, 384
Moorfields 118
Moro P. 87
Muir J. 155, 165
multi-objective planning 15, 109, 116, 167, 189, 251, 284, 319, 391
Mumford L. 28, 37, 133, 343
Muthesius S. 386

Nairn I. 386
Nash J. 65, 140, 143
National Environmental Policy Act (NEPA), 32, 80, 189
national parks 58, 61, 92, 117, 130–4, 146, 147, 155, 157, 161, 187, 194, 196, 215, 233, 263, 274, 343
National Playing Fields Association 115
natural process plans 36
New Ash Green 378
New Forest 260, 264
New South Wales 73, 189
new towns 363
    capital investment 384

Crawley 12
cycleways 379, 380
cycling 339
footpaths 267
forestry 377
innovation 137
landscape of 356
New Towns Act (1946), 358
reservoir new towns 178
roads 379, 382, 385
streets 331, 350, 382
surface water runoff, 301
zoning 390
New York 68, 126, 128, 334
Newman O. 386
Nicholas III 19
Nisbet J. 253
Nissan car plant 79
Nolli Plan of Rome 64
Norfolk Broads 188, 198, 207
Nuttgens P. 384

Odysseus 5
Olmsted F.L. 142, 144, 145
Olsen D. 66
opencast mining 200
Ottawa greenbelt 146
overlay maps 15, 101, 124
Oxford 68

Paley W. 78
Palladio 125, 365, 366
Parc de la Villette 17
Paris 52, 64, 65, 68, 93, 103, 128, 132,
    138, 142, 144, 280, 329, 331, 343,
    363, 376, 381
park belts 143
park systems 144
parkways 142
patterns 37, 47, 60, 80
pattern language 48, 99, 329
patterns 36, 102, 169
    Alexander 47, 100, 104, 396
    archetypal 152, 396
    drainage 81
    landscape 325
    paving 345
    spatial 61
Paxton. J. 124, 136. 310
pedestrianization 345
Philadelphia squares 127
Philosopher's Way 150

picturesque theory 89, 90, 91, 93, 254,
    389
Pinchot G. 249, 276
planning
    early-modern 10
    high-modern 10
    late-modern 11
planning information system (PIS), 104
planning-by-database 26
Plato 5, 60
Platte River Greenway 146
Pompidou Centre 52
Pope A. 90
Popper K. 3
porous paving 47, 95, 137, 295, 305, 399
Poundberry (Dorchester), 52
Price U. 254, 262, 389
Prince of Wales 51, 97, 256
private pleasure grounds 134
Prospect Park 142
public gardens 114, 128
public goods vii, xi, 16, 28, 35, 44, 111,
    152, 220, 221, 223, 237, 243, 250,
    279, 296, 317, 334, 391, 393, 394,
    398
public park re-engineering 117–20
Pulteney Bridge Bath 312
Punter J. 83, 87

Queen Hatshepsut Temple of 138
Queen Mother Reservoir 175, 177

Rackham O. 227, 236, 238, 247, 319, 352
Rassmussen S.E. 332, 382
Reading 37, 38
recreation plans 36, 50
Redditch New Town 111, 363, 371–4,
    378
Regent Street 140, 143
Regent's Park 140, 143, 334, 350
Relph E. 18
Repton H. 92, 179, 261, 362
reservoirs
    archaeology 182
    children's play 180
    development potential 184
    forestry 179
    new-town 178
    parks 179
    planning 166
    recreation 180
    urban 174

wild 169
wild life 181
Reuss Valley Improvement Scheme 295
Richmond Park 132
Rio Tinto Zinc (RTZ), 186
River Lea 290
river reclamation 245, 317
River Wandle 293
River Wandse 291
rivers and floods
  bio-engineering 306
  Britain 290
  catchment planning 280
  channelization 289
  coastal defence 312
  control structures 309
  Denmark 290
  flood contours 298
  improvement 282, 295
  infiltration 303
  land drainage 284
  managed flooding 296
  maximum social benefit 296
  multi-purpose planning 295
  river reclamation 280, 290, 295
  rivers reclamation 245, 317
  river training 288
  riverworks 286
  runoff acceleration 294
  storm detention 300, 301
  swales 303
  urban drainage 286
  vegetated roofs 305
  wetlands 284
Riverside Chicago 142
Robin Hood 248
Rome 64, 65, 90, 132, 138, 331
roof contour plans 68
roofscape plans 36
Rosa S. 92
Royal Parks 132
Rules of Taste 61
Runcorn New Town 378
rural retirement 232
Ruskin J. 7, 114
Rutland Water 178, 181

Samuelson P. 32
San Antonio River Walk 145
scenic management 60
scenic plans 36, 57–8

scenic quality 57, 61, 104, 107, 167, 174, 220, 230, 237, 245, 250, 296, 395
Scenic Quality Assessment 58–60
science and planning 5
Scott Report on Land Utilisation in Rural Areas (1942), 191–3, 295, 201
Scott W. 252
Seaside (Florida), 52
set-aside 249, 276
Shaw B. 128
Sheerness sea defences 315
Shepherd P. 368
Shepley C. 359
Sherwood Forest 248
side effects 15, 30, 31, 33, 51, 89, 152, 185, 250, 319, 322, 390
sidewalks 48
Silver Jubilee Walkway 146
Similarity Identity and Difference (SID), 52, 88, 102, 230, 395
Simpson J. 253
single-purpose planning 14, 109
Sitte C. 64, 65, 127
Sixtus V, 64
skateways 342
Skelmersdale New Town 366
skyline plans 36, 67, 72, 395
Smith A. 321
social process plans 36
South Downs The 218
Spain 186, 232
spatial plans 36, 61, 62, 83
special area plans 51
Spirn A.W. 37
squares and plazas 124
St James's Park 133, 140, 143
Stebbing E. P. 255, 264
Steiner G. 6
Stevenage New Town 378
Stevens Report 1976, 200
Stevenson R. L. 307, 332
stormwater management 39
strategic environmental assessment 82
streets 350
structuralism 16
Stuttgart air plan 44, 45
surface water 224
  impact questions 395
  infiltration 39, 57, 84, 107, 224, 295, 303, 399
  management 40, 94, 300
survey-analysis-plan 9, 28

sustainability x, 36, 52, 53, 249, 395
Sustrans 340
Sweden 303
swimming 50, 119, 155, 159, 162
Switzerland 93, 241, 295, 334
Sydney Opera House 33, 88, 103

Talla Reservoir 171
Tapiola 380
Tarn Howes 263
Team Valley Trading Estate 391
Teeside Whitewater Course 313
Tenessee Valley Authority 162
Thamesmead 379
Thameside cement belt 203
Thirlmere Reservoir 165
Tivoli Gardens 135
Tolkien J.R.R. 144
topography 37, 173, 362, 364, 401
tourism 57, 73, 107, 188, 357
Town and Country Planning Act (1947),
    83, 92, 134, 201, 390
traffic calming 14, 347
Trancik R. 64
Transition Style 91
transport planning 318, 350
  avenues 331
  BaTaPaC roads 345
  bridges 352
  bridleways 329
  canals 343
  contextual design 328, 329
  cycleways 95, 320, 335, 380, 385
  design criteria 19, 142, 324, 347, 382
  EID, 325
  footways 344
  The good roads guide 328
  green commuting 336
  green roads 330
  historic conservation 340
  impact questions 395
  leisure roads 332
  McHarg I. 318
  multi-mode design 328
  multi-purpose roads 320, 351
  names for route types 319
  off-road driving 333
  panoramic roads 332
  park roads 334
  pedestrianization 345
  railways and EID 335
  roads and civilization 318

skateways 342
speed roads 334
sustrans 340
traffic calming 321, 331, 347
Trimpley Reservoirs 175
Troup R.S. 272, 273
Tschumi B. 17, 99
Tunnard C. 19, 65
Turner T. 42, 65, 329

UK National Cycling Strategy 336
Union of Soviet Socialist Republics
    (USSR), 111
Unwin R. 143, 145, 386
urban fringe 107, 118, 153, 234, 243, 244
urbanization 137, 353
  advance tree-planting 376
  city parents 360
  commerce 386
  cycleways 380
  earthmoving 368
  EID 353, 391
  greenways 388
  housing 386
  industry 388
  lakes 375
  land acquisition 360
  land ownership 383
  location 356, 358
  morphology 365
  New Towns Act (1946), 358
  parks 367
  roads 378
  settlement size 358
  site appraisal 361
  streams 372
  streets 382
  topographic plans 362
  US Housing and Urban Development
    Act (1968), 384
US Coastal Zone Management Act
    (1972), 316
US Forest Service 249
Utrecht 337, 349

Vauxhall Gardens 135
vegetated roofs 40, 44, 95, 137, 295, 304,
    305, 306
Venice 343, 363
Venn diagrams 15, 16, 21
Versailles 132, 133
Vienna 331, 381

viewshed areas 59
village greens 130
Villette parc de la 17, 99
visual plans 36, 57
Vitruvius 35, 361, 365
Vladivostock 111
von Hayck F. viii

Walthamstow Reservoirs 175
Warrington New Town 378
Washington D.C. 381
watchmaker argument 78
Water Act (1973), 161, 287
Water Act (1989), 164, 287
Water City 38
waterspace plans 36, 38
Weddle A. vii
West Point Reservoir Georgia 182

Whyte W.H. 126, 146, 147, 362
wild food 51, 116, 236, 243, 245, 254,
    279, 398, 399
Williams Ellis C. 386
wonder tales 246
Woodlands Texas 375
Wordsworth W. 78, 133, 255

York 383
Youngman P. 364, 369, 378

zero runoff 300
Zola E. 114
Zone of Visual Influence (ZVI) 59
zoning 78, 79, 108, 190, 195, 207, 220,
    223, 241, 244, 358, 364, 384, 392,
    395
Zootermeer New Town 137